THE REALM OF PRESTER JOHN

THE REALM OF
PRESTER JOHN

Robert Silverberg

OHIO UNIVERSITY PRESS

ATHENS

OHIO UNIVERSITY PRESS, ATHENS, OHIO 45701
© 1972 BY ROBERT SILVERBERG
ALL RIGHTS RESERVED
PRINTED IN THE UNITED STATES OF AMERICA

FIRST PRINTED IN 1972 BY DOUBLEDAY AND COMPANY, INC.
FIRST PAPERBACK EDITION PUBLISHED
BY OHIO UNIVERSITY PRESS IN 1996

02 01 00 99   5 4 3 2

THIS BOOK IS PRINTED ON RECYCLED, ACID-FREE PAPER ∞

LIBRARY OF CONGRESS CATALOG CARD NUMBER: 78-171271

ISBN 0-8214-1138-1 PBK.

For L. Sprague de Camp

Contents

BENEDICK—Will your Grace command me any service to the world's end? I will go on the slightest errand now to the Antipodes that you can devise to send me on; I will fetch you a toothpicker now from the furthest inch of Asia; bring you the length of Prester John's foot; fetch you a hair off the Great Cham's beard; do you any embassage to the Pigmies. . . . You have no employment for me?

SHAKESPEARE, *Much Ado About Nothing,*
Act II, Scene I

Prologue

No one could say where the letter had come from or what messenger had carried it to Europe. But copies of it were circulating everywhere, in the closing years of the twelfth century, and the excitement it stirred was intense. It was addressed to Manuel Comnenus, the Emperor of Byzantium, and it had supposedly been sent by Prester John, the legendary Christian king and high priest of India. And among the things that Prester John wished to tell the Byzantine emperor were these:

"If indeed you wish to know wherein consists our great power, then believe without doubting that I, Prester John, who reign supreme, exceed in riches, virtue, and power all creatures who dwell under heaven. Seventy-two kings pay tribute to me. I am a devout Christian and everywhere protect the Christians of our empire, nourishing them with alms. We have made a vow to visit the sepulchre of our Lord with a great army, as befits the glory of our Majesty, to wage war against and chastise the enemies of the cross of Christ, and to exalt his sacred name.

"Our magnificence dominates the Three Indias, and extends to Farther India, where the body of St. Thomas the Apostle rests. It reaches through the desert toward the place of the rising of the sun, and continues through the valley of deserted Babylon close by the Tower of Babel. Seventy-two provinces obey us, a few of which are Christian provinces; and each has its own king. And all their kings are our tributaries.

"In our territories are found elephants, dromedaries, and camels, and almost every kind of beast that is under heaven. Honey flows in our land, and milk everywhere abounds. In one of our territories no poison can do harm and no noisy frog croaks, no scorpions are there, and no serpents creep through the grass. No venomous reptiles can exist there or use their deadly power.

"In one of the heathen provinces flows a river called the Physon, which, emerging from Paradise, winds and wanders through the entire province; and in it are found emeralds, sapphires, carbuncles, topazes, chrysolites, onyxes, beryls, sardonyxes, and many other precious stones. . . .

"During each month we are served at our table by seven kings, each in his turn, by sixty-two dukes, and by three hundred and sixty-five counts, aside from those who carry out various tasks on our account. In our hall there dine daily, on our right hand, twelve archbishops, and on our left, twenty bishops, and also the Patriarch of St. Thomas, the Protopapas of Samarkand, and the Archprotopapas of Susa, in which city the throne of our glory and our imperial palace are situated. . . .

"If you can count the stars of the sky and the sands of the sea, you will be able to judge thereby the vastness of our realm and our power."

Thus spake Prester John, circa 1165. And all Europe took note of his words in awe and wonder.

ONE

First News of Prester John

EARLY in the year 1145 a certain clergyman of Syria set out on a journey to western Europe, seeking aid for the beleaguered Christian states that the Crusaders had established in the Near East. He was Hugh, Bishop of Jabala—a small coastal town which in ancient times had been the great Phoenician port of Byblos, and which today is the Lebanese village of Jubayl. Though his see was in the Orient, the bishop himself was a Westerner, born in France; in the terminology of the times he was deemed a Latin, one who accepted the supremacy of the Pope and worshiped according to the Roman Catholic rite. During his career among the Crusaders, Bishop Hugh had distinguished himself as a capable and tough-minded diplomat, involved in matters both secular and churchly. As one of the chief spokesmen for Latin interests, he had fought the attempts of the Emperor of Byzantium to gain power over the various Crusader principalities: the Greek-speaking Byzantines, although fellow Christians, were sometimes looked upon by the Latin Crusaders as more dangerous than the Saracens themselves. And Bishop Hugh had also protected the interests of the Pope against the encroachments of the Byzantine Greek Orthodox Church in the Near East. The Byzantine and Roman churches had been bitter rivals for many years, and to a good Latin like Bishop Hugh, a Byzantine Christian was, if not actually a heretic, then certainly a schismatic, not to be trusted in doctrinal questions.

The bishop's mission came at a tense time for the Crusaders. Not since their conquest of the Holy Land, nearly fifty years before, had they been in such peril. In 1095 the Byzantine Emperor Alexius Comnenus had asked Pope Urban II for a few hundred experienced knights, to assist him in a project he was organizing for the reconquest of Byzantium's lost eastern provinces. In the seventh century the Arabs had taken Egypt, Syria, and the rest of the Near East from the Byzantines; later, Turkish warriors out of Central Asia had seized much of the Arab-held territory; by the late eleventh century, though, the Turks were quarreling bitterly among themselves, and Emperor Alexius saw a good chance to drive the Moslems out of his nation's former lands. Since one of the places Alexius hoped to recapture was Jerusalem, Christianity's holiest shrine, Pope Urban lent enthusiastic support to the scheme, urging all of Western Christendom to take part in the campaign. The results were dismaying for Byzantium. An uncouth army of thousands of European soldiers marched east in 1096 and 1097, overrunning Byzantine territory and sweeping devastatingly onward through Asia Minor into Syria. The Saracens (as the Crusaders termed all Moslems, of whatever nation) were defeated at every turn, and the leaders of the invading army began to establish themselves as princes in the conquered land, with only the most tenuous allegiance to Byzantium. Thus there came to be a Count of Edessa, a Prince of Antioch, a Count of Tripoli, and a King of Jerusalem—all of them rough Latin warriors who set up little feudal states of the European sort in the Near East.

These states survived, and even flourished, despite Saracen harassment and fierce dynastic squabbles among the leading Crusaders. New settlers came to the Holy Land, and in a couple of generations a curious hybrid society had taken form. As the chronicler Fulcher of Chartres wrote, "We who were westerners find ourselves transformed into Orientals. The man who had been an Italian or a Frenchman, transplanted here, has become a Galilean or a Palestinian. A man from Rheims or Chartres has turned into a citizen of Tyre or Antioch. We have already forgotten our native lands. To most of us they have be-

come territories unknown, or places never heard mentioned any more."
The Latins of the Crusader states still observed the Roman Catholic
rituals and still maintained the structure of the European feudal system, but otherwise they had come to imitate the ways of the Saracens;
they fancied silken draperies, richly ornamented carpets, tables hand-
somely carved and inlaid with precious metals, dinnerware of gold and
silver, vessels of porcelain imported from China. The knights, when
they were not in armor, dressed in silk robes, Saracen style, and
shielded their heads from the sun with turbans.

But life was precarious in this odd enclave of western European
Christendom. The Crusader states, all together, were no more than a
narrow strip at the eastern end of the Mediterranean. To the east and
to the south lay hostile Moslem principalities, waiting for an opportunity
to drive the Crusaders into the sea. The Crusaders' neighbors immediately to the west were the crafty Byzantines, who had little love for
the Latin barons. Byzantium, sprawling from the Black Sea to the borders of Italy, was an immense barrier between the Latins of the Near
East and their kinsmen and coreligionists of the Western countries.

Under the leadership of the Turkish General Imad ad-din Zengi,
the Saracens began seriously to threaten the Crusader states in the
1130s. Taking advantage of feuding among the Crusader princes, Zengi
made himself master of a great deal of territory in northern Syria, and,
late in 1144, laid siege to Edessa, the capital of the northernmost Crusader state. This ancient city in eastern Asia Minor (now the Turkish
town of Urfa) was strategically located on the Syrian frontier, dom-
inating a buffer zone that separated Crusader-held Syria from the Moslem world to the east; its population was largely Christian, though not
Christians of the Latin rite, and it had been ruled since 1098 by the family of the Crusader General Baldwin of Lorraine. On Christmas Eve,
1144, the Turks broke through Edessa's walls; the citizens were thrown
into confusion as sword-wielding Saracens burst into their city, and
thousands were slain or trampled to death. Zengi ordered the execu-
tion of all Latins caught in the city, though he spared the native Christian inhabitants.

The fall of Edessa sent shock waves through the entire Crusader
world. Never before had the Saracens succeeded in ousting the Crusaders from a major city. The tide of battle had always gone the other
way, from the time of the first invasion by the Latins in 1097. Now,
with Zengi rampaging in the north, a real prospect existed that the

whole conquest might be undone. Already Saracen troops were test-
ing the defenses of the great Syrian city of Antioch. There had been
a shift of momentum, and Zengi suddenly seemed invincible. The Crusaders, in panic, dispatched emissaries to the rulers of western Europe
in quest of Christian reinforcements. Nothing less than a second Crusade, it seemed, would save the endangered Latin states of the Holy
Land.

Among those emissaries was Bishop Hugh of Jabala, whom Prince
Raymond of Antioch sent to enlist the support of Pope Eugenius III.
In the autumn of 1145 Bishop Hugh reached Italy and learned that a
popular revolutionary uprising directed against the secular authority of
the Pope had forced Eugenius, who had been in office less than nine
months, to flee from Rome. The meeting between the bishop and
the pontiff therefore took place in the central Italian town of Viterbo,
on November 18, 1145. We know a good deal about what was said at
this conference, because, fortunately, one of the most trustworthy and
learned historians of medieval times happened to be in Viterbo that
autumn, and he made a careful record of Bishop Hugh's words. He was
the German churchman Otto, Bishop of Freising, who, by virtue of
his chance encounter with the Bishop of Jabala at Viterbo, became the
vehicle by which the remarkable tale of Prester John first was made
known in Europe.

Otto belonged to the Hohenstaufen family, which for centuries
would dominate Germany and the Holy Roman Empire. He had had
a lengthy and intensive education before taking up his ecclesiastic re-
sponsibilities, and his famous book, *Historia de Duabus Civitatibus*
(*The History of the Two Cities*), an account of the world from the
Creation to the year 1146, is an extraordinarily rich and detailed
chronicle, the product of a supple and well-stocked mind. (The Two
Cities of Otto's title were Jerusalem and Babylon, which he regarded
symbolically as the city of God and the city of the Devil; he interpreted
all the events of history as stages in the conflict between the heavenly
powers and those of the Inferno, and believed that the twelfth-century
world was on the verge of an apocalyptic era in which Antichrist would
appear on earth.)

The account of Bishop Hugh's visit to Viterbo is found in the seventh book of Otto's chronicle. There we are told that Hugh spoke eloquently of the plight of the Latins of the Holy Land since the fall of
Edessa, and asked the Pope's help in making Western rulers aware of

the dangers now facing the Christian realms of the Near East. According to Otto, the Syrian bishop then went on to relate this story:

"Not many years ago a certain John, a king and priest who lives in the extreme Orient, beyond Persia and Armenia, and who, like all his people, is a Christian although a Nestorian, made war on the brothers known as the Samiardi, who are the kings of the Persians and Medes, and stormed Ecbatana, the capital of their kingdom. . . . When the aforesaid kings met him with Persian, Median, and Assyrian troops, the ensuing battle lasted for three days, since both sides were willing to die rather than flee. At last Presbyter John—for so they customarily call him—put the Persians to flight, emerging victorious after the most bloodthirsty slaughter.

"He [Bishop Hugh] said that after this victory the aforesaid John had moved his army to the aid of the Church in Jerusalem, but when he had come to the river Tigris he had not been able to take his troops across it in any vessel. Then he had turned to the north, where, he had heard, the river sometimes froze over in the winter cold. He had tarried there for some years, waiting for the frost, but on account of the continued mild weather there was very little, and finally, after losing much of his army because of the unaccustomed climate, he had been forced to return home.

"He is said to be a direct descendant of the Magi, who are mentioned in the Gospel, and to rule over the same peoples they governed, enjoying such glory and prosperity that he uses no scepter but one of emerald. Inspired by the example of his forefathers who came to adore Christ in his cradle, he had planned to go to Jerusalem, but was prevented, so it is said, by the reason mentioned above. But that is enough of this."

2

Thus the Western world had its first news of that extraordinary and mysterious Christian potentate of the Orient, Presbyter Ioannes—in the Latin of Otto of Freising—or Prester John, to give him the form of his name by which he was best known in medieval times. Who was this "Priest John," this monarch and ecclesiastic, this great warrior, this possessor of enormous wealth, this descendant of the Magi, this follower of the Nestorian heresy? Where was his kingdom? How long had his nation existed? For the next five hundred years men would seek the answers to these questions. The quest for the realm of Prester John would become one of the great romantic enterprises of the middle ages, a geographical adventure akin to the search for El Dorado, for King Solomon's mines, for the Fountain of Youth, for the Holy Grail, for the Seven Cities of Cíbola, for the land of the Amazons, for the lost continent of Atlantis. Men would look through the whole length of Asia for his glittering kingdom, and, not finding anything that corresponded to the legends of magnificence they had so often heard, they would hunt the land of Prester John in Africa as well; eventually they would persuade themselves they had discovered it.

Tracing the origins of the legend of Prester John leads the scholar on a quest nearly as exhausting and difficult as those undertaken by the medieval explorers. For, although there is little doubt that the chronicle of Otto of Freising provides the first written account of the famous king, the story of Prester John was surely not invented by Bishop Hugh of Jabala, and must have been in oral circulation long before Otto heard it from Hugh in Viterbo in 1145. But to uncover the sources of the tale Hugh told requires a lengthy voyage on a treacherous sea of conjecture.

It appears that Bishop Hugh's main purpose in speaking of Prester John to the Pope may have been to dispel rumors of Prester John's omnipotence that had already begun to spread through Europe. It would do the imperiled Crusaders no good to have the French, Italian, and German kings believe that an invincible Christian sovereign reigned in glory east of the Holy Land. So long as Europe thought that the devout (if heretical) Prester John, descendant of the Magi, was available to protect Jerusalem against the Saracens, there would be no need to send European armies in defense of the Crusader states.

Bishop Hugh's narrative, therefore, seems designed to puncture Europe's existing faith in the power of Prester John. He had tried to go to Jerusalem, Bishop Hugh declares, after defeating the Persians and the Medes; but he had been unable to get across the Tigris, and ultimately had had to return to his own kingdom without achieving his goal of visiting the Holy Land. Therefore it was dangerous for Europe to place credence in the hope that Prester John would aid the Crusaders; help must come from the West, or Jerusalem would surely fall to the infidels.

If Hugh's aim was thus to discourage excessive dependence on the might of Prester John, he was successful. On December 1, 1145, Pope Eugenius issued a bull urging all princes of Western Christendom to join in a new Crusade. Two kings, Louis VII of France and Conrad III of Germany, agreed, after conferring with Bishop Hugh, to organize armies and lead them in person. A celebrated monk, Bernard of Clairvaux, known to us as St. Bernard, became the spiritual voice of the Crusade, recruiting hundreds of knights and thousands of common people by the fervor and piety of his sermons. In the spring of 1147 an immense force set out for the East. Otto of Freising himself was among the Crusaders, accompanying King Conrad, his half brother, to the Holy Land.

This mighty endeavor, however, ended disastrously. Most of the German troops were wiped out in their first battle with the Turks. The French army was thinned by starvation before it got east of Constantinople. The survivors of both forces then consumed their remaining resources in a badly conceived attack on the Saracen stronghold of Damascus, which produced a dispute among the Crusaders over strategy and a quick, ignominious retreat, during the course of which the Moslems inflicted heavy losses. King Conrad left the Holy Land in disgust in September 1148, and King Louis went back to France the following summer. The Second Crusade had been nothing but a vast waste of energy and money, costing the lives of thousands of men and gaining not an inch of territory for Christianity. The frictions developing out of it left the Crusader inhabitants of the Near East in a more precarious position than ever. They might just as well have relied on the mercies of Prester John, for all the good the intervention of the European princes did them.

3

Since the early nineteenth century, historians have recognized in Bishop Hugh's story of Prester John's victory over the Persians the distorted outlines of an authentic historical event: the defeat of Sanjar, the Seljuk Turk ruler of Persia, by the forces of the empire of Kara-Khitai, in 1141.

The Seljuks were the strongest of the Turkish tribes who swept into western Asia in the eleventh century. By the middle of that century they had made themselves masters of most of Persia; then they moved into Iraq, and in 1055 forced the Caliph of Baghdad, nominal head of the Moslem world, to accept their "protection," becoming a Seljuk puppet. Next they invaded Asia Minor, which was part of Byzantium; in 1071 they smashed a Byzantine army and captured Emperor Romanus IV Diogenes, thereby stripping Byzantium of her easternmost provinces. Syria and Palestine followed; by 1076 the Seljuks were in possession of Jerusalem. Their drive toward universal empire was halted, though, at the borders of Egypt in the south and at the outskirts of Byzantine Constantinople in the west. At the end of the eleventh century the warriors of the First Crusade succeeded in pushing the Seljuks out of the Holy Land and some of the surrounding territory, and the partition of the remaining empire among members of the Seljuk royal family further weakened its power; but the Persian Seljuk realm, under the strong leadership of Sanjar, flourished throughout the early decades of the twelfth century and greatly expanded its area at the expense of its neighbors.

Eventually the Persian Seljuks, as they extended their power eastward, came into conflict with the warriors of an equally dynamic and expansionist realm, that of Kara-Khitai. This was an empire founded by the Khitan, a tribe that once had governed much of China. Originally a nomadic pastoral people of Manchuria, the Khitan had organized a strong military confederation in A.D. 907, and their well-trained troops broke through the Great Wall a few years later. By 960 they ruled all of northern China. Styling themselves the Liao Dynasty, the Khitan emperors adopted Chinese dress and writing, took Chinese wives, and were converted to the main Chinese religions, Confucianism, Buddhism, and Taoism. This process of cultural blending seems to have softened the once warlike Khitan, and in time they were challenged by a fiercer and more primitive Manchurian tribe, the Jurchen, who began to make war on them in 1115. In less than a decade the grip of the Khitan on northern China had been broken. The Liao Dynasty fell and the Jurchen ascended the imperial throne; nothing remained to mark Khitan rule in China except the name, "Khitai," by which China still is known in Russian, Greek, and several other languages today. (The medieval "Cathay" is derived from the same word.)

In 1124, as the Liao Dynasty was collapsing, a member of the Khitan imperial family escaped with about two hundred followers into Central Asia, and, winning the support of the Turkish tribes that occupied the region, established the empire of Kara-Khitai, "Black Cathay." ("Black" appears to have been a term of honor and distinction in twelfth-century Turkish.) The founder of this empire was Yeh-lü Ta-shih, born about 1087, a descendant in the eighth generation from the first Khitan Emperor of China. Yeh-lü Ta-shih, according to the official Chinese history of the Liao Dynasty, was an outstanding horseman and archer, and in addition had a thorough grounding in Chinese literature; it also appears that he was a shrewd, ruthless man who, while other Khitan princes were planning a last-ditch effort against the Jurchen, made a quick and cool exit from China once he was convinced that his dynasty's cause was lost. In his new domain far to the west, he obtained the submission of a great many minor tribes whose chieftains recognized his superior powers of leadership, and rapidly created a kingdom composed largely of people of Turkish stock. In 1134 he made a half-hearted attempt to reconquer the Khitan possessions in China, but nothing came of it, and he abandoned the project; the real thrust of Yeh-lü Ta-shih's imperial ideas was westward, ever deeper into Central Asia.

A collision between Kara-Khitai and the Seljuks of Persia was in the making for many years. It finally came on September 9, 1141, at Qatawan, near the rich city of Samarkand, which lay on the main caravan route between China and the Near East. Yeh-lü Ta-shih's subjects had been raiding Samarkand for some time; at last the Khan of Samarkand, a Seljuk vassal, asked his master, the Sultan Sanjar, to come to his aid. Sanjar thereupon marched east from Persia at the head of a large army made up of Moslem troops drawn from many lands. Yeh-lü Ta-shih met him with the army of Kara-Khitai, and in the battle that followed the Seljuks suffered a terrible defeat. Sanjar escaped, but his wife and many of his highest nobles were captured, and the power of the Persian Seljuks was seriously impaired.

Merchants traveling the ancient caravan routes carried the news of this battle westward, until within a year or two it must have reached the Crusader principalities in Syria, two thousand miles west of Samarkand. These Christian outposts would find good reason to rejoice in the smashing of an Islamic army by the forces of Kara-Khitai. Sanjar had been the pre-eminent Moslem warrior of his era, and, though all his military activities had been carried out in regions of Asia far removed from the Crusader lands, the downfall of the great Seljuk sultan removed a major potential menace at the Crusaders' backs. But how strangely the story of Yeh-lü Ta-shih's victory was transformed, in the course of its journey from Samarkand to Syria! Sanjar the Seljuk was turned into a pair of brothers, the "Samiardi." Yeh-lü Ta-shih, who was a Buddhist, had become Prester John—a Christian, a priest, and a Nestorian to boot. The scene of the battle had been shifted from distant Samarkand to nearby Ecbatana, just on the far side of Mesopotamia in western Persia, and it was said that Prester John had afterward come even farther west, to the banks of the Tigris in Mesopotamia, in his unsuccessful attempt to undertake the pilgrimage to Jerusalem. Accounting for these discrepancies has occupied the students of the Prester John legend for more than a century and a half.

Some of them can be explained fairly easily, such as the cleaving of Sanjar into brother-kings called "Samiardi." In some manuscripts of Otto's chronicle this term is given as *Saniardi,* a recognizable plural form of Sanjar, and perhaps this is the spelling that should be preferred. The plural usage possibly is an acknowledgment of the Seljuk custom of sharing power among brothers: the eleventh-century warrior Togrul Beg, first of the great Seljuk sultans, ruled in conjunction with his brother Chagri, and in the early twelfth century the Seljuk realm had been divided among Sanjar and two of his brothers, although Sanjar was the only one who still lived at the time of the battle at Samarkand.

Yeh-lü Ta-shih's supposed Christianity, it seems fair to say, was merely wishful thinking on the part of those who brought the story westward. The official Chinese history of the Liao Dynasty explicitly states that Yeh-lü Ta-shih received a classical academic Chinese education, and it would have been most unusual for such a background to have led him to Christianity; certainly, had he been a Christian, that fact would have been noted in the dynastic annals. Instead, the dynastic history reveals that in 1130, while setting out on a military expedition, Yeh-lü Ta-shih "sacrificed a gray ox and a white horse to Heaven and Earth and to his ancestors," which does not sound like the practice of a Christian. In all probability he was loyal to the shamanistic tribal religion of the Khitan, and also, like many of the Liao Dynasty nobles, had embraced Buddhism. But there certainly were Christian tribes in Central Asia in his day—most notably the Keraits, a Mongol tribe living south and east of Lake Baikal. In 1007-08 missionaries from Syria, accompanying a party of merchants, had converted the chieftain of the Keraits and many of his people to the Nestorian form of Christianity, an event that was widely publicized in the Near East. It is not hard to see that the Christian travelers who spread the news of Sanjar's defeat would readily assume that anyone making war against Moslems must surely be a Christian; and, having claimed Yeh-lü Ta-shih for their own faith, they would necessarily have concluded that Sanjar's "Christian" vanquisher was likely to be one of those Central Asian Nestorians of whom so much had been heard.

Since Yeh-lü Ta-shih never came as far west as Ecbatana (he apparently remained in the vicinity of Samarkand after defeating Sanjar, and died in 1143 or 1144), there is no ready explanation for the transplantation of his battle with Sanjar from Samarkand to the Persian city. This may have been an error of the sort that often arises when a tale is told and retold many times, undergoing slight distortions at each new telling.

The most complex of the story's mutations is the most significant one of all, that which produced for Yeh-lü Ta-shih the name that Otto of Freising rendered as "Presbyter Ioannes," or "Prester John." During his career the Khitan prince used a variety of titles, but none of them can convincingly be interpreted as any form of "Ioannes" or "John," though scholars have tried to make several fit the phonetic mold. When first he fled into Central Asia after the Liao collapse, Yeh-lü Ta-shih awarded himself the title of *wang*, or "king" in Chinese, which Khitan chieftains had used since the late seventh century. Later, when his new realm had grown considerably, he bestowed on himself the Chinese imperial title, *huang ti*, "august sovereign," to indicate his kinship with the fallen Liao Dynasty. As emperor he adopted a formal imperial name in the Chinese manner—T'ien-yu. The dynastic annals show that Yeh-lü Ta-shih, while emperor, employed still another title of honor, by which he was more widely known. This was rendered in Chinese characters as *ko-erh-han*, and in the Mongol-Turkish speech of his subjects as *gur-khan*. It can best be translated as "supreme ruler."

Much ingenuity has been expended to conjure "John" or "Ioannes" out of this roster of names and titles. Gustav Oppert, who in 1864 published the first extensive examination of the Prester John myth, argued that *gur-khan*, softened in West Turkish pronunciation to *yur-khan*, had undergone a subtle change while the story was making its way westward, emerging finally as Yochanan, which is the Hebrew form of "John." This theory has a convincing ring, but acceptance of it is hampered by the ease with which so many other possible derivations of the name of Prester John can be constructed. In the 1930s, for example, the Italian medievalist Leonardo Olschki, rejecting Oppert's *gur-khan* derivation, suggested that Yeh-lü Ta-shih was known by the composite title of *wang-khan,* made up of the Chinese and Mongol words for "king": "The term was changed to Johannan by the Nestorians of Central Asia, who passed it on in this form, as a proper name, to their fellow believers and the other Christians of western Asia," Olschki wrote. Not only is it difficult to find a phonetic resemblance between *wang-khan* and Johannan, however, but Olschki's entire line of reasoning is gravely injured by the fact that nowhere in contemporary documents can Yeh-lü Ta-shih be found mentioned by the title of *wang-khan.* That title was indeed used by a Central Asian ruler, as we will see—a genuine Nestorian, far more suited to wear the mantle of Prester John than Yeh-lü Ta-shih; but the earliest known usage of the title dates from fifty years after Bishop Hugh's journey to Viterbo.

In 1876 the Russian scholar Philipp Bruun published a work entitled *The Migrations of Prester John,* in which he challenged the whole notion that Bishop Hugh's story was a distorted version of the exploits of Yeh-lü Ta-shih. According to Bruun, the prototype of Prester John was the general Ivané (John) Orbelian, commander-in-chief of the army of the kingdom of Georgia. This John Orbelian is one of his country's national heroes, who fought valiantly for many years to drive the Turks from the Caucasus. In 1123–24 he recaptured from the Seljuks a wide strip of territory in eastern Georgia, including the cities of Tiflis and Ani, and his grateful monarch, King David the Restorer, bestowed on him large grants of land in the reconquered region.

Bruun raised the interesting point that Otto of Freising apparently confused the Georgian city of Ani with the old Persian city of Ecbatana. In a passage of Otto's chronicle somewhat earlier than the Prester John anecdote, Otto, in providing some geographical information apparently received from Bishop Hugh, remarked, "The kings of the Persians . . . have themselves established the seat of their kingdom at Ecbatana, which . . . in their tongue is called *Hani.*" The defeat of the Seljuks at Ani in 1123 thus begins to seem a more plausible source for Prester John's victory at Ecbatana than does the triumph of Yeh-lü Ta-shih outside Samarkand. Moreover, John Orbelian was a Christian —Greek Orthodox, though, and not Nestorian. And, though he was neither a king nor a priest, the Georgian general did conduct himself in regal fashion: he dined on silver dishes, had the privilege of sitting on a couch at royal banquets while other princes sat merely on cushions, and the Orbelian family held the hereditary right to preside over the coronations of Georgia's kings. As for the "Samiardi" whom Prester John defeated, it was true that Orbelian had never done battle against Sultan Sanjar, but there were two other Seljuks who could qualify as Bishop Hugh's brother-kings: Sanjar's nephews Mas'ud and Da'ud, one of whom was the chief administrator of western Persia and the other of Seljuk-occupied Armenia and Azerbaijan. There is no record of Orbelian's actually having vanquished these princes on the battlefield, but he certainly engaged in battle with the soldiers of Da'ud, if not with Da'ud himself, during his campaigns of 1123–24. Lastly, Bruun pointed out, Georgia lies not too far to the north of Syria and the Holy Land, and it is considerably more likely that the Crusaders would have looked to John Orbelian for military aid than to the Gur-Khan of Kara-Khitai. It would even have been necessary for Orbelian to cross the Tigris in journeying from Georgia to Jerusalem.

Despite the cleverness of Bruun's reasoning, his identification of John Orbelian as the prototype of Prester John never attained wide acceptance. Though Orbelian's career fit the requirements of the story in many minor ways, it failed to coincide with the major ones: he was not a king or a priest, nor had he fought any single climactic battle in which a huge Moslem army had been destroyed, nor had he vanquished the brother-kings of Persia, nor could he claim descent from the Three Magi of the Gospel, nor did he wield an emerald scepter. It seems mere coincidence, then, that this Georgian warrior can be made to seem the model for Prester John.

How are we to explain, in that case, the discordant features of Bishop Hugh's narrative?

Perhaps we would do best to regard that narrative as a blend of fact and fantasy, a synthesis of history and legend. Its basis is an authentic event: the smashing of Sanjar the Seljuk's army near the city of Samarkand in 1141 by Yeh-lü Ta-shih, the Gur-Khan of Kara-Khitai. To this was welded another indisputable datum: the existence of Christian settlements, most of them of the Nestorian creed, in remote and obscure regions of the Far East. From these two nuclei sprang the romantic concept of a Christian monarch of the Far East, who combined in his person the dignities of king and priest, as in fact was not uncommon in the Orient. Mythical attributes now were attached to this warlike presbyter: an emerald scepter, descent from the Magi. For a storyteller to credit Prester John with a scepter of emerald would be no great feat of imagination, but indeed a source of inspiration must have been close at hand in *The Thousand and One Nights,* which already was in wide oral circulation in the Near East. On the sixth voyage of Sindbad the Sailor, he comes to the isle of Sarandib—which can be identified with Ceylon—and observes that the king's attendant is carrying "a great mace of gold, at the top of which is an emerald a span in length, and of the thickness of a thumb." The legendary wealth of Prester John may spring in part from Sindbad's account of the opulence of the court of Sarandib. As for Prester John's connection with the Three Magi, that may be derived, as will shortly be demonstrated, from another body of legend having to do with the Christians of the Far East. The name John itself may also be drawn from that group of myths.

Thus, by a circuitous process of accretion, the story of Prester John's victory over the Persian kings reached the Crusader lands, somewhat embellished and transmogrified, a year or two after the battle near Samarkand. The worried Latins of the Near East, seeing the Saracen menace on their borders growing more threatening all the time, quite naturally indulged in the pleasant hope that this valiant Christian warrior would one day bring his legions to the defense of Jerusalem. When Edessa fell to the Turks in 1144, and Bishop Hugh of Jabala set out to obtain reinforcements in western Europe, it became necessary to add one more strand to the story: Prester John's unsuccessful attempt to reach the Holy Land. Touring Europe in 1145, Bishop Hugh made it clear to the princes of Christendom that no help could be expected in the Near East from Prester John; and, the metamorphoses of the tale now being complete, Otto of Freising embedded it in his chronicle.

4

Christianity originated in Palestine, spread quickly to Syria, was carried by missionaries to Asia Minor and Greece, and took deep root in Rome, all during the first century after the Crucifixion. One hundred years later there were Christian churches throughout the length of the vast Roman Empire, from Egypt to Gaul and Britain. By the early fourth century Christianity was the official religion of Rome, and the whole Mediterranean world was penetrated by the teachings of Jesus.

While the structure of the Church was thus taking form in Europe and the Near East, Christianity also was traveling to the farther Orient, through Mesopotamia and Persia to India and even China. The immensities of the distances involved and the difficulties of communication after the breakdown of the Roman imperial system left these Oriental Christians cut off from the Western centers of the faith, so that their theological concepts developed along radically different lines; and by the year 1100 the Christians of the Orient had come to seem strange, unreal, and virtually mythical to their brethren in the West. It was out of this fantasy-shrouded Oriental Christianity that the essential features of the Prester John legend arose, and it is impossible for us to understand the convolutions of that legend without a detailed examination of the course taken by Christianity in the Far East, particularly in the fabled land of India.

The traditional founder of Indian Christianity was St. Thomas, the apostle who doubted the resurrection of Jesus, he who said upon hearing that Jesus had left his tomb, "Except I shall see in his hands the print of the nails, and put my finger into the print of the nails, and thrust my hand into his side, I will not believe." The story of Thomas' career in India is told in an apocryphal work, the vivid, romantic *Acts of Thomas*, which apparently dates from the first part of the third century. This extraordinary tale, probably composed at the city of Edessa in eastern Asia Minor, was written in Syriac, one of the dialects of the Semitic language known as Aramaic, which was spoken in much of the Near East in the early Christian Era; Syriac remains to this day the liturgical language of several Oriental Christian sects. Later the book was translated into Greek, Latin, Armenian, and several other languages, and achieved great popularity throughout the Christian world.

The *Acts* declares that after the Crucifixion the disciples of Jesus divided the world into missionary regions, and it fell to Thomas to carry the faith to India. The apostle was unwilling to go, saying that his health was too poor and that he could speak only Hebrew; it was necessary for Jesus to appear and to sell the reluctant Thomas as a slave to a merchant from India named Habban, whose master, King Gundafor of India, had sent him to Palestine to obtain a skilled carpenter. Habban and Thomas sailed to India, and, when they arrived at Gundafor's court, the monarch asked Thomas if he would build him a new palace. Reluctant no longer, the apostle replied, "Yes, I shall build it,

and finish it; for because of this I have come, to build and to do carpenter's work."

Gundafor provided Thomas with a large sum to cover the cost of
the construction. However, Thomas chose to distribute this money
among the needy, which so infuriated the king that he had the apostle
flogged and imprisoned. Gundafor's brother Gad, sorely distressed by
Thomas' squandering of the royal treasury, took to his bed and died of
chagrin, and was carried off to heaven. On his journey heavenward
Gad beheld a magnificent palace and asked the name of its owner; he
was told that the palace was that of Gundafor, and its architect was the
Apostle Thomas. Gad then asked permission to return to worldly life,
so that he could tell his brother of the splendid palace that awaited
him in the heavenly realms. This request was granted, and, after hearing the story of the celestial palace from Gad, Gundafor urged Thomas
to receive him into Christianity. The apostle baptized both Gundafor
and Gad, and many of the subjects of the Indian king.

After some further miraculous adventures among Gundafor's people, Thomas was invited to visit the land of a king named Mazdai—a
Persian name, though the *Acts* indicates that Mazdai's kingdom was
in another part of India. Here Thomas converted to the Christian faith
King Mazdai's wife Tertia and their son Vizan, whom he ordained a
deacon. Thomas preached the virtues of celibacy to such effect that
Tertia withdrew from the king's bed. Enraged, Mazdai ordered Thomas
to persuade Tertia to return to him; this Thomas refused to do, whereupon the angry monarch sent four soldiers to put the apostle to death.
Before he was slain, Thomas entrusted the Christian Church in India
to the young deacon Vizan and to an Indian named Sifur, whom
Thomas had ordained a priest. The martyred apostle was buried by
Vizan, Sifur, and his other disciples in a tomb where former kings had
been interred. King Mazdai later opened Thomas' grave but could not
find the martyr's bones, "for one of the brethren had taken them away
secretly and carried them into the regions of the West." Afterward
the repentant Mazdai embraced Christianity and his kingdom became
an important center of the faith in India.

How much of this story can be accepted as a genuine historical
record? To the native Christian population of India, virtually all of it
must be regarded as an accurate documentary account of the origin
of their religious heritage. Several hundred thousand Christians still
live along India's Malabar Coast—southwestern India, southwest from

Goa—and call themselves "the Christians of St. Thomas." Most of them acknowledge the Syrian Orthodox Patriarch of Antioch as their spiritual leader, though some belong to the Syrian Roman Catholic Church, which acknowledges the supremacy of the Pope. All, however, trace their faith to the missionary work done by St. Thomas. They place the date of his arrival in India at A.D. 52, and in December 1952, Syrian Christians everywhere celebrated the nineteen hundredth anniversary of his death. Just one piece of evidence exists to confirm the authenticity of the tale of Thomas' visit to India. The name of King Gundafor is found in no document of the Western world other than the Acts of Thomas. In the nineteenth century, however, archaeologists discovered that this king actually existed and was approximately contemporary with Thomas. Coins in first-century style bearing the Indian form of his name—Gudaphara—were unearthed in the Indus Valley, and an inscription at Peshawar indicated that his reign had lasted at least twenty-six years; historians now place it as from A.D. 19 to 45.

St. Thomas may well have been the one who brought Christianity to India. Beyond doubt it would have been possible for him to make such a voyage, for in his time there was considerable sea traffic between the Near East and India: out of Egypt down the Red Sea to Arabia, and around the coasts of the Arabian Sea to India's western coast, or else by land across Syria to the Euphrates, and down the river to the Persian Gulf, which gives access to the Arabian Sea. Some historians of the Church feel, though, that whatever Christian outposts St. Thomas may have managed to found in India were short-lived, and that the large Christian population there stems from missionary activity of a later time.

Certainly there were Christians there in the sixth century. Our authority for that is a sixth-century monk, Kosmas of Alexandria, surnamed Indicopleustes, "the Indian traveler." Kosmas had been a mariner before taking holy orders and had visited India, Ceylon, and Ethiopia; about 530, while dwelling in a monastery on Mount Sinai, he produced a bizarre geographical work, the Christian Topography, which is a strange mixture of factual information and grotesque theories about the shape and nature of the world. Concerning the island of Ceylon, which is immediately south of India, he declares, "The island has also a church of Persian Christians who have settled there, and a Presbyter who is appointed from Persia, and a Deacon and a complete ecclesiastical ritual. But the natives and their kings are heathens."

Speaking of India proper, Kosmas says, "In the country called Malê [Malabar], where the pepper grows, there is also a church, and at another place called Calliana [Kalyana, near Bombay] there is moreover a bishop, who is appointed from Persia. In the island, again, called the Island of Dioscorides [Socotra], which is situated in the same Indian sea, and where the inhabitants speak Greek, having been originally colonists sent thither by the Ptolemies who succeeded Alexander the Macedonian, there are clergy who receive their ordination in Persia, and are sent on to the island, and there is also a multitude of Christians. I sailed along the coast of this island, but did not land upon it. I met, however, with some of its Greek-speaking people who had come over into Ethiopia. And so likewise among the Bactrians and Huns and Persians, and the rest of the Indians, Persarmenians, and Medes and Elamites, and throughout the whole land of Persia there is no limit to the number of churches with bishops and very large communities of Christian people, as well as many martyrs, and monks living also as hermits."

These Christians of the Orient whom Kosmas describes were Nestorians, although the modern Christians of St. Thomas no longer adhere to the Nestorian rite, most of them having been affiliated since the seventeenth century with either the Roman Catholic or Monophysite factions of the Church. The origin of these factions lies in the stormy theological disputes that repeatedly split Christianity in the years when it was first developing into a religion of major significance.

The early church fathers differed most bitterly over the nature of the relationship of Jesus Christ to God. Was Jesus himself divine, or merely a human prophet through whom God had spoken? Was he the son of a mortal man and woman or the son of God? Should he be worshiped as God's equal? If one spoke of a Holy Trinity—the Father, the Son, and the Holy Ghost—was one worshiping one god or three? By the fourth century, angry feuding over these points threatened to divide the Church into rival and hostile branches. This was contrary to the policy of the Roman Emperor Constantine, who, having successfully brought the immense Roman Empire under his sole control after a period in which it was ruled by a committee of emperors governing different sections, had chosen Christianity to be the state religion in the hope of imposing yet another level of unity on the realm. In 325, therefore, Constantine summoned the leaders of the Church to an "ecumenical," or universal, council over which he would preside, at which

an attempt would be made to arrive at a commonly acceptable definition of the nature of Jesus. The city of Rome had long since lost its
place as the chief capital of the empire, and Constantine, who spent
most of his time in the eastern half of his domain, was then in the process of building a grand new capital to be known as Constantinople
at the gateway to the Black Sea. Since Constantinople was still un-
finished, the emperor chose Nicaea, in nearby Asia Minor, as the site
of the ecumenical council.

The chief theological business of the Council of Nicaea was a debate over the teachings of Arius, a priest of Alexandria in Egypt. Arius
was unable to accept the idea that Jesus was fully divine, the equal of
God Himself. That notion seemed to him dangerously close to the
assertion that Christians worship more than one god. If Jesus were the
son of God, Arius insisted, there must have been a time when Jesus
did not exist, and therefore he could not be God's equal, but rather
merely a messenger who had been sent to this world to instill the love
of God in mankind. This doctrine had won many followers, particularly in Egypt and other Near Eastern lands. However, the majority of
bishops insisted that Jesus was both man and god, and that one could
not be a true Christian without acknowledging his divine nature. By
a nearly unanimous vote the council denounced Arianism as a heresy
—an unacceptable and forbidden doctrine—and decreed that the
Father and the Son were *homoousios*, "of the same substance."

The next challenge to orthodoxy arose about a century later,
coming from Nestorius, a Syrian-born priest who in 428 had been ele-
vated to the rank of Patriarch of Constantinople. By this time the Roman Empire had been partitioned into eastern and western realms,
and the Patriarch of Constantinople was the highest ecclesiastical figure of the eastern (or Byzantine) sector, regarded by all Christians of
the East as on a level of parity with the Pope. Nestorius made use of
his position to promote the thesis that Christ had had two distinct natures, one human, one divine. Mary, he said, had been merely the
mother of the mortal Jesus, and so it was improper to hail her as
"Mother of God." Only later in life had Christ taken on a divine nature. Not only did Nestorius attempt to divide Jesus into two persons,
a man and a god, but he stressed the lesson for mankind to be found in
the Saviour's human life of growth, temptation, and suffering. Orthodox Christians found Nestorius' humanization of Jesus intolerable, and
at the request of the Pope another ecumenical council was called at

Ephesus, in Asia Minor, to deal with it. This council met in 431, and, after unusually violent debates, the Nestorian teachings were condemned, Nestorius himself being forced into retirement.

The doctrines of Nestorius, however, had attracted many followers east of Constantinople. A school of Nestorian theology flourished at Edessa until 489, when it was closed by order of the Byzantine Emperor Zeno; the Nestorian professors then moved eastward across the border into Persia, which had already been considerably penetrated by their teachings. Persia thereupon became the chief center of Nestorianism, virtually the entire Christian community there accepting its tenets and severing contact with the orthodox Christianity of the West. Syriac-speaking Nestorian missionaries carried their beliefs to neighboring lands, and churches of the Nestorian rite were established in eastern Syria, Arabia, and Mesopotamia. Nestorians also reached the coast of India at some time prior to the voyage of Kosmas Indicopleustes, and succeeded in imparting their ideas to the existing congregations of the Christians of St. Thomas. (Or, if Christianity had perished in India since St. Thomas' day, the Nestorians converted heathens to their faith.) By the early eighth century there were colonies of Nestorian Christians in China as well.

When the Arabs began their conquest of the Near East in the middle of the seventh century, therefore, they found Nestorian Christianity well entrenched. Mohammed himself had had instruction from a Nestorian monk in Arabia, and he gave the Church the status of a privileged minority, allowing it to function without interference after Persia came under Arab rule in 651. When Baghdad became the capital of the Moslem world in the latter part of the eighth century, the Catholicos of the East, as the head of the Nestorian hierarchy was known, transferred his headquarters to that city. Under Arab protection, Nestorian scholars carried out a great deal of important work, particularly in the translation of Greek scientific and philosophical treatises into Arabic; thus they played a significant role in the remarkable cultural development of the Arabs in the ninth and tenth centuries. The Church of the East—that has always been the official name of the Nestorians—continued to expand, and by the end of the tenth century its hierarchy was divided into fifteen provinces, ten within the Moslem world and the others in China, India, and Central Asia. Penetration of Nestorian missionaries to the Mongol steppes early in the eleventh century resulted in the celebrated conversion of the Kerait tribe. During all this time the Church of the East had no dealings whatever with Western Christendom, and its rites and sacraments came to differ considerably from those promulgated in Rome and Constantinople: veneration of the Virgin Mary was forbidden, the worship of images and holy ikons likewise, and services were performed in the Syriac tongue.

Nestorianism was not the only heresy that successfully established itself in the face of condemnation by the orthodox leaders of the Church. After the Council of Ephesus of 431, a monk named Eutyches proposed a doctrine that was so extreme in its opposition to Nestorianism that a new ecumenical council had to be called in 451 to protect Christians once again against heresy. Eutyches' teaching, known as the doctrine of Monophysitism, held that it was folly to think of Christ as having been a man at all; his human nature had been so consumed in the divine that it was sufficient to regard the Saviour as having had but one nature, a divine one.

This Monophysite belief in a wholly divine Christ quickly won a host of adherents in Egypt and western Syria. To the orthodox, though, it was just as unacceptable as the Arians' belief in a human Christ and the Nestorians' belief in a Christ of dual nature, and the ecumenical council, held just across the Bosphorus from Constantinople at Chalcedon, proclaimed Eutyches' theology to be heretical. The Council of Chalcedon offered a new formula which said, "Jesus Christ is one and the same Son, the same perfect in Godhead and the same perfect in manhood . . . made known in two natures without confusion, without change, without division, without separation." Yet the Monophysite beliefs could not be eradicated. Syrian Monophysites contemptuously referred to orthodox Syrians as "Melkites," that is, "the king's men," because they remained in communion with the church that was supported by their ruler, the Byzantine emperor. Rejecting the authority of the orthodox Patriarch of Antioch, the Syrian Monophysites set up their own patriarch in the same city. The division prevails to this day, Syria having one patriarch whose church is in communion with the Greek and other Eastern Orthodox churches, and another who presides over the Syrian Orthodox Church, which is Monophysite.

The same split occurred in fifth-century Egypt. Those Egyptians who spoke Greek and were loyal to Byzantine rule remained orthodox—"Melkites." Those who had never willingly accepted Byzantine authority, and who still spoke Coptic, the ancient language of Pharaonic times, became Monophysites. Two rival patriarchs thus presided in Alexandria. The Arabs, when they conquered Egypt in the seventh century, did not interfere in internal Christian affairs, but nevertheless many Melkites found it advantageous to convert to a church distinguished by its opposition to Egypt's former Byzantine masters, and the Coptic Church, as the Egyptian Monophysite faction called itself, came to include a majority of Egypt's Christians. The Coptic Church also was responsible for the planting of Christianity in nearby Ethiopia, which thereby became another outpost of Monophysite belief.

The orthodox Christian world itself underwent serious dissension during the centuries when the Nestorian and Monophysite heresies were establishing themselves in the East. The problem sprang from the struggle for power between the Pope, or Bishop of Rome, and the Patriarch of Constantinople. The division of the old Roman Empire in 395 into two independently governed realms had created a natural rivalry between these powerful prelates, which intensified after the western empire dissolved late in the fifth century into an array of small barbarian-ruled kingdoms. Traditionally, the Bishop of Rome had been head of the Church; but now the Patriarch of Constantinople could argue that he still presided over the true Roman Empire of the Caesars, for Byzantium was the only seat of imperial power left, while the Pope was merely a bishop with local supremacy in the chaotic West. By 484 matters were so critical that the Pope excommunicated the Patriarch of Constantinople, and the patriarch responded by declaring that the Pope had no authority over the Eastern Church. Occasional attempts were made to heal the breach, but relations between the two branches of orthodoxy were rarely amiable, and the final break came in 1054, after a quarrel over relatively minor matters of ritual. Michael Cerularius, the Byzantine patriarch, attacked the Roman Church on such questions as the mixing of water in the sacramental wine, the use of unleavened bread in communion, and the marriage of clergymen. Pope Leo IX responded to the aggressive patriarch by sending an equally aggressive Italian ecclesiastic, Cardinal Humbert, to Constantinople to defend Roman practices. Soon the two were engaged in a furious quarrel involving personal abuse of the most insulting kind. Finally, on July 16, 1054, Humbert and his fellow delegates from Rome entered Constantinople's great cathedral, Hagia Sophia, and laid on the altar a document in Latin that pronounced dire curses upon "Michael the pseudo-patriarch," his fellow clergymen, "and all who follow them in the heresies aforesaid and the crimes aforesaid." The Romans then hurriedly left the Byzantine capital. Patriarch Michael promptly pronounced equally resonant curses against the heads of the Church of Rome, and with that display of mutual ill temper all contact between the Greek and Latin branches of Christianity was sundered. Efforts at reconciliation were sporadically made, but they were futile. The two churches drifted rapidly apart in many aspects of ritual and doctrine, while each firmly maintained that it alone was the true Christian Church, in apostolic succession to the original disciples of Jesus. (The curses uttered in 1054 were not retracted until December of 1965, when Pope Paul VI and the Patriarch Athenagoras resolved to work toward some form of harmony between Eastern and Western Christianity; however, this ecumenical movement has shown few tangible results since then.)

A twelfth-century Christian such as Bishop Hugh of Jabala thus inhabited a world of fragmented faith. In western Europe the Roman Catholic Church was supreme, from the shores of the Mediterranean northward to the frosty land of the wild Norsemen, and from the British Isles eastward to Italy. In eastern Europe, though, from what now is Yugoslavia to the coast of the Black Sea, the Greek-speaking Emperor of Byzantium held sway, and ecclesiastical affairs were under the authority of his appointee, the Greek Orthodox Patriarch of Constantinople. At the eastern end of the Mediterranean, on the Syrian and Palestinian coasts, were a few tiny enclaves of Roman Catholicism: the Crusader states. But the native Christians of the Near East owed no allegiance to the Pope of the Latins. Some were "king's men," loyal even now to the Byzantine Church. Most, though, espoused doctrines that both the Roman Catholic and Greek Orthodox churches branded as heresies. In Egypt, Armenia, and western Syria they were Monophysites. In eastern Syria they were Nestorians.

Surrounding the Near East, with its tangle of conflicting Christian sects, lay Islam like a scimitar, cutting Europe off from all knowledge of farther Asia. The Arabs, who first had erupted into this region in the seventh century when all of it was part of the Byzantine Empire, still controlled Egypt, North Africa, and some of the key cities of Syria and Palestine that never had fallen to the Crusaders. Most of the Monophysite Christians lived under their rule. The Seljuk Turks, who had supplanted the Arabs as conquerors in many places, ruled in certain other parts of Syria, such as the cities of Aleppo and Damascus;

they had also lately reconquered from the Crusaders the region around Edessa, where Syria met Asia Minor; and they were masters of Mesopotamia and Persia, the two territories immediately east of the Crusader states. From the point of view of the western European Christian, the Seljuk-held country on the far side of the Euphrates was as remote and inaccessible as the moon, and the Nestorian Christians who lived in the Seljuk domain were alien beings, who might just as well have been moon-men for all that Europe knew of their way of life.

Beyond the Seljuk realm, everything dissolved, for a western European, into mist and myth. Somewhere to the east, out past Persia, there supposedly were great empires, and supposedly too there were Christian lands, but scarcely anything was known of them. Even their names were mysteries. Anyone familiar with the Orient knew of India, because it was mentioned in the *Acts of Thomas*, but no European could say precisely where India might be, and the name was applied loosely to many regions east of Persia, or often to the entire Far East. There once had been contact between Byzantium and China, in the seventh and eighth centuries, when China was enjoying a golden age under the T'ang Dynasty. But the T'ang had fallen under a barbarian onslaught in the early tenth century, and during the reign of the Khitan emperors of the Liao Dynasty the trade routes between China and the West had been snapped, so that in Bishop Hugh's time Europe had only the haziest of information about the far-off land of "Cathay," which was thought to be somewhere near India, or perhaps a part of it. In this epoch of geographical vagueness, the belief in Nestorian Christian kingdoms of the remote Orient came to glow like a brilliant beacon on the eastern horizon; and the apocryphal accounts of the missionary activities of St. Thomas in India served to lay the foundation on which the legend of the invincible priest-king Prester John arose.

5

Long before the Prester John story made its appearance in Europe, Christians everywhere had come to regard the burial place of St. Thomas as a shrine where miracles regularly occurred, and revered it as a place of holy pilgrimage. There were, however, *two* shrines of St. Thomas, one in India and one at Edessa, each claiming to hold the authentic relics of the apostle's body.

Of the Indian shrine, of course, no European of the twelfth century had exact knowledge. Several travelers of early medieval times had had claimed to have reached it, but the accounts of their journeys lack substantial detail. St. Gregory of Tours, who lived in the latter part of the sixth century, wrote in his *De Gloria Martyrum* that one Theodore had undertaken a pilgrimage to India, returning to declare, "In India is a place where the body of the Blessed Apostle Thomas was resting first, and in that place there is a monastery and a church of a wondrous size and elaborate architecture and decoration. In this sanctuary our Lord performs a great miracle. An oil lamp stands in front of the burial place and illuminates it constantly day and night and it burns without being refilled; neither wind nor accident can extinguish it and yet the oil does not decrease." And the twelfth-century English chronicler William of Malmesbury noted in his *De Gestis Regum Anglorum* that in the year 883 King Alfred, "being addicted to giving of alms . . . sent many gifts beyond the seas unto Rome, and unto [the shrine of] St. Thomas in India. His messenger in this business was Sighelm, Bishop of Sherborne, who with great prosperity (which is a matter to be wondered at in this our age) traveled through India, and returning home brought with him many strange and splendid gems, and aromatic oils and spices, such as that country plentifully yields." However, the first Western traveler who unquestionably visited the shrine of St. Thomas in India was the indefatigable Venetian Marco Polo, who saw it late in the thirteenth century while on his way home from his stay at the court of the Emperor Kublai Khan in China. Marco found the shrine not on India's Malabar or western coast, where the Christians of St. Thomas have always been most heavily concentrated, but on the eastern one, then known by the Arabic name of Maabar. His account declares, "The body of Messer St. Thomas the Apostle lies in this province of Maabar at a certain little town having no great population; 'tis a place where few traders go, because there is very little merchandise to be got there, and it is a place not very accessible. Both Christians [native to India] and Saracens, however, greatly frequent it in pilgrimage. For the Saracens do also hold the saint in great reverence, and say that he was one of their own Saracens and a great prophet, giving him the title of *Avarian*, which is as much as to say 'Holy Man.' The Christians who go thither in pilgrimage take of the earth from the place where the saint was killed, and give a portion thereof to anyone who is sick of a quartan or a tertian fever; and by the power of God and of St. Thomas the sick man is instantly cured." Marco goes on to speak of several miracles credited to the saint, describes the apostle's death (by accident, according to Marco, and not through martyrdom), and mentions that before coming to India Thomas had served as a missionary in Nubia.

The place Marco Polo visited was undoubtedly Mylapur, now a suburb of the city of Madras, which the Christians of St. Thomas continue to venerate as the place of their patron's death. An ancient shrine of St. Thomas existed at Mylapur when the Portuguese came to India at the beginning of the sixteenth century; finding it half in ruins, they erected a new one on a hill not far away. In 1522 a Portuguese commission excavated at Mylapur for the bones of St. Thomas, located them, and transferred them to Goa, the capital of Portuguese India, where they still are preserved in that city's Church of St. Thomas.

According to the apocryphal *Acts of Thomas*, though, the apostle's body did not remain at the place of his death in India but were secretly taken away by one of his followers and carried into "the regions of the West." Both of the sixth-century Latin translations of the *Acts* specifically state that Thomas' remains were taken to Edessa, the great center of Syrian Christianity, where Nestorianism would later win its first partisans. Etheria, an abbess from Gaul who made a pilgrimage to the Holy Land about A.D. 386, saw the shrine of St. Thomas at Edessa and reported that "his body is laid entire." The theologian St. Ephraim, who died in 373, suggested in one of his works that the body of St. Thomas might be resting in India and at Edessa simultaneously. There is indeed the possibility that the apostle's bones were divided, part remaining at the place of his martyrdom in Mylapur, and part being transferred to Edessa. Western Christians appear to have regarded both shrines as equally sacred. St. Gregory of Tours, writing in the sixth century and relaying the story of the pilgrim Theodore's journey to India, clearly indicates that the shrine in India is the place where the apostle *first* was buried, but that his remains since had gone to Edessa; Theodore had been to that shrine too, and witnessed another miracle there, the sudden increase of water in the city's wells at the time of the annual feast of St. Thomas. Edessa continued to display the relics of St. Thomas until 1142, when, with the chances of a Seljuk conquest of the city increasing, the saint's bones were transferred for safekeeping to the Aegean island of

Chios; in 1258 they were moved again, to the cathedral of the Italian city of Ortona, where they still remain. The Roman Catholic Church apparently recognizes the Ortona relics as the authentic bones of the apostle, relegating the bones at Goa dug up by the Portuguese to a condition of highly uncertain sanctity.

The miraculous nature of St. Thomas' shrine in India was described in detail in two twelfth-century texts, both of which contributed themes to the developing legend of Prester John. One of these is an anonymous Latin tract, *De adventu patriarchae Indorum ad Urbem sub Calixto papa secundo* ("On the Arrival of the Patriarch of the Indians in Rome under Pope Calixtus II"), and the other is a letter from Odo of Rheims, Abbot of St. Remy, to a certain Count Thomas, which also speaks of the visit of a prelate of India to Rome, and of his meeting with the Pope. *De adventu* declares that this meeting took place during the fourth year of the pontificate of Calixtus II, that is, the year beginning February 1122. The letter of Odo gives no year but fixes the date of the event at May 5.

According to the unknown author of *De adventu*, this Patriarch of the Indians, whose name was John, left his homeland so that he might travel to Constantinople, pay homage to the Greek Orthodox patriarch there, and receive from him his pallium, the ecclesiastical vestment that is a high prelate's badge of office. The journey from India to Constantinople is said to have taken a year. While at the Byzantine capital, Patriarch John encountered ambassadors from the Pope, who had come to try to heal the breach between the Greek and Roman Churches. After speaking with these Latin churchmen awhile, John asked to be allowed to go in their company back to Rome, so that he might be introduced to the Pope. This request was granted, and when he reached Rome John was entertained by Calixtus II and many of his cardinals at the Lateran Palace, where, through an interpreter, he offered a lengthy description of his native country.

The city over which he presides, said Patriarch John, is called Hulna. It is the capital of India, and is so large that a journey around its circumference would take four days; the wall that protects it is of such a size that two Roman chariots could be driven side by side along its top. Through the heart of the city flows the river Physon, which is described in the second chapter of Genesis as being one of the four great rivers that emanate from Eden. The clear waters of the Physon "cast forth most precious gold and gems, which make the regions of

India passing rich." No one but an orthodox Christian may live in Hulna; if an unbeliever or heretic comes there, "either he speedily comes to his senses or falls by sudden chance into mortal sickness." Outside the city's wall there is a lofty mountain, wholly surrounded by the waters of a deep lake, and at the summit of this peak is the mother church of St. Thomas the Apostle. On the shores of the lake are twelve monasteries.

Throughout the year the lake renders the mountain and its church inaccessible by foot, nor does anyone dare to approach by boat; but, eight days before the feast day of St. Thomas, the volume of the lake diminishes, "so that it is difficult to discern that water had been there," and "from every quarter there comes thither a concourse of people, believers and unbelievers, from distant parts, all sick, confidently expecting remedy and cure, by the merit of the blessed Apostle Thomas, for their infirmities." The church contains a "holy of holies, marvelously wrought, constructed of gold and silver and decorated with various precious stones, such as the same river of Paradise, called Physon, casts up. Within is a very precious silver shell which hangs by silver chains, a precious metal indeed, but more worthy is the treasure deposited within. For there, as on the day on which it was placed there, is still preserved the holy body of the apostle, unchanged and uncorrupted." He stands erect as in life, and before him hangs a golden lamp full of balsam, suspended by silver cords; since the day it was lit, the lamp has never gone out, nor has the balsam diminished. On the day of the feast of St. Thomas, the patriarch enters the shrine and withdraws some of that oil, anointing with it the ill, who straightaway are healed.

Accompanied by his bishops, the patriarch then solemnly opens the silver shell that holds St. Thomas' body, and, "in much fear and with great reverence," they place the apostle's body in a golden chair by the altar. "The face shines like a star, having red hair hanging almost down to the shoulders, a red beard, curly but not long, the whole appearance being beautiful to behold: the clothes as firm and whole as when they were first put on." They proceed now to celebrate the Mass; the patriarch brings the consecrated wafers to St. Thomas in a golden dish, and, kneeling, offers them to the saint, who, "by dispensation of the Creator, receives them in his extended right hand so carefully that one would take him to be not dead but living. Having received them, he keeps them in his extended palm, offering them freely to each." The whole gathering advances, and one by one each worshiper receives the wafer from the saint, except only that if a sinner or infidel or heretic should draw near, the saint will close his hand. "Such a sinner cannot evade him. Either then and there he repents and in penitence receives the communion from the apostle, or before he leaves that place he dies. Which many infidels perceiving and, terrified by the dread of so great a miracle, leave the error of their heathenism and are at once converted to the faith of Christ, and, demanding without ceasing the water of sanctification, are with one accord baptized in the name of the holy and undivided Trinity." When this has been done, and all the other holy rites and mysteries pertaining to the feast of St. Thomas have been performed, the body of the saint is replaced in its silver shell, the worshipers leave the church, and the waters of the lake shortly resume their former level. *De adventu* concludes, "The Patriarch of the Indians having thus related in the Roman Curia, Pope Calixtus II, with the rest of the Roman church who were present, raising their hands to heaven, together glorified Christ, who continues to work such and so great miracles through his holy apostle Thomas year by year, and who lives, with the Father and Holy Ghost, for ever and ever."

Taken at face value, *De adventu* seems to be nothing more than a pious miracle tract, of no particular historical importance. The city of Hulna is unknown to geographers; the story of the miraculously replenished oil lamp was probably borrowed from St. Gregory of Tours's account of the pilgrim Theodore's journey to the shrine of St. Thomas in India; two other passages of the tale were surely taken from one of the sixth-century Latin translations of the *Acts of Thomas*—in which, referring to the transfer of the saint's body to Edessa, it is noted that the body "was placed into a silver casket that hung on silver chains," and that in the city of Edessa "no heretic, no Jew, no idolator can stay alive." Even the motives for Patriarch John's visit to Constantinople must be dismissed as implausible. If he really had been a Christian of St. Thomas from southern India, he would have gone for his pallium not to the Greek Orthodox patriarch in Byzantium, who would have regarded him as heretical, but to his own Nestorian catholicos in Baghdad, if any such journey had been at all necessary.

However, a contemporary document, the letter of Odo of Rheims to Count Thomas, forces us to take at least some of *De adventu* more seriously. Odo, who lived from 1118 to 1151, probably wrote the letter between 1126 and 1135. In it he tells of being present at the court of the Pope when a delegation of ambassadors from Byzantium arrived, bringing with them a certain Archbishop of India, whom Odo does not name. Already the story deviates from *De adventu*, in which Patriarch John is said to have come to Rome with a group of returning papal legates, not with a Byzantine embassy. Odo's explanation for the Indian prelate's presence in Constantinople is also quite different. He declares that the ruler of the archbishop's country had died, leaving no heir, and the archbishop had gone to Byzantium to obtain a new prince for his land from among the Byzantine emperor's entourage. Twice the monarch had received the archbishop graciously and had nominated one of his courtiers to the Indian throne, but each time the designated candidate had perished en route to India. The emperor had declined to select a third; but instead of setting out immediately for his homeland, the archbishop had gained permission to visit Rome in the company of the Byzantine ambassadors.

Odo says he was present in Rome when the Indian archbishop had an audience with the Pope and told him about the shrine of St. Thomas. Odo's version of the miracles of the shrine is similar to that of *De adventu*, but somewhat less flamboyant. Not a lake but a river blocks access to the mountain on which the shrine is located, and an annual drought permits pilgrims to cross its bed safely. The body of the apostle is preserved within, but Thomas does not distribute communion wafers to the faithful; rather, he receives gifts from them in his open hand, and, the archbishop maintained, he closes the hand when a heretic tries to place an offering in it. Odo relates that the Pope and his cardinals refused to believe these tales until the archbishop swore an oath that convinced them.

The differences between the story told in *De adventu* and that in the letter of Odo of Rheims rule out the possibility that one was derived from the other. The miraculous aspects of the tale probably stem from some common source, now lost, which combined legends of St. Thomas' two shrines in India and Edessa into a single narrative. But what are we to make of the report of Patriarch John's visit to Rome? There is no reason to doubt Odo's statement that someone claiming to be a high ecclesiastic from India did pay a call on the Pope. Documentation exists for the alleged exchange of ambassadors between Byzantium and Rome; a letter written in May 1124 by the Byzantine Emperor John Comnenus to Pope Calixtus II apologizes for the tardiness of his reply to an earlier embassy the Pope had sent. But this does not necessarily mean that the episcopal visitor, if he did travel with one of these embassies, was actually from India. *De adventu*'s notion that the Patriarch of the Indians would have gone to the Western world to seek a pallium from the Patriarch of Constantinople is, of course, nonsense. The motive Odo gives, that the Indian archbishop had come to ask the Byzantine emperor to nominate a prince for his land, seems nearly as implausible. Perhaps the stranger who visited Rome in 1122 was an impostor, as more than one medievalist has suggested; or perhaps the deficiencies of his interpreter caused him to be misunderstood, and he came from some place other than India.

One modern student of these matters, Vsevolod Slessarev, proposed in 1959 the view that the mysterious Eastern prelate came not from India but from Edessa, or some district near Edessa in northern Syria. Much that seems unlikely or incomprehensible is thereby explained. Edessa, in 1122, was ruled by a Crusader prince, Count Joscelyn I, who at least in theory was a vassal of the Byzantine emperor. "On September 13, 1122," Slessarev points out, "Count Joscelyn and several of his companions were captured by the Turks. Would it not be possible that some Syrian or Armenian churchman from Edessa took this occasion to petition the Byzantine emperor to restore Greek rule over the city that only a generation before had been taken from the Greeks by a breach of agreement? This conjecture would conflict chronologically with May 5, 1122, as the time when the Patriarch visited Pope Calixtus II in Rome, but . . . this date is by no means reliable." If the Pope's visitor did indeed come from Edessa, he would naturally have discussed with the Pope some of the miracles credited to the shrine of St. Thomas in that city, and out of that conversation the author of *De adventu* could easily have produced the highly embroidered fantasy that has come down to us.

The story of Patriarch John bears on the legend of Prester John in several ways. The name of the prelate, obviously, is one. In the 1120s, evidently, word was circulating in Europe that a high-ranking priest from India named John had paid a call on the Pope; it is not beyond imagination to think that this story may have got back to Syria in garbled form and provided the name of John for the supposed priest-king of the extreme Orient, to whom the actual military exploits of Yeh-lü Ta-shih were being credited. This, naturally, is a slender hypothesis. What is more noteworthy about the Patriarch John narrative is the fanciful imagery it employs in describing St. Thomas' shrine in India— imagery which, as we shall soon see, recurs in the most famous of the medieval accounts of the realm of Prester John. The river of gems, the annual resurrection of St. Thomas, the all-healing balsam and other miracles, all find their place in the Prester John stories, and in one version the "Patriarch of St. Thomas" rules as regent for Prester John whenever the great monarch goes out of his country to wage war.

There are other links, besides *De adventu*, joining the legend-cycles of 'St. Thomas and Prester John. On the authority of Bishop Hugh of Jabala, Otto of Freising reported that Prester John "is said to be a direct descendant of the Magi." These were the wise men from the East who, the Gospel of Matthew relates, came to Jerusalem at the time of the Nativity, "saying, Where is he that is born King of the Jews? for we have seen his star in the east, and are come to worship him," and, finding the infant Jesus, presented him with gold and frankincense and myrrh. By the third century apocryphal traditions had arisen to the effect that the Magi were kings, and were three in number; by the sixth, their names appeared in apocryphal literature as Balthasar, Melchior, and Gaspar. In at least two late apocryphal works, the *Book of Seth* and the eighth-century Syrian *Chronicle of Zuqnin*, it is told that after the resurrection of Christ St. Thomas traveled to the homeland of the Three Magi, baptized them, and accepted their aid in the conversion of their subjects. Some scholars have pointed out that in Armenian texts of the legend the name of Gaspar appears as "Gathaspar," which they see as a variant of the Indian "Gudaphara"—who is the King Gundafor of the *Acts of Thomas*. By this process Prester John emerges as a descendant of one of the Indian kings whom St. Thomas converted to Christianity; and an account of Prester John's kingdom written less than a generation after Bishop Hugh's visit to Viterbo explicitly states that the palace of Prester John is patterned after the heavenly edifice that Thomas designed for Gundafor.

Vsevolod Slessarev has cautiously extended the theory that even the name of Prester John may have been drawn from the cycle of St. Thomas legends. He notes that in the *Acts of Thomas* the dying apostle is shown naming two young men as his spiritual successors in India: Sifur, his guide to King Mazdai's land, whom he ordains as a priest, and Vizan, King Mazdai's son, whom he makes a deacon. In several later versions of the story, however, it is Vizan who becomes the priest, Sifur the deacon; since Vizan was of royal birth, it is more probable that Thomas would have given him the higher ecclesiastical rank. Interestingly, "Vizan" is the Persian equivalent of "John," and in some versions of the story John and not Vizan is the name used for King Mazdai's son. Thus we see St. Thomas designating a certain John, who is both a priest and a future king, as one of the heads of the Christian Church in India. "An original Prester John belonging to the cycle of legends created around St. Thomas," Slessarev has written, "would solve many difficulties that so far have complicated the previous identifications. If it was he who inspired the image of the later Prester John, one could dispense entirely with the tenuous derivations of his name from the foreign titles; at the same time he would have had those vital ingredients which made the later Prester John a Christian king and priest."

6

There is one final place where we may seek the antecedents of Bishop Hugh's "Presbyter Ioannes," and that is in a work to which the good bishop certainly had access: the New Testament. For there we find the very name of John the Presbyter.

Five books of the New Testament are traditionally credited to John the son of Zebedee, one of the original twelve apostles, the first disciples of Jesus. These are the Gospel According to St. John; the Revelation of St. John the Divine; and the three short Epistles of John. The actual authorship of these five works has perplexed biblical scholars for centuries—indeed, almost since they were composed. The evidence that the Gospel of St. John was really written by the apostle is most uncertain, and, in any event, it appears that the text as we have it was substantially revised and extended by someone who was not its original author. There is considerable doubt that the author of the Gospel, whoever he may have been, was also responsible for writing the Book of Revelation. The three Epistles of John are possibly the work of the same man who produced the Gospel of St. John, but there is some cause to think that they were done by a later writer, who perhaps was one of St. John's followers. Some authorities believe that the First Epistle is by one hand and that the Second and Third are by another, although it has also been proposed that the First and Second have common authorship and the Third is separate, and that all three are the work of one individual.

It is in the Second and Third Epistles of John that the apostle, or the writer who speaks in his name, identifies himself as a "presbyter."

This was a title used from the earliest days of Christianity to designate an elder of the Church, one who has the responsibility for the management of the affairs of a local congregation, and who perhaps also does some teaching. Presbyters held a rank intermediate between bishops and deacons; that is, they were priests, and the word "priest" is derived from the Latin *presbyter*, itself derived from the Greek *presbyteros*, "an older man." The original form of the word survives today in the name of the Presbyterian Church, founded in the sixteenth century as a reformist movement whose aim was to restore Christianity to the ideals of the apostolic era.

In most English translations of the Bible, *presbyteros* is rendered as "elder." Hence, in the King James version, the Second Epistle of John begins, "The elder unto the elect lady and her children, whom I love in the truth; and not I only, but also all they that have known the truth . . ." and the Third Epistle opens, "The elder unto the well-beloved Gaius, whom I love in the truth. . . ." But a twelfth-century reader would not have had access to a translation of the Bible into English or any other secular European tongue of the time. The only text in use in Roman Catholic lands then was St. Jerome's Latin translation, the Vulgate, in which the author of the Second and Third Epistles of John speaks of himself as a *presbyter*, and anyone who consulted the original Greek text of the epistles would find the term *presbyteros* employed.

The identity of this John the Presbyter was a topic of learned inquiry when the New Testament still was young. Eusebius, Bishop of Caesarea in Palestine, devoted some lines to the matter in the classic *History of the Church* that he wrote early in the fourth century. Eusebius quotes a passage written about the year 130 by the theologian Papias of Hierapolis in Asia Minor, whose works are otherwise lost. Describing the way he learned the tenets of the faith in his obscure village, Papias said, "Whenever anyone came who had been a follower of the presbyters, I inquired into the words of the presbyters, what Andrew or Peter had said, or Philip or Thomas or James or John or Matthew, or any other disciple of the Lord, and what Aristion and the presbyter John, disciples of the Lord, were still saying. For I did not imagine that things out of books would help me as much as the utterances of a living and abiding voice." On the evidence of this passage Eusebius concluded that there had been *two* Johns, since two are mentioned by Papias: one the apostle (who could also be called a presbyter), and another, a younger man, "the presbyter John." The original apostles must all have been dead in Papias' time, but it would seem from Papias' phrase "were still saying" that Aristion and the presbyter John were alive in the early second century. Eusebius' interpretation has been challenged by some later commentators, who maintain that despite the curious double mention of John by Papias he nevertheless was referring to only one man, the apostle and presbyter; others, however, accept the presbyter as the author of the Epistles of John, though not the Gospel.

These matters aside, it is important here to consider the existence of a persistent apocryphal tradition that the Apostle John did not die but was chosen by Jesus to wander in the world as an immortal until the Second Coming of Christ. One source of this belief is the ninth chapter of the Gospel of Mark, in which Jesus, speaking with John and several of the other apostles, declares, "Verily I say unto you, That there be some of them that stand here, which shall not taste of death, till they have seen the kingdom of God come with power." And in the final chapter of the Gospel of John, Jesus seems to hint that he has conferred immortality upon John, and the Gospel notes, "Then went this saying abroad among the brethren, that that disciple should not die."

In fact, the Gospels of Mark and John both explicitly deny that John is to be granted life eternal. In the tenth chapter of Mark, Jesus tells John and his brother James, "Ye shall indeed drink of the cup that I drink of," meaning that they too shall be martyrs. Again, in the final chapter of the Gospel of John, Jesus is shown taking pains to quash the rumor that John, described as "the disciple whom Jesus loved," would be spared from death. The scene is a conversation between Jesus and some of his disciples at the shore of the Sea of Galilee, after the Resurrection, in which Jesus asks Peter to follow him into death, and the full passage, in the modern translation of Father Raymond E. Brown, is this:

"Then Peter turned around and noticed that the disciple whom Jesus loved was following (the one who had leaned back against Jesus' chest during the supper and said, 'Lord, who is the one who will betray you?'). Seeing him, Peter was prompted to ask Jesus, 'But Lord, what about him?' 'Suppose I would like him to remain until I come,' Jesus replied, 'how does that concern you? Your concern is to follow me.' This is how the word got around among all the brothers that this disciple was not going to die. As a matter of fact, Jesus never told him that he was not going to die; all he said was: 'Suppose I would like him to remain until I come [how does that concern you]?"

The implication is clear: Jesus has chosen Peter to be the next martyr but has not called upon John to die, and the subject of John's death is not Peter's business. But the entire passage has the earmarks of an editorial emendation, designed to explain to Christians of the late first or early second century how it has come to pass that the Apostle John has died, despite the widespread belief that he was not supposed to die. That is, it may have been the impression among the earliest members of the Church that Jesus had given John immortality with some such phrase as, "Remain until I come." But when the apostle did in fact die and the Second Coming was obviously not yet at hand, the closing section of the Gospel of John was amended to show that Jesus' phrase must not be interpreted literally. Despite this, the tradition of an undying John could not be eradicated.

At the city of Ephesus in Asia Minor the alleged tomb of the Apostle John was a sacred shrine as early as the second century; indeed, by the third there were two rival tombs of John at Ephesus, an embarrassment which Eusebius accounted for by suggesting that one was the apostle's tomb and one the tomb of that later John, John the Presbyter. No matter how many tombs of St. John were adduced, however, people went on believing that the apostle had been exempted from mortality and roamed the earth unrecognized, awaiting the return of the Saviour.

Now we have all the known material out of which the tale told by Bishop Hugh of Jabala could have been woven. There was St. John, who refers to himself twice in the Bible as John the Presbyter, who perhaps was still alive more than ten centuries after the Crucifixion. There were the Nestorian Christians of St. Thomas in India, who had been brought to their faith long ago by another of the twelve apostles. There was King Gundafor, said to have been one of the Three Magi, whom St. Thomas had baptized and for whom St. Thomas had built a wondrous celestial palace. There was Vizan/John, prince and priest, son of the ruler of a neighboring Indian kingdom. There was Patriarch John of India, who had come to Rome to speak of the miraculous shrine at Hulna where St. Thomas' incorruptible body was preserved. There was the ruler of the isle of Sarandib, whom Sindbad the Sailor saw to possess an emerald-tipped scepter. Lastly, there was the doughty

Yeh-lü Ta-shih, Gur-Khan of Kara-Khitai, who in 1141 had dealt the Moslem Seljuks of Persia so terrible a blow that it was worthy of a mighty champion of Christendom. Out of some or all of this the legend of Prester John was fashioned, possibly over a period of many centuries, gaining new levels of meaning with each retelling, until, by the time Bishop Hugh of Jabala paid his call on Pope Eugenius III in 1145, it had taken the form of a story of a distant Christian ruler, combining in himself the functions of priest and king, whose exploits on the field of battle were unparalleled, and who would, if only he had been able to find some way of crossing the Tigris, surely have come to the assistance of the troubled Crusaders in the Holy Land.

TWO

Prester John Sends a Letter

I<small>N THE</small> chronicle of Albéric of Trois Fontaines, written between 1232 and 1252, one finds this entry for the year 1165:

"At this time Presbyter Ioannes the King of the Indians sent his letters full of marvelous things to different kings of Christendom, but especially to Manuel the Constantinopolitan Emperor, and to Frederick, the Emperor of the Romans."

Whether Prester John's letter can actually be dated to 1165 is open to question. Albéric was not the most precise of scholars, and he was writing some seven decades after the fact, nor would it have been easy even for a meticulous historian to determine the exact year when Prester John's letter began to circulate in Europe. Hence 1165 must be considered only an approximation, though probably a fairly good one. Certainly the letter could not have been written much earlier, for its main addressee, Emperor Manuel Comnenus, did not come to the Byzantine throne until 1143. Nor could the letter date from a much later time, since Manuel died in 1180. The 1160s, the middle of his reign, are the most likely years for its composition.

The letter of Prester John became one of the most widely read documents of medieval times. Friedrich Zarncke, the great nineteenth-century German philologist whose examination of the Prester John myth can still be regarded as definitive, located and compared nearly one hundred surviving manuscripts of the letter in its Latin text alone. In addition, it was translated into French, German, English, Russian, Serbian, and many other languages, even Hebrew; it enjoyed a multitude of editions in the centuries prior to the introduction of printing, and then, in the fifteenth and sixteenth centuries, it went through innumerable printed editions in many lands. Beyond all this, the letter was plagiarized on a number of occasions by fantasists and myth-spreaders who borrowed freely from it for their own purposes. Its influence on the imagination of medieval Europe was immense, and ultimately it served as one of the great motivating forces behind the era of exploration and discovery that commenced in the fifteenth century.

Since no twelfth-century manuscripts of the letter are known to exist, we are not completely certain of the original form of the text. Through heroic labors Zarncke succeeded in demonstrating that in the course of the centuries five interpolated sections were added to the basic document, each designed to make the kingdom of Prester John seem all the more wondrous; by the time the last of these interpolations was introduced, in the fourteenth century, the letter was a veritable compendium of medieval geographical and historical folklore. We will consider these interpolations in a later section. This was the original text as reconstructed by Zarncke:

"John the Presbyter, by the grace of God and the strength of our Lord Jesus Christ, king of kings and lord of lords, to his friend Manuel, Governor of the Byzantines, greetings, wishing him health and the continued enjoyment of the divine blessing.

"Our Majesty has been informed that you hold our Excellency in esteem, and that knowledge of our greatness has reached you. Furthermore we have heard from our secretary that it was your wish to send us some objects of art and interest, for our pleasure. Since we are but human we take this in good part, and through our secretary we forward to you some of our articles. Now it is our desire to know whether you hold the true faith, and adhere in all things to our Lord Jesus Christ; for while we know that we are mortal, your little Greeks regard you as a god; still we know that you are mortal, and subject to human weaknesses.

"If you should wish to come here to our kingdom, we will place you in the highest and most exalted position in our household, and you may freely partake of all that we possess. Should you desire to return, you shall go laden with treasures. If indeed you wish to know wherein consists our great power, then believe without doubting that I, Prester John, who reign supreme, exceed in riches, virtue, and power all creatures who dwell under heaven. Seventy-two kings pay tribute to me. I am a devout Christian and everywhere protect the Christians of our empire, nourishing them with alms. We have made a vow to visit the sepulchre of our Lord with a very great army, as befits the glory of our Majesty, to wage war against and chastise the enemies of the cross of Christ, and to exalt his sacred name.

"Our magnificence dominates the Three Indias, and extends to Farther India, where the body of St. Thomas the Apostle rests. It reaches through the desert toward the place of the rising of the sun, and continues through the valley of deserted Babylon close by the Tower of Babel. Seventy-two provinces obey us, a few of which are Christian provinces; and each has its own king. And all their kings are our tributaries.

"In our territories are found elephants, dromedaries, and camels, and almost every kind of beast that is under heaven. Honey flows in our land, and milk everywhere abounds. In one of our territories no poison can do harm and no noisy frog croaks, no scorpions are there, and no serpents creep through the grass. No venomous reptiles can exist there or use their deadly power.

"In one of the heathen provinces flows a river called the Physon, which, emerging from Paradise, winds and wanders through the entire province; and in it are found emeralds, sapphires, carbuncles, topazes, chrysolites, onyxes, beryls, sardonyxes, and many other precious stones.

"There is also a sandy sea without water. For the sand moves and swells into waves like the sea and is never still. It is not possible to navigate this sea or cross it by any means, and what sort of country lies beyond is unknown. And though it lacks water, yet there are found, close to the shore on our side, many kinds of fish which are most pleasant and delicious for eating, the like of which is not seen in other lands.

"Three days' journey from this sea there are mountains from which descends a waterless river of stones, which flows through our country to the sandy sea. Three days in the week it flows and casts up stones both great and small, and carries with it also wood to the sandy sea. When the river reaches the sea the stones and wood disappear and are not seen again. While the sea is in motion it is impossible to cross it. On the other four days it can be crossed.

"Between the sandy sea and the mountains we have mentioned is a desert. Underground there flows a rivulet, to which there appears to be no access; and this rivulet falls into a river of greater size, wherein men of our dominions enter, and take therefrom a great abundance of precious stones. Beyond this river are ten tribes of Jews, who, although they pretend to have their own kings, are nevertheless our servants and tributaries. In another of our provinces, near the torrid zone, are worms, which in our tongue are called salamanders. These worms can only live in fire, and make a skin around them as the silkworm does. This skin is carefully spun by the ladies of our palace, and from it we have cloth for our common use. When we wish to wash the garments made of this cloth, we put them into fire, and they come forth fresh and clean.

"In a plain lying between the sandy sea and the mountains is a stone of incredible medical virtue, which cures Christians or would-be Christians of whatever ailments afflict them, in this fashion. There is in the stone a cavity of the shape of a mussel, in which the water is always four inches deep, and this is kept by two holy and reverend old men. These ask the newcomers whether they are Christians, or do desire to be so, and then if they desire the healing of the entire body, and if the answer is satisfactory they lay aside their clothes and get into the shell; then if their faith is sincere, the water begins to increase and rises over their heads; when this has taken place three times, the water returns to its usual height. Thus everyone who enters, leaves it cured of whatsoever disease he had.

"For gold, silver, precious stones, beasts of every kind, and the number of our people, we believe that we are unequaled under heaven. There are no poor among us; we receive all strangers and pilgrims; thieves and robbers are not found in our land, nor do we have adultery or avarice.

"When we ride forth to war, our troops are preceded by thirteen huge and lofty crosses made of gold and ornamented with precious stones, instead of banners, and each of these is followed by ten thousand mounted soldiers and one hundred thousand infantrymen, not counting those who have charge of the baggage and provisions.

"Flattery finds no place in our land; there is no strife among us; our people have an abundance of wealth; our horses, however, are few and wretched. We believe that there is none to equal us in wealth and numbers of people.

"When we go out on horseback on ordinary occasions, there is borne before us a wooden cross, without decoration or gold or jewels, so that we may be reminded of the passion of our Lord Jesus Christ, and also a single golden vase full of earth to remind us that our flesh must one day return to its original substance, the earth. But in addition there is also carried before us a silver bowl full of gold, that all may know that we are lord of lords. Our magnificence surpasses all the wealth which is in the world.

"There are no liars among us, nor does anyone dare to tell an untruth, for he who speaks a lie dies forthwith, or is regarded by us as dead. His name is not mentioned, nor is he honored among us. It is our pleasure to follow truth and to delight therein.

"The palace in which our sublimity dwells is built after the pattern of that which the apostle Thomas erected for King Gundafor, and resembles it in its offices and the rest of its structure. The ceilings, pillars, and architraves are of *shittim*-wood. The roof is of ebony, which cannot be injured by fire. At the extremities, above the gables, are two golden apples, set in each of which are two carbuncles, so that the gold shines by day and the carbuncles shine by night. The greater gates of the palace are of sardonyx inlaid with the horn of the serpent called *cerastes*, so that none may enter with poison; the lesser gates are of ebony; the windows are of crystal. The tables at which our court dines are some of gold and some of amethyst; the columns supporting them are of ivory. In front of the palace is the square where we watch the judicial contests of the trial by combat: the square is paved with onyx, in order that the courage of the fighters may be increased by the virtue of the stone. In our palace there is no light burning, except what is fed by balsam. The chamber in which our sublimity reposes is marvelously bedecked with gold and all manner of precious stones. But whenever an onyx is used for ornament, four cornelians are set about it, so that the evil virtue of the onyx may be tempered. Balsam burns perpetually in our chamber. Our bed is of sapphire, because of its virtue of chastity. We possess the most beautiful women, but they approach us only four times in the year and then solely for the procreation of sons, and when they have been sanctified by us, as Bathsheba was by David, each one returns to her place.

"We feed daily at our table 30,000 men, besides casual guests; and all of these receive daily sums from our treasury, to nourish their horses and for other expenses. This table is made of precious emerald, with four columns of amethyst supporting it; the virtue of this stone is that no one sitting at the table can fall into drunkenness.

"During each month we are served at our table by seven kings, each in his turn, by sixty-two dukes, and by three hundred and sixty-five counts, aside from those who carry out various tasks on our account. In our hall there dine daily, on our right hand, twelve archbishops, and on our left, twenty bishops, and also the Patriarch of St. Thomas, the Protopapas of Samarkand, and the Archprotopapas of Susa, in which city the throne of our glory and our imperial palace are situated. Each of them returns to his dwelling every month in his turn; otherwise no one departs from our side. Abbots, in the same number as the number of days in the year, minister to us in our chapel.

"If you ask us how it is that the Creator of all things, having made us the most supreme and the most glorious over all mortals, does not give us a higher title than that of *presbyter*, 'priest,' let not your wisdom be surprised on this account, for here is the reason. At our court we have many ministers who are of higher dignity than ourselves in the Church, and of greater standing in divine office. For our household steward is a patriarch and a king, our butler is an archbishop and a king, our chamberlain is a bishop and a king, our marshal is a king and an archbishop, our chief cook is a king and an abbot. And therefore it does not seem proper to our Majesty to assume those names, or to be distinguished by those titles with which our palace overflows. Therefore, to show our great humility, we choose to be called by a lesser name and to assume an inferior rank. If you can count the stars of the sky and the sands of the sea, you will be able to judge thereby the vastness of our realm and our power."

2

The letter of Prester John is a clever fabrication, as scholars have recognized for centuries. It was written not by some splendid potentate of the Orient but, in all likelihood, by a western European monk whose identity we shall never know.

That the letter was a work of imaginative literature, not even intended to be taken seriously as an actual example of royal correspondence, seems evident from the text. Certain conventions of diplomatic usage had been established long before the twelfth century, and most of them are ignored in Prester John's missive. It bears no date, nor is the place from which it supposedly was sent indicated; and the lofty, boastful tone of Prester John's description of his realm does not have the ring of truth. No monarch, not even one so puissant as Prester John, would be likely to take such an overbearing way of speaking about himself and his land to a fellow prince with whom he hopes to have friendly relations. The grand hyperbole of the final section ("our butler is an archbishop and a king, our chamberlain is a bishop and a king") and the mock humility of the same passage ("we choose to be called by a lesser name") are examples of literary, not diplomatic, craft, as are the gaudy tales of a miraculous stone and a sandy sea in earlier passages.

Furthermore, the literary sources of much of the letter can be traced to books available in Europe at the time of the work's composition. Zarncke showed that three passages in the original text were borrowings from a fanciful biography of Alexander the Great to be found in the *Chronicon Universale*, written early in the twelfth century by the German historian Ekkehard of Aura. Other sections, and several actual phrases, apparently came from the *Historia de Proeliis* ("History of the Battles") of Leo the Archpriest, another retelling of the deeds of Alexander dating from the latter half of the tenth century. The British scholar Malcolm Letts, in an essay published in 1945, identified a number of parallels between the letter and the writings of Isidore of Seville, Marbod of Rennes, and other medieval authors. The letter therefore is an ingenious compilation, a synthetic blend of wonders and amazements drawn from many sources.

Some students of the text have concluded that it was originally written in Greek, and thus was probably the work of a Byzantine author. The proofs offered to sustain this notion, however, are circumstantial and unconvincing. They rest on the presence of some words of Greek derivation in the Latin manuscripts that are the oldest known versions of the letter, and on a phrase that was added to the letter when the fifth interpolated section was affixed to it in the fourteenth century: "Here ends the book or history of Prester John that was translated from the Greek into Latin by the Archbishop Christian of Mainz."

No Greek manuscript of the letter has ever been recorded, though. Even the Russians and the Serbs, who were within the Byzantine cultural orbit, were forced to make use of Latin versions of the document in making translations of it into their own languages. The reference to Christian of Mainz is inconclusive and probably apocryphal; he was a German prelate who visited Constantinople on a diplomatic mission in 1170, but there is no contemporary evidence that he obtained a Greek copy of Prester John's letter while there, that he brought back to western Europe even a Latin copy, or that he ever translated the letter from Greek into Latin. Pretending that the Latin text had antecedents in other languages was probably one of the devices by which medieval readers were encouraged to believe in the letter's authenticity. A twelfth-century manuscript from Paris declares on its title page, "Here begins the letter of the Emperor John of India . . . translated first into Greek and into Latin." Another Paris manuscript claims to be a translation into Latin from the Arabic. This is not at all plausible.

A look at the Latin text casts further doubt on the notion that there could ever have been a prior Greek version. The unknown author was plainly hostile to the Byzantines, and such words of Greek origin as he used must have been chosen merely to lend an exotic texture to his style. For example, in the salutation of the letter Prester John addresses Emperor Manuel as *Romeon gubernator*, literally, "Governor of the Romans"—that is to say, "Governor of the Byzantines," since the Byzantine monarch took pains to preserve the idea that his Greek-speaking eastern European realm was the legitimate successor to the Roman Empire. But no Byzantine emperor ever styled himself "Governor of the Romans." The proper imperial title was *Basileus ton Romeon*, "Emperor of the Romans," as any Byzantine writer would certainly know. Possibly the origin of the term used in Prester John's letter lies in Leo the Archpriest's work on Alexander the Great: in a letter said to be from Alexander to his teacher Aristotle, taking the form of the Macedonian emperor's last will and testament, Alexander is made to say, "Since I have often thought of a ruler to govern you after my death, I bequeath that Ptolemy be the guardian of my tomb and your governor." The implication is that the designated "governor" was inferior in rank to Alexander himself, for Ptolemy was merely a general and inherited only a part of Alexander's empire. Use of the same word in connection with Manuel Comnenus may be construed as an attempt to deprecate the Byzantine ruler. Similarly, in one of the first passages of the letter we find Prester John speaking slightingly of Manuel's subjects: "For while we know that we are mortal, your little Greeks [*Graeculi*] regard you as a god." A Byzantine writer would not have caused Prester John to sneer that way at the Byzantines; but a writer of the Latin West, living at a time when relations between Greek Orthodox Byzantium and Roman Catholic Europe were severely strained, might well have relished doing so.

The use of the Greek *Romeon* in place of the Latin *Romanorum* in the salutation is one example of the employment of Greek words for, it would seem, purely decorative purposes. Another is Prester John's use of the term *apocrisiarii* for "messengers," instead of the expected Latin *nuntii* or *legati*. But this word had been taken over from the Greek by Leo the Archpriest; it appears nine times in the Latin text of his work on Alexander. Several other Greek words found in the letter, such as *diadema* ("diadem") and *lechitos* ("oil jar"), had similarly passed unaltered into medieval Latin before the time when the letter was written, and so cannot be used as evidence of the existence of a prior Greek text.

In discussing the high prelates who dine at his court, Prester John mentions the Protopapas of Samarkand and the Archprotopapas of Susa. These are Greek ecclesiastical titles, roughly equivalent to "bishop" and "archbishop." Plainly they were selected merely for their resonance, though, since both Samarkand and Susa then were episcopal sees of the Nestorians, whose high prelates did not bear Greek Orthodox titles; the proper rank for these ecclesiastics would have been "metropolitan." Susa, which according to the letter was Prester John's capital, was a city of Persia. At the time the letter was written Susa had been in decline for many centuries, and was partly in ruins; but it had been the Persian capital fifteen centuries earlier, under the dynasty of the Achaemenids, and in Leo the Archpriest's book the opulent palace of the Persian King Darius at Susa is described in elaborate detail—the apparent inspiration for situating Prester John's palace there.

Despite the casual mislabeling of the prelates of Samarkand and Susa, and the placing of Prester John's capital in a city whose best days were a millennium and a half behind it, the author of the letter must have had, for a European, more than ordinary familiarity with the

Orient. The reference to Samarkand shows that. This great Central Asian city, a major trading center on the old silk road that linked China to the Near East, had been known to the Greeks and Romans but cannot be found mentioned in any European document earlier than the letter of Prester John. Even the Crusaders, living at the western rim of the Orient, seemed to have no knowledge of the city, which may have been how Yeh-lü Ta-shih's victory over Sanjar at Samarkand came to be transferred to the Persian city of Ecbatana. The author of the letter could not therefore have borrowed his reference to Samarkand from some existing Latin geographical work but must have had access to travelers' reports unknown to us.

Prester John's unexpected statement, "Our horses, however, are few and wretched," in the midst of a catalogue of his country's riches, also hints at special knowledge. For in fact India had no great stock of horses and found it necessary to import them from Persia and Arabia, which was well known to merchants and travelers who visited the Orient. Marco Polo commented on it, some hundred and fifty years after the letter was written: "Here [Maabar] are no horses bred; and thus a great part of the wealth of the country is wasted in purchasing horses." If the author of the letter had access to the *Christian Topography* of Kosmas Indicopleustes, he might have made use of the reference to one of the kings of India: "Horses they bring to him from Persia, and he buys them, exempting the importers of them from paying custom." But Kosmas' book was then some six hundred years old, and perhaps some more recent oral source was used. (Curiously, the line about Prester John's horses seemed so incongruous amidst the recital of plenty that in later medieval versions of the letter it was changed to read, "We have many and swift horses.")

The form of the letter itself has led some scholars to ascribe to its author a familiarity with Oriental literature—specifically, to *The Thousand and One Nights*. In the sixth voyage of Sindbad, the same that cites the King of Sarandib's emerald-tipped scepter, Sindbad quotes the text of a letter he was asked to carry from that potentate to the Caliph Harun al-Rashid. Though brief, it is in the florid style of the Prester John letter and, like it, dwells on the wealth of its sender. In Richard Burton's translation: "The missive was written . . . with ink of ultramarine and the contents were as follows. 'Peace be with thee from the King of Al-Hind [India], before whom are a thousand elephants and upon whose palace-crenelles are a thousand years. But after (laud to the Lord and praises to His Prophet!): we send thee a trifling gift which be thou pleased to accept. Thou art to us a brother and a sincere friend; and great is the love we bear for thee in heart; favour us therefore with a reply. The gift besitteth not thy dignity: but we beg of thee, O our brother, graciously to accept it and peace be with thee.' And the present was a cup of ruby a span high the inside of which was adorned with precious pearls; and a bed covered with the skin of the serpent which swalloweth the elephant, which skin hath spots each like a dinar and whoso sitteth upon it never sickeneth; and an hundred thousand miskals of Indian lign-aloes and a slave girl like a shining moon." Later in the same tale, when Sindbad has reached Baghdad and has his audience with the Caliph Harun, he offers this description of the King of Sarandib's court: "For state processions a throne is set for him upon a huge elephant, eleven cubits high: and upon this he sitteth having his great lords and officers and guests standing in two ranks, on his right hand and on his left. At his head is a man hending in hand a golden javelin and behind him another with a great mace of gold whose head is an emerald a span long and as thick as a man's thumb. And when he mounteth horse there mount with him a thousand horsemen clad in gold brocade and silk; and as the King proceedeth a man precedeth him, crying, 'This is the King of great dignity, of high authority!'" Sindbad also informs Harun that there is no need for judges in the Indian king's capital, since all his subjects are able to distinguish between truth and falsehood. The tale of Sindbad, which is echoed in so many ways by the Prester John letter, was composed in the ninth or tenth century.

The tale of the river of stones likewise indicates that the author of the letter was acquainted with the literature of the East. The earliest known references to this myth are to be found in the writings of two Roman authors of the first century. Pliny, in his great compendium, *Historia Naturalis*, notes, "In Judaea there is a river that is dry every Sabbath day." The Jewish historian Flavius Josephus provides somewhat more detail, locating the wondrous river in Lebanon and declaring, "When it runs, its current is strong, and has plenty of water; after which its springs fail for six days together, and leave its channel dry, as anyone may see. After this it runs on the seventh day as it did before, and as though it had undergone no change at all, and it has been observed to keep this order perpetually and exactly: whence they call it the Sabbatic River, so naming it from the sacred Sabbath of the Jews."

This story, apparently based on the existence of actual intermittent (though far less regular) rivers or streams in the Near East, bobbed up frequently in the reports of later travelers. But the specific source used by the author of the Prester John letter seems to have been the narrative of Eldad the Danite, a Jewish traveler and philologist of the second half of the ninth century. Eldad, a native of Arabia or Palestine, spent some years traveling in Egypt, Mesopotamia, North Africa, and Spain, and is credited with having written a romantic and fabulous account of his adventures, in which, after having been captured by and rescued from cannibals, he discovers the ten lost tribes of Israel scattered throughout the Orient. The tribe of Levi, according to Eldad's account, lived in "the land of Havila," somewhere "beyond the rivers of Ethiopia," and the Levites were cut off from the rest of the world by the river Sambation, which is described in this fashion: "The river Sambation is two hundred yards broad, about as far as a bowshot. It is full of sand and stones, but without water; the stones make a great noise like the waves of the sea and a stormy wind, so that in the night the noise is heard at a distance of half a day's journey. There are sources of water which collect themselves in one pool, out of which they water the fields. There are fish in it, and all kinds of clean birds fly round it. And this river of stone and sand rolls during the six working days and rests on the Sabbath day. As soon as the Sabbath begins, fire surrounds the river, and the flames remain until the next evening, when the Sabbath ends." Eldad's work was written in Hebrew, and the first known Latin translation was not published until the sixteenth century; yet from the resemblances between this passage and the pertinent sections of the Prester John letter it appears likely that the author of the latter had at least secondhand knowledge of the story as told by Eldad.

On the other hand, he neglected two obvious sources: the Prester John story in the version of Bishop Hugh of Jabala, and *De adventu*, the account of Patriarch John of the Indians and the miraculous shrine of St. Thomas. Both of these narratives were in circulation twenty years or more before the supposed date of Prester John's letter. But nowhere in the original text of the letter do we find references to Prester John's descent from the Magi, his defeat of the Persians, or his unsuccessful attempt to reach Jerusalem, and we may be sure that at least the first of those would have found its way into the letter had the author known of it; indeed nothing of Bishop Hugh's story enters the letter except the name of Prester John itself and the priest-king's vow to visit the Holy Land. Nor can we recognize in the letter the mountain-in-the-lake on which St. Thomas' shrine is situated in *De adventu*, or the ghostly Mass at which the apostle annually presides, and the capital city of Hulna is not mentioned. Two minor traces of *De adventu* do appear in the letter: the jewel-bearing river Physon out of Paradise, and the reference to the "Patriarch of St. Thomas" being present at Prester John's court. But these must have reached the author of the letter through some other source, since it is hard to believe that he would have ignored the gaudy wonders of *De adventu* had he had access to that text.

Who, then, was responsible for writing Prester John's letter? Friedrich Zarncke, after making the closest possible study of the existing manuscripts, found himself unable to decide with any confidence whether the original text had been composed in Latin or in Greek. A twentieth-century student of the letter, Alexander A. Vasiliev, reached the conclusion that "both the direct and indirect evidence . . . testifies that the original text was Greek," and suggested that the author was a Nestorian living in Constantinople. However, most scholars have accepted the 1923 verdict of the American medievalist Lynn Thorndike: "This letter even in its earliest and briefest form seems without doubt a western forgery and bears the marks of its Latin origin, since despite the use of a few Greek ecclesiastical and official terms and the attempt to rehearse unheard-of wonders, the writer indulges in a sneer at Greek adoration of the emperor and is unable to conceive of Prester John except as a feudal overlord with the usual kings, dukes and counts, archbishops, bishops and abbots under him." But the frequent recourse in the letter to special knowledge of the Orient that would not have been available in Latin works of the time leads one to doubt that it was produced by some monk of literary inclinations working in the well-stocked library of a French or German abbey. More probably the author lived in one of the Latin states of the Near East, where he would have access to the books of the West and to the oral traditions, at least, of the East. And very likely he was in holy orders, for at that time clerics held a near monopoly on literacy, and besides were generally more hostile to the schismatic Byzantines than most Latin laymen. Beyond these hypotheses we cannot go. There are no further clues to the identity of Prester John's invisible amanuensis.

3

And why was the letter written? What was its unknown author's real intent?

The simplest assumption, and the one most frequently heard, is that he was attempting to perpetrate a literary hoax—that the letter was, to use Lynn Thorndike's phrase, "a western forgery," purporting to be an actual letter from Prester John to Emperor Manuel Comnenus. This is not easy to accept, in view of the letter's departures from conventional diplomatic form and its numerous exaggerations and absurdities, which ought to have aroused suspicions even in credulous medievals. What would be the purpose of such an exercise? To stimulate European interest in the Orient? To initiate a quest for the realm of Prester John? To induce Western rulers to send ambassadors to that fabled monarch? In fact, these were the consequences of the letter's wide distribution; but one is reluctant to assert that its author had any such goals in mind.

One school of thought holds that the letter had no particular purpose: that it was never intended to be passed off as an authentic piece of diplomatic correspondence, but rather was merely a literary endeavor, whose author had stitched together an assortment of current legends to make a pretty tale. Its readers would derive nothing but entertainment from it, or, at most, some knowledge of the supposed miracles of the Orient. That seems to have been the attitude of the letter's first known translator, Roau d'Arundel. During the Third Crusade (1190–92), one of whose leaders was King Richard the Lion-Hearted of England, a party of English knights stopped in Constantinople on the way home, and a butler named Gillibert somehow obtained in that city a copy of the Latin text of the letter. He turned it over to Roau, one of the Crusaders in the group, who produced a rendering of it into Anglo-Norman verse. In a prologue that he added to the letter, Roau indicated that the work's chief value lay in the diverting and instructive portrait it provided of "the great miracles of the Orient." It was, to him, no more than a quaint narrative of exotic wonders, which one could take at face value or accept as a fantasy, as one chose.

Another line of reasoning has it that the letter was composed by a Crusader to bolster the morale of his fellow Crusaders, by instilling in them the hope that a mighty Christian monarch of the East might at any moment ride to their aid. In 1145, Bishop Hugh of Jabala had taken pains to deny this very supposition during his tour of western Europe. Thus persuaded that they were the only succor the Crusader states might find, the rulers of Germany and France had organized the Second Crusade—which, however, ended in complete failure by 1149. Since then the position of the Crusaders had shown no improvement. In January 1153, King Baldwin III of Jerusalem had captured the Palestinian port of Ashkelon, the only city on the coast of the Holy Land that had remained in Saracen hands, but that was to be the last moment of glory the Kingdom of Jerusalem would know. Within a few years the Crusaders found themselves hemmed in by strong Moslem foes on two fronts. A Turkish general, Nur ed-Din, had assembled a domain that stretched down the entire eastern border of the Latin Near East from Edessa to the deserts beyond the Jordan River. No one Moslem leader had ever before controlled that whole region, which took in all the territory that today comprises eastern Turkey, eastern Syria, and the Kingdom of Jordan. To the south, in Egypt, the old Arab dynasty had come upon evil times, creating an opportunity for Nur ed-Din to extend his power even further. After a series of assassinations the Egyptian throne had fallen, in 1160, to a nine-year-old boy, and all was chaos there: the real control of the country was in the hands of the vizier, or chief minister, but within the space of two years two viziers were slain and a third was driven from the country. In 1163 Nur ed-Din sent one of his lieutenants, a certain Shirkuh, into Egypt to restore order. Shirkuh, leading a strong Turkish army, set himself up as Egypt's "protector," ruling through a puppet Egyptian vizier in the name of the boy caliph. This presented the Crusaders with the frightening prospect that all the Saracen lands would come under the direct rule of Nur ed-Din, thereby ending the feuding that had until then prevented the Moslems from launching a single organized attack against the Crusader intruders in their midst. To the Crusaders, no less than to the Israelis in a similar position today, such a unified concerted attack was the ultimate threat.

King Amalric of Jerusalem was able to forestall that threat in 1164 through diplomatic intrigue, forming an alliance with Shawar, a former Egyptian vizier, in order to oust the Turks from Egypt. With the aid of Amalric's troops Shawar forced Shirkuh to withdraw, ending for the moment the possibility of a united Saracen front. Even so, the uncomfortable likelihood remained that the Moslems would eventually come together to crush the Crusaders; and, perhaps, the letter of Prester John was designed to encourage the harried Latins gloomily contemplating that eventuality. (In fact, the worst was to come to pass within a generation after Prester John's letter was written. Saladin, Shirkuh's nephew, succeeded in gaining control of Egypt in 1169, and a few years later inherited Nur ed-Din's Syrian domain. Gradually he conquered much of the area belonging to the Crusaders; in 1187 he captured Jerusalem itself, leaving the Latins only Antioch, Tripoli, Tyre, and a few other outlying towns.)

The Italian scholar Leonardo Olschki proposed in 1931 that Prester John's letter was neither a hoax nor a literary romance nor an inspirational work for Crusaders, but rather a piece of utopian literature, postulating an ideal commonwealth in order to level moral criticism against twelfth-century Europe. According to Olschki, the figure of Prester John, uniting in his person the roles of king and priest, was conceived as a comment on "the bitter controversy then raging between church and state, respectively personified in the Pope and the Holy Roman Emperor. It was just when the struggle for power between Frederick Barbarossa and Pope Alexander III had reached its climax that there came to their attention this literary image of an exemplary ruler who combined both the kingly and the priestly office for the good of his peoples, practiced the highest public virtues, and abstained from evil— quite in accord with the Western imperial ideal and the political literature of the Middle Ages." In his portrayal of the realm of Prester John, Olschki maintained, the author of the letter offered his vision of the perfect society. Europe then was torn by religious factionalism and by political squabbling; the people of the Christian West were given over to envy, greed, violence, and lust; and here, in Prester John's own words, was a description of a land in which poverty and strife were unknown, where the teachings of Jesus were universally obeyed, where adultery and avarice found no place, and where the pious king, who abjured sexual intercourse except for the sake of siring progeny, was content to be known by the humble title of "priest." It was a land where virtue reigned and where virtue was rewarded, since the rivers themselves overflowed with precious gems and every man possessed abundant wealth. The letter, therefore, was a political allegory, Olschki said, the prime purpose of which was to induce the people of Europe to abandon discord and pride and adopt the principles of justice and humility so splendidly exemplified by that extraordinary monarch, Prester John.

4

The geographical location of the realm of Prester John was a matter of some concern to the medieval readers of his letter. The original text of that letter supplies only three clues. One is the reference to the Persian city of Susa as the site of Prester John's capital. The second is the information that the river Physon runs through one of his provinces. The third is the passage which declares, "Our magnificence dominates the Three Indias, and extends to Farther India, where the body of St. Thomas the Apostle rests. It reaches through the desert toward the place of the rising of the sun, and continues through the valley of deserted Babylon close by the Tower of Babel."

From this evidence we are meant to conclude that Prester John's kingdom begins just east of Syria and stretches far to the east. Babylon was a city of Mesopotamia, situated on the Euphrates River near the present city of Baghdad in Iraq. Susa lay a few hundred miles farther east, at the foot of the Zagros Mountains in what is now Iran. From Susa to the western borders of India is a distance of more than fifteen hundred miles. That the author of the letter should have placed Prester John's capital in Susa is an indication of how hazy the geographical notions of twelfth-century Europeans were: for all his apparent knowledge of the Orient, the author of the letter must have thought that India proper was just on the other side of Persia, a litle way beyond Susa. (Otto of Freising seems to have had the same compressed view of Asia. He quotes Bishop Hugh of Jabala as saying that Prester John "lives in the extreme Orient, beyond Persia and Armenia." But in another section of his chronicle he records the visit of a delegation of Armenian bishops to the Pope and describes them as coming *ab ultimo pene oriente*, "almost from the farthest East," as if he believed that the farthest East itself could not be very much farther than Armenia.)

The citation of the river Physon tells us that the author of the letter wanted his readers to regard Prester John as ruler over India proper, since medieval geographers always placed that river in India, even when they had no idea of where India might be. The Physon, or Pison, is mentioned in the second chapter of the book of Genesis as one of the four great rivers flowing out of Eden, the others being the Gihon, the Hiddekel, and the Euphrates. From the biblical description it is evident that the Gihon is the Nile and the Hiddekel is the Tigris; and at least as early as the sixth century such Christian geographers as Kosmas Indicopleustes were identifying the Physon as the Indus, which then formed the boundary between Persia and India, though other writers of the era thought it to be the Ganges. In *De adventu*, the Physon is said to flow through the middle of Prester John's capital, Hulna; Prester John's letter, which of course places the capital far to the west of the Indus at Susa, locates the Physon merely "in one of the heathen provinces" of his realm.

The letter also declares that Prester John rules over "the Three Indias." Few phrases more ill defined than that can be found in the archives of medieval European geography. The term "India" itself was loosely applied to virtually every part of the Far East, as well as to a good deal of what we would consider the Near East, and some of Africa as well. From early Christian times it was generally agreed that this immense tract was divided into three (or sometimes two) regions of distinctly different character, but the definitions of the regions varied enormously. One writer of the early Christian Era known to us only as the Pseudo-Abdias quoted "certain historiographers" to the effect that the first of the three Indias faces Ethiopia, the second faces the country of the Medes, and the third occupies the end of the earth, with the realm of darkness on one side and the ocean on the other. The mapmaker Lambert of St. Omer, working about 1130, showed *India Prima*, the land of the pygmies; *India Secunda*; and *India Ultima*, the land "of the trees of the sun and moon." Another map of the twelfth century paradoxically depicted *India Ultima*, "Farthest India," as the territory closest to Europe: it extended from the Indus to the "Hipanis," in Persia, thus comprising what now are Afghanistan and West Pakistan. *India Inferior* lay between the Indus and the Ganges, taking in most of what today is India, and *India Superior* lay to the northeast, running from the Ganges to the Caucasus. Still another system divided India into Nearer or Lesser India, Farther or Greater India, and Middle India. The first of these was the northern half of the Indian subcontinent; the second was the southern half, where the Christians of St. Thomas were to be found; and by Middle India was meant, apparently, Ethiopia. Medieval geographers had no very clear concept of the distance between Ethiopia and India, and tended to regard everything east of the Nile—including Ethiopia—as being part of Asia. This confusion of Ethiopia with India would eventually have an important effect on the development of the legend of Prester John.

Prester John's claim to hold sway over the Three Indias, as expressed in his letter to Emperor Manuel Comnenus, therefore gave twelfth-century Europeans no specific idea of the boundaries of his realm. They could conclude only that it was immense, and ran from Mesopotamia and Persia to the uttermost end of the earth in the east, taking in virtually every Oriental land of which anyone had heard. Surely this must be a king of kings!

5

A dozen years after the supposed date when Prester John's letter began to circulate in Europe, Pope Alexander III made the first attempt on the part of a major European figure to open communication with the fabled Oriental monarch. From Venice, on September 27, 1177, Pope Alexander dispatched a letter to Prester John, manuscript copies of which have survived in the libraries of Cambridge and Paris, and summaries of which were embedded in the chronicles of such medieval annalists as Roger of Hoveden, Benedict of Peterborough, and Matthew Paris.

Alexander III, who had ascended to the papacy in 1159, had been a celebrated professor of theology at Bologna, and later, as cardinal and then as papal chancellor, had helped to direct the fortunes of the Church through one of its most trying periods, the time of conflict between the Pope and the Holy Roman Emperor. The medieval papacy was both a temporal and a spiritual office; the Pope had become a feudal lord, who by the twelfth century had more vassals than any other European prince. Under the feudal contracts between Pope and vassal, St. Peter, acting through the person of the reigning Pope, was deemed to confer his protection upon the vassals, in return for military service or monetary payments. The involvement of the papacy in European secular affairs inevitably created friction between the Pope and the so-called Emperor of the Romans, who had pretensions of his own to political supremacy in western Europe.

The western half of the original Roman Empire had collapsed in the fifth century, and for the next three hundred years the only emperor to be found in Christendom was the Byzantine monarch who ruled from Constantinople. His authority in Europe did not extend west of the Balkans, but he was universally acknowledged to be the successor to the Roman Caesars, and the kings of the western European countries that had formed out of the old Western Roman Empire regarded him, in theory if not in fact, as their sovereign. But, in 800, Pope Leo III suddenly crowned Charlemagne, the Frankish king, as emperor, thereby claiming to have revived the Western Empire. Charlemagne ruled over a considerable area; his empire, however, was dissipated by his descendants, yet the concept of an Emperor of the West remained alive, to the great displeasure of Byzantium. German princes invariably were elected to the imperial title, and by the latter half of the tenth century the Western Empire consisted essentially of Germany and northern Italy, with Burgundy being added after 1032. Italy south of the Alps was the domain of the Pope and his vassals.

The struggle between the papacy and the empire was a fluctuating one; there were long intervals of peace, punctuated by bitter strife whenever some strong-willed individual came to either throne. One of the most famous crises was the battle between the Emperor Henry IV and the sturdy reformist Pope Gregory VII late in the eleventh century. At one stage in the dispute Henry declared Gregory deposed, and Gregory retaliated by excommunicating Henry. In 1077, Henry was forced to beg forgiveness from the Pope, making the celebrated pilgrimage to Canossa, but later he succeeded in sending Gregory into exile and established a puppet anti-Pope at Rome. Difficulties between the two great powers eased for some time thereafter, but in 1157 they erupted again. Adrian IV, the only Englishman ever to become Pope, had granted the imperial title to the German King Frederick Barbarossa in 1155, on the condition that Barbarossa swear fealty to him. But soon Frederick denied that he was Adrian's vassal and rejected the Pope's authority as a secular monarch. It was Barbarossa who added the adjective *sacrum* to the name of his realm, making it for the first time the *Holy* Roman Empire, by way of establishing its equality with the holy domain over which the Pope presided.

Adrian IV died in 1159, and his chancellor, Ronald Cardinal Bandinelli, was elected to succeed him as Alexander III. But the new Pope had been one of Frederick Barbarossa's most vehement opponents, and Barbarossa refused to accept his election, recognizing another prelate instead as Pope Victor IV. For this he was excommunicated by Alexander in 1160. What followed was, essentially, a war between Germany and Italy, with Pope Alexander the symbol of Italian resistance to domination by the German Emperor Frederick. Frederick invaded Italy, besieging and razing Milan, and chasing Alexander into exile. Since it was apparently about this time that the letter of Prester John was composed, it may well be that that document was a political fantasy designed to contrast the peace and serenity of his realm with the unseemly turmoil of Western Christendom, where church and state were not only separate powers but at one another's throats.

Frederick did not succeed in conquering Italy, but he maintained his defiance of Pope Alexander: when Victor IV died in 1164, Frederick procured the election of another anti-Pope, Paschal III, and two years later he stormed Rome and seated Paschal on the papal throne. Two more anti-Popes, Calixtus III and Innocent III, followed, while Alexander was compelled to withdraw to France for a prolonged stay. But eventually the defiant Barbarossa suffered grave reverses; in yet another attempt to invade Italy in 1176 his army was defeated at Legnano and he himself was wounded and nearly slain on the battlefield. He found no choice but to yield to the durable Alexander, and the long schism came to an end at Venice in July 1177, when Frederick knelt before Alexander, kissed his feet, and acknowledged him to be Pope. It was the most thorough surrender of civil power to clerical authority since Henry IV's submission at Canossa exactly one hundred years earlier.

Two months after his triumph over Barbarossa, Pope Alexander dictated his letter to Prester John—as though, finally having established his supremacy in Western Christendom, the Pope wished to bring the great monarch of the Orient under his sway as well. The letter is addressed *carissimo in Christo filio Iohanni, illustri et magnifico Indorum regi:* "to his dearest son in Christ, John, illustrious and magnificent King of the Indians." It opens with a conventional statement of the doctrine of the Pope's authority over all Christians, in line of succession from the first pontiff, St. Peter. Then Alexander declares that he has heard from many persons and by common report that John is a pious Christian, and eager to do good works. The Pope's own physician and confidant, Master Philip (*magister Philippus, medicus et familiaris noster*), had provided him with a great deal of information about John, for Master Philip had spoken with great and honorable men of John's kingdom *in partibus illis,* "in those parts," by which the Pope apparently means in John's own land, or some neighboring territory. Philip had reported that John devoutly wished instruction in the tenets of Roman Catholic belief, so that he and his kingdom might in all ways

Respicer Iohānes potē
cia dei z virtute dñi nr̄i
iħu xp̄i Rex regū z dñs
dñanciū amico suo Ema
nueli Rome guberna-
tozi salutē gaude' z gr̄a
dirādi ad vlterioza trā-
sire Nūciabat' apud ma
iestatē nr̄am ꝙ dilige-
bas vide' excellēciā no-
strā· z mencio altitudi-
ms nr̄e erat apud te Sz p apocrifariū nr̄m ꝯgnoui
m⁹ ꝙ ꝙdā ludicra z iocūda volebas nob' mittere
ꝙb⁹ delectaret² iusticia nr̄ā · Et em̄ si hō sum ꝓ bo
no habeo · z de nr̄is per apocrifariū nr̄m aliꝙ tibi
trāsmittim⁹ · ꝙ scire volum⁹ z desideram⁹ si rectā
fide nobiscū habeas · z si p omnia credas in dñm
nr̄m iħm xp̄m Cū em̄ nos hōies esse cognoscamus
querculi tui te deū estimāt · cū te moztalē z hūani
cozrupcōm subiace' cognoscā⁹ de ꝯsueta largita-
tis nr̄e mūificēcia si aliquoꝫ ꝙ ad gaudia ꝑtinent
nullā habes indigēciā p apocrifariū tuū z p cedu
lā dilectōis tue nos certifica z impetrab' Accipe
hyperūcā in nōie nr̄ō z ure' ꝙ libent' utim² lecbico
tuo ut sic ꝯfoztem⁹ z cozrozoborem⁹ ꝰirtutes nr̄as ad
inuicē Tigna quoꝗ nr̄m respice z ꝯsidera ꝙ si ad
dñatoziū nr̄e maiestatis venire volueris · maiozis
z digmozis nr̄e dom⁹ dñm te ꝯstituem⁹ z potens
frui abūdācia nr̄ā ex his ꝙ ap⁰ nos sunt z abun-
dāt · z si redire volueris locupletat⁹ redibis Si ve
ro vis cognosce' in ꝙb⁹ dñet² potencia nr̄ā crede si
ne dubitacōe ꝙ e⁰ p̄sbit' Ioħes dñs dñanciū ꝓcel
lo oēs ꝙ sub celo sunt ꝰirtute diuicijs z potencia ·

1. First page of the first printed edition of Prester John's letter in Latin (c. 1480).

2. Pope Alexander III meeting the Doge of Venice. BETTMANN ARCHIVE.

3. Genghis Khan. BETTMANN ARCHIVE.

4. "Men Whose Heads Do Grow Beneath Their Shoulders," illustration from Otto von Diemeringen's German translation of Mandeville, 1484.

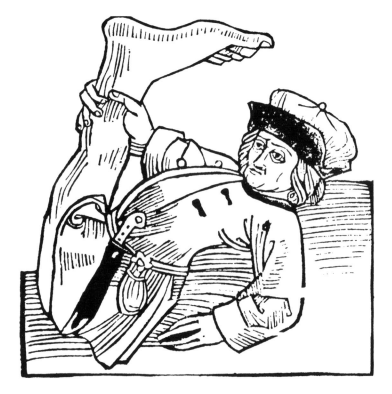

5 and 6. A sciapod, from Von Diemeringen's Mandeville, and a flat-faced man from Velser's German translation of Mandeville, 1482.

practice their faith in accordance with the doctrines of the Apostolic See—that is, of the papacy. Also, according to Philip, John desired to have a church in Rome and an altar in Jerusalem, for the use of those of his subjects who might come to those cities to receive the apostolic teachings. Pope Alexander goes on to say that because of the difficulties and dangers of the long and laborious journey he did not at present find it feasible to dispatch anyone of ecclesiastical rank to John's land; but he would, however, send Master Philip to serve as John's instructor in Roman Catholicism. Upon Philip's arrival at John's court, the Pope says, the king should send envoys to Rome bearing letters sealed with his seal, in which his wishes should be expressed at length. "The more nobly and magnanimously you conduct yourself," the Pope concludes, "and the less you boast of your wealth and power, the more readily shall we regard your wishes both as to the granting of a church in the city and of altars in the Church of Sts. Peter and Paul, and in the Church of the Lord's Sepulchre at Jerusalem, and as to other reasonable requests." Master Philip thereupon was dispatched to Prester John's kingdom bearing the Pope's letter, but what befell him on that journey we cannot say, since nothing is known of the success or failure of his mission.

Pope Alexander's letter has commonly been taken to be a direct response to the letter of Prester John, but there are no strong reasons for thinking that that was the case. Prester John had addressed himself to Manuel Comnenus; why, therefore, should the Pope answer someone else's mail? (In the various later medieval versions of Prester John's letter, it is addressed not only to Manuel but to Frederick Barbarossa, and sometimes to other European monarchs, but never to Pope Alexander; the early manuscripts are addressed to Manuel alone.) There is internal evidence that the Pope was aware of Prester John's letter: the phrase, "the less you boast of your wealth and power, the more readily shall we regard your wishes," seems a clear rebuke to Prester John's expansive self-praise. But Pope Alexander makes no other references, veiled or otherwise, to the earlier letter, and indicates that all his information about Prester John has come "from many persons and by common report" and from his beloved friend Master Philip. The Pope chooses to ignore John's mock-humble boast of being content with the rank of priest: he hails John solely as a king, never as a priest, and nowhere in his letter does he call John by the title of Presbyter or any of its variations. (One of the late twelfth-century chroniclers who quotes the letter, Roger of Hoveden, includes in the salutation the phrase, *sacerdoti sanctissimo*, "holy priest," after "King of the Indians," but this is found in no other contemporary manuscripts and is probably an apocryphal insertion.) It would seem, then, that the Pope did not regard himself as replying to any previous letter, but was taking the initiative in making contact with Prester John, having become interested in John through hearing the stories told by Master Phillip.

One wonders who Master Philip was and where he got the information about John, King of the Indians, that led Pope Alexander III to send his letter. The only knowledge we have about this physician to the Pope is that which is contained in Alexander's letter itself. Lynn Thorndike has pointed out that in the twelfth century a certain Philip, a cleric of the crusader city of Tripoli on the Lebanese coast, obtained in Antioch the manuscript of an old Greek scientific text spuriously attributed to Aristotle, *The Secret of Secrets*, and translated it into Latin. *The Secret of Secrets* was greatly prized in medieval times for its medical sections; was this Philip of Tripoli the same Philip who was Pope Alexander's doctor? It is impossible to say. But if we are to make any sense of the Pope's letter, we must assume that his Philip was a man who on some occasion had visited the East.

Where had he gone, though? The Pope's reference to *partibus illis*, "those parts," is ambiguous. It could be taken to mean Prester John's own kingdom, or merely some Oriental land close by it. What if Master Philip had traveled no farther from Italy than Syria or Egypt? Would he have had occasion to talk with "great and honorable men of John's kingdom" in one of those countries?

It appears that he would. There was indeed one Christian monarch living in those parts of the world which Europeans included in their notion of "India," and this ruler might very well have had ambassadors in Egypt or Syria at the time when Master Philip was there. He was the king of the African realm of Ethiopia: a Monophysite, not a Nestorian, but otherwise well qualified to play the part of Prester John, for he was a Christian, a valiant warrior, and, by European geographical thinking, a native of India. Furthermore, Ethiopian annals show that in the twelfth century the Ethiopians were quarreling with their spiritual leader, the Coptic Patriarch of Alexandria, so they might well have been considering shifting their allegiance to the Pope, as Master Philip reported. Also it is a matter of record that the Ethiopians at that time wished to obtain a church in Jerusalem. The Crusaders, regarding them as heretics, gave them no such privileges; but in 1187 the Saracen leader Saladin, having extinguished the Latin Kingdom of Jerusalem, granted the Ethiopians a chapel in the Church of the Holy Sepulchre at Jerusalem and a station in the grotto of the Nativity at Bethlehem. From this it seems clear that the "great and honorable men" Master Philip met while he was *in partibus illis* were Ethiopians, traveling on some mission on behalf of their exalted and Christian sovereign, and that "John, King of the Indians," of whom Philip spoke to the Pope, was in truth the black-skinned Negus of Ethiopia.

6

We cannot say whether Master Philip actually delivered the Pope's letter to Prester John, but we may be sure that no reply from that monarch reached the Pope, for, had a second letter from Prester John arrived, every contemporary chronicler would have made much of it, and no such letter is mentioned by anyone. Prester John remained silent.

In the absence of a new letter from the fabulous potentate, the old one continued to circulate, both in Latin and in humbler tongues. As we have seen, the first known translation of the letter into a vernacular language was the Anglo-Norman one produced by the Crusader Roau d'Arundel about 1192. By the early thirteenth century it had been joined by French and Italian versions, and perhaps others.

The letter, passing through the hands of its many copyists and translators, tended to grow longer, and Prester John's realm thereby became more wondrous. The first interpolation to enter the text concerned the techniques of producing pepper in the land of Prester John:

"In another of our provinces pepper is grown and gathered, to be exchanged for corn, grain, cloth, and leather. But that district is thickly wooded and full of serpents, which are of great size and have two heads and horns like rams, and eyes which shine as brightly as lamps. When the pepper is ripe, all the people come from the surrounding countryside, bringing with them chaff, straw, and very dry wood with which they encircle the entire forest, and, when the wind blows strongly, they light fires inside and outside the forest, so that the serpents will be trapped. Thus all the serpents perish in the fire, which burns very fiercely, except those which take shelter in their caves.

"And behold, when the fire has burned itself out, men and women, large and small, go into the forest carrying forks in their hands and spear the roasted serpents with these forks, and pile them in huge heaps, like the heaps which lie on the threshing floor after the grain has been threshed from the chaff. The wise Indians grind these serpents cunningly with certain health-giving herbs, and make meal from them, which meal is used as a medicine mainly to cure those who are afflicted with sterility, but also for all other infirmities, if it is applied in the way proper to each infirmity. The pepper is taken from the burned trees and carried to a barn, and is washed two or three times, and left to dry in the sun. In this way it becomes black, hard, and biting."

The second interpolation, like the first, entered the letter toward the close of the twelfth century. It tells how Prester John's father, Quasideus, fell asleep and was visited in his dreams by an angel, who instructed him to build a palace for his unborn son, "who will be the greatest king on earth and enjoy long life." Whoever stays in the palace, Quasideus was told, would never suffer hunger, thirst, or death. Upon awakening, Quasideus at once began to build the palace which Prester John now inhabits. Its walls and floor are of crystal and the ceiling is adorned with precious stones; there are no windows or doors (!), and the roof is supported by twenty-four columns of gold set with gems. "We live there," Prester John declares, "during the great holidays of the year, and in the midst of it St. Thomas preaches to the people. And inside our palace there is water and the best wine on earth, and whoever drinks of it has no desire for worldly things, and no one knows the source of the water."

This passage has several ties to the legends of St. Thomas. The dream in which Quasideus is ordered to build a palace for his future son has analogies to the visit to heaven that Gad, King Gundafor's brother, makes when he sees the palace on high that St. Thomas has built for Gundafor, in the *Acts of Thomas*. The curious name Quasideus, "godlike," may be, according to Vsevolod Slessarev, a corruption of "Mazdai"—the name of the king in the *Acts of Thomas* whose son, Vizan or John, was perhaps a prototype of Prester John. Lastly, St. Thomas himself is present at the palace, alive at least on great holidays, and preaching to the people—a theme that seems derived from the miracle tract, *De adventu*.

What Zarncke terms Interpolation C, which brought a mass of

new material into the text, became part of the letter no later than 1221. Added now is a description of the wild animals and zoological monstrosities of the Three Indias, such as "lions that are red, green, black, and blue in color," and "swift horses with two little horns, who can outrun all other animals," and "birds known as griffins, which can without difficulty lift an ox or a horse into their nest to feed their young." This section, in its Latin version, speaks of three beasts whose names have never ceased to baffle medievalists: *methagallinarii, cametheternis,* and *thinsiretae.* It is assumed that these are corrupt forms of the names of some mythological creatures, much garbled by copyists; the early vernacular translators of the letter usually dealt with these three textual excrescences by ignoring them.

Another new section tells of one of Prester John's provinces that is inhabited by "horned men, who have but one eye in front and three or four in the back. There are also women who look similar." Such fanciful anthropology follows a tradition established more than a thousand years earlier by the Roman geographers Pliny and Pomponius Mela, who were in the habit of populating unexplored territories with bizarre variants on the human form.

Interpolation C also introduces into the Prester John story one of the most ubiquitous myths of the Middle Ages:

"We have in our country yet another kind of men who feed only on the raw flesh of men and women. . . . And when one of them passes away, even if it be their father or mother, they devour him without cooking him. They say that it is good and righteous to eat human flesh and they do it for the redemption of their sins. This nation lives under God's curse and it is called Gog and Magog and they are more numerous than any other people. When the Antichrist comes they will spread over the face of the earth, for they are his friends and allies. These are the people who were walled in by King Alexander of Macedonia, for the safety of us all. When they burst forth God will hurl lightning and scorching fire upon them, which will sear and scatter them along with the Antichrist, and in this fashion they will be destroyed and routed. Nevertheless we take many of them with us into battle, whenever we wish to make war, and we grant them permission to eat our enemies, so that of a thousand foes not one remains who is not devoured and consumed. But later we send them home, because, if we let them stay longer with us, they would eat us all."

Gog and Magog are biblical names. In Genesis we are told that Magog was one of the sons of Japheth, and in Ezekiel is found the prediction that Gog, of the land of Magog, the prince of Rosh, Meshech, and Tubal, shall come forth from his place "out of the uttermost parts of the north, thou [Gog] and many peoples with thee, all of them riding upon horses, a great company and a mighty army. . . . Surely in that day there shall be a great shaking in the land of Israel . . . and the mountains shall be thrown down, and the steep places shall fall, and every wall shall fall to the ground." In the book of Revelation, too, it is predicted that the innumerable hordes of Gog and Magog shall be loosed upon the world by Satan.

Early in the Christian Era, Gog and Magog found their way into the growing cluster of legends dealing with Alexander the Great. In one of these apocryphal tales, the Syrian *Christian Legend Concerning Alexander*, written about 514, the great Macedonian king leads his troops into the high mountains of the Caucasus and discovers that beyond the highest peak of all dwells a savage and barbarous tribe. Questioning a native of the place, Alexander learns that the barbarians are the Huns, and that among their many kings are "Gog and Magog and Nawal the kings of the sons of Japhet." Alexander then declares, "Let us make a gate of brass and close up this breach." He summons three thousand smiths who work in iron, and three thousand who work in brass, and they fashion an immense wall from mountain to mountain, sealing in the Huns; on the colossal gate of this wall the king causes an inscription to be engraved, saying that at the end of eight hundred twenty-six years the Huns would break forth and "make the earth tremble," and that in nine hundred forty years "the world shall come to an end by the command of God." Variations on this story were incorporated into many medieval romances, the most popular of them being the one that goes by the name of the *Pseudo-Callisthenes,* because it is ascribed apocryphally to Callisthenes, a companion of Alexander. The tale of Alexander's wall against Gog and Magog even became embedded in the Koran, evidently as a borrowing from one of the Syrian manuscripts. Since those who loved to dwell on the exploits of Alexander were the ones most likely to be attracted by the new hero, Prester John, it was perhaps inevitable that one of the best-known episodes of the Alexander mythos should wander into the narrative of Prester John; and so it was that Gog and Magog became citizens of his kingdom.

The third interpolation has Prester John declare that each year he goes into the desert to pay homage to the tomb of the prophet Daniel, a figure of some mystical significance with a considerable apocryphal literature of his own. In the late twelfth century the Jewish traveler Benjamin of Tudela had been shown a tomb said to be Daniel's while he was in the Persian city of Susa, and this, possibly, led to the linking of Daniel and Prester John. In making his annual pilgrimage, Prester John says, "We are accompanied by ten thousand priests and the same number of knights, and two hundred towers built on the elephants which also carry a turret to protect us against the seven-headed dragons."

Another place Rabbi Benjamin visited was the Pharos, the famed lighthouse of Alexandria; writing of it about the year 1173, he described its great mirror and said, "All vessels which approached with hostile intentions from Greece and from the western side could be observed at fifty days' distance by means of this glass mirror." The lighthouse, which was built about 270 B.C. and rose to a height of more than four hundred feet, apparently did have some sort of huge mirror, most likely a curved sheet of polished metal, which was used in amplifying the beam the Pharos cast to aid ships nearing the port. Benjamin of Tudela's account of the lighthouse may have been the inspiration for the description of Prester John's magic tower that is found for the first time in Interpolation C. This tower, thirteen stories high, stood in front of his palace, and contained an enchanted mirror in which Prester John could observe the schemes of his enemies.

Interpolation C added a few medical miracles to the letter: "You should know that in our country we do not need doctors, for we have precious stones, herbs, fountains, and trees of so great virtue that they prevail against every infirmity and against poisons and wounds. And we have books which instruct us and distinguish between the potencies and virtues of the herbs." One of the herbs cited is called *assidios*: it has the property of enabling anyone who carries it to bind the devil or any other evil spirit in a spell that will force him to reveal who he is, where he is going, and what business he is about. Because of this, the devil does not dare to visit Prester John's land. In the medieval pharmacopeia this property of exorcising the devil is credited to the herb known as wormwood, *apsinthios* in Greek; *assidios* is evidently a corruption of that word. Also, according to Interpolation C, there are certain stones known as *midriosi*, which eagles seek and take to their nests; these greatly sharpen the vision, can restore the blind to sight, and, with the appropriate spells, have the power of making a person invisible. Friedrich Zarncke could find no direct derivation for *midriosi* and suggested the term was a corrupt form of *nidiosi*, from *nidus*, the Latin word for "nest." This theory is supported by the writings of a fourteenth-century German naturalist, Konrad of Megenberg, who told of stones called *nides*, which eagles keep in their nests to help them hatch their eggs, and by a German folk tale of a stone of invisibility found in birds' nests; it raises the possibility of a north European origin for all of Interpolation C.

7

While these fantasies were gaining circulation in Europe, Christendom was entering upon a dark time—indeed, a veritable reign of Antichrist, a veritable loosing of Gog and Magog. A new enemy was coming forth from Asia: the Mongols in their invincible hordes, more deadly than the Arabs who had harried Byzantium in the seventh century, more mighty than the Turks who had engulfed Persia and the Holy Land three centuries later, more terrifying than any conquerors since the frightful Huns who had smashed deep into Europe in the fourth and fifth centuries. Yet so befuddled were the people of thirteenth-century Europe by the tales of Prester John that at first they hailed these all-consuming Mongols as saviors, identified their chieftain as the true Prester John, coming to save Christendom from the Saracens—and recognized the nature of their mistake only when the Mongol horsemen were actually upon them.

It was the Saracens, not the still unknown Mongols, who most sorely troubled the Western world in the early thirteenth century. In 1187 the peerless general Saladin, of Turkish ancestry, had driven the Crusaders out of Jerusalem, ending eighty-eight years of Latin rule in the Holy City. The fall of Jerusalem led to the organization of the Third Crusade, whose commanders were King Philip II of France and King Richard of England, called *Coeur-de-Lion*, "the Lion-Hearted." They set out for the Holy Land in June 1190. Another who enrolled as a Crusader at this time was the venerable and fiery Holy Roman Emperor, old Frederick Barbarossa, who headed for the East in May of 1189, leading a German army that was the largest single force yet to go on a Crusade. But in the spring of 1190, riding ahead of his troops through Asia Minor, Barbarossa tumbled into a river and was drowned; most of the German princes, stunned by the loss, returned to Europe at once. Meanwhile King Richard and King Philip were accomplishing little. They added their forces to those of the Crusaders who had been besieging the city of Acre since August 1189; but the Saracens held on stubbornly, and Acre did not surrender until July of 1191. The long ordeal left Philip exhausted, and he returned to France forthwith; Richard the Lion-Hearted continued the Crusade without him, getting within a dozen miles of Jerusalem by the winter of 1191–92, but he came to see that Saladin could not be defeated and in September 1192 signed a five-year peace treaty with the Saracen leader. It provided that Jerusalem would remain in Moslem hands but that Christian pilgrims would be allowed to visit the city's shrines. This, and the capture of Acre, were the only tangible gains for Christendom in the Third Crusade.

In 1199, the treaty having expired and Saladin having died, Pope Innocent III called for a new Crusade to liberate the Holy City. An army of French and German barons and knights was duly formed; but the Crusaders fell under the domination of the crafty old Doge of Venice, Enrico Dandolo, who persuaded them to forget about the Saracens and invade Christian Byzantium instead, thus crippling Venice's chief commercial rival. The most grotesque episode of these holy wars ensued: in 1203 the Crusaders broke into Constantinople, the first time in that city's long history that invaders had succeeded in entering it, and the following spring, after sacking and looting and setting fire to it, they drove out the anointed Greek emperor. In his place they sat one of their own number, Count Baldwin of Flanders, who became the first Latin Emperor of Byzantium. The new patriarch of the Greek Orthodox Church was a Venetian named Morosini, one of Dandolo's lieutenants, who was, of course, a Roman Catholic, and not even a priest. Most of the Crusaders then went home, heavy with the spoils of Constantinople, Christendom's wealthiest city. Those who remained took possession of huge estates in the former Byzantine Empire, and for the next fifty-seven years Byzantium suffered under the misrule of these Latin warriors, until at last they were expelled and a prince of the old Greek dynasty regained the throne. None of the men of the Fourth Crusade ever did battle in the Holy Land.

An uneasy truce prevailed there between Saracen and Latin until 1215. Then, at the instigation of Pope Innocent, plans were drawn for a Fifth Crusade, and upon the death of Innocent the following year his successor, Honorius III, renewed the call for another attempt to regain Jerusalem. By the spring of 1218 thousands of soldiers from France and Germany were arriving at the port of Acre. King John of Jerusalem, the leader of the Latins of the Near East, informed them that their first target was to be Egypt, richest land in the Moslem world. If the Saracens could be driven from Egypt, the Crusaders would be able to launch a two-pronged offensive against Jerusalem, striking eastward from Acre and northward from Suez. The way to capture Egypt, King John said, was to seize Damietta, the port that was the gateway to the Nile.

In 1169, when the Crusaders first tried to take Damietta, Saladin had had a huge chain strung across the Nile as a barrier to naval attack. The Saracens employed the same strategy now. It was August 1218 before the Crusaders broke through the chain and proceeded up the Nile to the walls of Damietta, but not until November of 1219 did the heavily protected city fall to its attackers. At this point the Sultan of Egypt, Malik al-Kamil, Saladin's nephew, made an extraordinary offer: if the Crusaders would call off their invasion of Egypt he would hand over the entire Holy Land, Jerusalem and all, to them! King John and most of the Crusaders, seeing that by this treaty they would accomplish their whole purpose in a single stroke, were eager to accept. But the Pope's personal representative, a fierce Portuguese cardinal named Pelagius, would not give his consent. This harsh, narrow-minded man angrily denounced anyone who dared to negotiate with infidels. He wanted nothing less than unconditional surrender: let the Saracens hand over Egypt and Syria as well as Palestine, he said, or there could be no deal. The Crusaders begged Pelagius to yield, but he was firm, and threatened to excommunicate anyone who disagreed with him. The struggle between Pelagius and King John grew violent, and in February of 1220 John gave up and angrily returned to Acre. Pelagius now ruled Damietta. He called for an all-out attack on Cairo, but the knights would not obey. They said they would fight only under King John, and King John had departed. For a year and a half the Crusaders remained at Damietta, stalemated. In the summer of 1221, King John let himself be persuaded to return to Damietta. He was unhappy about having to co-operate with Pelagius, but he did not wish to be accused of ruining the Crusade. The army at last began to march south to attack Cairo. It was the wrong time to be fighting a war in Egypt, since the Nile was about to begin its annual flood, but Pelagius would not listen to advice.

The outcome was the catastrophe King John expected. Unable to get the fiery Pelagius to turn back, he watched the Crusaders plunge deeper and deeper into Egypt, until eventually they were face to face with the main body of the Saracen army. Then they discovered that a second Saracen force had circled behind them and lay between them and their base at Damietta. Cut off and surrounded, they broke into a panicky retreat and most of them were slaughtered as they fled northward. Upon reaching Damietta with the survivors, Cardinal Pelagius had no choice but to surrender the city to the Egyptians and withdraw from the country. On September 8, 1221, the remaining men of the Fifth Crusade took their leave of Egypt, having failed utterly to achieve any of their goals, even though possession of Jerusalem had for a time been in their grasp.

During this dismal adventure, however, one of the Latin invaders managed to find some good news to send back to Europe. He was Jacques of Vitry, Bishop of Acre, a French prelate who had come to the Near East just before the launching of the Fifth Crusade, and who had been one of Pelagius' chief supporters in the dispute with King John of Jerusalem. In the spring of 1221 this bishop relayed hopeful and happy tidings in letters he sent to Pope Honorius, to King Henry III of England, to Duke Leopold of Austria, and to his former colleagues at the University of Paris. "A new and mighty protector of Christianity has arisen," Jacques de Vitry announced. "He is King David of India, who has taken the field of battle against the unbelievers at the head of an army of unparalleled size."

This King David was a Christian, the bishop reported, and was either the son or the grandson of Prester John—although, Bishop Jacques pointed out, "King David was himself commonly called Prester John." His kingdom was deep in Asia. His involvement in the affairs of the Near East had come about because the Caliph of Baghdad had been threatened with war by a fellow Moslem prince, the Shah of Khwarizm; seeing no other ally at hand, the caliph had requested the Nestorian Catholicos—or Patriarch—of Baghdad to summon King David to his aid, and the king had agreed to defend the caliph against the Khwarizmians.

Khwarizm then was one of the mightiest realms of Central Asia. Located northeast of Persia, in what now is the Uzbek Soviet Socialist Republic of the U.S.S.R., Khwarizm had expanded vastly in the early twelfth century at the expense of the Seljuk Turks of Persia. The victory of "Prester John" (Yeh-lü Ta-shih) over the Seljuks in 1141 had left the latter in disarray, but Yeh-lü Ta-shih's own realm of Kara-Khitai took relatively little advantage of that. The Khwarizmians, making use of the opportunity Yeh-lü Ta-shih had created for them, finished off the Seljuks and, under their great leader Shah Mohammed, conquered Persia to give themselves an empire stretching from the Indus to the Tigris. Then, in the second decade of the thirteenth century, Shah Mohammed's son Jelal ad-Din decided to conquer Mesopotamia as well. It was at this point, according to Jacques de Vitry, that the Caliph of Baghdad asked the local Nestorian patriarch to seek the help of King David, said to be the descendant of the king who had smashed the Turks in 1141.

And, so the bishop continued, King David, a loyal Nestorian, had responded to the appeal of the Catholicos of Baghdad. He had invaded the Khwarizmian territories, had defeated the shah, and had seized control of Persia. But the caliph who had summoned King David was to be the next to feel his power. Now, said the bishop, King David was only five days' march east of Baghdad and had sent envoys to the caliph demanding that he surrender five sixths of his land, including the city of Baghdad, which would become the center of the Nestorian faith. When he was finished with his conquest of Mesopotamia, King David planned to continue on to the Holy Land, vanquish the Saracens, and rebuild the recently razed walls of Jerusalem, using the gold and silver that he had extracted from the Moslem kingdoms.

These letters from Jacques of Vitry sent a frenzied wave of joy through Europe. Prester John was coming at last! Or, in any event, his grandson King David. Perhaps "Prester John" was the title by which this whole dynasty of Asian kings was known. That was an unimportant detail. What mattered was the basic information, gathered by the trustworthy Jacques of Vitry, that a Christian warrior had emerged from the farthest part of the Orient to crush the despicable Moslems. Already he had wiped out the Khwarizmians, whoever they might be; now he was about to deal with the Caliph of Baghdad; next he would cleanse the Holy Land and make it safe once again for Christians. Was this not reason enough for Christendom to rejoice?

Even Europe's customary victims and scapegoats, the Jews, took heart from the news of King David's triumphant westward march. Was there any name more likely to stir pride and hope in a Jew than that of King David? Was there not an ancient Messianic tradition that a "son of David" would someday return and claim the throne of Israel? By a copyist's error in Damietta, two of Jacques de Vitry's letters went forth describing the new King David as *rex Judaeorum* instead of *rex Indorum* —King of the Jews, not King of the Indians—and word of this astounding phrase passed rapidly through the ghettos of Europe, inspiring a belief in the imminence of the Messiah's long-awaited coming.

Who was this Messiah, this Prester John, this enemy of Saracens and deliverer of the Christians and Jews—this King David of the Indies? Was he one more phantasmagoric figure, the product of rumor and fable passed off as fact? No, not this time. The essence of Jacques de Vitry's report was accurate. In truth there was a new conqueror on the march in the Orient, and in truth he had attacked the Khwarizmians, the greatest Moslem power in Central Asia, and in truth he had destroyed their army and sent their shah fleeing into exile. These things had actually happened. But in other respects Bishop Jacques had been deceived. This warrior-king was no Christian, nor was he Prester John, nor even the grandson of Prester John. He was the fierce and terrible Genghis Khan, the scourge of Asia, the lord of the Mongol hordes, and when he had finished conquering the lands of Islam he proposed to begin on the lands of Christendom, for it was his plan to conquer all the world.

THREE

Prester John of the Steppes

In the middle of the thirteenth century the English monk Matthew Paris made this entry in his historical chronicle under the heading *Anno 1240:*

"The detestable people of Satan, to wit, an infinite number of Tartars, brake forth from their mountain-compassed and rock-defended region, like devils loosed out of hell . . . and like grasshoppers covering the face of the earth, spoiling the eastern confines with fire and sword, ruining cities, cutting up woods, rooting up vineyards, killing the people both of city and country. . . . They are rather monsters than men, thirsting and drinking blood, tearing and devouring the flesh of dogs and men; clothed with ox-hides, armed with iron plates; in stature thick and short, well set, strong in body; in war invincible, in labor indefatigable. . . ."

Matthew Paris wrote at a time when all Europe trembled before the Mongol menace. They had come out of the steppes of Central Asia and had speared deep into Europe, reaching Poland, Hungary, and the Danube Valley by 1241 before casually abandoning their drive and retreating undefeated. Some tribes of these Mongols called themselves Tatars, which to men like Matthew Paris suggested a ready pun, *Tartars*, or beings out of Tartarus, one of the medieval names for hell. The pun passed into the languages of Europe; as "Tartars" men knew and dreaded them, only twenty years after they had been hailed, in ignorance and from a great distance, as the warriors of Prester John and the saviors of Christendom.

As late as the middle of the twelfth century, these future world-conquerors had been simple nomads of the open steppe, living in small family groups, each family occupying a *yurt*, a tent made of felt stretched over a wooden framework. They drifted from pasture to pasture as the needs of their herds of horses required. Family clans tended to move together during these seasonal migrations, forming a larger tribal unit. The society was a fluid one; adoption from clan to clan was common. So was petty warfare between clans and between tribes. Now and again some strong chieftain succeeded in bringing several Mongol tribes into a confederation, but these unions always were short-lived. The Persian historian Juvaini, who was born in the year Genghis Khan died and lived at the royal court in Mongol-ruled Persia, wrote, "Before the appearance of Genghis Khan the Mongols had no chief or ruler. Each tribe or two tribes lived separately; they were not united with one another, and there was constant fighting and hostility between them. Some of them regarded robbery and violence, immorality and debauchery, as deeds of manliness and excellence. The Khan of Khitai [northern China] used to demand and seize goods from them. Their clothing was of the skins of dogs and mice, and their food was the flesh of those animals and other dead things."

By race the Mongols were kin to the Chinese, the Japanese, and other Oriental peoples, but their centuries of harsh nomadic life had hardened them, making them stocky and tough, with big bodies and short limbs. John of Plano Carpini, an Italian friar who visited the Mongol homeland in 1246, declared, "The Mongols or Tartars, in outward shape, are unlike to all other people. For they are broader between the eyes, and the balls of their cheeks, than men of other nations be. They have flat and small noses, little eyes, and eyelids standing straight upright. They are shaven on the crowns of their heads like priests. They wear their hair somewhat longer about their ears than upon their forehead, but behind they let it grow long like woman's hair."

In the second half of the twelfth century a Mongol chieftain named Yesukai managed to organize a confederation of tribes in northeastern Asia, in the vicinity of the Onon and Amur rivers. About the year 1167 a son was born to Yesukai and given the name of Temujin. He came into the world clutching a lump of clotted blood in his fist, which the tribal shaman said was an omen that he would become a mighty warrior; and so it would be, for Temujin was the future Genghis Khan.

Temujin had the customary education of a Mongol warrior: he was taught to ride, to handle the long, wickedly curved Mongol sword, to use a bow and a hand ax. Legend has it that when he was only nine Temujin was capable of riding a speeding horse without touching the reins, while showering arrows unerringly in all directions. Meanwhile, Yesukai, through valor and shrewd diplomacy, was gradually extending the power of his confederation. Tribe after tribe acknowledged Yesukai's supremacy. One tribe was too strong for him to subjugate, but he won their friendship by other means. These were the Keraits, who lived to the west of the Mongol territory. Converted to Nestorian Christianity at the outset of the eleventh century, the Keraits were somewhat more settled and civilized than most of the peoples of the region. About 1170, when the Kerait khan died, his son Togrul found himself challenged for his inheritance by his brothers and uncles. Yesukai gave his support to Togrul and helped him obtain the Kerait throne; Togrul and Yesukai then took an oath of brotherhood, and, with the power of the Keraits now behind him, Yesukai was in a position to make himself khan over most or all of the Mongol tribes. But he was poisoned before he could accomplish this. His son Temujin was only thirteen (or, according to one version of the story, nine).

Because of his youth, Temujin was unable to assert his claim to the chieftainship. The confederation his father had put together collapsed, and even in his own tribe and family Temujin found opponents. A mere handful of followers gave their allegiance to him. He spent hard years in exile, several times coming close to death at the hands of tribal rivals. But through strength and cunning and, occasionally, treachery, he acquired a position of authority, first in his own tribe, then in the neighboring tribes which once had been subject to Yesukai. He built a system of alliances, linking family and family, clan and clan, tribe and tribe, using the device of blood brotherhood to rivet his Mongols together.

One tribe of Turkish stock, the Merkits, who lived by Lake Baikal, not only defied him but raided his camp, carrying off Temujin's own wife Bortei in his absence. In dealing with this insult Temujin drew on his friendship with his father's old blood brother, Togrul, the khan of the Keraits, whom Temujin had come to regard as a foster father, and who now was the most powerful of the many khans of the Asian steppes. An army of Mongols and Keraits attacked and vanquished the Merkits, and Temujin regained his wife. During her months of captivity, however, she had been delivered of a son, whose legitimacy was suspect. Nevertheless Temujin accepted the child as his first-born, naming him Juchi, "the guest."

In the guise of Togrul's protégé, Temujin rapidly became the second most influential khan of the Mongol region. When Togrul was driven from the Kerait throne in 1197, it was Temujin who returned him to power, and together they conquered all the remaining independent tribes. Inevitably, jealousies developed between the two great khans, and in 1203 they quarreled. War between the Mongols and the Keraits followed; Temujin wiped out the Kerait army on its own home ground, and Togrul was killed as he tried to escape. By 1204, Temujin was supreme over all the tribes of Mongolia. His domain was bounded on the east by the river Amur in Manchuria, on the south by the Great Wall of China, on the north by the mountains of Siberia, and on the west by the parched wasteland of the Tarim Basin.

At a *khuriltai*, or meeting of all tribes, held on the banks of the Kerulen River in central Mongolia in 1206, Temujin's imperial status was formally confirmed. By common agreement he was acclaimed as Genghis Khan, the "universal ruler." Among the Mongols every chieftain wore the title of *khan*, "prince," but Genghis was awarded a unique designation: *khaghan*, "great khan," "khan of khans."

He offered the *khuriltai* a vision of world empire. "Man's highest joy is in victory," he declared. "To conquer one's enemies, to pursue them, to deprive them of their possessions, to make their beloved weep, to ride on their horses, and to embrace their wives and daughters." He had welded clan to clan, tribe to tribe; now he proposed to bring every nation in the world under Mongol authority, not out of greed for wealth or the hunger for luxuries, but, so it seemed, out of sheer love of conquest for its own sake. To make himself lord of Mongolia, he had climbed aboard a juggernaut that could not be slowed. Ceaseless warfare, endless outward expansion—only thus could the empire be held together. So Genghis looked toward this land and that, planning to add them to his domain, and after the nearby ones had been taken there were the nations yet beyond, and so onward to all horizons.

As a foundation for his empire, Genghis proclaimed a code of laws, the *yasas*. The Persian historian Juvaini declares: "In accordance and agreement with his own mind he established a rule for every occasion and a regulation for every circumstance; while for every crime he fixed a penalty. And since the Tartar peoples had no script of their own, he gave orders that Mongol children should learn writing from the Uighurs [a Turkish tribe who used an alphabet based on Syriac letters]; and that these *yasas* and ordinances should be written down on rolls. These rolls are called the *Great Book of Yasas* and are kept in the treasury of the chief princes."

All tribes were to be united as one. Keraits, Merkits, Tartars, Naimans, Uighurs, Oirats, Urianguts, and all the rest would be known simply as Mongols. Every Mongol was to consider himself a soldier. Men between fourteen and seventy were chosen for active duty, some to fight, some to care for the roads and the horses. Women, boys, old men, and weaklings were given the tasks of maintaining the pastures and the home encampments. The Mongol army was built out of units of ten men, drawn from different tribes in such a way as to replace the old tribal loyalties with a new loyalty to the Mongol state. One man of each ten was the leader of the group; every unit of ten was part of a unit of a hundred, with its own leader, and units of a thousand and ten thousand warriors were formed from these. At the top of the pyramid were a hundred or so great commanders, reporting directly to Genghis Khan. The organization was tight and efficient; no man could shirk his duty, none could do less than his share. If any soldier betrayed his trust, his commander was held responsible, and even a commander of ten thousand might suffer for the faults of an underling.

The core of the Mongol army was the *ordo*—an elite band of ten thousand picked warriors. When the Mongol *ordos* began to invade Europe in the middle of the thirteenth century, Europeans turned the word into "hordes" and spoke of the Mongols as if their numbers were boundless—the "grasshoppers covering the face of the earth" of Matthew Paris. But actually the Mongol "hordes" that conquered so much of the world were quite small. At the height of his power, Genghis Khan never commanded more than about 250,000 men, and only half of these were Mongols, the rest allies from other nations. When the Mongols conquered China, their total population was no greater than two million, as against a hundred million Chinese.

The secret of Mongol might was their iron discipline and superb horsemanship, not the great numbers that a frightened Europe imagined to exist. Theirs was an army of superb archers and lancers, mounted on swift ponies and covering immense distances as though the rigors of travel were unknown. "They are excellent soldiers," wrote Marco Polo seventy years after Genghis' death, "and passing valiant in battle. They are also more capable of bearing hardships than other nations; for many a time, if need be, they will go for a month without any supply of food, living only on the milk of their mares and on such game as their bows will win them. . . . When they are going on a distant expedition they take no gear with them except two leather bottles for milk; a little earthenware pot to cook their meat in; and a little tent to shelter them from rain. And in case of great urgency they will ride ten days on end without lighting a fire or taking a meal."

Mongol boys learned to ride almost as soon as they could walk. They trained their horses so well that beast seemed part of man, both under the command of a single brain. A Mongol steed could wheel and charge with the greatest agility—"just like a dog," according to Marco— while its master fired arrows with phenomenal speed and accuracy, arrows that could slay at a distance of two hundred yards. In battle, the Mongols burst forward in well-ordered columns, showering arrows with such ferocity that their terrified victims bolted in panic; the horsemen maneuvered their foes into a herd, ringing them for the slaughter. Where the enemy refused to panic, the Mongols would pretend to retreat, drawing their opponents after them. Then, at a given signal, they would swing around and charge once more, uttering terrifying cries. "In this sort of warfare," Marco Polo observed, "the adversary imagines he has gained a victory, when in fact he has lost the battle." Terror was another Mongol weapon: they put whole cities to the sword, not out of innate cruelty as Europeans thought, but for propaganda purposes: enemies who were shivering at the mere rumor of Mongol ferocity were half beaten before the first blow was struck. As conquerors, however, the Mongols proved to be far less bestial than their advance reputation had led men to think. All atrocities ceased, and pointless butchery was prohibited. A district under Mongol control was allowed to live very much as it had before, but for the change of masters. Nor did the Mongols impose any particular religious orientation on their victims. Genghis himself had no strong religious convictions but was content to observe the simple pagan shamanism of his forefathers. He married his sons to Christian Keraits, and sometimes consulted the Christian priests who served the spiritual needs of the Nestorian Mongols at his court; he also had Moslems and Buddhists around him as advisers, and seems to have regarded one religion as about as good as another.

2

As they began their campaign of world conquest, the Mongols had three major nations on their borders. To the east and southeast was China. To the southwest, in what is now the Chinese province of Kansu, was the kingdom of Hsi-Hsia, where a Tibetan dynasty ruled over a mixed agricultural and nomadic population of Turks, Mongols, and Chinese. And due west was Kara-Khitai, the realm founded some eighty years earlier by Yeh-lü Ta-shih; his descendants, using the title of gur-khan, still governed this region, most of whose people were of Uighur Turkish stock.

In choosing his targets, Genghis Khan commenced by attacking the weakest of the three, Hsi-Hsia. By 1209 the Mongols were masters there. Next came the invasion of the huge, unwieldy Chinese Empire. This was a divided realm. In the warm rice-growing south an old native dynasty, the Sung, was in command. From the Yangtze to the Great Wall China was under the Jurchen, barbarian conquerors from Manchuria, who also held sway in their homeland north of the Great Wall. Like most of China's conquerors, the Jurchen had been softened by their contact with the civilized delights of that ancient land: in 1125 they had been rugged warriors coming in to throw out an earlier set of nomad conquerors, the Khitai, who had become decadent, and now, contaminated by civilization themselves, the Jurchen were vulnerable to attack by the hard-eyed Mongols.

Genghis invaded China in 1211. The Great Wall, recently reinforced by the Jurchen, proved to be a stronger barrier than he had expected, but eventually he broke through and inflicted heavy damage on the Jurchen forces. By 1214 the Mongols were at the gigantic walls of Yenching, the capital, now called Peking. The city seemed impregnable; but in May 1215 traitors within the walls opened its gates to the

Mongols, who looted and burned it, and slew thousands of its citizens. The Jurchen emperor fled. All of China north of the Yellow River fell into Mongol hands, and nothing was left of the Jurchen realm except Manchuria and a thin strip of China sandwiched between the Mongol and Sung territories.

Instead of going on to complete his conquest of China at that time, Genghis left one of his lieutenants in charge of the Mongol-occupied district and led his armies westward. There was trouble in Kara-Khitai from which the Mongols could profit. The gur-khan had come into conflict with his powerful neighbor on the west, the Shah of Khwarizm, who coveted his territory. Khwarizmian agents had incited the gur-khan's own vassals to rebel against him; in the confusion that followed, Khwarizm seized the southern part of Kara-Khitai, and, in the remaining section of the country, the gur-khan was overthrown and replaced by a certain Kuchluk, a Naiman Turk, thus ending the dynasty of Yeh-lü Ta-shih. Kuchluk, though a Nestorian Christian by birth, had become a Buddhist upon his marriage to a Kara-Khitai princess, and when he took power he began persecutions of those of his subjects who were Christians or Moslems. His reign was an unpopular one; when Genghis and his Mongols arrived, they were welcomed in Kara-Khitai as liberators, and Kuchluk was deposed.

Now that Kara-Khitai was part of the Mongol realm, the two most puissant warriors in Asia were on a collision course, for the empire of Genghis had come to border on the empire of Shah Mohammed of Khwarizm. Each monarch claimed the other as his vassal, and, after a few cold and formal interchanges of ambassadors, each began to test the other's resolve by offering provocations to war. When a party of Mongol emissaries were slain by order of one of Shah Mohammed's local governors in 1218, Genghis ordered a total mobilization of his forces. By the summer of 1219 he was leading some 200,000 soldiers toward Khwarizm, and Shah Mohammed, with an army said to number half a million men, was waiting on his frontier. The highly mobile Mongol troops easily outmaneuvered the Khwarizmians and quickly captured the key cities of Bokhara and Samarkand, while Shah Mohammed withdrew to his capital, Urgenj, on the Oxus. The sons of Genghis laid siege to that city and after some months took it as well; the shah, in despair, slipped away to an obscure island in the Caspian Sea, where he died virtually unattended in December 1220.

One branch of the Khwarizmian army, under Mohammed's son

Jelal ad-Din, resisted the Mongol thrust and staged an orderly retreat into Afghanistan. The Mongols followed, pausing to massacre the inhabitants of every city they conquered along their route. In the autumn of 1221 they caught up with Jelal ad-Din on the banks of the Indus, and in a climactic battle on November 24 the Khwarizmian soldiers were almost wholly wiped out; Jelal ad-Din himself fled across the river to take refuge with the King of Delhi. Genghis spent the next year pacifying Afghanistan. The city of Herat, having first submitted readily to the Mongols and then rebelled against their rule, was besieged and taken in June of 1222; the entire population, several hundred thousand, was put to death in a week-long bloodbath. After placing Mongol governors in charge of the former Khwarizmian provinces, Genghis called a halt to his westward thrust and began slowly to return to the Mongolian heartland, reaching the steppes in the spring of 1225.

It was the news of the Mongol obliteration of Khwarizm in 1219–21, getting to the Near East in distorted and incomplete form, that inspired Jacques de Vitry's tale of the all-conquering Christian hero, King David, grandson of Prester John. Only one aspect of that tale was true: that a warrior-king from some remote part of Asia had attacked and shattered the great Moslem realm of Khwarizm. The rest—that this warrior-king was a Christian, that he was about to attack Baghdad, that the Holy Land would be his next objective—was mere wishful fantasy.

Those who were heartened by Jacques de Vitry's letters of 1221 must have felt no little dismay when further reports of the exploits of the armies of "King David" came out of Asia the following year. In the summer of 1220 Genghis Khan had sent one party of troops under two of his best generals into Persia to capture the fleeing Shah Mohammed. When the shah eluded them, the Mongols simply passed on through Persia to the west, sacking cities as they went. In February 1221—just about the time Jacques de Vitry was beginning to write his jubilant letters—they penetrated the Caucasus and fell upon the Christian principalities of Georgia and Armenia. The Georgians were routed in a battle near their capital of Tiflis; the Mongols, having annihilated this Christian army, then plundered Christian cities and slew Christian citizens. With the Caucasus in ruins they turned back for further pillaging of northwestern Persia; then, early in 1222, they passed through the Caucasus a second time and followed the western coast of the Caspian northward into Russia. On May 31, 1222, they smashed a huge

Russian army on the banks of the Kalka River, near the Sea of Azov. Afterward the Mongol marauders raided the Crimea, sacking a Genoese trading depot there, and destroyed an army of Bulgars before returning, early in 1223, to the main encampment of Genghis Khan. This savage raid through the Caucasus and Crimea was odd behavior for the supposed saviors of Christendom, for nearly all its victims had been Christians; but those in Europe who wished to see the Mongols as their deliverers from the Moslem menace chose to believe that the violent western campaign of this Mongol army had been an isolated adventure, an aberration of the generals, some sort of cataclysmic accident or error that would not be repeated.

By 1225 the Mongols ruled an empire that stretched from Korea to Persia, from Siberia to the middle of China. No one, neither Alexander the Great nor any of the Caesars, had ever been lord of so much territory as had been conquered by Genghis Khan. Now nearing sixty and troubled by weakening health, Genghis called a great *khuriltai* of the Mongol clans to decide the question of the imperial succession. By tradition, supreme authority was to descend to the eldest son. But Juchi, the firstborn of Genghis, was of doubtful legitimacy; and in any case he did not attend the *khuriltai*, for he was on his deathbed in the mountainous country of the far northwest. Chagadai, the second son, was a brilliant general, but Genghis deemed him too hot-tempered and merciless a man to make a satisfactory khaghan. Therefore Genghis persuaded the assembled Mongol chieftains to accept his third son, Ogodai, a strong, slow-witted, patient, and good-willed man, as their next leader.

He decreed that to Ogodai would fall not only the title of khaghan, carrying with it supremacy over all Mongols throughout the vast empire, but also the specific responsibility for governing China and Tibet. Chagadai was to be given command over the former Kara-Khitai realm and neighboring territories in Central Asia. To Tului, Genghis' youngest son, would go authority over the original Mongol homeland north of the Great Wall. The country in the far west, up to the frontiers of Russia, was awarded to Juchi's eldest son Batu, the first of the grandsons of Genghis Khan to emerge as an important Mongol leader.

The old khagan's illness grew worse, and on August 18, 1227, Genghis Khan died while leading a campaign in the hills of the Hsi-Hsia country, where rebellion had broken out. In autumn his body was carried northward into Mongolia and buried at a place known only to his closest kin. Another *khuriltai* was called to ratify the decisions of 1225, and Ogodai became khaghan. He commenced his reign by decreeing the establishment of the first Mongol city—Karakorum, near the Orqon River in western Mongolia. Supposedly he did this at the behest of his wife, Turakina, a Naiman Turk who disliked the nomadic Mongol ways and was weary of living in tents. Juvaini's history of the Mongols declares that a great palace was constructed at Karakorum, containing a throne for Ogodai reached by three flights of steps. Twice a year the great khan would go there to hold court for a month at a time, but he was always restless and uncomfortable amid such unfamiliar splendor.

In 1230, Ogodai resumed the Mongol conquest of China. The Jurchen now were confined to a narrow region south of the Yellow River, but this was well defended by nature on three sides: the Yellow River in the north, mountains in the west, the Yellow Sea on the east. The only ready access to their territory was from the south, which was still under the control of the native Chinese dynasty, the Sung. So strongly did the Sung rulers hate the barbarians who had displaced them a century before that they readily granted permission for the Mongols to cross their domain in order to attack the Jurchen. Ogodai thereupon launched a two-pronged onslaught: while one Mongol army fought its way across the Yellow River and battered the Jurchen from the north, a second force set out on a huge detour around the western end of China, came up through the Sung realm, and hit the Jurchen from below. Caught between two armies, the Jurchen were annihilated. The survivors took refuge behind the walls of their capital, Kaifeng, a city forty miles in circumference with a population of four million. The Mongols laid siege to it and, in 1234, seized it. The last Jurchen emperor took his own life. His dynasty was ended; China was divided between the Mongols and the Sung.

For the time being the invasion of China went no deeper. The hot, swampy, densely populated south did not tempt the Mongols, and they knew its terrain was unsuitable for the kind of cavalry-charge warfare on which they invariably relied. Once again they turned their attention westward.

The Khwarizmians, led by Shah Jelal ad-Din, had undergone a brief resurrection since Genghis' withdrawal from their territory in 1222. Jelal ad-Din had managed to reassert his power in western Persia, had made himself overlord of Mesopotamia, and in 1225 had invaded the

Caucasus, annexing Azerbaijan and much of Georgia. But this second Khwarizmian regime collapsed as soon as the Mongol hordes returned to Persia in 1231. Jelal ad-Din was slain; the remnants of his army fled into northern Syria and took up banditry; Persia and Azerbaijan came under Mongol rule, and, a few years later, so did Georgia and Armenia. Now, with Jurchen China out of the way, the Mongols moved onward past the Caucasus into the Western world. Commanded by Genghis' grandson Batu, they entered Russia in the autumn of 1237. City after city fell, and their inhabitants were massacred: Riazan, Kolomna, Vladimir, Moscow, Rostov. Batu's army, which called itself the Golden Horde, reached the Ukraine late in 1240, and that December sacked the great city of Kiev. One branch of the army then went northward into Poland, burning Krakow and Sandomir, and swung about to the south to devastate Moravia and northern Hungary. The main Mongol force moved westward across the Carpathians from the Ukraine into the plains of eastern Hungary, and, after smashing the Hungarian army, swept on into Croatia, getting as far west as the shores of the Adriatic. Batu Khan set up a capital in Hungary and looked about for the next project. Where would the invasion end, the people of Europe asked? Would the Mongols simply ride on and on, into France and Spain and Scandinavia, and then swarm across the Channel to overwhelm England, and go boiling into the sea to conquer whatever nations might lie at the ends of the world? The Mongols were everywhere at once, and no army could stand before them. It seemed that millions upon millions of the yellow-skinned horsemen had come pouring forth on this campaign of world conquest.

Early in 1242, though, just as it appeared certain that all of Europe must shortly be incorporated into the Mongol realm, the invasion suddenly halted. The Mongols struck camp and began heading eastward. "We are called away," they shouted to the dumbstruck people of eastern Europe, "and we spare you war."

What had happened was the death of the Khaghan Ogodai at Karakorum in December 1241. Couriers had hastened the news to every Mongol army in the field, for, under the *yasas*, the code promulgated by Genghis Khan, it was incumbent upon all tribal leaders to return at once to the ancestral lands for the *khuriltai* that would choose the new monarch. It had taken two and a half months for word of Ogodai's death to reach Batu in his camp five thousand miles west of

Karakorum. Reluctantly, he broke off the sacking of Europe and ordered the voluntary retreat.

The succession was uncertain; many of the grandsons and even the great-grandsons of Genghis Khan were jockeying for power. Just before his death Ogodai had expressed a wish to have his favorite grandson, Shiramun, follow him as khaghan. His father, Ogodai's son by one of his secondary wives, had been killed fighting in China. But few of the Mongol khans wanted to give the throne to this untried boy. Ogodai's chief widow favored the claim of her son Kuyuk, the eldest of the late khaghan's children. She argued that it was unreasonable to let the supreme power go to a grandson of Ogodai while one of his sons still lived; also on her mind was the fact that Kuyuk was of her blood and Shiramun was not. Kuyuk's cousin Batu, as the senior among Genghis' grandsons, had imperial hopes of his own despite his clouded ancestry—he was the son of Juchi the dubious—and several other princes of the line of Genghis put forth their own claims. So complex were the rivalries that more than three years passed before the *khuriltai* could be held. During this interregnum Ogodai's chief widow, Turakina, served as regent, as provided also by the *yasas* of Genghis. In this she had the powerful support of old Chagadai, the last surviving son of Genghis Khan, who defended her right to rule pending the election of the new khaghan. Turakina—who, like most of the wives of Genghis' sons, was a Christian—used her time in power to gather backing for her son Kuyuk. In 1245, after considerable politicking, she finally won the votes of enough of the Mongol princes to bring about Kuyuk's election, and at a *khuriltai* held at Karakorum the following year the Mongol world formally acclaimed him as the khan of khans.

A visitor from Christendom was on hand to witness the ceremony by which Kuyuk assumed his exalted rank. He was John of Plano Carpini, a Franciscan monk from Italy, who had come as the Pope's ambassador, seeking to negotiate an alliance between Mongols and Christians against the Saracens.

3

The extraordinary journey of John of Plano Carpini was a tribute to Europe's naïve but persistent faith that the salvation of the Christian world would somehow come from an Asian king. It was quite clear now that the "King David" of whom Jacques de Vitry had written in 1221 was neither Prester John nor any of his relatives, but rather the ferocious Genghis Khan, whose grandson Batu had just laid waste to Russia, Poland, and Hungary. It was equally apparent that these frightful Mongols, who had come almost to the gates of Italy before Ogodai's sudden death had interrupted their steady advance, were bloodthirsty savages, not the most desirable sort of allies. Nevertheless, was it not the case that many of the wives of the great Mongols were Christians? Nestorian heretics, yes, but still Christians. And it was known that many Nestorian priests served as advisers at the Mongol court. Therefore hope endured, despite everything the Mongols had just inflicted on Europe, that they could be transformed into good Christians, Christians loyal to the Pope, and could be enticed into making common cause with Christian Europe against the followers of Islam.

From the point of view of Sinibaldo Fieschi of Genoa, who had become Pope Innocent IV in June 1243, Christendom had rarely been so much in need of help as at that moment. Half of Europe lay in smoldering ruins, and, although many of the cities Batu had destroyed were populated by Greek Orthodox schismatics whose tragedies were no problem of the Pope's, a good number had been Roman Catholic cities, whose inhabitants cried out now to the Pope for succor. The papacy itself, meanwhile, was embroiled in a new battle with the Holy Roman Empire. Emperor Frederick II, Barbarossa's grandson, had once again challenged the doctrine of papal supremacy and since 1236 had been making war intermittently in Italy, seizing a great deal of territory owned by the Pope. For this he had been excommunicated, but that had not discouraged him, and now Frederick was preparing to invade Rome and expel the Pope. (He would succeed in this endeavor in the summer of 1244.) In the Holy Land the Crusaders were going through one of their periodic catastrophes. They had, in 1229, regained Jerusalem, Bethlehem, and Nazareth without striking a blow in battle, thanks to a clever treaty that the same Emperor Frederick II had negotiated with the Sultan of Egypt. (The sultan, who was being threatened with invasion by his half brother, the Sultan of Damascus, handed over Jerusalem to the Christians in return for Frederick's promise to help him in case war broke out.) But Christian control of the Holy City was doomed to be short-lived this time. The friendly Egyptian sultan died in 1238, and his successor, determined to dislodge the Crusaders, hired an army of Moslem mercenaries: the Khwarizmian warriors who had been roaming Syria since their second defeat by the Mongols. These freebooters proceeded south into the Holy Land, burning villages and leaving a trail of chaos. Soon they were at Jerusalem. In July 1244 the Khwarizmians broke into the city, forced the Crusader garrison to surrender, drove out the entire Christian population, and ravaged the holy shrines. Leaving Jerusalem ablaze, they sped on toward Gaza and joined the Egyptian army in inflicting upon the Crusader forces one of the most terrible defeats they had suffered since Latin soldiers first had entered the Near East. By the end of 1244 the Crusaders once more were limited to a few coastal towns in the Levant, and their total expulsion seemed near. To Pope Innocent, seeing Emperor Frederick lording it in Rome and the Khwarizmians dancing through burning Jerusalem, these were apocalyptic times, and the Mongols appeared to be the only saviors available.

In 1245 the Pope presided over the Council of Lyons, which had two primary purposes: to deal with the misdeeds of Frederick II and to propose ways of gaining the friendship of the Mongols. The 150 bishops assembled duly voted to condemn the emperor, to excommunicate him once again, and to strip him of his imperial title, which would prove to be a serious blow to his prestige and power. The council also resolved to send two embassies to the Mongols. One, led by the Franciscan monk John of Plano Carpini, would travel across Poland, Russia, and Central Asia to Karakorum; the other, under the direction of a Dominican, Ascelin of Lombardy, would go by way of Syria and Armenia.

Friar John was the first to depart. Clad in his coarse brown robe, his head shaved, his feet bare but for sandals, he mounted a donkey and, on Easter Sunday, 1245, set out from Lyons for the Mongol realms. The papal ambassador was a man in his sixties, already widely traveled; he had served the Order of St. Francis in Saxony, Bohemia, Hungary, Norway, Lorraine, and Spain, and had shown himself impervious to hardship and risk. He would meet plenty of both on this journey, for he had only a single companion—a monk known as Benedict the Pole, who would serve as his interpreter—and was riding into regions where no European had gone before except when being carried off into slavery. Yet Friar John was destined to complete his arduous mission safely, and, upon his return to the papal court at Lyons at the end of

1247, to produce one of the most valuable works of medieval travel literature, his famous *History of the Mongols*.

By late spring of 1245, Friar John was jogging through the devastated regions of Bohemia and Poland. At the city of Krakow he presented himself to the duke, who provided him with an escort as far as the Russian city of Kiev. In February 1246 the friar crossed into Mongol-held territory, and not long afterward he had his first encounter with the conquerors: "Armed Tartars came rushing upon us in uncivil and horrible manner, being very inquisitive of us what manner of persons, or of what condition we were: and when we had answered them that we were the Pope's legates, receiving some victuals at our hands they immediately departed." The next day a Mongol officer asked them to state their business. Friar John replied—the translation is the sixteenth-century one of Richard Hakluyt—"We are the legates of our lord the Pope, who is the father and lord of the Christians. He hath sent us as well unto your emperor, as to your princes, and all other Tartars for this purpose, because it is his pleasure, that all Christians should be in league with the Tartars, and should have peace with them. It is his desire also that they should become great or in favor with God in heaven, therefore he admonisheth them as well by us, as by his own letters, to become Christians, and to embrace the faith of our Lord Jesu Christ, because they could not otherwise be saved." Friar John also conveyed the Pope's displeasure at the Mongols' "monstrous slaughters and massacres of mankind, and especially of Christians. . . . And because the Lord God is grievously offended thereat, he adviseth them henceforth to beware of such dealing, and to repent them of that which they had done."

Apparently amused and perplexed by the friar's audacity, the Mongols gave him permission to proceed eastward. With nothing to defend him but his letter from the Pope, Friar John moved unharmed through the Mongol lines and traveled down the Dnieper River, frozen by winter's grip, to the Black Sea, which was also covered with an icy sheet. There he found the camp of the terrifying Batu Khan, and on Good Friday came before the grandson of Genghis Khan to explain his mission. "This Batu carries himself very stately and magnificently," Friar John later reported, "having porters and all officers after the manner of the emperor, and sits in a lofty seat or throne together with one of his wives. . . . The said Batu is courteous enough unto his own men, and yet he is had in great awe by them: he is most cruel in fight:

he is exceedingly prudent and politic in war, because he hath now continued a long time in martial affairs."

Batu allowed Friar John to go on to Karakorum to confer with the newly elected Khaghan Kuyuk. "Upon Easter day, having said our prayers, and taken a slender breakfast . . . we departed with many tears, not knowing whether we went to death or to life. And we were so feeble in body, that we were scarce able to ride. For all that Lent through, our meat was millet only with a little water and salt. And so likewise upon other fasting days. Neither had we ought to drink, but snow melted in a skillet." Onward he rode, across the Volga Basin, into what had been Kara-Khitai, then into Mongolia proper. Despite the shortage of provisions, the Pope's ambassador traveled at the merciless pace set for him by two Mongols whom Batu had assigned as guides: five changes of horses a day were necessary, for "we spared no horse-flesh, but rode swiftly and without intermission, as fast as our horses could trot." On July 22, 1246, they arrived at Karakorum, to find the Mongol lords gathered in a grand *khuriltai*, for the coronation of Kuyuk was about to take place.

The scene was an astonishing one: an Oriental fantasy of tents and pavilions, of haughty, richly garbed Mongol chieftains, of ambassadors from many lands come to pay homage to the khan of khans. Friar John saw "Duke Jeroslav of Susdal in Russia, and a great many dukes of the Cathayans and of the Solangi. The two sons also of the King of Georgia, the ambassador of the Caliph of Baldach [Baghdad], who was a sultan, and (as we think) above ten sultans of the Saracens besides. And, as it was told us by the agents, there were more than four thousand ambassadors, partly of such as paid tributes, and such as presented gifts, and other sultans, and dukes, which came to yield themselves, and such as the Tartars had sent for, and such as were governors of lands."

The envoys from the Pope were received courteously and given a tent of their own, but they were told they could not see Kuyuk until after the coronation. Friar John did catch a glimpse of him as he paid a visit to his mother, for whom "there was maintained a very solemn and royal court" in "an huge tent of fine white cloth . . . of so great quantity that more than two thousand men might stand within it." For four weeks the Franciscan observed in wonder the festivities at Karakorum. Whenever Kuyuk appeared, "he had a noise of music, and was bowed unto, or honored with fair wands, having purple wool upon the tops of them." Some Mongol "dukes" took a fancy to the friar and his companion, and invited them to one of the celebrations, at which they were offered *khumiss*, the fermented mares' milk on which the Mongols doted. Friar John, watching the daylong drinking bout, said the Mongols drank "in so great quantity, as it was wonderful. And they called us in unto them, and gave us of their ale, because we could not drink their mares' milk. And this they did unto us in token of great honor. But they compelled us to drink so much, that in regard of our customary diet, we could by no means endure it. Whereupon, giving them to understand that it was hurtful to us, they ceased to compel us any more."

During this time of waiting, Friar John gathered as much data as he could about Mongol customs and history, for his instructions from the Pope called upon him to act as a sort of anthropologist as well as a diplomat. The information he collected was copious and fascinating. ("Their victuals are all things that may be eaten: for we saw some of them eat lice.") In his report he described the Mongols' clothing, their physical appearance, their manners ("They seldom or never fall out among themselves, and, as for fightings or brawlings, wounds or man-slaughters, they never happen among them") and their laws ("Whatsoever man or woman be manifestly taken in adultery, they are punished with death. A virgin likewise that hath committed fornication, they slay together with her mate"). He offered an account of Mongol religion: "They know nothing concerning eternal life and everlasting damnation, and yet they think, that after death they shall live in another world, that they shall multiply their cattle, that they shall eat and drink and do other things which living men perform here on earth. At a new moon or a full moon they begin all enterprises that they take in hand, and they call the moon the Great Emperor, and worship it upon their knees."

Friar John's account also contains a history of the rise of Genghis Khan, his conquests, and the succession to power of Ogodai. In general outline it is reasonably accurate, though peppered with myths, errors, and distortions. The friar is most trustworthy in his description of Mongol military tactics, which is superb in detail, and least reliable when he speaks of the fabulous monsters that the Mongols allegedly encountered while doing battle in remote parts of the world. Medieval Europe, endlessly fascinated by monsters, must have relished Friar

John's story of creatures in the deserts near Armenia who "had each of them but one arm and one hand growing out of the midst of their breast, and but one foot. Two of them used to shoot in one bow, and they ran so swiftly that horses could not overtake them. They ran also upon that one foot by hopping and leaping, and being weary of such walking, they went upon their hand and their foot, turning themselves round, as it were in a circle." Then there were the Parossitae, people of the Arctic, "who having little stomachs and small mouths, eat not anything at all, but seething flesh they stand or sit over the pot, and receiving the steam or smoke thereof, are therewith only nourished, and if they eat anything it is very little." Also there were "certain monsters, who in all things resembled the shape of men, saving that their feet were like the feet of an ox, and they had indeed men's heads but dogs' faces. They spake, as it were, two words like men, but at the third they barked like dogs."

Curiously, considering the interest he took in wonders of all sorts, John of Plano Carpini gave relatively short shrift to Prester John. That fabulous prince, so much on the minds of Europeans throughout the century prior to Friar John's journey, appears in his narrative only once, in a subordinate role: he is merely an Indian king whose main distinction is that he was able to repel an invasion by a Mongol army led by one of the sons of Genghis Khan:

"But he [Genghis] sent his other son [Chagadai?] with an army against the Indians, who also subdued India Minor. These Indians are the black Saracens, which are also called Ethiopians. But here the army marched forward to fight against Christians dwelling in India Major. Which the king of that country hearing (who is commonly called Presbyter John) gathered his soldiers together, and came forth against them. And making men's images of copper, he set each of them upon a saddle on horseback, and put fire within them, and placed a man with a pair of bellows on the horseback behind every image. And so with many horses and images in such sort furnished, they marched on to fight against the Mongols or Tartars. And coming near unto the place of the battle, they first of all sent those horses in order one after another. But the men that sat behind laid I wot not what upon the fire within the images, and blew strongly with their bellows. Whereupon it came to pass, that the men and the horses were burnt with wildfire, and the air was darkened with smoke. Then the Indians cast darts upon the

Tartars, of whom many were wounded and slain. And so they expelled them out of their dominions with great confusion, neither did we hear, that ever they returned thither again."

4

The coronation of Kuyuk Khan finally took place late in August 1246. There was, Friar John wrote, "a huge multitude standing with their faces towards the south. And a certain number of them being a stone's cast distant from the residue, making continual prayers, and kneeling upon their knees, proceeded farther and farther towards the south. Howbeit we, not knowing whether they used enchantments, or whether they bowed their knees to God or to some other, would not kneel upon the ground with them. And having done so a long time, they returned to the tent, and placed Cuyne [Kuyuk] in his throne imperial, and his dukes bowed their knees before him. Afterward the whole multitude kneeled down in like manner, except ourselves, for we were none of his subjects."

Kuyuk, according to the Franciscan, "seemed to be about the age of forty or forty-five years. He was of a mean stature, very wise and politic, and passing serious grave in all his demeanor." His sympathies toward Christianity encouraged the papal envoy: "Certain Christians of his family earnestly and strongly affirmed unto us that he himself was about to become a Christian. A token and argument whereof was, that he retained divers clergymen of the Christians. He had likewise at all times a chapel of Christians near unto his great tent, where the clerics (like unto other Christians, and according to the customs of the Greeks) do sing publicly and openly, and ring bells at certain hours. . . ."

Now the khaghan began to receive the ambassadors who had come to him in such great numbers from many lands. Each approached the imperial tent, was searched for concealed weapons, and entered to present his gifts: "Robes of purple, and of Baldakin cloth, silk girdles wrought with gold, and costly skins, with other gifts also. Likewise there was a certain sun canopy, or small tent (which was to be carried over the emperor's head) presented unto him, being set full of precious stones. . . . And we were demanded whether we would bestow any gifts upon him or no? But we were not of ability so to do, having in a manner spent all our provision." Nevertheless the monks were granted an audience with the khaghan, who had read their letter from the Pope, and also a letter from Batu explaining in the Mongol language the purpose of Friar John's mission. The meeting was a chilly one. When asked if he were a Christian, Kuyuk replied, "God knows," and invited the Pope to come to Mongolia to find out for himself. He let it be known that the Mongols planned to conquer the world, and that only the death of Ogodai had caused them to abstain from warfare for these few years past. In reply to the Pope's letter Kuyuk dictated a harsh statement, which he made Friar John take down word for word in Latin, and then had retranslated into his own tongue to be sure that the Franciscan had got it right. The letter, which is still preserved in the Vatican archives, made this demand upon the Pope:

"You must come yourself at the head of all your kings and prove to us your fealty and allegiance. And if you disregard the command of God and disobey our instructions, we shall look upon you as our enemy. Whoever recognizes and submits to the son of God and lord of the world, the Great Khan, will be saved, and whoever refuses submission shall be wiped out."

Kuyuk added:

"You inhabitants of the western lands consider yourselves alone to be Christians and despise others. How then do you know who is worthy in the sight of God to partake of His mercy? When you say to yourselves, 'I am a Christian, I pray to God and serve Him, and I hate the others,' how do you know whom God considers righteous and to whom He will show His mercy?"

Having received this dismaying message, Friar John was compelled to spend another month at Karakorum before being granted leave to return to the Pope. During this time the emissaries were "in such extreme hunger and thirst that we could scarce hold life and soul together. For the provision allowed us for four days was scantly sufficient for one day. Neither could we buy us any sustenance, because the market was too far off. Howbeit the Lord provided for us a Russian goldsmith named Cosmas, who being greatly in the emperor's favor, procured us some sustenance." In November, at last, they began their homeward journey, and "traveled all winter long, lying in the deserts oftentimes upon the snow, except with our feet we made a piece of ground bare to lie upon." On June 8, 1247, they reached Kiev, where the citizens "rejoiced over us, as over men that had been risen from death to life," and westward they went, coming finally to Pope Innocent at the end of the year. John of Plano Carpini had little cheer to offer. Prester John, it seemed, was a shadowy figure dwelling somewhere in India Major, and no help could be expected from him. As for Kuyuk, the Great Khan of the Mongols, he might perhaps have inclinations toward Christianity, but he had no love for Europe, as could be seen from his frosty letter with the grim declaration, "God has commanded my ancestors and myself to send our people to exterminate the wicked nations."

5

Pope Innocent's other ambassador to the Mongols, Ascelin of Lombardy, who had not traveled nearly so far as Friar John, returned with more encouraging news. He had journeyed through Syria and Armenia into Persia, and in May 1247 had met with the Mongol general Baichu at the Persian city of Tabriz. Baichu, though personally discourteous and offensive to the Dominican monk, seemed interested in negotiating a Mongol-Christian military alliance aimed at the Turkish family, descendants of Saladin, who controlled much of the Near East. The Mongol warrior was just then planning an attack on Baghdad, and felt that it would be useful to distract the Moslems of Syria by new warfare while he made his move against Mesopotamia. When Ascelin went back to Europe, he brought with him Aibeg and Serkis, a pair of Mongol envoys from Baichu, of whom at least one was a Nestorian Christian. They spent a year at the papal court but lacked the authority to draw up a treaty, and in November 1248 the Pope sent them home bearing word that he was still interested in an alliance.

Meanwhile a new Crusade was getting under way. Its prime mover was Louis IX, King of France, whose life was so virtuous that he was known even in his own day as St. Louis. This pious monarch, who wore a shirt of hair beneath his royal robes and each night was chastised by priests wielding a whip of flexible chain, had fallen ill in 1244 and was close to death before miraculously recovering. In gratitude for being delivered he vowed to free the Holy Land, which had just been overrun by the Khwarizmians. Four years of preparations followed; the dockyards of six cities, from Barcelona to Venice, were put to work building ships for Louis's fleet. In the summer of 1248 the French Crusaders set sail from Marseilles. Their initial goal was the same as that of the Crusade of 1218–21: the port of Damietta, the gateway to Egypt.

The Crusaders spent the winter of 1248–49 on the island of Cyprus, in the eastern Mediterranean. During this time another Mongol general named Aljighidai, the khaghan's commissioner at the Mesopotamian city of Mosul, learned that a Christian army would soon be landing in Egypt to make war against the Saracens. Like Baichu, he saw this as helpful to the Mongols' proposed attack on Baghdad, and he sent two more emissaries, Nestorians named David and Mark, to discuss terms for a joint anti-Saracen offensive. They arrived in Cyprus in December 1248. The chief chronicler of St. Louis's expedition, John of Joinville, who fought in Louis's Crusade and wrote a memoir of it half a century later, tells us that the Mongol envoys gave the French king to understand "that they would help him to conquer the Kingdom of Jerusalem from the Saracens. The king sent back these envoys, and sent with him, by his own envoys, a chapel which he had caused to be fashioned all in scarlet; and in order to draw the Tartars to our faith, he had caused all our faith to be imaged in the chapel: the Annuciation of the angel, the Nativity, the baptism that God was baptised withal, and all the Passion, and the Ascension, and the coming of the Holy Ghost; and with the chapel he sent also cups, books, and all things needful for the chanting of the mass, and two Preaching Brothers to sing the mass before the Tartars."

The friars whom Louis sent were Dominicans from France, Andrew of Longjumeau and his brother, both of whom were fluent in Arabic. They set out for Mosul in January 1249, were received by Aljighidai, and were sent by him to Karakorum to pay homage to the Khaghan Kuyuk. By many reports, including those of the envoys David and Mark, Kuyuk had recently embraced Christianity, so perhaps he would be less arrogant now than he had been three years earlier at the time of the visit of John of Plano Carpini.

But when Andrew of Longjumeau and his brother arrived in Karakorum they found that Kuyuk had died some months before; that the Mongol world was in confusion over electing his successor; and that Kuyuk's widow, Oghul Gaimish, was serving as a regent during the interregnum. She was attempting to engineer the election of the only remaining prince of Ogodai's line, the boy Shiramun, who had been passed over in 1245 in favor of Kuyuk. But she was opposed in this by

the oldest and most powerful of Genghis' grandsons, Batu Khan. Batu
had long hated Kuyuk; they had quarreled when they fought in Europe,
and Batu had insolently refused to come to the *khuriltai* that had made
Kuyuk khaghan. He loathed Oghul Gaimish as well, and was determined not to let her candidate be chosen, for if Shiramun became
khaghan he would be nothing but Oghul Gaimish's puppet. Too old
to be khaghan himself, and tainted by his father Juchi's uncertain ancestry, Batu had thrown his support to his cousin Mangu, the son of
Genghis' youngest son Tului. This dissension among the leading Mongols prevented the calling of a *khuriltai*.

When King Louis's ambassadors came before Oghul Gaimish in
1249, therefore, they found her preoccupied with a dynastic crisis and
hardly interested in making treaties with distant potentates. She seems
to have accepted Louis's gifts in a gracious but absent-minded way,
regarding them as the tribute from some remote vassal to his sovereign.
Ignoring all requests for military alliance, she handed Andrew a patron-
izing letter to the French king in which she thanked him for his presents and reminded him that similar offerings would be expected every
year.

In a somewhat distorted way this incident entered Joinville's
chronicle. Unable to believe that the Mongols were under a woman's
rule, Joinville said that the envoys had come before "the King of the
Tartars," and that he had made this reply:

"A good thing is peace; for in the land where peace reigns those
that go about on four feet eat the grass of peace; and those that go
about on two feet till the earth—from which good things do proceed—
in peace also. And this thing we tell thee for thy advertisement; for
thou canst not have peace save thou have it with us. For Prester John
rose up against us, and such and such kings"—and he named a great
many, says Joinville—"and we have put them all to the sword. So we
admonish thee to send us, year by year, of thy gold and of thy silver,
and thus keep us to be thy friend; and if thou wilt not do this, we will
destroy thee and thy people, as we have done to the kings already
named." To which Joinville adds, "And you must know that it repented
the king sorely that he had ever sent envoys to the great King of the
Tartars."

The destruction of Prester John by the Mongols, alluded to in
this supposed letter from the Tartar king, enters the record for the first

time in Joinville's pages. The story, which he claims to have heard from Andrew of Longjumeau, is this:

"They [the Tartars] were subject to Prester John, and to the Emperor of Persia, whose land came next to his, and to several other misbelieving kings, to whom they rendered tribute and service every year, for the pasturage of their beasts, seeing they had no other means of livelihood. This Prester John, and the King of Persia, and the other kings, held the Tartars in such contempt that when they brought their rents they would not receive them face-wise, but turned their backs upon them.

"Among the Tartars was a wise man, who journeyed over all the plains, and spoke with the wise men of the plains, and of the different places, and showed them in what bondage they stood, and prayed them all to consider how best they might find a way of escape from the bondage in which they were held. He wrought so effectually that he gathered them all together at the end of the plain, over against the land of Prester John, and explained matters to them. And they answered that whatever he desired, that they would do. And he said that they would achieve nothing unless they had a king and lord over them. And he taught them after what manner they might obtain a king; and they agreed.

"And this was the manner: out of the fifty-two tribes that there were, each tribe was to bring an arrow marked with its name; and by consent of all the people it was agreed that the fifty-two arrows so brought should be placed before a child aged five years; and the arrow that the child took first would mark the tribe from which the king would be chosen. When the child had so lifted up one of the arrows, the wise men caused all the other tribes to draw back; and it was settled that the tribe from which the king was to be chosen should select among themselves fifty-two of the wisest and best men that they had. When these were elected, each one brought an arrow marked with his name. Then it was agreed that the man whose arrow the child lifted up should be made king. And the child lifted up one of the arrows, and it was that of the wise man by whom the people had been instructed. Then were the people glad, and each rejoiced greatly. And the wise man bade them all be silent, and said: 'Lords, if you would have me to be your king, swear to me by Him who made the heavens and the earth, that you will keep my commandments.' And they swore it.

"The ordinances that he established had for purpose the maintenance of peace among the people; and they were to this effect: that none should steal another man's goods, nor any man strike another, on penalty of losing his fist; that no man should have company with another's wife or daughter, on penalty of losing his fist, or his life. Many other good ordinances did he establish among them for the maintenance of peace.

"After he had established order and arrayed them, the king spoke in this wise: 'Lords, the most powerful enemy that we have is Prester John. And I command you to be all ready, on the morrow, to fall upon him; and if it so happens that he defeats us—which God forbid!—let each do as best he can. And if we defeat him, I order that the slaying last three days and three nights, and that none, during that space, be so rash as to lay hand on the booty, but all be bent on slaying the people; for after we have obtained the victory, I will distribute the booty, duly and loyally, so that each shall hold himself well paid.' To this they all agreed.

"On the morrow they fell upon their enemies, and, as God so willed, discomfited them. All those whom they found in arms, and capable of defense, they put to the sword; and those whom they found in religious garb, the priests and other religiouses, they slew not. The other people belonging to Prester John's land, who were not in that battle, made themselves subject unto the Tartars."

6

This story shows us a new Prester John: no longer the invincible priest-king, but rather an Asian monarch who was defeated and overthrown by the Mongols in the early days of their quest for empire. In Joinville's chronicle, then, we see the burying of the original form of the myth that had obsessed Europe since the middle of the twelfth century, since Bishop Hugh of Jabala's sojourn at Viterbo and the circulation of the supposed letter of Prester John to Emperor Manuel of Byzantium. Prester John would not, as Jacques of Vitry had foretold in 1221, come riding to the defense of Christendom. Prester John, to whom seventy-two kings were tributaries, who entertained thirty thousand men daily at his table, who had an archbishop for his cupbearer and a patriarch for his steward, was dead—slain by his rebellious subjects, the Mongols.

It is not difficult to recognize Genghis Khan as the prototype for the "wise man" who, in Joinville's story, unified the Mongol tribes. Who, then, was this Prester John whom he defeated? Surely it can be none other than Genghis' godfather, Togrul, the khan of the Christian Keraits, to whom Genghis once was subject, and whom he overthrew and killed in 1203. For a confirmation of that theory, however, we must examine the report of the next ambassador of Christendom to the Mongols.

King Louis IX, during the absence of Andrew of Longjumeau, had enjoyed varied fortunes in his Crusade. In June of 1249 he had captured Damietta with surprisingly little resistance, and then had begun to move slowly up the Nile toward Cairo. By December the Crusaders had advanced only thirty-five miles, to the town of Mansourah, where they were blocked for two months by a large Saracen army. Many of Louis's leading knights were slain there in a battle in February, but the valor of the saintly king turned a rout into a victory. Then the Saracens blockaded the Nile, and the Crusaders, making camp between two branches of the river, found themselves trapped without food or water. "The flesh of our legs dried all up," Joinville wrote, "and the skin of our legs became mottled with black like an old pair of boots. . . . No one could escape the disease, except by dying." The disease that ran through their camp was typhoid fever, contracted by eating eels that had fed on the rotting bodies of dead Crusaders in the river. Louis was compelled to surrender and, in May 1250, bought his freedom by paying a ransom of a million gold bezants—some $15,000,000 in modern money—as well as giving Damietta back to the Saracens. The survivors of the ill-fated adventure now withdrew to Acre, one of the few cities of the Holy Land still controlled by the Crusaders, to consider their next steps. For most, the next step was an immediate journey back to France, but Louis, feeling bound by his vows, remained in the Holy Land. He took part in no further combat but dipped liberally into his treasury to strengthen the coastal fortresses of Acre, Tyre, Jaffa, and Sidon, and served as a moderating force in the endless quarrels among the Latin barons. It was his main hope that reinforcements would come from Europe, but the French nobles, stunned by Louis's debacle in Egypt, were unwilling to become involved in further Crusading, and King Henry III of England, who with many of his subjects had taken the Cross in 1250, found reasons to postpone his departure for the Near East indefinitely. Hence, when word reached Louis at Acre early in 1253 that one of the Mongol princes, Sartaq, the son of Batu, had been converted to Christianity, Louis at once dispatched ambassadors to Sartaq's camp in pursuit of the old dream of a Mongol-Christian alliance.

The envoys were two Franciscan monks: William of Rubruck, a native of French Flanders, and an Italian, Bartholomew of Cremona. Of Bartholomew we know very little, but William of Rubruck, who left us an extensive and important account of the journey, was a fat and sturdy man, physically inexhaustible, and a shrewd, sharp-eyed observer. He was well prepared for his mission: before departing he conferred with Andrew of Longjumeau, newly returned from Kara-korum, and read the manuscript of John of Plano Carpini, who had died in 1252.

Friar William and Friar Bartholomew went first to Acre, then to Constantinople, and in May 1253 they set out across the Black Sea, accompanied by three servants, one of whom they had bought in Con-stantinople. The following month they landed at the Italian trading outpost of Soldaia in the Crimea, where they quite possibly encoun-tered two wealthy Venetian merchants who did business there, the brothers Niccolò and Maffeo Polo. (Niccolò's son Marco had not yet been born.) The traders at Soldaia advised the monks to travel into Mongolia in carts drawn by oxen, instead of on horseback, for thus they "should ride a more gentle pace." So indeed they went, to Friar Wil-liam's regret, for the journey to Sartaq's camp took twice as long by ox-cart as it would have by horse.

Three days east of Soldaia they found themselves in Mongol-held territory. "When I met Tartars for the first time," Friar William wrote, "I thought myself entered into another age." With the example of John of Plano Carpini before him, he took careful notes on all he saw, set-ting down an analysis of Mongol customs even more detailed than Friar John's. He described their marital ways, their household goods, their food and drink, their manner of hospitality, their styles of dress and hair, and much else. Mongol women, he wrote, "are exceeding fat, and the lesser their noses be, the fairer are they esteemed: they daub over their sweet faces with grease too shamefully, and they never lie in bed for their travail of childbirth." Concerning marriages, he reported that "no man can have a wife among them till he hath bought her: whereupon sometimes their maids are very stale before they can be married, for their parents always keep them till they can sell them." When a man did purchase a bride, it was usually necessary for him to gain her by rape, for she would hide among her kinsmen during the wedding feast. "Then saith her father unto the bridegroom: Lo, my daughter is yours, take her wheresoever you can find her. Then he and his friends seek for her till they can find her, and having found her he must take her by force and carry her, as it were, violently unto his own house."

The first Mongols the friars met "began impudently to beg our victuals from us. And we gave them some of our biscuit and wine, which we had brought with us from the town of Soldaia. And having drunk off one flagon of our wine they demanded another, saying that a man goeth not into the house with one foot." The envoys finally halted this raid on their provisions and, explaining that they sought Sartaq to give him letters from King Louis of France, were permitted to pass. Eastward they rode, through lands inhabited by pagan tribes wilder and more barbarous than the Mongols, and came to Sartaq near the Volga River. Sartaq's major domo, a Nestorian Mongol named Coiat, interviewed them and agreed to present them to his master, though he was irked that they could offer Sartaq no gifts richer than biscuit and wine. Then the friars went before Sartaq. "I myself putting on our most precious ornaments," Friar William declared, "took in mine arms a very fair cushion, and the Bible which your Majesty [Louis] gave me, and a most beautiful psalter, which the queen's grace bestowed upon me, wherein there were goodly pictures. Mine associate took a missal and a cross: and the clerk having put on his surplice, took a censer in his hand. . . . Then we entered, singing Salve Regina. And within the entrance of the door, stood a bench with cosmos [khumiss], and drinking cups thereupon. And all his [Sartaq's] wives were there assembled. Also the Moals [Mongols] or rich Tartars thrusting in with us pressed us sore. Then Coiat carried unto his lord the censer with incense, which he beheld very diligently, holding it in his hand. Afterward he carried the psalter unto him, which he looked earnestly upon, and his wife also that sat beside him. After that he carried the Bible; then Sartaq asked if the Gospel were contained therein. Yea (said I) and all the holy scriptures besides. He took the cross also in his hand, and demanded concerning the image, whether it were the image of Christ or no? I said it was. The Nestorians and the Armenians do never make the figure of Christ upon their crosses. Wherefore either they seem not to think well of his passion, or else they are ashamed of it. Then he caused them that stood about us, to stand aside, that he might more fully behold our ornaments. Afterwards I delivered unto him your Majesty's letters, with the translation thereof into the Arabic and Syriac tongues."

Sartaq's apparent keen interest in the Christian articles the friars showed to him did not necessarily mean that he was, as rumor had had it, a Christian himself. "Whether he believes in Christ, or no, I know not," Friar William admitted. "This I am sure of, that he will not be called a Christian. Yea rather he seemeth unto me to deride and scoff at Christians." Nor would this junior prince commit himself in regard to King Louis's request for an alliance; these matters were too delicate for Sartaq, and he told Friar William to proceed eastward to the camp of his father Batu. The emissaries went down the Volga in a barque, past villages of Moslem Bulgars ("I wonder what devil carried the religion of Mahomet thither"), and came at length to the court of Batu, which Friar William "was astonished at the sight thereof: for his houses or tents seemed as though they had been some huge and mighty city, stretching out a great way in length, the people ranging up and down about it for the space of some three or four leagues."

They found Batu sitting "upon a seat long and broad like a bed, gilt all over, with three stairs to ascend thereunto, and one of his ladies sat beside him." Barefoot and bareheaded in their monkish habits, Friar William and Friar Bartholomew approached the Mongol khan in his splendid tent and were told to kneel and speak. Friar William amiably went down on one knee, but the Mongol interpreter "signified that I should kneel upon both knees: and I did so, being loath to contend about such circumstances." As long as he was kneeling, Friar William delivered himself of a brief prayer, and then admonished Batu, "Be it known unto you of a certainty, that you shall not obtain the joys of heaven, unless you become a Christian: for God saith, Whosoever believeth and is baptized, shall be saved, but he that believeth not, shall be condemned." At this Batu smiled, "but the other Moals began to clap their hands, and to deride us. And my silly interpreter, of whom especially I should have received comfort in time of need, was himself abashed and utterly dashed out of countenance."

Undaunted, Friar William explained that he had come to see Sartaq, having heard that he was a Christian, and that Sartaq had sent him on to Batu to consider the import of King Louis's letters. Batu questioned the monk courteously, and asked him to be seated, and gave him, as a special sign of favor, the fermented mares' milk to drink, this last causing Friar William no pleasure. But Batu, like his son, refused to take the responsibility for dealing with the ambassadors: there was no help for it, but the weary friars must journey on, all the way to Karakorum, to say their piece to the khaghan himself. (By this time the dynastic crisis had been resolved to Batu's satisfaction. He had helped to bring his cousins, the sons of Genghis' son Tului, into power over the opposition of the descendants of Ogodai and Chagadai. At a *khuriltai* in 1251 Tului's eldest son, Mangu Khan, had become khaghan, with Oghul Gaimish and the other members of the defeated faction reluctantly acquiescing. Mangu then parceled out the Mongol world among his brothers: China to Kublai, Mongolia to Arik-buga, Persia to Hulagu. Batu and his family, of course, retained control over Russia and the other western provinces. Soon after the *khuriltai*, Oghul Gaimish and nearly everyone else of the house of Ogodai were put to death on charges of conspiring to assassinate the new khaghan.)

For five weeks the friars traveled down the Volga in Batu's company. The Mongols were sparing with their hospitality, evidently because Friar William had neglected to bestow a gift on a certain functionary of the court, and so, he wrote, "Sometimes mine associate [Friar Bartholomew] was so extremely hungry, that he would tell me in a manner weeping, that it fared with him as though he had never eaten anything in all his life before." Some Hungarians who had long lived as slaves to the Mongols rescued the friars from their plight with meat and *khumiss*. Worse hardships were ahead: when they parted from Batu's entourage, a Mongol came to the envoys, introduced himself as the guide who was to lead them to Karakorum, and said, "We have thither a journey of four months long to travel, and there is such extreme cold in those parts, that stones and trees do even rive asunder in regard thereof. Therefore I would wish you thoroughly to advise yourselves, whether you be able to endure it or no." To which Friar William responded, "I hope by God's help that we shall be able to brook that which other men can endure," and the Mongol blandly replied, "If you cannot endure it, I will forsake you by the way."

Wrapped in a sheepskin jacket, socks of felt, and leather boots, Friar William and Friar Bartholomew withstood the cold, and the other difficulties also. "Of twenty or thirty horses we had always the worst, because we were strangers. For everyone took their choice of the best horses before us. They provided me always of a strong horse, because

I was very corpulent and heavy, but whether he ambled a gentle pace or no, I durst not make any question," Friar William wrote. "Of hunger and thirst, cold and weariness, there was no end. For they gave us no victuals, but only in the evening. In the morning they used to give us a little drink, or some sodden millet to sup off. In the evening they bestowed flesh upon us, as namely, a shoulder and breast of ram's mutton, and every man a measured quantity of broth to drink." Through all the thousands of miles of the journey he recorded penetrating observations on the customs of the tribes through whose territory he passed—Uighurs, Tanguts, Keraits, and others. He checked on John of Plano Carpini's stories of strange beings: "I was inquisitive of the monsters or monstrous men. . . . They told me they never saw any such, whereof we much wonder, whether it be true or not." The natives questioned Friar William, too, "concerning the great Pope, whether he was of so lasting an age as they had heard? For there had gone a report among them, that he was five hundred years old. . . . Concerning the Ocean Sea, they could not conceive of it, because it was without limit or banks."

He watched Buddhists and tribal shamans at their rites, and described them with as much sympathy as he could give the doings of idolaters. His deepest contempt he reserved for the Nestorians, of whom he saw a great number while traveling among such Christian tribes as the Uighurs and the Keraits: "The Nestorians there know nothing. They say their offices, and have sacred books in Syriac, but they do not know the language, so they chant like those monks among us who do not know grammar, and they are absolutely depraved. In the first place they are usurers and drunkards; some even among them who live with the Tartars have several wives like them. When they enter church, they wash their lower parts like Saracens; they eat meat on Friday, and have their feasts on that day in Saracen fashion. The bishop rarely visits these parts, hardly once in fifty years. When he does, they have all the male children, even those in the cradle, ordained priests, so nearly all the males among them are priests. Then they marry, which is clearly against the statutes of the fathers, and they are bigamists, for when the first wife dies these priests take another. They are all simoniacs, for they administer no sacrament gratis. They are solicitous for their wives and children, and are consequently more intent on the increase of their wealth than of the faith. And so those of them who educate some of the sons of the noble Moals, though they teach them the Gospel and the articles of the faith, through their evil lives and their cupidity estrange them from the Christian faith, for the lives that the Moals themselves and Tuins or idolaters lead are more innocent than theirs."

In December 1253, William and Bartholomew reached Mangu Khan's encampment, a few miles south of Karakorum. The great khan received them on January 4 in a handsome tent: "The house was all covered inside with a cloth of gold and there was a fire . . . in a grate in the center of the dwelling. . . . Mangu was seated on a couch and was dressed in a skin spotted and glossy, like a seal's skin. He is a little man, of medium height, aged forty-five years, and a young wife sat beside him." The khaghan "appeared to me to be tipsy," and so also did the interpreter, so the meeting was inconclusive. One of the Mongols questioned Friar William lengthily "about the kingdom of France, whether there were many sheep and cattle and horses there, and whether they had not better go there and take it." As the audience ended the friars were informed, "Mangu Khan takes compassion on you and allows you to stay here for the space of two months: then the great cold will be over."

The envoys soon moved with the court to Karakorum itself, which left Friar William unimpressed: "You must know that, exclusive of the palace of the khan, it is not as big as [the Parisian suburb of] St. Denis, and the monastery of St. Denis is ten times larger than the palace." But an awesome corps of diplomats was in attendance on Mangu: ambassadors from Byzantium and Baghdad, from the King of Delhi, from the Seljuks of Asia Minor, from emirs of Syria and Iraq, from princes of Russia. There was even a colony of European residents who apparently had been brought back as captives during the Mongol raids of the previous decade: a goldsmith from Paris who had a Hungarian wife, an Alsatian woman married to a Russian architect, and a certain "Basil, the son of an Englishman, who was born in Hungary."

Eventually Friar William was permitted a second audience with Mangu. The great khan, whose mother had been a Christian, examined William's cross "without seeming to worship it in any way." There followed a religious debate, as Buddhists and Moslems and Nestorians and representatives of other faiths at Mangu's court put forth the advantages of their creeds. Friar William took part, and found himself agreeing with the Nestorians and even the Moslems on at least one

basic point—that there was only one God. He spoke intolerantly, however, and angered the easygoing Mongols, who accepted most religions
with equal willingness.

Mangu himself declared, "We Mongols believe that there is only
one God, by whom we live and by whom we die, and we have an upright heart towards him. As God hath given the hand many fingers, so
hath he given many ways to men. God hath given the Scriptures to you
Christians, and you keep them not. . . . To us he has given sooth-
sayers, and we do that which they bid us, and we live in peace."

Plainly Mangu was no Christian, though his chief wife was. (Friar
William professes to have seen her reeling home drunkenly from High
Mass, confirming his belief that the Nestorian rite was mere debauchery.) But the great khan did indeed intend to make war against the
Moslems of the Near East, and indicated a willingness to have Christendom join its forces to his. There was one minor problem, though:
the Mongol prince regarded himself as supreme sovereign of the world,
and all other princes, the King of France included, were expected to
pay homage to him. If King Louis would not declare himself Mangu's
vassal, alliance was impossible, for anyone who was not Mangu's vassal
was, by definition, his enemy. Ultimately, said Mangu, "the whole world
shall be at one, in peace and rejoicing," under the benign reign of the
Mongols. Friar William, aware that Louis would never accept an alliance
on such terms, realized his mission had failed, and in the summer of
1254 he departed from Karakorum, bearing a letter from Mangu to
Louis that warned the princes of Europe to prepare themselves to submit to Mongol government or be destroyed. Friar Bartholomew remained in Mongolia as a missionary, and of his fate nothing is known.
William of Rubruck reached Acre in the summer of 1255, with the discouraging news that the Mongols were beyond all understanding: sympathetic to all religions, but subject to none, and following some divine
plan from which they would not swerve. There would be no converting
them to Catholicism, nor could the Crusaders hope for much comfort
from them.

7

While among the Mongols Friar William obtained further details of the
Asian king whom Genghis Khan had overthrown and whom John of

Plano Carpini had identified as Prester John. This is the story as William heard it:

"At the same time when the Frenchmen took Antioch, a certain man named Con Can had dominion over the northern regions, lying thereabouts. Con is a proper name: Can is a name of authority or dignity, which signifieth a diviner or soothsayer. All diviners are called Can among them. Whereupon their princes are called Can, because that unto them belongeth the government of the people by divination. We do read also in the history of Antioch, that the Turks sent for aid against the Frenchmen, unto the kingdom of Con Can. For out of those parts the whole nation of the Turks first came.

"The said Con was of the nation of Kara-Catay. Kara signifieth black, and Catay is the name of a country. So that Kara-Catay signifieth the black Catay. This name was given to make a difference between the foresaid people, and the people of Catay, inhabiting eastward over against the Ocean Sea. . . . These Catayans dwelt upon certain Alps, by the which I traveled. And in a certain plain country within those Alps, there inhabited a Nestorian shepherd, being a mighty governor over the people called Yayman, which were Christians, following the sect of Nestorius. After the death of Con Can, the said Nestorian exalted himself to the kingdom, and they called him King John, reporting ten times more of him than was true. For so the Nestorians which come out of those parts, use to do. For they blaze abroad great rumors, and reports upon just nothing. . . . So likewise there went forth a great report concerning the said King John. Howbeit, when I traveled along by his territories, there was no man that knew anything of him, but only a few Nestorians. . . .

"This John had a brother, being a mighty man also, and a shepherd like himself, called Vut, and he inhabited beyond the Alps of Kara-Catay, being distant from his brother John, the space of three weeks' journey. He was lord over a certain village, called Cara Carum, having people also for his subjects, named Crit, or Merkit, who were Christians of the sect of Nestorius. But their lord abandoning the worship of Christ, followed after idols, retaining with him priests of the said idols, who all of them are worshippers of devils and sorcerers. Beyond his pastures some ten or fifteen days' journey, were the pastures of Moal, who were a poor and beggarly nation, without governor, and without law, except their soothsayings, and their divinations, unto the which detestable studies all in those parts do apply their minds. Near unto Moal were other poor people called Tartars.

"The foresaid King John died without issue male, and thereupon his brother Vut was greatly enriched, and caused himself to be named Can: and his droves and flocks ranged even unto the borders of Moal. About the same time there was one Cyngis, a blacksmith among the people of Moal. This Cyngis stole as many cattle from Vut Can, as he could possibly get: insomuch that the shepherds of Vut complained unto their lord. Then provided he an army, and marched up into the country of Moal to seek for the said Cyngis. But Cyngis fled among the Tartars, and hid himself amongst them. And Vut having taken some spoils both from Moal, and also from the Tartars, returned home. Then spake Cyngis unto the Tartars, and unto the people of Moal, saying: Sirs, because we are destitute of a governor and captain, you see how our neighbors do oppress us. And the Tartars and Moals appointed him to be their chieftain. Then having secretly gathered together an army, he broke in suddenly upon Vut, and overcame him, and Vut fled into Catay. At the same time was the daughter of Vut taken, which Cyngis married unto one of his sons, by whom she conceived, and brought forth the Great Can, which now reigneth, called Mangu-Can. Then Cyngis sent the Tartars before him in all places where he came: and thereupon was their name published and spread abroad: for in all places the people would cry out: Lo, the Tartars come, the Tartars come."

Here is a wondrous mixture of half-truths, misapprehensions, and errors! Only through a line-by-line gloss can this tangled tale be properly unsnarled, and reveal to us the figure of Prester John lurking behind William of Rubruck's muddled anecdotes.

when the Frenchmen took Antioch: the "Frenchmen" are the soldiers of the First Crusade, who captured the Syrian city of Antioch in 1098.

a certain man named Con Can: in some manuscript versions of William of Rubruck's narrative, this name is given as *Coir Can* or *Coir Cham.* In this form it may more readily be recognized as *gur-khan,* the title taken by Yeh-lü Ta-shih when he founded the realm of Kara-Khitai in 1125.

Can is a name of authority. . . . All diviners are called Can among them. Whereupon their princes are called Can, because that unto them belongeth the government of the people by divination: here

Friar William introduces a delicious bit of etymological confusion. In the Mongol tongue a *khan* was a prince and a *kham* was a shaman or soothsayer. By confounding the two separate words, William provides a false philological basis for the notion that Prester John was both king and priest.

The said Con was of the nation of Kara-Catay: further indication that by "Con Can" is meant the Gur-Khan Yeh-lü Ta-shih.

the people called Yayman: the Naiman Turks of Central Asia, whom Genghis Khan ultimately defeated and absorbed.

After the death of Con Can: here William goes astray again. No Naiman took control of Kara-Khitai when Yeh-lü Ta-shih died, about 1143. He was succeeded by his wife, ruling as regent for their son, I-lieh. However, the dynasty of Yeh-lü Ta-shih *was* finally extinguished by a Naiman, Kuchluk, in 1211. Friar William has apparently telescoped seventy years of Asian history.

they called him King John, reporting ten times more of him than was true: in another part of his account, William refers to this Naiman usurper as "King or Presbyter John," so this can be taken as a deflation of the exaggerated stories of Prester John's might that were circulating in Europe in his day.

This John had a brother, being a mighty man also, and a shepherd like himself, called Vut: there are more difficulties here. If we are to accept Kuchluk the Naiman as the prototype for Friar William's King John, we cannot identify this supposed brother, Vut. William tells us that upon John's death Vut succeeded him and proclaimed himself to be Vut Can. But history records nothing about Kuchluk's brothers; and after Kuchluk was slain by the Mongols in 1219 his realm passed into the possession of Genghis Khan, who certainly cannot be identified with Vut. So we must discard the notion that Vut was John's brother.

Some variant texts of Friar William's narrative give us the name *Ung Can* in place of Vut, and herein lies the explanation. For "Ung Khan" is the Mongol form of the composite title *wang-khan*, that is, the Chinese and Mongol words for "king." All Central Asian princes called themselves khan, and some called themselves *wang* as well, but the first recorded use of the double form dates from the final decade of the twelfth century. The Chinese Emperor Ts'ang Tsung, a Jurchen who ruled from 1190 to 1200, bestowed it upon his vassal Togrul Khan, the chieftain of the Keraits. This was Genghis' godfather, whom he later overthrew; and so the Vut or Ung Can of William of Rubruck can be assumed to be the Wang-Khan Togrul, the master of much of Mongolia immediately before Genghis' ascendancy. As we have already seen, Togrul was the chieftain whom John of Joinville, retelling the account of Andrew of Longjumeau, regarded as the real Prester John. John of Plano Carpini, on the other hand, said nothing about Togrul and did not look upon Prester John as a native of Mongolia at all, but rather of the lands beyond the Indus.

How are we to account for William's linking of Togrul and Kuchluk the Naiman ("King or Presbyter John")? They were in fact not brothers, nor of the same tribe, nor of the same generation, nor could Togrul, who died in 1203, possibly have succeeded to the throne of Kuchluk, who outlived him by sixteen years. Friar William must have woven the two improperly together. A clue to the source of his error can be found in the *Chronicon Syriacum* of the Syrian cleric Gregory Abulfaraj Bar-Hebraeus, who lived from 1226 to 1286: speaking of the conversion of the Keraits to Christianity, he notes that in the time of the Mongol dominion they were ruled by an "Ung Khan who is called *Malik Yuhanna*," that is, "King John." Leonardo Olschki and other modern scholars have raised the suggestion that Yuhanna, or Johannan, was merely a Central Asian Nestorian corruption of the title, *wang-khan*; but somehow the concept took root that King John was an alternative designation for the *wang-khan*, the Kerait chieftain. And William of Rubruck, mysteriously, assigned these titles to a pair of brothers conjured up for the occasion, calling them John and Vut (or Ung). Another possibility was proposed by the nineteenth-century British Sinologist Alexander Wylie, who pointed out that Kuchluk's father, the Naiman king before him, had been known as Tai-yang Khan. This, said Wylie, is literally "Great King John," as near as *John* can be rendered in Chinese.

Crit or Merkit: the Keraits and the Merkits, both tribes ultimately conquered by the Mongols.

Moal: Mongols.

Cyngis: Genghis. William offers a romanticized version of Genghis' rise to power in Mongolia and his defeat of the Wang-Khan Togrul of the Keraits. Genghis was, of course, the grandfather and not the father of Mangu Khan, as William has it here.

In William of Rubruck's narrative, then, is embedded a jumbled account of the important events of Central Asian history in the twelfth and thirteenth centuries. He speaks first of the Gur-Khan (Con or Coir Can) Yeh-lü Ta-shih's founding of Kara-Khitai in 1125, then introduces the conquest of Kara-Khitai by Kuchluk the Naiman (King or Presbyter John) out of its proper sequence in time, and wrongly credits the Wang-Khan Togrul the Kerait (Vut or Ung Can) with being Kuchluk's brother; then he tells of Togrul's downfall at the hands of Genghis Khan (Cyngis). It is interesting to note that of these four, Yeh-lü Ta-shih, Kuchluk, Togrul, and Genghis, all had previously been identified in some fashion in the European world as Prester John, except only Kuchluk, to whom Friar William awards the title. But the essential point emerging out of this maze of identities is this: that Prester John had been a nomad chieftain of Mongolia, a man of no great power or importance, who had been swept away by Genghis Khan.

8

Under Mangu Khan, the Mongols resumed their war against the world. For a decade their expansion had been reined, first because of Ogodai's death and the dynastic dispute that followed it, then because of the illness and death of the next khaghan, Kuyuk, and then because of the period of feuding preceding Mangu's election. In January 1256, Mangu's brother Hulagu led a huge Mongol army westward to obliterate the Islamic states of the Near East. Another brother, Kublai, was already in China, planning the conquest of that half of the country still under the rule of the Sung Dynasty.

Hulagu swept into Persia, which had come under the control of a sinister sect of Moslem fanatics, the Assassins. These he exterminated with the aid of his most trusted general, Kit-buga, a Nestorian Naiman who was said to be descended from one of the Three Magi of the Gospel. When Persia was satisfactorily pacified, Hulagu moved on toward Mesopotamia, where, since the collapse of the Khwarizmians, the Caliph of Baghdad had managed to revive the authority of his ancient dynasty, which still claimed pre-eminence in the orthodox Moslem world. Late in 1257 the Mongol army defeated that of the caliph about thirty miles from Baghdad and, in February 1258, Baghdad itself, the capital of the caliphate, yielded under a fierce Mongol bombardment. The Caliph al-Mustasim, thirty-seventh ruler of the Abbasid line, was put to death, though only after Hulagu had extracted from him the hiding places of all his wealth. The immense treasures accumulated by the caliphs through five centuries thus fell into Hulagu's hands. He sent a generous share to Mangu at Karakorum and carried the rest into the Caucasus, where he built a castle in Azerbaijan as his treasury. Mongol officials were placed in charge of Baghdad. At the urging of his principal wife, Dokuz Khatun—the granddaughter of Togrul Khan, and a devoted Nestorian—Hulagu turned one of the late caliph's palaces over to the Nestorian catholicos, Makika, to be his residence and church, and endowed the patriarch with a rich helping of the caliph's wealth. (Hulagu himself had the Mongol khan's customary neutrality in religious matters, dabbling both in shamanism and in Buddhism. But his wife and mother both were Christians, and they aroused in him strong sympathies for Nestorianism, as well as an antipathy for Islam that deepened as he did battle against the Moslem states.)

The destruction of the caliphate aroused familiar hopes in Christendom. Once more a warrior-king seemed to be coming out of Asia to shatter the infidels. The fall of Baghdad left the entire Moslem world in shock and inspired Christians everywhere with the belief that Hulagu would shortly complete the eradication of Islam. Hulagu gave no reason to doubt that bold expectation. In September 1259 he invaded northwestern Syria, and soon Mongols were laying siege to the Saracen-held cities of Aleppo and Damascus, which the Crusaders even in their strongest days had never been able to capture. By the spring of 1260 both had fallen to Hulagu. The only remaining Crusader prince of any importance, Bohemond VI of Antioch, came to pay homage to Hulagu, and rode happily through the streets of Damascus next to the Mongol Christian general Kit-buga. Hulagu bestowed on Bohemond various territories that had been stripped from his principality by the Moslems in Saladin's time, but he also forced the prince to make an unpalatable concession: a Greek Orthodox patriarch would have to be installed in Antioch in place of the Roman Catholic one who had presided there under the Crusaders. Hulagu had no personal interest in raising the Greek Church above the Latin, since both regarded his wife's favorites, the Nestorians, as heretics; however, Nestorians were not an important factor in this part of Syria, and the Latin Crusaders were only a thin ruling minority, while a great many of the native Syrian Christians were Greek Orthodox. Hulagu, deft politician of religion that he was, sought to win the support of this large group by granting their patriarch so prestigious a see. Bohemond had no choice but to obey, though his submission was humiliating to all Crusaders and to Roman Catholics generally.

Hulagu now began to plan the downfall of the only remaining major Saracen land in the area, Egypt. A man of Turkish ancestry, Qutuz, once a slave, had made himself sultan there. Early in 1260, Hulagu sent an ambassador to Qutuz, asking him to submit to Mongol authority. Qutuz put the envoy to death. The Mongol army, under Kit-buga, thereupon began to move southward into Palestine, which was controlled by the Egyptians except for the few coastal towns still under Crusader rule. Kit-buga captured the town of Nablus and then took Gaza, which commanded the land route from Palestine to Egypt. Presumably the liberation from Moslem rule of the rest of Palestine, including Jerusalem, would have followed. At this point, however, Hulagu received news of trouble in the Mongol homeland. Mangu Khan was dead, and his brothers Kublai and Arik-buga had each proclaimed themselves khaghan: a civil war threatened. Hulagu could not plunge deeper into the Near East with such a crisis to his rear. Leaving Kit-buga to hold down Palestine and Syria with only a small garrison, Hulagu turned back toward Persia with the bulk of his troops, so that he could hasten into Mongolia if the situation demanded his presence.

Kublai was the logical successor to Mangu. He was the oldest and most powerful living grandson of Genghis Khan, the formidable Batu having died in Russia in 1255. But he had many opponents among the Mongols: those who still kept to their nomad ways, living in tents, scorning all luxuries. How, they asked, could Kublai dare claim the throne once held by Genghis? He was no true Mongol, this Kublai. He was soft, scholarly, fond of comfort. Could he ride by day and night for weeks? Could he endure hunger and thirst? Could he inspire terror?

Indeed Kublai had never shared his brothers' love for warfare. He had seen his first military action when he was only thirteen, in the last year of Genghis Khan's life, but he had no real taste for battle. Mangu and Hulagu and Arik-buga loved to be in the thick of things, shedding enemy blood and roaring violent songs, but not Kublai. He had stayed home on the greatest of all Mongol expeditions, the one that made Europe tremble. He was more comfortable in the pleasures of his palace and in the delights of the hunt than he was on the field of battle.

Mangu Khan, in 1253, had assigned him the task of finishing the conquest of China. It was an assignment Kublai welcomed, for he loved

China and relished the idea of dwelling there, surrounded by fine porcelain vases, elegant painted scrolls, clever Chinese poets, and lovely Chinese women. He led his army through the terrible mountains of Tibet into the region the Chinese called Yunnan, "south of the clouds," and conquered it, thereby taking up a strategic position on the southwestern frontier of Sung China. But he did not take the next step—a simultaneous attack on the Sung domain from the southwest and from the north. Instead he retired to the palace he had built for himself at a place known as Keibung, not far north of the Great Wall—a sumptuous palace that the conquered Chinese of the north called Shang-tu, "the Upper Court," and that would become Xanadu in the writings of medieval Europeans who visited China. Ruling from Shang-tu, Kublai concentrated on consolidating the Mongol grip on the sectors of China already under Mongol rule, thus infuriating more belligerent Mongols who wished him to get on with the war. Mangu, troubled by the outcries against Kublai, summoned him to Karakorum to explain his inactivity. Kublai said that he preferred to rule by kindness rather than by terror, since in no other way could the millions of Chinese be governed, and so he had delayed his destruction of the Sung while establishing a trustworthy bureaucracy in the north. But at Mangu's urging he agreed to resume the military campaign, late in 1257. Kublai would attack from the northeast, his general Uriangkatai would come up out of Yunnan to pierce the southwestern frontier, and Mangu himself would lead an army into China from the northwest.

It was in 1259, during this three-pronged assault, that Mangu Khan died of dysentery while laying siege to the sturdy Sung fortress of Ho-chow. Kublai hurried back into Mongolia to establish his claim to the title of khaghan. As the senior surviving brother of Mangu, he did not anticipate rivalry: Hulagu seemed content to rule the Near East, and Arik-buga, who had command of Mongolia proper, could hardly expect to rise above his two older brothers. Nor was trouble likely to come from the other main branch of the family, that which ruled in Russia. Kublai's cousin Batu had always recognized the suzerainty of Mangu, though remaining almost entirely independent. Now Batu was dead, and his son Sartaq had quickly followed him—poisoned, some said. The Khan in Russia was Batu's brother, Bereke, holding court on the banks of the Volga. Bereke, the first descendant of Genghis Khan to be converted to Islam, was a man of self-sufficient ways. It mattered little to him who the khaghan might be. He would pay lip service to the man and go on ruling in imperial splendor in the west, heedless of anything that might happen at Karakorum.

Kublai had journeyed only as far north as Shang-tu when stunning news came from Karakorum: the friends of Arik-buga, including many members of the families of Ogodai and Chagadai, had called a quick rump *khuriltai* and proclaimed him khaghan. Mangu's own sons had sworn allegiance to him, as had Mangu's widow. From Russia, Bereke Khan had sent messengers acknowledging Arik-buga's election. Kublai's response was to stage a *khuriltai* of his own at Shang-tu, attended only by his officers, in June 1260. They elected him supreme khan, and the civil war began. Quickly Kublai defeated an army that the sons of Mangu led; then he met and scattered the troops of Arik-buga in a decisive encounter. Next he surrounded Karakorum and starved the city into submission. Arik-buga escaped into the Gobi Desert, which became his base for guerrilla operations.

In Persia, Hulagu waited anxiously for word of the struggle in the homeland. He supported Kublai and, if necessary, would go to his aid. But then came disturbing news from the other front. The full Egyptian army, led by Sultan Qutuz and his ferocious general Baibars, had crossed into Palestine, had wiped out the small Mongol force stationed at Gaza, and was on its way up the coast to attack the rest of the slender Mongol garrison under Kit-buga in the northern part of the Holy Land. There was no way for Hulagu, with his large and capable army, to intervene in time. On September 3, 1260, the Egyptians overwhelmed Kit-buga's garrison at a place called Ain Jalud; nearly all the Mongols were slain, and Kit-buga himself was captured and beheaded.

The battle of Ain Jalud was one of history's turning points. Had the Mongols succeeded in invading Egypt, there would have been no significant Moslem state left in the world east of Morocco; and had the Christian Kit-buga survived and become the governor of a Mongol Near East under the pro-Christian Hulagu, Islam might well have given way to Christianity all through Iraq, Syria, Palestine, and Egypt. But the dissension between Kublai and Arik-buga had induced Hulagu to withdraw most of his troops at a critical moment; the Egyptians took advantage of that to strike down Kit-buga and halt the Mongol thrust; and Hulagu never regained the momentum of his earlier campaigns. As a result, Moslem Egypt dominated the Near East for the next two centuries, until the coming of the Ottoman Turks, who also were Moslems, and the last hope of Christendom to take possession of that region was lost.

Hulagu was unable to resume the offensive, even after the triumph of Kublai in Mongolia, because he was having military problems on another frontier. His Moslem cousin Bereke Khan, leader of the Golden Horde that had conquered Russia, disapproved of Hulagu's Christian sympathies and of his warfare against Moslem states. There was friction between Hulagu and Bereke in the Caucasus, where their spheres of influence met, and it was necessary for Hulagu to fortify this frontier against possible attack by the Golden Horde. The difficulties with Bereke prevented him from taking revenge against the Egyptians. After their victory at Ain Jalud, Qutuz and Baibars had forced the Mongols to withdraw from Aleppo and Damascus as well, and now all of Syria and Palestine were under Egyptian rule except for the increasingly exiguous Crusader states. In the fall of 1260 Baibars assassinated his master and made himself sultan; this savage warrior then turned on the Crusaders and stripped them of nearly all their territory, including their prized city of Antioch, while Hulagu was compelled to remain on the sidelines. By 1267 nothing survived of the Crusader principalities except some isolated fortresses and six cities: Acre, Tyre, Sidon, Tripoli, Jabala, and Tortosa. These holdings were extinguished over the succeeding quarter of a century, and in 1291, with the fall of Acre to the Saracens, the two-hundred-year-old adventure of the Latin kingdoms of the Near East came to its end.

While Hulagu had been watching Baibars undo the Mongol conquests in the Near East, Kublai Khan was taking a firm grasp in the Mongol homeland. By 1264 the rebellion of Arik-buga was crushed, and soon Kublai was ready to return to his campaigning in China. From 1268 through 1273, Mongol forces moved steadily southward, compressing the Sung realm in ever smaller confines. By 1271, Kublai felt it was proper to proclaim himself Emperor of China, calling his dynasty the Yüan, meaning "The First Beginning," or "The Origin." Genghis Khan, as founder of the dynasty, was posthumously awarded the imperial Chinese title of T'ai Tsu, "Grand Progenitor." Kublai chose Peking as his southern capital. Since Genghis had sacked it in 1215, it was necessary to build a new city on its site, which Kublai named Khan-baliq, "City of the Khan." This became Cambaluc in the accounts of such European travelers as Marco Polo.

In 1274 the Sung emperor died and the throne passed to his three-year-old son. This was the signal for an all-out Mongol offensive. Nan-king and Hangchow, the last great Sung cities, were taken by 1276; the boy emperor went to Khan-baliq as a prisoner. A strong Sung navy still existed, and a brother of the emperor, escaping, presided over a ghostly seaborne court that slipped from port to port for two years, until a ty-phoon sank his ship. One more imperial heir was found and enthroned aboard a Sung vessel; but the Mongols closed in, and in 1279 captured the fleet. A loyal minister, taking the eight-year-old emperor on his back, jumped into the sea, and the Sung Dynasty came to its end. The Mongols ruled all of China—the first of that nation's many foreign con-querors to have achieved total control of every province.

A great empire had fallen to the Mongols, and they made it the crowning gem of an even greater one. The center of the Mongol world shifted from Mongolia to China, as Kublai turned his back on Kara-korum and the rest of his ancestral homeland. The khaghan, from his two capitals at Shang-tu just north of the Great Wall and Khan-baliq not far south of it, ruled all of China, Korea, Mongolia, Manchuria, and Tibet, with Burma, Java, and Indochina paying tribute. The de-scendants of Chagadai Khan reigned in Central Asia, Turkestan, and Afghanistan. Much of Persia, Asia Minor, and Mesopotamia was under the authority of Hulagu's son Abaka, Hulagu having died in 1265. In Russia and the Caucasus, Bereke Khan was the lord of the Golden Horde.

9

The era of the Mongol Empire opened Asia to Westerners as never before. When Seljuks and Khwarizmians and other Moslems had gov-erned Persia and Mesopotamia, no travelers from the Western world had dared to enter their territories, and Islam became an impassable barrier separating the Near East from the Far East. But the Mongols, while they might have no great love for Western visitors, had no reason to hate or fear them, and they prided themselves besides on the effi-ciency of communications throughout all their vast realm. Now that a single empire ran all the length of Asia, it became possible to travel un-der Mongol protection even to fabled Cathay. Some travelers took the hard way through southern Russia and the steppe; others crossed the Black Sea and followed the line of oases known as the Old Silk Road in Central Asia; some went overland via Baghdad and Persia to reach the same highway. The way was open for Christians to search Asia for the storied realm of Prester John.

The first to come were John of Plano Carpini, William of Rubruck, and the other diplomat-friars seeking to forge an alliance between the Mongols and Christendom. But shortly it was the turn of the merchants. Of all the mercantile cities of Europe, the most dynamic was Venice in the thirteenth century, and of all the merchants of Venice the most adventurous were the brothers Niccolò and Maffeo Polo, jewelers, who owned a house in the Italian commercial colony at Soldaia, on the Black Sea. In 1260 they set off into Russia to pay their respects to Bereke Khan and perhaps to do some business at his court. He welcomed them cordially, and they spent a year among the Golden Horde. When war broke out in the Caucasus between the forces of Bereke and those of his cousin Hulagu, the Polos found their homeward route cut off by battle, and so they decided to make the best of their situation and continue eastward. For three years they were stranded in Bokhara, because the fighting between Kublai and Arik-buga made the caravan route unsafe; but by 1264 Kublai had triumphed, and shortly there arrived in Bokhara a party of ambassadors on their way from Hulagu Khan to see the Great Khan Kublai in far-off China. These envoys invited the Polos to accompany them to Kublai's court, saying, "The great khan has never seen any Latins and is exceedingly eager to meet one." And so they were taken to Kublai Khan. He was "greatly pleased at their arrival," according to the account written many years later by Niccolò's son Marco, and "they were entertained with feasts and honored with other marks of distinction." Kublai questioned them in detail about European life and customs, and "above all he questioned them particularly respecting the Pope, the affairs of the Church, and the religious worship and doctrine of the Christians." The Polos, who spoke the Mongol language well, answered so eloquently that the khaghan began to consider the idea of becoming a Christian, Christianity having been his mother's religion.

Kublai asked the brothers to return to their own land and bring him "some hundred wise men learned in the law of Christ" to instruct the Mongols, and also some holy oil from the sacred sepulchre in Jerusalem. The westward journey took them three years, though they had a golden safe-conduct tablet from the great khan, and when they reached Acre, in 1269, they learned that the Pope had just died. They continued on to Venice to await the election of his successor. Coming home after an absence of more than a dozen years, Niccolò Polo found that his wife was dead and his baby son Marco had grown into a strapping youth of fifteen, who listened excitedly to his tales of the Mongols and their khans.

Papal politics were intricate in the thirteenth century, and two years went by without the choosing of a new pontiff. The brothers decided to return to Asia without further wait, and took with them Niccolò's boy Marco, to his delight and our great fortune—for the elder Polos were merchants, not men of letters, and never wrote a word about their travels. Marco, though, was a different sort—less of a tradesman, more of a student. He planned to take notes on all he saw and someday to write a book; and, unlike many travelers who make such resolutions, he kept his word, though he needed the help of a professional writer to get his book into shape.

By 1271 the three Polos were in Acre. They made a pilgrimage to Jerusalem to get the holy oil. Then they learned that a Pope had been elected—conveniently, he was Theobald of Piacenza, the Church's representative in Acre. Theobald, now Pope Gregory X, had learned of the Polos' dealings with Kublai Khan when they passed through Acre two years before. He could not spare the hundred priests Kublai wanted, but he offered two Dominican friars.

The Dominicans, too easily frightened, soon turned back, but the Polos pressed on, past Mount Ararat in Armenia, through Baghdad and Mosul, through the salt deserts of Persia, into the icy reaches of the Pamirs, on to the oasis cities of Kashgar, Khotan, and Yarkand, rich with jade and gems, and then into the grim desert of the Gobi, said to be haunted by phantoms and nameless terrors. To the right and the left of the caravan track lurked unknown spirits, and strange sounds were heard afar—the tinkling of invisible bells, the beat of mysterious drums. The Polos plodded forward, unscathed by demons. The borders of Kublai's own realm drew near. To the travelers' left was desolate Mongolia; to the right lay populous China. They followed the frontier line, probably traveling along the Great Wall, and in May 1275 they arrived at Shang-tu, Kublai's summer capital, the Xanadu of Coleridge's poem. "In this city," Marco wrote, "Kublai Khan had an immense palace made of marble and stone, with halls and rooms all gilt and adorned with figures of beasts and birds, and pictures of trees and flowers of different kinds. It is most wondrously beautiful and marvelously decorated. On one side it is bounded by the city-wall, and from that point another wall runs out enclosing a space of no less than sixteen miles, with numerous springs and rivers and meadows. And the great khan keeps all kinds of animals in it, namely stags and fallow-deer and roebucks."

Presiding over all this splendor was the khan himself, plump and dignified, vigorous despite his sixty years. He was delighted with young Marco, and enrolled him among his attendants. It pleased the great khan to see Marco asking many questions, studying languages, taking notes of Mongol ways. He called Marco to his side and they spoke for long hours, the khan questioning Marco about Europe, and Marco daring to question the khan about the Mongol world.

As lord of most of Asia, Kublai was in an excellent position to feed his insatiable curiosity with facts about strange and remote places. Yet, he told Marco, he had had difficulties in getting the information he wanted. He sent ambassadors everywhere, but when they returned they spoke only of the official business they had transacted, and told him nothing about the customs and unusual features of the lands they had visited. Such ambassadors, Kublai said, were nothing but fools and dunces. Marco agreed. What was the use of traveling to a distant place, he wondered, if you gathered no diverting information there? He himself would not be so foolish as to blind his eyes to the wondrous sights of strange lands. It occurred to Kublai, then, that Marco might be a useful ambassador, since he already spoke several languages, was wise beyond his years, and had the inestimable gift of curiosity.

So began Marco Polo's career in the service of Kublai Khan. He went from city to city in China, collecting data for the great khan. He passed through the provinces of Shansi, Shensi, and Szechuan; he trekked along the Tibetan frontier to Yunnan, and thence to northern Burma. He went by sea to southern India; he spent three years in Central Asia and three more as governor of the huge city of Yangchow; he stayed awhile at the old Mongol capital of Karakorum. Wherever he went, he searched out matters of interest, to the eternal profit of future generations. For seventeen years he served Kublai; then he and his father and uncle, homesick at last, won permission to return to Venice, arriving in 1295 after a three-year journey. In 1298, Marco went to sea during a naval war between the rival cities of Venice and Genoa and was captured; in prison he had the leisure to write the book he had promised to give the world. An author of chivalrous romances, one Rustichello, was in the same prison, and Marco dictated his memoir to him. Rustichello gave it courtly phrases, but the material itself was Marco's, and the book they produced by this collaboration is an imperishable document of Asia in the time of Mongol supremacy.

10

It is not surprising that Marco, in the course of his years of Asian exploration on behalf of Kublai Khan, should have devoted some effort to searching for Prester John. Indeed Marco succeeded in turning up the traces of this elusive monarch; it would seem, in fact, that he located more than one to whom he could attribute that name. The first reference to Prester John appears fairly early in his book, in the section in which he describes Karakorum and explains how the Mongols acquired their empire and spread through the world:

"Originally the Tartars dwelt in the north on the borders of Chorcha [in Manchuria]. Their country was one of great plains; and there were no towns or villages in it, but excellent pasture-lands, with great rivers and no lack of water; in fact it was a very fine and extensive region. But there was no sovereign in the land. They did, however, pay tax and tribute to a great prince who was called in their language Unc Can, which simply means Great Lord. This was that Prester John, of whose great empire all the world speaks. The tribute he had of them was one beast out of every ten, and also a tithe of all their other gear.

"Now it came to pass that the Tartars multiplied exceedingly. And when Prester John saw how great a people they had become, he began to fear that he should have trouble from them. So he made a scheme to distribute them over sundry countries, and sent one of his barons to carry this out. When the Tartars became aware of this they took it much amiss, and with one consent they left their country and went off across a desert to a distant region towards the north, where Prester John could not get at them to annoy them. Thus they revolted from his authority and paid him tribute no longer. And so things continued for a time.

"Now it came to pass in the year of Christ's Incarnation 1187 that the Tartars chose themselves a king whose name was Chinghis Kaan. He was a man of great worth, and of great eloquence and valor. And as soon as the news that he had been made king was spread abroad through those countries, all the Tartars in the world came to him and owned him for their lord. And right well did he maintain the sovereignty they had given him. What shall I say? The Tartars gathered to him in astonishing multitude, and when he saw such numbers he equipped them with spears and arrows and such other arms as they used, and set about the conquest of all those regions until he had conquered eight provinces. When he conquered a province he did no harm to the people or their property, but merely established some of his own men in the country along with a proportion of theirs, whilst he led the remainder to the conquest of other provinces. And when those whom he had conquered became aware how well and safely he protected them against all others, and how they suffered no ill at his hands, and saw what a noble prince he was, then they joined him heart and soul and became his devoted followers. And when he had thus gathered such a multitude that they seemed to cover the earth, he began to think of conquering a great part of the world. Now in the year of Christ 1200 he sent an embassy to Prester John and desired to have his daughter to wife. But when Prester John heard that Chinghis Kaan demanded his daughter in marriage he waxed very wroth, and said to the envoys, 'What impudence is this, to ask my daughter to wife! Wist ye not well that he was my liegeman and serf? Get ye back to him and tell him that I had rather set my daughter in the fire than give her in marriage to him, and that he deserves death at my hand, rebel and traitor that he is!' So he bade the envoys begone at once, and never come into his presence again. The envoys, on receiving this reply, departed straightway, and made haste to their master, and related all that Prester John had ordered them to say, keeping nothing back.

"When Chinghis Kaan heard the brutal message that Prester John had sent him, such rage seized him that his heart came nigh to bursting within him, for he was a man of a very lofty spirit. At last he spoke, and that so loud that all who were present could hear him: he proclaimed that never more might he be prince if he took not revenge for the brutal message of Prester John, and such revenge that insult never in this world was so dearly paid for. And before long Prester John should know whether he were his serf or no!

"So then he mustered all his forces, and levied such a host as never before was seen or heard of, sending word to Prester John to be on his defense. And when Prester John had sure tidings that Chinghis was really coming against him with such a multitude, he still professed to treat it as a jest and a trifle, for, quoth he, 'these be no soldiers.'

Natheless he marshalled his forces and mustered his people, and made great preparations, in order that if Chinghis did come, he might take him and put him to death. In fact he marshalled such an host of many different nations that it was a world's wonder.

"And so both sides got them ready to battle. And why should I make a long story of it? Chinghis Kaan with all his host arrived at a vast and beautiful plain which was called Tenduc, belonging to Prester John, and there he pitched his camp; and so great was the multitude of his people that it was impossible to number them. And when he got tidings that Prester John was coming, he rejoiced greatly, for the place afforded a fine and ample battleground, so he was right glad to tarry for him there, and greatly longed for his arrival.

"But now leave we Chinghis and his host, and let us return to Prester John and his people.

"Now the story goes that when Prester John became aware that Chinghis with his host was marching against him, he went forth to meet him with all his forces, and advanced until he reached the same plain of Tenduc, and pitched his camp over against that of Chinghis Kaan at a distance of twenty miles. And then both armies remained at rest for two days that they might be fresher and heartier for battle.

"So when the two great hosts were pitched on the plains of Tenduc as you have heard, Chinghis Kaan one day summoned before him his astrologers, both Christians and Saracens, and desired them to let him know which of the two hosts would gain the battle, his own or Prester John's. The Saracens tried to ascertain, but were unable to give a true answer; the Christians, however, did give a true answer, and showed manifestly beforehand how the event should be. For they got a cane and split it lengthwise, and laid one half on this side and one half on that, allowing no one to touch the pieces. And one piece of cane they called Chinghis Kaan and the other piece they called Prester John. And then they said to Chinghis: 'Now mark! and you will see the event of the battle, and who shall have the best of it; for whose cane soever shall get above the other, to him shall victory be.' He replied that he would fain see it, and bade them begin. Then the Christian astrologers read a psalm out of the psalter, and went through other incantations. And lo! whilst all were beholding, the cane that bore the name of Chinghis Kaan, without being touched by anybody, advanced to the other that bore the name of Prester John, and got on the top of it. When the prince saw that he was greatly delighted, and seeing how in this matter he found the Christians to tell the truth, he always treated them with great respect, and held them for men of truth ever after.

"And after both sides had rested well those two days, they armed for the fight and engaged in desperate combat; and it was the greatest battle that ever was seen. The numbers that were slain on both sides were very great, but in the end Chinghis Kaan obtained the victory. And in the battle Prester John was slain. And from that time forward, day by day, his kingdom passed into the hands of Chinghis Kaan till the whole was conquered."

This story has many familiar elements; we have already encountered it, in somewhat different form, in the narratives of John of Joinville and William of Rubruck. It is, of course, an account of Genghis Khan's overthrow of his godfather and one-time ally, the Wang-Khan Togrul of the Keraits, to which Marco has added a few features not previously reported. Oriental sources, such as the Mongol chronicle compiled at the court of Ogodai Khan in 1240 and known to us as *The Secret History of the Mongols*, confirm that Genghis, who had been Togrul's vassal, did rebel against his master out of personal resentment as well as for reasons of political ambition. Marco says that "Prester John" (the wang-khan) refused Genghis his daughter's hand. The actual story at the base of this is that, about 1202, when Genghis and Togrul still theoretically were in alliance, Genghis asked for Togrul's daughter Jaur Bigi as a bride for his eldest son Juchi, and offered his own daughter Kijin Bigi to become the wife of Togrul's grandson Kush-buga. The proposals were rejected, and this double affront to Genghis Khan's dignity was one of the causes of the breach between him and Togrul. (There had, however, been a number of marriages between Kerait princesses and members of Genghis' family prior to this incident. One of Genghis' own wives was a niece of Togrul. Juchi also had married one of the nieces of the wang-khan. Still another niece, Syurkuk Teni, the wife of Genghis' youngest son Tului, was the mother of Mangu, Kublai, Hulagu, and Arik-buga.)

Marco does not tell us by what authority he identifies the wang-khan as Prester John. He merely declares that "Unc Can" is the same man as "that Prester John, of whose great empire all the world speaks." He could not have got that notion from William of Rubruck, even if he had read Friar William's narrative, which is doubtful; for the good friar, as we have seen, erroneously distinguished between Prester John and his supposed brother and successor, Vut or Ung Can. Probably Marco, discussing this aspect of Mongol history with Nestorians at Kublai's court, heard them refer to the wang-khan as Malik Yuhanna, "King John," and drew the obvious conclusion. Another possibility is that the Mongols, having heard so many queries about Prester John from Andrew of Longjumeau, William of Rubruck, and others, had themselves concluded that Togrul must have been this Prester John in whom the Europeans were so interested, and told Marco as much.

The second reference to Prester John appears a few chapters later in Marco's book, after he has finished his description of Mongolia and has begun to speak of the provinces that lie just west of China proper:

"Tenduc is a province which lies towards the east, and contains numerous towns and villages; among which is the chief city, also called Tenduc. The king of the province is of the lineage of Prester John, George by name, and he holds the land under the great khan, not that he holds anything like the whole of what Prester John possessed. It is a custom, I may tell you, that these kings of the lineage of Prester John always obtain to wife either daughters of the great khan or other princesses of his family. . . .

"The rule of the province is in the hands of the Christians, as I have told you; but there are also plenty of idolaters and worshippers of Mahomet. And there is also here a class of people called *Argons*, that is to say 'halfbreeds,' who are a blend of the race of the idolaters of Tenduc and that of the worshippers of Mahomet. They are handsomer men than the other natives of the country, and having more ability, they come to have authority; and they are also excellent merchants.

"You must know that it was in this same capital city of Tenduc that Prester John had the seat of his government when he ruled over the Tartars, and his heirs still abide there; for, as I have told you, this King George is of his line, in fact, he is the sixth in descent from Prester John.

"Here also is what we call the country of Gog and Magog; they, however, call it Ung and Mungul, after the names of two races of people that existed in that province before the migration of the Tartars. Each of these two provinces was inhabited by a separate race: in Ung lived the Gog, in Mungul the Tartars. And therefore the Tartars are sometimes called Munguls."

Tenduc, Marco has told us earlier, was the scene of Genghis' defeat of Unc Can, or Prester John. Now he asserts that Prester John's descendants still govern there as Kublai's vassals. These two statements are incompatible: evidently there were two Tenducs, one in Mongolia and one close by China, which Marco fused into a single place. Togrul, Marco's Prester John, was of course a Kerait; his tribal homeland was in the heart of Mongolia, south of Lake Baikal along the Orqon River, not far from the future site of Karakorum. His supposed descendant, King George, was a real figure, and Marco was not the only European to visit his kingdom; but he was no Kerait, and he did not live on the Mongol steppes. King George was an Öngut Turk—his name actually was Görgüz—and modern geographers have identified Tenduc, his capital, as T'ien-te, in the great bend of the Yellow River on China's northwestern border, hundreds of miles south of the Kerait country. Like Togrul, Görgüz was a Nestorian, whose tribe had converted to Christianity in the eleventh century, and that, along with the apparent coincidence of the two Tenducs, must have led Marco to credit King George with descent from Prester John. The muddled reference to "Ung" (Öngut?) and "Mungul" in Marco's text may point to some association in Marco's mind between Togrul's title of "Unc Can" and the name of Görgüz' tribe. Perhaps here he is also trying to draw a distinction between the Turks and the Mongols, the two nomadic and distantly related groups that came forth as conquerors from Central Asia over a period of some hundreds of years.

Much farther on, in his account of China proper, Marco refers to Prester John a third time, offering a story new to Europeans:

"On leaving Pianfu [P'ing-yang-fu, in the province of Shansi] you ride two days westward, and come to the noble castle of Caichu, which was built in time past by a king of that country, whom they used to call the Golden King, and who had there a great and beautiful palace. There is a great hall of this palace, in which are portrayed all the ancient kings of the country, done in gold and other beautiful colors, and a very fine sight they make. Each king in succession as he reigned added to those pictures.

"This Golden King was a great and potent prince, and during his stay at this place there used to be in his service none but beautiful girls, of whom he had a great number in his court. When he went to take the air about the fortress, these girls used to draw him about in a little carriage which they could easily move, and they would also be in attendance on the king for everything pertaining to his convenience or pleasure.

"Now I will tell you a pretty tale concerning the Golden King and his dealings with Prester John, as it was related by the people of the castle.

"It came to pass, as they told the tale, that this Golden King was at war with Prester John. The Golden King was subject to that Unc Can who, as I have already told you, called himself Prester John, but through arrogance and presumption he rebelled against his master. And the king held a position so strong that Prester John was not able to get at him or do him any harm; wherefore he was in great wrath. So seventeen gallants belonging to Prester John's court came to him in a body, and said that they were ready to bring him the Golden King alive. His answer was, that he desired nothing better, and would be much bounden to them if they would do so.

"So when they had taken leave of their lord and master Prester John, they set off together, this goodly company of gallants, and went to the Golden King, and presented themselves before him, saying that they had come from foreign parts to enter his service. And he answered by telling them that they were right welcome, and that he was glad to have their service, never imagining that they had any ill intent. And so these mischievous squires took service with the Golden King; and served him so well that he grew to love them dearly.

"And when they had abode with that king nearly two years, conducting themselves like persons who thought of anything but treason, they one day accompanied the king on a pleasure party when he had very few else along with him: for in those gallants the king had perfect trust, and thus kept them immediately about his person. So after they had crossed a certain river that is about a mile from the castle, and saw that they were alone with the king, they said one to another that now was the time to achieve the purpose for which they had come. So they laid hand to hilt, and told the king that he must go with them and make no resistance, or they would slay him. The king at this was in alarm and great astonishment, and said: 'How then, good my sons, what thing is this ye say? and whither would ye have me go?' They answered, and said: 'You shall come with us, willy-nilly, to Prester John our lord.'

"And on this the Golden King was so sorely grieved that he was like to die. And he said to them: 'Good my sons, for God's sake have pity and compassion on me! Have I not done you honor enough under

my roof, that you should wish to betray me into the hands of my enemies? Assuredly, if you do this, you will be guilty of great wrong and
great disloyalty.' But they answered only that so it must be, and away
they had him to Prester John their lord.

"And when Prester John beheld the king he was right glad, and
told him that he had earned a cold welcome. The king answered not a
word, as if he knew not what to say. So Prester John ordered him to
be taken forth straightway, and to be put to look after cattle, but to be
well looked after himself also. So they took him and set him to keep
cattle. This did Prester John of the grudge he bore the king, to heap
contempt on him, and to show what a nothing he was, compared to
himself.

"And when the Golden King had thus kept cattle for two years,
Prester John sent for him, and treated him with honor, and clothed
him in rich robes, and said to him: 'Now, Sir King, art thou satisfied
that thou wast in no way a man to stand against me?' 'Truly, my good
lord, I know well and always did know that I was in no way a man to
stand against thee.' And when he had said this Prester John replied: 'I
ask no more; but henceforth thou shalt be waited on and honorably
treated.' So he caused horses and harness of war to be given him, with
a goodly train, and sent him back to his own country. And after that
he remained ever friendly to Prester John, and held fast by him."

Marco Polo tells us that the Prester John of this pleasant courtly
romance is the same as that who was overthrown by Genghis Khan; or,
at least, one of Marco's early editors tells us so, for the line, "The Golden
King was subject to that Unc Can who, as I have already told you, called
himself Prester John," appears only in the printed edition of Marco's
book produced by Giambattista Ramusio and published in 1553. Ramusio claimed to have access to a Latin manuscript of the book more extensive than the fourteenth-century French one then in general circulation, although some critics have accused him of fabricating the extra
material himself. In any case, regardless of Marco or Ramusio, if the
Prester John of this story existed at all he must have been someone
other than Togrul of the Keraits.

No original of the story of the capture of the Golden King by Prester
John's henchmen has ever been located in Chinese or Mongol annals.
The identity of the Golden King therefore is most uncertain. However,
when the Jurchen nomads came down out of Manchuria to overthrow

the Khitan and replace them as lords of northern China, their leader, A-ku-ta, proclaimed himself Emperor of China in 1122 and gave his dynasty the name of Chin, "golden" in Chinese. Perhaps one of these Jurchen emperors of the Chin Dynasty can be identified as the Golden King of Marco's book. But, although the Jurchen did capture a rival monarch (Chao Huan, a Sung Dynasty emperor, whom they seized in 1126), there is no record of the capture of a Jurchen ruler by someone else; when the dynasty finally was extinguished by the Mongols in 1234, as we have seen, the last Chin emperor committed suicide rather than surrender. Certainly no member of the Chin Dynasty was ever taken prisoner by Togrul Khan. According to one medieval source—the thirteenth-century Arab historian Rashid-ud-din—the *grandfather* of Togrul, Merghuz Boiruk Khan, was delivered to the Jurchen emperor of the time by treachery and put to death. But the same author relates that Togrul got his title of wang-khan from a later emperor of that line, so whatever bitterness had existed between the Keraits and the Jurchen had subsided by Togrul's day.

There is, though, one event in the history of Kara-Khitai that might have generated the story of Prester John and the Golden King. The dynastic annals of Kara-Khitai for the year 1211 report that in that year the last emperor of the family of Yeh-lü Ta-shih, whose name was Chih-lu-ku, "was captured during the autumn hunt by the Naiman prince Ch'ü-ch'u-lü, who used eight thousand soldiers to ambush him. Ch'ü-ch'u-lü assumed the title gur-khan, adopted the dress and customs of western Liao [Kara-Khitai], and made Chih-lu-ku the imperial father and his wife the empress dowager. As long as they lived he attended them every morning and evening like a respectful son." This Ch'ü-ch'u-lü is already known to us by the Turkish form of his name, Kuchluk. It was he (or perhaps his father Tai-yang Khan) whom William of Rubruck named as Prester John, with Ung Can (Togrul) alleged to be his brother. If Kuchluk here is playing the role of Prester John for Marco, and the last Kara-Khitai monarch is meant to be the Golden King, then the circle of confusions has closed in on itself, and the interchange of identities among these Asian princes is complete.

11

No matter how tangled Marco Polo's accounts of Prester John might have been, one thing is clear from his book: Marco was certain that

Prester John was a khan of the Mongolian steppes. He did not live in southern India among the Christians of St. Thomas, nor was he an Ethiopian, the ruler of that Christian nation to whom Pope Alexander III had apparently sent Master Philip as an ambassador in 1177.

Marco could speak with some authority about southern India because he visited it in the 1290s, on his way home by sea from the court of Kublai Khan. He found the shrine of St. Thomas at Mylapur, and plenty of Christians living in its vicinity, but the king of the region was a pagan and there was no one thereabouts who fit any of the descriptions of Prester John.

He did not actually visit Ethiopia, but he came close to it, for the ship in which he traveled home crossed the Indian Ocean to the Persian Gulf, stopping at such places as Aden and Socotra, where Marco could easily have obtained reliable information about the nearby Ethiopian realm. In his book he calls it Abash, or Abyssinia, the name by which it was generally known in Europe, and says:

"Abash is a very great province, and you must know that it constitutes the Middle India; and it is on the mainland. There are in it six great kings with six great kingdoms; and of these six kings there are three that are Christians and three that are Saracens; but the greatest of all the six is a Christian, and all the others are subject to him.

"The Christians in this country bear three marks on their face; one from the forehead to the middle of the nose, and one on either cheek. These marks are made with a hot iron, and form part of their baptism; for after that they have been baptised with water, these three marks are made, partly as a token of gentility, and partly as the completion of their baptism. There are also Jews in the country, and these bear two marks, one on either cheek; and the Saracens have but one, to wit, on the forehead extending halfway down the nose.

"The Great King lives in the middle of the country, the Saracens toward Aden. St. Thomas the Apostle preached in this region, and after he had converted the people he went away to the province of Maabar, where he died; and there his body lies, as I have told you in a former place. . . .

". . . in the year of Christ, 1288 . . . this Christian king, who is the lord of the province of Abash, declared his intention to go on pilgrimage to Jerusalem to adore the Holy Sepulchre of Our Lord God Jesus Christ the Savior. But his barons said that for him to go in person would be to run too great a risk; and they recommended him to send some bishop or prelate in his stead. So the king assented to the counsel which his barons gave, and despatched a certain bishop of his, a man of very holy life. The bishop then departed and traveled by land and by sea till he arrived at the Holy Sepulchre, and there he paid it such honor as Christian man is bound to do, and presented a great offering on the part of his king who had sent him in his own stead. . . ."

Marco also tells us of Ethiopia's natural wonders, in terms that remind us of the spurious letter of Prester John:

"It abounds greatly in all kinds of victual; and the people live on flesh and rice and milk and sesame. They have plenty of elephants, not that they are bred in the country, but they are brought from the islands of the other India. They have however many giraffes, which are produced in the country; besides bears, leopards, lions in abundance, and many other passing strange beasts. They have also numerous wild asses; and cocks and hens the most beautiful that exist, and many other kind of birds. For instance, they have ostriches that are nearly as big as asses; and plenty of beautiful parrots, with apes of sundry kinds, and baboons and other monkeys that have countenances all but human."

It is not to our purpose here to sort fact from fantasy in Marco Polo's description of Ethiopia. What is significant is that Ethiopia was a kingdom of great wealth, in what he took to be India, and that it was ruled by a pious Christian whose military exploits Marco recounts in another passage; and yet Marco did not succumb to the temptation to identify this monarch as Prester John. For Marco, Prester John was a khan of the steppes, and he was dead, and his descendant of the sixth generation, King George, ruled the insignificant principality of Tenduc as Kublai Khan's vassal.

12

The Polos did not succeed in their attempt to convert Kublai Khan to Christianity. Perhaps if the Pope had been able to send the hundred diligent friars to Cathay, things might have gone differently; but as it was, Kublai never developed more than a dilettante's interest in the faith of Jesus. Through much of his reign he was under the influence of a Tibetan lama named Phags-pa, who seems to have been something of

7. Medieval representations of Mandeville's human monsters.

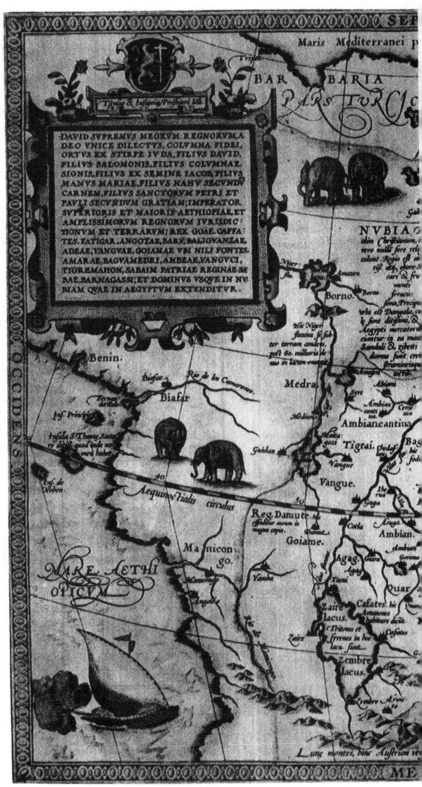

8. Map of the kingdom of Prester John: Ortelius, the Netherlands, 1573.

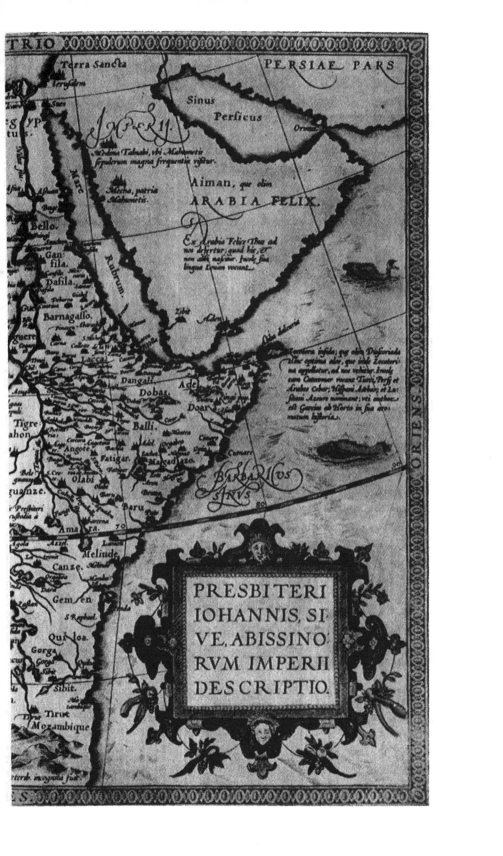

Terra Sancta

PERSIAE PARS

Hierusalem

Sinus

Suez

Persicus

Ormus

gypto

tus.

IMPERII

Medina Talnabi, vbi Mahometis
sepulcrum magna frequentia visitur.

Mecha, patria
Mahometis.

Aiman, que olim

ARABIA FELIX.

Ex Arabia Felice Thus ad
nos defertur, quod hic, &
non alibi nascitur. Incolæ, sua
lingua Louan vocant.

Mare

Bello.

Gan-
fila.

Dafila.

Rubrum.

Zibit

Aden

Barnagasso.

guere

Lacca

Dangali

Dobas

Ade

Doar

Tigre

ahon

Balli.

Angote

Fatigar.

Magadazo.

Olabi

Daru

BARBARICVS
SINVS

Amara.

Melinde

Canze

Gem en

Qui loa.

Gorga

Sibit.

Tirut

Mozambique

PRESBITERI
IOHANNIS, SI
VE, ABISSINO-
RVM IMPERII
DESCRIPTIO.

ORIENS

9. Prince Henry the Navigator: probably the only portrait of him drawn from life, c. 1450. From the Paris manuscript of Gomes Eannes de Azurara's *Chronicle of Guinea*.

a sorcerer, devious and scheming; at Phags-pa's urging Kublai came to prefer Lamaistic Buddhism over other religions, even to the point of persecuting those of his subjects who were Moslems, Taoists, Confucianists, or Chinese Buddhists, and would not follow Phags-pa's belief.

Kublai died in 1294, while the Polos were sailing home to Venice, and was succeeded by his grandson Timur, who became Great Khan of the Mongols and Emperor of China. Under Timur, Kublai's lamas ceased to enjoy special favor and an energetic new Catholic missionary, John of Monte Corvino, was welcomed at the court.

This John was an Italian Franciscan, born about 1247, the year of John of Plano Carpini's return from Mongolia. His first overseas duty on behalf of the Church had taken him to Constantinople, where in 1272 he served as a papal legate attempting to heal the breach between the Greek and Latin faiths; afterward he was a missionary in the Near East, assigned to the task of the conversion of the Saracens, and in 1289 Pope Nicholas IV sent him eastward as ambassador-general to all of Asia. He carried a sheaf of papal epistles: to the King of Armenia; to the Nestorian hierarchy of Persia; to the Monophysite Patriarch of Syria; to "the Emperor of Ethiopia"; to Arghun Khan, the Mongol ruler of Persia—Hulagu's grandson, and friendly to Christianity; to Kublai Khan; and even to a rebel Mongol chieftain named Kaidu, Ogodai's grandson, who, refusing to accept the election of Kublai, had set up an independent kingdom in Turkestan and Siberia. But he bore no letter addressed to Prester John.

Friar John traveled overland to Tabriz in Persia, where he met with Arghun Khan. This prince, a few years earlier, had sent a Nestorian Turk to Europe to suggest once again an alliance between Mongols and Christians against the Saracens, with the liberation of Jerusalem a prime objective. As usual, nothing came of this proposal, and the final collapse of the Crusader states at this time ended even the possibility of such an alliance; nevertheless, John of Monte Corvino reported to the Pope that Arghun was a plausible candidate for conversion. (In fact Arghun was a Buddhist, and his successors were converts to Islam.) Taking ship at the Persian Gulf port of Ormuz in 1291, Friar John sailed to India. He spent thirteen months among the Christians of St. Thomas and succeeded in persuading about a hundred Hindus to let him baptize them. Then he set out by sea for Cathay.

By the time he arrived at the Chinese capital, in 1295, Kublai Khan was dead, and the missionary presented his credentials to Timur instead. Thus he began the career in China that would occupy him to the end of his long life. In a letter of January 1305 that he sent from Khan-baliq (Peking) to a group of Catholic missionaries in Persia, Friar John described the progress of his mission, saying that he had invited Timur Khan "to adopt the Catholic faith of our Lord Jesus Christ, but he had grown too old in idolatry. However he bestows many kindnesses upon the Christians. . . . I have built a church in the city of Cambaliech, in which the king has his chief residence. This I completed six years ago; and I have built a bell-tower to it, and put three bells in it. I have baptised there, as well as I can estimate, up to this time some 6000 persons; and . . . I am often still engaged in baptizing. Also I have gradually bought one hundred fifty boys, the children of pagan parents, and of ages varying from seven to eleven, who had never learned any religion. These boys I have baptized, and I have taught them Greek and Latin after our manner. . . . Eleven of the boys already know our service, and form a choir and take their weekly turn of duty as they do in convents, whether I am there or not. . . . His Majesty the Emperor moreover delights much to hear them chanting. I have the bells rung at all the canonical hours, and with my congregation of babes and sucklings I perform divine service, and the chanting we do by ear because I have no service book with the notes."

In this way John of Monte Corvino planted Roman Catholicism in China. The only hindrance he met came from fellow Christians: "The Nestorians, a certain body who profess to bear the Christian name, but who deviate sadly from the Christian religion, have grown so powerful in these parts that they will not allow a Christian of another ritual to have ever so small a chapel, or to publish any doctrine different from their own. . . . And so the Nestorians aforesaid, either directly or through others whom they bribed, have brought on me persecutions of the sharpest. For they got up stories that I was not sent by our lord the Pope, but was a great spy and impostor; and after a while they produced false witnesses who declared that there was indeed an envoy sent with presents of immense value for the emperor, but that I had murdered him in India, and stolen what he had in charge. And these intrigues and calumnies went on for some five years." Friar John persevered, however, and eventually Timur ordered his persecutors to desist. The missionary even won away from the Nestorians one of their most celebrated members:

"A certain king of this part of the world, by name George, belonging to the sect of Nestorian Christians, and of the illustrious family of that great king who was called Prester John of India, in the first year of my arrival here attached himself to me, and being converted by me to the truth of the Catholic faith, took the lesser orders, and when I celebrated mass he used to attend me wearing his royal robes. Certain others of the Nestorians on this account accused him of apostasy, but he brought over a great part of his people with him to the true Catholic faith, and built a church on a scale of royal magnificence in honor of our God, of the Holy Trinity, and of our lord the Pope, giving it the name of the Roman Church."

A fantasy come true! For here we see King Görgüz of the Öngut Turks, said by Marco Polo to be a descendant of Prester John, not only enrolling in the Latin faith but also taking holy orders, and thus becoming the Asian king-and-priest of the legend. Alas, the effects of this were short-lived, for the king died in 1298, Friar John declares, "leaving as his heir a son scarcely out of the cradle, and who is now nine years old. And after King George's death his brothers, perfidious followers of the errors of Nestorius, perverted again all those whom he had brought over to the Church, and carried them back to their original schismatical creed."

13

Had he not been virtually alone in his far-off mission, John of Monte Corvino might have transformed Cathay into one of the gems of the papal crown. But his first companion, Nicolas of Pistoia, had died while they were still in India, and Friar John had to work alone in China for eleven years until he was joined by a German monk, Friar Arnold of Cologne. "Indeed if I had had but two or three comrades to aid me 'tis possible that the Emperor Cham would have been baptized by this time!" he wrote. "I ask them for such brethren to come, if any are willing to come. . . . I have myself grown old and gray, more with toil and trouble than with years; for I am not more than fifty-eight. . . ."

In 1307, Pope Clement V, learning of John's achievements, awarded him the resounding titles of Archbishop of Cambaluc and Patriarch of All the Orient, and sent him seven Franciscans as his suffragan bishops. Three of these reached Khan-baliq safely, three perished en route in India, and one, apparently, turned back at the outset. When a rumor—baseless, as it developed—came to the Pope in 1312 that the great khan himself had been converted by Friar John, three more Franciscans went forth to China. With this corps of priests the missionary was able to found Catholic dioceses in several Chinese cities, although there is no record of his luring back to the Latin faith any of the Öngut subjects of "Prester John's" descendants at Tenduc.

Among the priests who arrived in China during John of Monte Corvino's long archepiscopal reign at Khan-baliq was a certain Odoric of Pordenone, who left an account of his travels second in interest only to the narrative of Marco Polo. Odoric was born about 1286 in the Friuli region of eastern Italy, close to the Austrian border. As a young man he took the Franciscan vows and distinguished himself for piety and asceticism, scourging himself severely and living mainly on bread and water. Several miracles were ascribed to him and he was locally regarded as a saint. In 1316 or 1317 he began his travels by departing for Constantinople. After some years in Persia and Mesopotamia he sailed to India in 1321, and then, by way of Sumatra, Java, and Borneo, journeyed to China, where he served for three years in one of the churches founded by John of Monte Corvino. Carrying a letter from the Archbishop of Cambaluc to the Pope requesting fifty more missionaries for China, Odoric then set out westward, passing through Tenduc, Tibet, the oasis cities of Central Asia, and Persia, and arriving ultimately in Venice in 1330. There he dictated the story of his wanderings to a fellow friar, and early in 1331 he died, an event that was followed by a host of miracles in the vicinity.

His narrative is a lovely mixture of fact and fable: what he saw himself he reported accurately, but he had a tendency toward gullibility in accepting the tales told by his guides. His errors, and there are many of them, are thus the result of innocence rather than guile, and much of what he wrote is clearly the product of careful observation.

On his way through Persia, for example, he came close to one of the remarkable natural wonders described in the letter of Prester John: "I traveled to a certain city called Iest [Yezd], which is the furthest city of Persia towards India, from which the Sea of Sand is but one day distant. Now that sea is a wondrous thing, and right perilous. And there were none of us who desired to enter on that sea. For it is all of dry sand without the slightest moisture. And it shifteth as the sea doth when in storm, now hither, now thither, and as it shifteth it maketh waves in like manner as the sea doth; so that countless people traveling thereon have been overwhelmed and drowned and buried in those sands." Had he borrowed this description from the letter, he might also have included Prester John's account of the tasty fish that dwell in the sandy sea, but Friar Odoric says nothing of them. And there is indeed a perilous desert not far from Yezd, whose dunes might easily seem to a traveler like the waves of a dry ocean.

In his account of India's Malabar Coast, however, he seems to have lifted the passage about the pepper forest wholly from the Prester John letter, for he describes the pepper plants growing among tall trees, and tells how there are "many serpents in the forest, which the men burn by kindling tow and straw, and so they are enabled to go safely to gather pepper." This is essentially the story as told in the letter. But Friar John of Marignolli, a missionary who passed the same way about twenty years later, made a point of writing, "There is no roasting of the pepper, as authors have falsely asserted, nor does it grow in forests, but in regular gardens." In stressing that his account of the pepper stems from his observations during a fourteen-month stay in India, John of Marignolli seems to imply that Odoric, whom he does not name, made use of secondhand information and spent little, if any, time in Malabar.

On India's opposite shore, the Maabar or Coromandel Coast, Friar Odoric visited the shrine of St. Thomas, which, he said, "is filled with idols, and beside it are some fifteen houses of the Nestorians, that is to say Christians, but vile and pestilent heretics." He says no more of it, though he devotes several pages to a nearby "church" of idolaters, which is described in terms reminiscent of the description of St. Thomas' shrine in *De adventu*. Odoric declares, "Hard by the church of this idol there is a lake, made by hand, into which the pilgrims who come thither cast gold or silver or precious stones, in honor of the idol, and towards the maintenance of the church, so that much gold and silver and many precious stones have been accumulated therein. And thus when it is desired to do any work upon the church, they make search in the lake and find all that hath been cast into it. But annually on the recurrence of the day when that idol was made, the folk of the country come and take it down, and put it on a fine chariot; and then the king and queen and all the pilgrims, and the whole body of the people, join together and draw it forth from the church with loud singing of songs and all kinds of music; and many maidens go before it by two and two chanting in a marvelous manner. And many pilgrims who have come to this feast cast themselves under the chariot, so that its wheels may go over them, saying that they desire to die for their god. And the car passes over them, and crushes and cuts them in sunder, and so they perish on the spot."

So he proceeds, telling many a marvelous tale: in Zampa (Champa, now part of South Vietnam), he saw "a tortoise bigger in compass than the dome of St. Anthony's church in Padua," and in the Nicobar Islands "both the men and the women have faces like dogs," and in Ceylon "there be also certain birds as big as geese, which have two heads." We see from these stories Friar Odoric's predisposition to believe in wonders, and we have just seen also his evident familiarity with the literature of Prester John. But of Prester John himself, the good friar could offer only modest news. He tells us first of the marvels of China. "The province of Manzi hath two thousand great cities, cities I mean of such magnitude that neither Treviso nor Vicenza would be entitled to be numbered among them. . . ." Canton is "as big as three Venices" and "indeed all Italy hath not the amount of craft that this one city hath." In this city "there be serpents bigger than anywhere else in the world, many of which are taken and eaten with great relish." The Yangtze is "the greatest river that exists in the world, for where it is narrowest it is some seven miles in width." The basement of the royal palace at Khan-baliq contains "four-and-twenty columns of gold, and all the walls are hung with skins of red leather, said to be the finest in the world. In the midst of the palace is a certain great jar, more than two paces in height, entirely formed of a certain precious stone called *Merdacas* [jade?] and so fine, that I was told its price exceeded the value of four great towns." At the summer palace of Shang-tu Friar Odoric saw, or claims to have seen, "six horses, each of which had six feet and legs. And I saw two very great ostriches, and two smaller ones behind them, that had each two necks and two heads with which they ate. . . ." After a recitation of many further marvels, Odoric comes at last to giving word of Prester John, and has only this to say:

"Departing from that land of Cathay and traveling westward for fifty days through many cities and towns, I arrived at the country of Prester John: but as regards him not one hundredth part is true of what is told of him as if it were undeniable. His principal city is called Tozan [Tenduc?], and chief city though it is, Vicenza would be reckoned its superior. He has, however, many other cities under him, and by a standing compact always receives to wife the Great Khan's daughter."

14

"But as regards him not one hundredth part is true of what is told of him as if it were undeniable. . . ." With that sad phrase Friar Odoric signaled the end of the quest for Prester John on the Asian steppes. That quest had begun a century earlier, when Jacques de Vitry in his optimism mistook the report of Genghis Khan's conquests for the deeds of a Christian hero. The delusive hope that the Mongols could be converted and made into the allies of Christendom then brought missionaries to Central Asia: Andrew of Longjumeau identified Prester John as a Kerait chieftain, the Wang-Khan Togrul, and William of Rubruck seemed to find him in the Naiman prince, Kuchluk. Marco Polo, who accepted the wang-khan as Prester John, claimed to have discovered his descendant in the sixth generation, King George of the Öngut Turks, and John of Monte Corvino led King George into the Roman Catholic fold, only to have that work undone upon the king's death. Lastly came Friar Odoric to the Öngut country in the time of King George's successor, the Prester John of the moment, and pronounced his coldly unromantic verdict: as regards Prester John, not one hundredth of what has been told of him is true. The evidence was unassailable, and no one now continued to pretend that a mighty Christian monarch held sway in that part of Asia. Yet the story of Prester John would not die. It was too firmly rooted by now in the European imagination. These chieftains of the Mongol steppes may have been Prester Johns of a sort, men admitted, but they must not be taken for the *real* Prester John, he of the grand palaces and the seventy-two tributary kings. But where was his realm? No one could say, except that if it was not in the Mongol country, then it must surely be somewhere else. And the search went on.

FOUR

Embellishments and Fantasies

Wʜɪʟᴇ Venetian merchants and Catholic missionaries plodded through the wastes of Mongolia hunting for Prester John, the supposed letter of that extraordinary monarch to Emperor Manuel of Byzantium continued to circulate in Europe, growing ever longer and more fabulous with each copying of the text. By the fourteenth century it had become an extensive anthology of medieval fable, thickly encrusted with myth and marvel.

One of the new interpolations was borrowed from a source some sixteen centuries old. In 302 B.C., Seleucus, who had succeeded Alexander the Great as ruler of Persia, negotiated a treaty of friendship with the Indian king Chandragupta. Seleucus sent an ambassador, Megasthenes, a Greek from Asia Minor, to live at Chandragupta's court at Patna in northern India. The ambassador was a man of consuming curiosity. During his stay in India, Megasthenes traveled widely and brought back a mass of information that was the foundation for all that the later Greek and Roman writers knew of India. His own writings have been lost, but extracts were quoted by Arrian and Strabo, and survive in their works. Among Megasthenes' tales was that of the ants of India, as big as foxes, with skins like panthers, that dug burrows in the ground and piled up heaps of dirt at the entrance. These heaps of dirt, Megasthenes said, were rich with gold, and the natives would sieve it by stealth. "The people take this gold very secretly," he wrote. "For if the animals notice it they pursue the thieves and kill them." In the fourteenth century someone with a classical education inserted the story in the text of Prester John's letter, as follows:

"In certain other of our provinces there are produced ants of the size of young dogs, having six feet and wings like sea locusts', and having teeth inside their jaws greater than dogs' teeth, with which they eat, and tusks outside the jaw larger than forest boars', with which they slay men as well as other animals. And those which they have killed they straightway devour. Nor is this the only wonder, for they are so fleet of foot that you would think they were flying, and therefore in those provinces men dwell only in safe and well-fortified places. And these ants, from sunset until the third hour of the day, remain underground, but all night they dig for the purest gold and bring it to light. From the third hour of the day until sunset they remain above ground, and then they feed. Afterwards they descend into ground to dig for gold. And so they do each day. By night the men leave their fortified places and collect the gold, which they load on elephants, hippopotami, camels, and other animals of great stature and power, to transport it to our treasuries. By night they [the men] labor, plough, sow, reap, and go and come, and do whatever they will. But by day none dare appear so long as the ants are above ground, because of the strength and ferocity of those same ants."

The celebrated story of the lion and the unicorn seems to have originated in another of the fourteenth-century interpolations into the text of the Prester John letter. This is how it was told in one French version of the letter:

"There are in our land also unicorns who have in front a single horn of which there are three kinds: green, black, and white. Sometimes they kill lions. But a lion kills them in a very subtle way. When a unicorn is tired it lies down by a tree. The lion goes then behind it and when the unicorn wants to strike him with his horn, it dashes into the tree with such a force that it cannot free itself. Then the lion kills it."

The conflict between the lion and the unicorn, which cannot be traced to any source earlier than Prester John's letter, took on a symbolic political significance in the late sixteenth century during the time of tension between England and Scotland, for the royal arms of England bore three lions, and those of Scotland a pair of unicorns. Thus Spenser, in his *Faerie Queene*:

> Like as a lyon, whose imperial powre
> A prowd rebellious unicorn defyes—

When King James VI of Scotland came to reign also as James I of England in 1603, he brought one of Scotland's unicorns with him. The shield in England's royal arms then was supported on one side by a lion and on the other by the red dragon of Wales; James replaced the dragon by a unicorn, and there the unicorn has remained.

In 1607, in his *History of Four-Footed Beasts*, the naturalist Edward Topsell solemnly retold the tale of how lions trap unicorns by causing them to embed their horns in the trunks of trees, using words not too different from those given above, and said, "These things are reported by the King of Ethiopia, in an Hebrew Epistle unto the Bishop of Rome." One must be familiar with the letter of Prester John in its various medieval mutations to realize that what Topsell means is *the King of India, in a Latin Epistle to the Emperor of Byzantium!*

The lion and the unicorn show up also, of course, in *Through the Looking Glass*. ("There was a pause in the fight just then, and the Lion and the Unicorn sat down, panting, while the King called out 'Ten minutes allowed for refreshments!'") But Tenniel's accompanying illustration makes it clear that Lewis Carroll was merely having some sport with his nation's coat of arms and meant no esoteric reference to Prester John.

Among the other natural wonders that entered the letter in its fourteenth-century redactions were birds "who rule over all other fowl in the world. They are fiery of hue, their wings are as sharp as razors, and they are known as Yllerion. There are but two of them in the entire world. They live for sixty years, after which span they fly off to plunge into the sea. But first they sit upon two or three eggs for forty days until the young ones hatch. Then the old pair, father and mother, take off and go to drown themselves in the sea. And all the birds who meet them fly as escorts with them until they are drowned. After this has taken place, the companions return and they go to the fledglings and feed them until they grow up and can fly and look after themselves." One fifteenth-century version of this passage added, "Likewise, you should know that we have other birds called tigers who are so strong and bold that they lift and kill with ease an armored man together with his horse." This is the only version that includes the odd reference to tigers as birds. The same manuscript curiously inverts the legend of Alexander the Great and the tribes of Gog and Magog by saying, "This was the people that enclosed the King Alexander in Macedonia and put him into prison from which he escaped."

A good deal of the cycle of St. Thomas mythology was imported into Prester John's letter in the fourteenth century. In the original twelfth-century text Prester John had mentioned the apostle only once, merely saying that the place where the body of St. Thomas rests is part of his empire. In that text also "the Patriarch of St. Thomas" is listed among those who dine at Prester John's table. One of the late twelfth-century additions to the original text declares that during the great holidays of the year St. Thomas is resurrected and preaches to the people from Prester John's palace. In the fourteenth-century text there are repeated references to the miracles of St. Thomas: "Know that God has performed many miracles for my lord St. Thomas, in fact, he has performed more of them than for any other saint of our country, for he preaches in person and he delivers a sermon to the people of the city where his body is resting." It is the income derived from "all the pilgrims who come to my lord St. Thomas and to the other saints of our land" that makes his country rich, Prester John admits. And when he leaves his land to make war, he appoints the Patriarch of St. Thomas as his regent. If by chance he should die without an heir, the patriarch is to succeed him as king. And we are informed, "Know that nobody dares to lie in the city of my lord St. Thomas, for he would soon die a miserable death"—a passage that seems plainly adapted from the old St. Thomas miracle-tract, *De adventu.*

The Amazons now enter the story in what Friedrich Zarncke termed Interpolation D. Herodotus had been one of the first to write of these warlike women, seventeen centuries earlier. He placed them in Pontus near the shore of the Euxine Sea, and described their raids against Scythia, Thrace, and the coasts of Asia Minor. No men were permitted to dwell in their country, though once a year the Amazons visited a neighboring nation for purposes of procreation, slaying all male children or returning them to their fathers, and recruiting the baby girls. Supposedly their name came from the Greek *amazos*, "without breast," from their custom of amputating the right breast to make the drawing of the bow more convenient, but several other derivations have been put forward. In the hands of one of the expanders of Prester John's letter the story turned into this:

"In another region of the wilderness we have a country that extends for forty-two days' journey and it is called the Grand Feminie. You must not think it is in the land of the Saracens, for the one of which we speak is in our country. In that land there are three queens and many other ladies who are their vassals. And when these three queens wish to wage war, each of them brings a force of one hundred thousand armed women, besides those who drive the carts, horses, and elephants with the equipment and provisions. And know that they fight bravely like men. No male can stay with them more than nine days, during which he can carouse and amuse himself and make them conceive. But he should not overstay, for in such a case he will die."

Adjoining the country of the Amazons, according to this text, is a land called Piconye, where "men are as small as seven-year-old children and their horses are as small as sheep, and yet they are good Christians and willing workers." The only enemies these people have are birds, who swoop each year to raid the grapes at harvest time. "Then the king of this country equips himself to the best of his ability against the said birds and they have a dreadful carnage. Later, however, the birds return." The fable of the pygmies and the cranes can be traced as far back as *The Iliad*.

Out of Greek mythology now came centaurs, too: "Bowmen who from the waist up are men, but whose lower part is that of a horse. They carry in their hands bows and arrows and they can pull harder than any human being and they live on raw flesh." The phoenix also was recruited, perhaps from the pages of Herodotus: "You should also know that in our country there is a bird called phoenix which is the most beautiful in the world. In the entire universe there is only one such creature. It lives for a hundred years and then it rises toward the sky so close to the sun that its wings take fire. Then it descends into its nest and is consumed; and yet from the ashes there emerges a worm which at the end of a hundred days becomes again as beautiful a bird as it ever was before." Also interpolated in the fourteenth century were men who tamed flying dragons by incantations, saddled and bridled them, and rode them through the air; five marvelous stones that could freeze or heat or reduce to an even state of temperature or turn light or dark everything within a span of five miles; five more stones, two of which were unconsecrated and turned water to milk or wine, and three of which were consecrated and would cause fish to congregate, or wild beasts to follow one, and, when sprinkled with hot lion's blood, produce a fire that could be doused only by sprinkling the stone with hot dragon's blood; a marvelous chapel of glass, always just big enough for as many persons as entered it; and a good deal more.

The Lost Tribes of Israel figured conspicuously in this expansion. The original text of Prester John's letter had said merely that ten tribes of Jews lived on the far side of a river of precious stones, and paid tribute to Prester John. Another passage told of a waterless river of stones that flowed three days a week, but could be crossed on the other four. In the fourteenth-century version of the letter these two themes were combined: the river of stones became the barrier between Prester John's country and the province of the Jews, and it was said to stand still only on Saturdays, being impassable the rest of the week. The author of this section seems unaware that Jews would be unlikely to launch an invasion on their Sabbath, for he reveals that Prester John found it necessary to fortify the banks of this river that could be crossed only on Saturdays, erecting forty-two castles and manning them with 10,000 knights, 6,000 crossbowmen, 15,000 archers, and 40,-000 troopers, "so that, if the great King of Israel would come with his men, he could not get across with his Jews, who are twice as numerous as the Christians. . . . Know that the great King of Israel has under him three hundred kings and four thousand princes, dukes, and counts, all of them Jews and obedient to him. And if the Jews could cross this passage, all the Christians and Saracens would be lost." Every Saturday, however, eight hundred or a thousand Jews are allowed across the river to engage in trade. "They do not, however, enter our strongholds, but exchange the wares outside, because we do not trust them. They buy exclusively with ingots of gold and silver, for they do not have real money. After they have made their purchases, they return home." Jewish women, the letter adds a few lines later, "are the most beautiful and passionate in the world."

It was now about two centuries since Europe first had heard of Prester John, and perhaps questions had been raised about the great king's extraordinary longevity. These could be met by giving him access to the Fountain of Youth: ". . . a clear fountain which has within itself every kind of taste. It changes its taste every hour by day and night, and is scarcely three days' journey from Paradise, whence Adam was expelled. Anyone who tastes three times of this fountain, while fasting, will suffer no infirmity thereafter, but remains as if of the age of thirty-two years as long as he lives." In a slightly later manuscript one finds, "Whoever drinks of its water three times without having eaten will have no illness for thirty years; and when he has drunk of it, he will feel as if he has eaten the finest meat and spices, for it is full of God's grace. A person who bathes in this fountain, whether he be of a hundred or a thousand years, will regain the age of thirty-two. Know that we were born and blessed in the womb of our mother 562 years ago and since then we have bathed in the fountain six times." Europe's difficulty in making contact with Prester John, then, was of no moment: for he was immortal, and could wait a while longer to be discovered.

2

From the beginning, the letter of Prester John had been received on at least two levels, and the space between those levels widened as wonder after wonder was added to the text. The sophisticated few regarded the letter primarily as an amusing fantasy, it would seem; certainly this must have been the attitude of the scholarly monks who playfully packed the centaurs and the Amazons and the pygmies into it. They had no travelers' reports on which to base those interpolations; on the contrary, every report coming out of Asia tended to make Prester John seem more prosaic and less fabulous. Therefore the expansion of the letter could only have been done for the sake of making a tall tale even taller, thus heightening the joke. Meanwhile the credulous many, who probably had word of Prester John only through the oral tradition, continued to regard the story as literal truth, and no amount of mythological padding could shake that belief. Either they chose to ignore the more implausible marvels or they accepted them at face value, but their faith in the existence of an authentic Prester John did not waver. He was part of the given and established body of data of geographical knowledge, like the great ocean that surrounded the world, and the inhabited antipodal continents that could never be reached because of the zone of fire across the equator. Even the sophisticates must have shared this curious doubleness of attitude: largely discounting the fanciful embellishments of Prester John's letter, its phoenixes and dragons, yet retaining their conviction that Prester John himself existed. And this outlook would persist for centuries, until all the possible prototypes of Prester John in the Orient had been investigated and the mythmaking brought to an end.

In any case, Prester John had now entered the public domain and was available for the free use of any storyteller. He began to appear in the pious fictions of the era, of which a good example is *The Legend of the Holy Three Kings* of Johannes of Hildesheim, written about 1378 and much republished over the following two centuries. This work drew Prester John, St. Thomas, and the Three Magi together in one elaborate construct.

It opens with the familiar story of St. Thomas' journey to bring the word of Jesus to India—or rather, to the Three Indies, the rulers of which were the Magi, Melchior, Balthasar, and Gaspar. These kings were converted to Christianity by the apostle (completing the identification of Gaspar with the King Gundafor of the earlier Thomas legends) and were made archbishops by him. After the martyrdom of St. Thomas, the three kings instructed their subjects to elect a "Patriarch Thomas" to be their lord in spiritual matters, and another as their temporal master, with the title of "Prester John." Johannes of Hildesheim declares, "For the Three Kings were priests and of their possessions they made him [Prester John] lord. For there is no degree so high as priesthood is in all the world, nor so worthy. Also he is called Prester John in honor of St. John the Evangelist that was a priest, the most specially chosen and beloved of God Almighty."

The three kings died and were given proper Christian burials, and Patriarch Thomas and Prester John ruled the Indies. However, many of their subjects were tempted by the Devil and abandoned Christianity, some reverting to paganism and some giving their allegiance to heretic sects like that of the Nestorians. After many years St. Helena, the mother of Emperor Constantine I of Rome, visited the Indies after a pilgrimage to the Holy Land, and reconverted a number of the backsliders. She wished to collect holy relics to bring to her son's newly founded city of Constantinople, and so she persuaded Patriarch Thomas and Prester John to let her have the bodies of the Magi Melchior and Balthasar. The villainous Nestorians, however, had made off with Gaspar's body, and in order to obtain it from them she was compelled to give in exchange the body of St. Thomas, which happened to be in her keeping. Then St. Helena brought the bodies of the Three Kings to Constantinople, where they were interred in the cathedral of Hagia Sophia.

(In fact the supposed relics of the Magi did rest in Hagia Sophia for many centuries. After the split between the Greek and Latin churches in the eleventh century, the Byzantines ceased to revere the bones, and one of the emperors allowed them to be transferred to Milan. About a hundred years later, when the German army of Frederick Barbarossa sacked Milan, the Archbishop of Cologne obtained the relics and took them to his city, where to this day they remain in the cathedral.)

Johannes of Hildesheim also tells of the rebellion of the Nestorians against the authority of Patriarch Thomas and Prester John. When the Tartars invaded their lands, though, the Nestorians appealed for help to Prester John. The three kings visited Prester John in a dream to warn him to give no aid to the heretics; but Prester John rashly sent his son David to free them. David was slain by the Tartars. Now the three kings manifested themselves to the Tartar emperor, urging him to make peace with Prester John, the son of one to marry the daughter of the other. The marriage was performed, an alliance was consummated between Prester John and his erstwhile foes, and the hapless Nestorians became fugitives.

3

Prester John figured prominently as well in the work of a fourteenth-century writer of less pious intent, the illustrious Sir John Mandeville. Samuel Purchas, the seventeenth-century compiler of explorers' journals, called Mandeville "the greatest Asian traveler that ever the world had," which most assuredly he was not; but if Mandeville was a charlatan, as seems indisputable, he was also an uncommonly gifted literary entertainer.

The prologue to Mandeville's *Travels* declares that he was born in the English town of St. Albans and set forth across the sea in 1332 (or 1322, in some manuscripts), "and since hitherward [I] have been long time over the sea, and have seen and gone through many kingdoms, lands and provinces and isles, and have passed through Turkey,

Armenia the less and the more, Tartary, Persia, Syria, Arabia, Egypt the high and the low, Libya, Chaldea, and a great part of Ethiopia, Amazonia, India the less and more, a great part, and through many other isles that are about India, where dwell many diverse manners of folk of diverse laws and shapes. . . ." Sir John offers us no other information about himself, except the statement in his epilogue that he completed his book thirty-four years after his departure from England—in 1366 according to one manuscript, 1356 according to another. There once was a tomb of Mandeville in a church near the Belgian city of Liège, which was much visited by travelers until its destruction during the French Revolution; Mandeville's tombstone identified him as a practitioner of medicine and gave the date of his death as November 17, 1372.

For further information about Sir John we must look to a notary and historian of Liège, Jean d'Outremeuse (1338–99), author of a vast world-chronicle in the French-Flemish dialect, *Myreur des Histors*. Only sections of the *Myreur* have survived to our time; Book IV, which mentioned Mandeville, is not among them, but the pertinent passage has come down to us through its quotation in a work by the Liège genealogist Louis Abry (d. 1720). Outremeuse asserts in this passage that in November 1372 he was called to the deathbed of his old friend Jean de Bourgogne, who had been a doctor in Liège since 1343, and was asked in his capacity as notary to receive the dying man's last will and testament. From Jean de Bourgogne then came a confession, said Outremeuse, that he was in fact "Master Jean de Mandeville, Knight, count of Montfort in England. . . . Having had the misfortune to kill, in his country, a count whom he did not name, he obliged himself to traverse the three parts of the world. . . . Although he was a man of distinguished nobility he preferred to keep himself hidden. For the rest, he was a great naturalist, a profound philosopher and astrologer, to which he added in particular a singular knowledge of medicine. . . ."

Some modern authorities have maintained that "Sir John Mandeville" was merely a pseudonym employed by Jean de Bourgogne, whose claim to have been an Englishman was fictitious. Others have insisted that "Mandeville" was in truth Sir John Mandeville of St. Albans, and that Outremeuse's attempt to claim him for Liège by way of Jean de Bourgogne's deathbed statement was a fraudulent bit of opportunistic home-town boosting. However, Malcolm Letts, the foremost Mandeville scholar of the twentieth century, concluded from internal evidence that the book was almost certainly written by an Englishman, who might just as well be considered to have been John Mandeville of St. Albans: "The more the problem is studied the clearer it becomes, at least to my mind, that Mandeville was a man of flesh and blood, born, as he says, at St. Albans, that he practiced medicine . . . , that he fled the country, and that de Bourgogne was a name invented or borrowed by Mandeville to conceal his identity." Pointing out that "where there is so much uncertainty one guess is as good as another," Letts observed that "after all these centuries it is the man as disclosed in his book that is important, not the man himself. The man himself can now never be anything but a ghost."

The book—whether it was the work of Mandeville living under the name of Bourgogne or Bourgogne writing under the name of Mandeville—was written after 1360, judging by certain events mentioned in it, and may well have been completed in the year Mandeville gives, 1366. A statement found in an English translation of the fifteenth or sixteenth century gave rise to the belief that the original language of the book was Latin, which the author then had translated into French and from French into his native English. This seems, though, merely to be a misunderstanding of a passage in the French version of the work, in which Mandeville says that he *should have* written the book in Latin but chose French instead to have a wider audience. French does appear to have been the original language of the *Travels*. This is no bar to regarding Mandeville as an Englishman, since a fourteenth-century English knight would have been as much at home in French as in English, and perhaps more so. French was not only then the language of the English upper class but had replaced Latin as the international tongue of Europe; Marco Polo's travels were evidently originally written in French, for example.

The whereabouts of Mandeville's original manuscript are unknown. The oldest surviving copy of the text, in French heavily flavored with Anglicisms, bears the date of 1371. Not long afterward a copy of this was made for the library of King Charles V of France, with the style corrected to a somewhat more Parisian brand of French. Sometime prior to 1396, Jean d'Outremeuse, the notary of Liège, obtained a copy of this text and produced a version of it in the dialect of his region—inserting, as we shall see, a good deal of new material. Translations into Spanish, Latin, Dutch, German, Bohemian, Danish, and Gaelic quickly followed. Three medieval English translations are known, none of them earlier than the fifteenth century. The universal popularity of the work is indicated by the existence of some three hundred manuscripts in all, today, whereas there are only seventy-seven manuscripts of Marco Polo extant and about a hundred of Prester John's letter. After the general introduction of printing in the late fifteenth century Sir John's memoir went through a host of new editions in many languages; it was still being offered in cheap popular form as late as the eighteenth century.

Though we are uncertain about its author's identity, we are sure of one thing: he was not the traveler he claimed to be. If he had really visited all the places he describes, he would not have had to borrow so freely from the writings of genuine travelers. His book is actually an unacknowledged compilation from a host of sources: a synthesis of the entire literature of travel of thirteenth- and fourteenth-century Europe, cunningly and artfully blended to form a single coherent narrative of one man's alleged voyaging. Sir John seems to have drawn most heavily on the gigantic encyclopedia called the *Speculum Mundi*, the work of Vincent of Beauvais, who died in 1264. Vincent had done much of Mandeville's preparatory work for him, albeit unintentionally, having digested and abridged an immense range of geographical data. In the *Speculum* could be found a lengthy extract from the journal of John of Plano Carpini, along with the accounts of many other travelers and quotations from Pliny, Solinus, Isidore of Seville, the romances of Alexander the Great, various bestiaries, and much more; Mandeville helped himself liberally from this huge trove to oddments of natural history and exotic lore. For his account of the countries east of the Levant, Mandeville relied chiefly on Odoric of Pordenone, shamelessly quoting him almost literally for long sections and, of course, giving the friar no credit for his observations. His text is so similar to Odoric's that it was once thought they had journeyed together, and Purchas, publishing both writers in his vast compendium of travel literature, accused Odoric of having plagiarized Mandeville! Sir John drew less copiously on William of Rubruck, and apparently took only one minor passage from Marco Polo; but dozens of less celebrated travelers were pillaged at his hands, and the anonymous authors of Prester John's letter were among the victims.

In its opening pages Mandeville's book pretends to be a guide for pilgrims to the Holy Land. Some scholars have maintained that Mandeville did at least make that part of his journey, and may really have been to Egypt as well; but, as Malcolm Letts points out, "If Mandeville did see the Holy Places with his own eyes, he either made little use of them or his memory was defective." Most of the information he provides was out of date in his own time, as might be expected, since it has been shown that he took most of it from writers of the eleventh and twelfth centuries. His sketch of the Greek Islands came from Brunetto Latini; his account of the route through Constantinople into Asia Minor was taken from Albert of Aix; his information on Cyprus came from Jacques de Vitry; his sections on Palestine and Egypt were adapted from the narrative of a German knight named William of Boldensele, padded with extracts from an early guidebook known as the *Old Compendium*, in standard use among pilgrims bound for Jerusalem. Identifying Mandeville's sources was a favorite activity of nineteenth-century historians of geography; they have shown that his text is a montage of fragments from a multitude of works.

Though in this section Mandeville is much concerned with giving detailed information on routes and accommodations, it is easy to perceive that his main interest lies in the anecdotal, the diverting, the fantastic: he is a storyteller, not a Baedeker. He interrupts a discussion of the tomb of St. John at Ephesus to speak of a princess who was transformed into a dragon, and on Cyprus he passes quickly over the cross of Dismas, the good thief, to examine the curious custom of the Cypriote aristocrats who took their meals knee-deep in trenches to avoid the heat. In Jaffa he notes the "bones of a giant that hight Andromedes; and one of his ribs is forty feet long." In Cairo he gives a paragraph to the Pyramids, which he says are "the barns of Joseph that were made for to keep corn in for the seven barren years that were betokened by the seven dead wheat ears, which King Pharaoh saw in dream, as the first book of Bible tells." And so on, with many a charming digression, to Mount Sinai, Bethlehem, and Jerusalem.

Once past the Holy Land, Mandeville began fully to indulge his love of the marvelous. By far the larger part of the book describes his "travels" through the Far East, even unto the realm of Prester John and the borders of the Terrestrial Paradise. (He did not visit that last place, "and I repent it not, for I was not worthy," but he did find the Fountain of Youth and take three sips of it, "and evermore since that time I feel me the better and the wholer.") Friar Odoric provides the underpinnings for much of this section, except for the tour of Tartary, which was copied from John of Plano Carpini; but, not content with the wonders described by those indefatigable Franciscans, our arm-chair traveler spliced in an array of marvels from other sources, perhaps even some of his own invention. Neither Odoric nor Friar John had toured the country of the Amazons, for example, but following his de-scription of Mesopotamia Mandeville declares, "Beside the land of Chaldea is the land of Amazonia, that is the land of Feminie. And in that realm is all women and no man; not, as some men say, that men may not live there, but for because that the women will not suffer no men amongst them to be their sovereigns." Although Mandeville was familiar with Prester John's letter, his extensive account of the Ama-zons was not based on the interpolated reference to them to be found there, but rather seems to have been drawn from an older source, since it goes into details not used in the letter.

On the other side of Chaldea, to the south, lay Ethiopia, where, he says, the people are black and short-lived because of the excessive heat. Here he introduces the first of his gallery of human monsters: the sciapods, folk with but one foot, who lie on their backs holding that foot aloft to shade them from the sun. In Ethiopia, also, "are young children white-haired, and when they are of eld, their hair waxes black. In this land of Ethiopia is the city of Saba, of which one of the three kings that offered to our Lord was king." Here Mandeville inserts a dis-quisition on diamonds, discussing their virtues in warding off venom or poison, and revealing that these gems "grow together male and fe-male . . . and they engender commonly and bring forth small children, and multiply and grow all the year."

Then he passes over into India, which he divides into three parts: "India the More, which is a high country and hot; India the Less, which is a temperate land, and it is toward the south; the third part is toward the north, and it is so cold a country that for the great cold and con-tinual frost the water congeals into crystal." By India the More he evi-dently meant the Indian subcontinent; India the Less appears to stretch from the Indus westward to Arabia and Ethiopia; the third India must have been the country beyond the Himalayas. Of India the More he says, "In India are many divers countries; and it is called India because of a water that runs through that land, the which men call Inde. In that water men find eels of thirty foot long. And folk that dwell near that water are ill colored, yellow and green." He tells the story of the pepper forests that must be burned, mainly following Odoric's version, though including some details found in the Prester

John letter that Odoric did not deign to use: however, he expresses
a rare bit of skepticism, saying that the story must be untrue, "for if
they thus made fires about the pepper, they should burn the pepper
and the trees that it grows on, or else dry them so that they should no
more bear fruit." It was near the pepper country that Mandeville found
the Fountain of Youth (his description is quoted from Prester John's
letter) and allowed himself his modest few sips. Then he claims to have
gone on to "Mabaron"—Maabar—and the shrine of St. Thomas. This
section is taken practically verbatim from Odoric, though Mandeville
does offer one story Odoric does not mention. The body of the apostle,
he says, was seized by the Assyrians and taken to Edessa, but afterward
was miraculously translated back to India, and it lies whole in a tomb
in Mabaron, except for St. Thomas' arm, the one with which he touched
Christ's wound. This arm rests outside the tomb in a special vessel. If
two men have a dispute at law, Mandeville declares, each writes a statement of his case on a scroll, and the scrolls are placed in the saint's
hand, and at once "the hand casts out the bill that contains the false
cause, and the other it holds still." Perhaps this is a variant of the old
tale of De adventu in which St. Thomas holds forth the communion
wafer but closes his hand when approached by infidel or heretic.

Still leaning heavily on Friar Odoric, Mandeville journeys on
through Java and its neighboring islands to Southeast Asia, and thence,
by a mysterious backtracking on his route, to Ceylon. In the course of
this voyaging he encountered an abundance of human monsters, all of
them lifted from the pages of Vincent of Beauvais, who had found
them in the works of Pliny, Solinus, and the Greek traveler Ctesias of
the fourth century B.C. Mandeville offers for his readers' delight "giants,
horrible and foul to the sight," that "have but one eye, and that is in
midst the forehead"; "foul men without heads," who have one eye in
each shoulder, and mouths of horseshoe shape in their chests; flat-faced
people, noseless and having two small holes instead of eyes; folk with
upper lips so large that they wrapped them about themselves as cloaks
when they slept in the sun; people with ears hanging down to their
knees; people with horses' feet, who run so swiftly they overtake wild
beasts; hermaphrodites, who alternately sire and bear children; eight-
toed people who crawl wondrous fast on their knees; and others of
divers sorts.

Cathay was Mandeville's next destination, and, skillfully shuffling
together the narratives of Odoric, John of Plano Carpini, and several

other travelers, he produces an exciting and elaborate account of the great khan's realm. "Under the firmament is not so great a lord, nor so mighty, nor so rich as is the great Chan," Mandeville observes. "Not Prester John, that is emperor of the high Ind, nor the Soldan of Babylon, nor the Emperor of Persia [is mightier]. All these be not in comparison to the great Chan, neither of might, nor of noblesse, nor of royalty, nor of riches; for in all these he passes all earthly princes." Mandeville discusses the opulence of China, the splendor of the emperor's court, the ancestry of the Mongol rulers beginning with "Chaanguys," the table habits of the Mongols, and a good deal more. For a touch of verisimilitude he adds that he himself enrolled in the great khan's army and fought for fifteen months in the Mongol conquest of Sung China; that conquest had been accomplished twenty or thirty years before Mandeville was born, but his readers were unlikely to know much about that, nor, in all probability, did he.

The section on Cathay is followed by a catchall couple of chapters summarizing the geography of Persia and the Caucasus. Unsurprisingly, Mandeville tells the story of how Alexander the Great penned up Gog and Magog behind the mountains of the Caucasus, but he gives the tale a novel twist by identifying Gog and Magog as "the Jews of the ten kindreds," who in the time of Antichrist shall come forth and overwhelm Christendom. ("And therefore all the Jews that dwell in divers parts of the world learn for to speak Hebrew, for they trow [believe] that these Jews that are enclosed among the hills shall come out and shall know them by their speech that they are Jews as they are. And then they shall lead them into Christendom for to destroy Christian men.") This is perhaps an inspired combining of two themes of the Prester John letter: Gog and Magog penned up in one of Prester John's provinces, and the ten tribes of Israel living on the far side of the river of stones in another. It was typical of Mandeville's method to blend his source material in this way, producing seemingly original stories through such juxtapositions. Certainly he had access to the Prester John letter in one of its expanded versions—for not only are pieces of it (the pepper forest, the Amazons, and so forth) scattered through the earlier part of his narrative, but whatever parts of the letter he did not use there appear intact in his account of his visit to the isle of Pentoxere, which he tells us is the name of Prester John's homeland.

4

"The Emperor Prester John has many divers countries under his empire, in the which are many noble cities and fair towns and many isles great and large. For this land of India is departed in isles because of the great floods that come out of Paradise and run through this land and depart it. And also in the sea he has many great isles. The principal city of the isle of Pentoxere is called Nise; and there is the emperor's see, and therefore it is a noble city and a rich. Prester John has under him many kings and many divers folk; and his land is good and rich, but not so rich as the land of the Great Chan of Cathay. For merchants come not so mickle to that land as to the land of Cathay, for it were too long way. And also merchants may find in the isle of Cathay all that they have need of, as spicery, cloths of gold and other rich things; and they let also for to go thither because of long way and great perils in the sea."

Thus Sir John Mandeville opens his description of the realm of Prester John. The English translation is the so-called Egerton Text, a manuscript dating from the fifteenth or sixteenth century, and, from the use of such words as "mickle," "ilk," and "kirk," evidently the work of a native of Scotland or northern England; the spelling has been somewhat modernized. The passage just quoted is not, of course, a borrowing from the Prester John letter, nor is the next:

"For there are in many places in the sea great rocks of the stone that is called adamant, the which of his own kind draws to him iron; and for there should pass no ships that had nails of iron there away because of the foresaid stone, for he should draw them to him, therefore they dare not wend thither. The ships of that country are all made of wood and none iron. I was one time in that sea, and I saw as it had been an isle of trees and brushes growing; and the shipmen told me that all was of great ships that the rock of the adamant had gert [caused to] dwell there, and of divers things that were in the ships were those trees and those brushes sprung."

The story of the sea of magnetic rocks—adamant or lodestone— was a familiar one in medieval times. Mandeville, who was the first to associate this perilous sea with the kingdom of Prester John, probably lifted the notion from the book of Vincent of Beauvais, but it appears in many other sources, most notably *The Thousand and One Nights*.

After discussing in a vague and incomprehensible way the land route to Prester John's kingdom via Persia, Mandeville offers a nugget mined from Odoric, who may have taken it from Marco Polo: "This ilk [same] royal king Prester John and the Great Chan of Tartary are evermore allied together through marriage; for either of them weds other daughter or other sister." The origin of this statement must lie in the frequent marriages between the family of Genghis Khan and that of Togrul, the Kerait chieftain. But, though Mandeville follows Odoric in this one detail, he chooses to ignore the friar's other statement about how everything said of Prester John is a hundredfold exaggeration; at this point Mandeville drops Odoric as his source and begins to paraphrase the famous letter:

"Now will I speak of some of the principal isles of Prester John's land, and of the royalty of his state and what law and belief he and his people hold. This emperor Prester John is a Christian man, and the most part of his land also, if all it be so that they have not all the articles of our belief so clearly as we have. Not forbye they trow in God, Father and Son and Holy Ghost; and full devout men they are and true ilk one to other, and there is nowhere with them fraud nor guile. This emperor has under his subjection seventy-two provinces, and in ilk one of them is a king. And these kings have other kings under them, and all are tributaries to the emperor Prester John. In the land of Prester John are many marvels. . . ."

The marvels are the customary ones: the sandy sea, the river of stones, the men with horns. We are told that from the waterless sea come savory fishes, "of other shape than fishes are of other waters. I John Mandeville ate of them, and therefore trow it." Some of the wonders that then were included in the letter Mandeville could not use, for he had already attributed them to other lands, but he made up for this by inserting some new ones, such as birds capable of human speech (clearly, from his description, parrots) and trees that sprout at sunrise, and "grow till midday, bearing fruit, but no man dare take of that fruit, for it is a thing of faerie. And after midday they decrease and enter again into the earth, so that at the going down of the sun they appear no more." These ephemeral trees came from the Alexander-romance of Pseudo-Callisthenes, by way of Vincent of Beauvais.

Closely following the letter, Mandeville speaks of how Prester John rides to battle with crosses of fine gold and precious gems borne before him, and how in peacetime a plain wooden cross is carried before him in remembrance of the passion of Christ. The description of Prester John's imperial palace at Susa is also taken wholesale from the letter, as are the details of life in Prester John's court ("and ilk a day there eat in his court twelve archbishops and twenty bishops"). Mandeville adds, "sickerly [assuredly] I saw it with mine eyes and mickle more than I have told you. For my fellows and I were dwelling with him in his court a long time and saw all this that I have told you and mickle more than I have leisure for to tell."

It is in his tales of the lands subject to Prester John that Mandeville most gloriously indulges his taste for fantasy. Not far from Susa, Mandeville relates, is the formidable Valley Perilous, where the sounds of invisible drummers and trumpeters are heard, and the cries of unseen participants at some hideous feast: "This vale is full of devils and always has been; and men say in that country that there is an entry to hell." Here may be seen the visage of a devil in a rock, "and out of his mouth and his nose comes so great plenty of fire of divers colors with so great stink, that no man may suffer it." Many travelers die horribly here, and their corpses, which do not decompose, lie scattered all about. Beyond this realm of demons is an island of naked giant cannibals, twenty-eight or thirty feet high; Mandeville says he did not care to visit them, or to tour a neighboring isle of cannibals *sixty* feet in height. Next is found a place where maidens once were in the custom of keeping venomous serpents in their vaginas to defend their chastity, and near that land is one where women have the power to slay men with an angry look, and the island next to that has women who mourn when their children are born and rejoice if the infants die. Continuing through Prester John's realms, Mandeville reports a race that refrains from eating the meat of hares, hens, and geese, yet raises these animals for the mere pleasure of beholding them—a passage that he borrowed almost verbatim, by way of Vincent of Beauvais, from Caesar's account of the ancient Britons in *De bello gallico*. He describes such exotic beasts as cocodrilles (crocodiles), which he says have no tongues, and orafles or gyrfaunts (giraffes), an animal which he declares "is a fair beast, well dappled, of the height of a great steed or higher; and his neck is twenty cubits long. . . . And he may well enough stand on the earth and look over a high house." Farther on one reaches the isle of Bragmans— Brahmans, it seems—inhabited by men who, though they are not Christians, "are folk of good virtue and flee all vices and sin and malice. . . .

They set nought by riches of this world, nor by having of earthly goods." So temperate and sober are they that they are the longest-living folk of the world, even without benefit of Prester John's Fountain of Youth. Near them is the isle of Pytan, "where the folk neither till nor sow no land, nor neither eat nor drink. And nevertheless they are right fair folk and well colored and well shapen after the stature that they are of; for they are little like dwarfs, somewhat more than the pigmens." They are nourished by the scent of wild apples, and wherever they travel they take their apples with them, for "as soon as they forgo the smell of them they die." In another island dwell people "all full of feathers and rough," who ate raw fish, and beyond lie the land of the Trees of the Sun and the Moon, which spoke to Alexander the Great and foretold his death. The keepers of these trees, who eat of their fruit, live four or five hundred years. Mandeville did not attempt to penetrate their country, for the route lay through a wilderness thick with dragons and unicorns and lions and many other dangerous creatures, including elephants both white and blue. Instead he went on to "an isle mickle and large and good, the which is called Taprobane"—Ceylon—whose king is subject to Prester John; it was a seven days' journey by sea from Prester John's land. Here, Mandeville says, the famed gold-digging ants are to be found. To the east of Taprobane, he tells us, is Tile, or Thule, "the furthest isle of the world inhabited with men." Here the imperial sway of Prester John reached its boundary; east of Thule "is nought but waste land and wilderness," in which nothing dwells but "dragons and other wild beasts, cruel and fell." If one were to go on and on, eastward across that wilderness, one would in time come to Eden, the terrestrial paradise. With becoming humility Mandeville says that he cannot properly speak of Eden, not having been there; but he has gathered enough information about it to be able to describe the great wall that encloses it and the well from which the four mighty rivers spring. To this he appends brief descriptions of Tibet and China, and brings his wondrous tale to its end.

5

In the course of his account of Prester John's land Mandeville provides a unique version of the etymology of that monarch's title. Once there was a pagan emperor, he says, who had many Christian knights in his service. While traveling with his retinue this emperor entered Egypt, then a Christian land, and, out of curiosity concerning the Christian rite, attended a service at an Egyptian church at which a bishop was ordaining new priests. "And the emperor beheld the service," Mandeville declares, "and the manner of the making of priests, how solemnly and how busily and how devoutly they were ordained. And then he asked the knight that was with him what manner of folk were those that were so ordained and what they hight; and he said that they were priests. And then the emperor said he would no more be called king nor emperor but priest, and also he would have the name of the first priest that came out of the kirk. So it fell that the first priest that came first out of the kirk hight John; and therefore that emperor and all other emperors since [in his land] have been called Prester John, that is as much as saying Priest John."

Quite a different story of Prester John's origin appears in the edition of Mandeville's book that was produced about 1396 by the notary of Liège, Jean d'Outremeuse. Outremeuse, who as we have already seen was a friend of the presumable author of the great work, doctored the text considerably in the course of his translation of it from the Parisian dialect of French to that of Flanders. In particular he introduced a number of stories concerning the exploits of the heroic Ogier the Dane.

Outremeuse had already written an epic poem, now lost, on the deeds of Ogier, and had dealt with him at length in his interminable chronicle, *Myreur des Histors*. Ogier, a figure out of the Charlemagne mythos, apparently was based on an actual ninth-century Frankish warrior, Autcher, who was probably born in what is now Belgium and had no connection with Denmark at all. Passing into myth as Ogier the Dane, Autcher became one of Charlemagne's famed Twelve Paladins; the Danes themselves revere him as their national hero, Holger Danske. According to one of the Ogier legends, he left Charlemagne's court to pursue a career of conquest in the Orient, and eventually was carried off to Avalon, where the sorceress Morgan le Fay introduced him to King Arthur and made him immortal. After passing two centuries among the knights of Avalon, Ogier was sent back to France by Morgan, for he was needed to defend that land against a Saracen invasion. Then he returned to Avalon, and there he remains, awaiting his next summons from a beleaguered Europe. Nowhere in Mandeville's original text are there any references to Ogier, but when the book had passed through the hands of Outremeuse it emerged with a host of Ogier interpolations, most of them drawn from Outremeuse's own earlier works, which themselves were deeply indebted to Mandeville.

In his *Myreur*, Outremeuse had acquired material for his tales of Ogier by ransacking Mandeville. What he did was to substitute Ogier for Mandeville for chapters at a time, turning a first-person account into a third-person one. Thus in Book III of the *Myreur* it is Ogier who visits the pepper forest, Ogier who drinks from the Fountain of Youth, Ogier who sees the body of St. Thomas in India, and so on. Later, when preparing his edition of Mandeville, Outremeuse reversed the process, cavalierly interpolating Ogier stories from the *Myreur* into Mandeville's narrative. The effect of this is greatly to distort the plan of Mandeville's book, which purports to be the account of his own adventures. Into it Ogier abruptly is thrust—marching through India and Java and Cathay and many other lands, subduing pagans, founding cities, erecting churches. Outremeuse causes Mandeville to tell us that in the year 816 Ogier conquered the part of India that became the nucleus of Prester John's empire, and offers this explanation of the derivation of that ruler's title:

"There was among the barons [in Ogier's army] one named John, the son of Goudebuef King of Frisia, and the said John was devoted to God. When opportunity occurred he was wont to enter the thresholds of churches, for which reason the barons, as in jest, gave him the name of Priest John. After Ogier had conquered the aforesaid regions he divided them among fifteen of his followers, and established whom he pleased from among them in his place and made him king, so that the Christian religion might be established there forever. He delivered upper India to Priest John . . . for which cause all his successors in India are called Priest [Prester] John."

This story first appeared in the *Myreur*, in which Outremeuse wrote, "And the king Goudebuef of Frisia delivered to him [Ogier] Presbyter John his son. He was called priest, because he went every day to pray in church and knelt in devotion before every altar. He was accustomed to call himself Prester John and was king of India because Ogier crowned him." After Outremeuse had introduced this into Mandeville's book, it naturally became part of all later translations that were based on the Outremeuse-edited text. Somewhere along the way a phrase entered the text crediting the story to a certain ancient chronicle, which is evidently a hazy reference to the *Myreur*. So in the first

German translation of Mandeville, done in the fifteenth century by Otto von Diemeringen, the tale has this form:

"Here it should be noted how the name Prester John came first into being. Ogier had a friend who was called King Godebuch of Frisia. He had a son called John. This same John was always to be found in churches: he prayed much and was very devout and performed many excellent priestly duties. And therefore, because he was so pious and was so often in church, he became a jest to other people. And therefore he was called Priest John or Prester John. Now it happened that this same John performed many doughty deeds, so that he grew in favor with his cousin Ogier who, when he departed, bestowed upon him the lands he had won, and Prester John retained these same lands, and the name remained, so that all his descendants are so called to this day. Thus was a jest turned to earnest. All this I read in that same country, in the Chronicles which are preserved in the town of Nyse, in Our Lady's Minster, and I believe none other than that the name itself came in this manner." Otto von Diemeringen must have had access to a non-Outremeuse text of Mandeville as well, for he goes on immediately to tell Mandeville's own version of the origin of Prester John's name, the one about the emperor who was so impressed by the humility of the newly ordained priests in Egypt that he adopted their title for his own. But he adds, "I prefer to believe the first story, since I have read it in the books." In this way does one fable drive another from circulation, as the maze of fantasy grows.

FIVE

Prester John in Ethiopia

ALL this mythmaking served well to keep alive the public hunger for the discovery of Prester John's realm. Fourteenth-century Europe was ringed round by enemies, real and imaginary, no less than the Europe of the twelfth and thirteenth centuries; if a puissant Christian monarch did exist in some remote corner of the world, it was as sensible then as ever to make contact with him and strike up an alliance. The steppes of Central Asia had been extensively searched and had yielded no one who seemed properly mighty enough to be the true Prester John, though many chieftains had been seen to fit this or that facet of the description of the legendary Prester. It might have been the part of reason to admit that Prester John was a fantasy, and to terminate the quest; but rather than abandon all hope of finding Prester John, fourteenth-century Europe simply ceased to look for him in Asia and turned instead toward Africa, toward the land of Ethiopia.

It was not an unreasonable move. Prester John was commonly thought to rule in India, but we have seen that the concept of "India" was a vague one in medieval times, and many geographers considered

Ethiopia to be one of the Three Indias, having no idea that a great sea separated eastern Africa from India proper. Then, too, Prester John was supposed to be a Christian emperor, and the Ethiopian monarch was in fact just that, though he was a Monophysite and not a subscriber to the Nestorian rite usually associated with Prester John. Furthermore, since Ethiopia was just beyond Egypt and contact between Europe and Egypt had continued throughout medieval times, it is highly likely that rumors of a Christian realm somewhere up the Nile had been circulating in Europe as long as, if not longer than, the Prester John tale itself. We have already noted that the Prester John to whom Pope Alexander III addressed a friendly letter in 1177 may well have been the Ethiopian emperor. Since the middle of the nineteenth century some scholars have argued that the Ethiopian emperor was the prototype of Prester John from the start, and that the diversion of the quest from Africa to Central Asia was the result of unfortunate geographical confusion. However, Marco Polo, writing at the outset of the fourteenth century, made it clear that he knew that Ethiopia was ruled by a Christian, and yet he continued to regard Prester John as a figure of the Asian steppes. Not until a generation after Marco's time did Europeans generally begin to turn away from the phantom of an Asian Prester John and to seek him in Ethiopia.

The Ethiopian phase of the Prester John story opens in 1306 with the arrival in Genoa of thirty Ethiopian envoys, homeward bound from western Europe. Their king, Wedem Ar'ad, had sent them to Europe to negotiate a mutual defense pact with "the King of the Spains." (Spain was then a patchwork of quasi-independent little kingdoms, and the country as a whole was properly referred to by the plural form, *las Españas*.) The rulers of the kingdoms of Castile and Aragon had slowly been extinguishing the power of the Moors who once had governed the entire Iberian Peninsula, and the Ethiopian king, somehow learning of the Spanish struggle against the Moslems, had sent his envoys to offer Ethiopia's aid, in the hope that Spain would subsequently help him in his own warfare with his Arab neighbors. A commercial treaty between Genoa and Egypt, concluded in 1290, provided the means by which the Ethiopians got to Europe. Evidently they had journeyed northward from their homeland to the Egyptian port of Alexandria, where, perhaps hiring passage in a Genoese ship, they sailed across to Europe. We do not know if they ever reached Spain, but they did get as far west as the French city of Avignon, where the Popes then made their headquarters, and also visited Rome. On their way home they were delayed some time in Genoa, awaiting favorable winds, and during this time they were interviewed by an Italian geographer, Giovanni da Carignano, who compiled from their replies a treatise on the government, customs, and religious practices of Ethiopia.

Carignano's treatise has not survived; but a summary of it was included in the *Supplementum Chronicarum* of Jacopo Filippo Foresti of Bergamo, published at Venice in 1483, and from Foresti's abstract we can see that Carignano was the first writer, so far as we know, to place Prester John in Ethiopia. This is the relevant passage:

"A certain priest [Carignano], the rector of St. Mark in Genoa, a truly excellent man, published a treatise, which he also called a 'map.' Among many things written in it about the state of this nation [Ethiopia] he reports that Prester John is set over that people as patriarch; and he says that under him are 127 archbishoprics, each of which has twenty bishops. Those who are to be reborn they baptize in the Roman manner, In the name of the Father and the Son and the Holy Spirit; and in the same way they celebrate the Sacrament of the Eucharist, with this one exception, that they sing the Paternoster before the elevation of the Sacrament. . . . It is said that their emperor is most Christian, to whom seventy-four kings and almost innumerable princes pay allegiance, except those kings who observe the laws of Mahomet but submit to the emperor in other things."

The next document in the record of Prester John's transplantation to Ethiopia is the *Mirabilia Descripta* of a Dominican missionary from France, Jordanus of Sévérac. Our knowledge of Friar Jordanus' life is sketchy, but it appears that he was born late in the thirteenth century, served for a time in the Catholic missions in Persia, and, about 1320 or 1321, set out by sea from Persia to China in the company of several other missionaries, both Dominican and Franciscan. Their plan was to attach themselves to the Cathayan archdiocese presided over by John of Monte Corvino, after making a short visit to India. Though their ship had been supposed to carry them to the port of Quilon, on India's southern tip, it was driven instead by storm to Tana, far up the coast near Bombay; here Jordanus briefly separated from his companions to pay a call on a Nestorian community, and when he returned to Tana he discovered the others had been martyred by Moslem fanatics. With the aid of a young Genoese whom he found in Tana he regained the bodies of his colleagues and gave them a proper burial; then, making his way with great difficulty to Quilon, he maintained a one-man mission there for some years, eventually being named a bishop by Pope John XXII. In the early 1330s Jordanus returned to Europe, and the course of his life thereafter is unknown to us.

His adventures in the Orient yielded three works: two letters to the missionaries in Persia, one dated 1321 and the other 1324, which describe his Asian travels and hardships, and the *Mirabilia,* or *Book of Wonders,* a brief but comprehensive geographical treatise on the lands he visited. In this he shows himself to be a careful observer and a discerning, ungullible reporter; his account of India in the fourteenth century is probably the most accurate we have. The *Mirabilia* also includes some sections on regions Jordanus knew only by secondhand report, and here he is more willing to admit marvels and prodigies to the record in the style of Odoric, although he is at least at pains to point out that he is working from hearsay. One such section deals with India Tertia, "the Third India," by which Friar Jordanus seems to have meant eastern Africa south of Ethiopia:

"Of India Tertia I will say this, that I have not indeed seen its many marvels, not having been there, but have heard them from trustworthy persons. For example, there be dragons in the greatest abundance, which carry on their heads the lustrous stones which be carbuncles. These animals have their lying-place upon golden sands, and grow exceeding big, and cast forth from the mouth a most fetid and infectious breath, like the thickest smoke rising from fire. These animals come together at the destined time, develop wings, and begin to raise themselves in the air, and then, by the judgment of God, being too heavy, they drop into a certain river which issues from Paradise, and perish there.

"But all the regions round about watch for the time of the dragons, and when they see one that has fallen, they wait for seventy days, and then go down and find the bare bones of the dragon, and take the carbuncle which is rooted in the top of his head, and carry it to the emperor of the Ethiopians, whom you call Prester John."

Whom you call Prester John. The choice of words is interesting. Friar Jordanus seems to be saying that the Ethiopian emperor corresponds in salient details to the monarch known in Europe as Prester

John, but that Prester John is not his true name or title. Of course, one may argue that Jordanus is no more to be taken seriously on the subject of Prester John than he is on that of fire-breathing dragons, or on the unicorns and elephant-lifting birds that he describes a few lines farther on. Yet we know from his letters to the Persian missionaries that he had learned something of Ethiopia from Latin merchants he met in India, and that he hoped to go there one day and preach the Gospel, for "the way is now open to Ethiopia." And in the *Mirabilia* he offers this account of Ethiopia and its king, which, inflated and mythologizing though it is, points to a Prester John of genuine substance for once:

"Of Ethiopia, I say that it is a very great land, and very hot. There are many monsters there, such as gryphons that guard the golden mountains which be there. Here, too, be serpents and other venomous beasts, of vast size and venomous exceedingly.

"There, too, are very many precious stones. The lord of that land I believe to be more potent than any man in the world, and richer in gold and silver and in precious stones. He is said to have under him fifty-two kings, rich and potent. He ruleth over all his neighbors towards the south and the west. In this Ethiopia are two burning mountains, and between them a mountain of gold. The people of the country are all Christians, but heretics. I have seen and known many folk from those parts.

"To that emperor the Sultan of Babylon giveth every year 500,000 ducats of tribute as 'tis said. I can tell nothing more of Ethiopia, not having been there."

The *Mirabilia* was probably written between 1330 and 1340. A decade or two later a Spanish Franciscan friar produced a somewhat similar work which shows how pervasive the idea of an Ethiopian Prester John was becoming. This was *The Book of the Knowledge of All the Kingdoms, Lands, and Lordships That Are in the World*, known to us in three manuscript versions in Madrid. Its author, whose name is unknown, claimed to have visited every part of the world, and his book is written, like Mandeville's, in the first person. Some scholars think that the text is entirely a compilation of other works, but others believe that the friar did indeed travel widely, though not quite as widely as he claims. Some of his geographical information is jumbled and incomprehensible; much, particularly concerning western and central Africa, is remarkably accurate for his day. (The latest date mentioned in the book is 1348.) If he did borrow from others, we are not in a position to name his sources, as we can do in the case of Mandeville; either the friar journeyed himself to Africa and India, or he spoke with obscure and forgotten Spanish and Italian explorers who have left us no accounts of their own of their voyages. Certainly he had access to unusually detailed information about regions that in his time Europeans had only just begun to visit: the Canary Islands and the Azores, the coasts of Africa, the Gulf of Guinea, Sierra Leone, the Sudan. He seems even to have had reliable word of the western Pacific, for concerning the ocean east of China he says it is "full of reefs and islands, and to the eastward there is no news of any lands, only waters as in the western sea." The kingdom of Prester John he explicitly locates in Africa. His description of it follows his account of Egypt and adjoining countries. After discussing a populous realm of black idolaters that he calls Amenuan, he tells of crossing a great river called the Euphrates—not to be confused with the Mesopotamian Euphrates—and coming to "a great city called Graciona which is the head of the empire of Abdeselib, a word meaning 'Servant of the Cross.' The Abdeselib is a defender of the church of Nubia and Ethiopia, and he defends Preste Juan who is Patriarch of Nubia and Abyssinia, and rules over very great lands and many cities of Christians. But they are Negroes as to their skins and burn the sign of the cross with fire in recognition of baptism. But although these men are Negroes, they are still men of intelligence with good brains, and they have understanding and knowledge."

From the land of these black vassals of Prester John, the friar declares, he "traveled over many lands and through many cities" until he arrived at last at Malsa, Prester John's own capital. "From the time I came to Malsa," the friar says, "I saw and heard marvelous things every day. I inquired what the terrestrial paradise was like, and wise men told me it consisted of mountains so high that they came near the circuit of the moon. No man has been able to see it all, for of twenty men who went, not more than three ever saw it, and that they had never heard tell of any man who had ascended the mountains. . . . They further told me that these mountains were surrounded by very deep seas, and that from the water of those seas come four rivers which are the largest in the world. They call them Tigris, Eufrates, Gion, and Ficxion. These four rivers irrigate all Nubia and Ethiopia. The waters which descend by these rivers make so great a noise that it can be heard at a distance of two days' journey. All the men who live near it are deaf, and cannot hear each other owing to the great noise of the waters. . . . They told me many other secrets of the stars both as regards judgments and magical virtues, also concerning herbs, plants, and minerals, and I saw several marvelous things." The most complete of the three manuscripts provides a drawing of Prester John's royal standard: a white flag bearing a black cross between two shepherds' crooks.

2

While the locale of Prester John's realm was shifting from Asia to Africa, the Catholic outpost in China established by John of Monte Corvino was entering its final decades of existence. The Mongol dynasty was collapsing, and when it fell, the period of Asian stability that had allowed missionaries and merchants to penetrate the farthest Orient would come to its end.

Timur Khan, Kublai's grandson and successor, who had encouraged the growth of John of Monte Corvino's mission in China, died in 1307, and in the following quarter of a century six Mongol emperors came and went. The blood of Genghis Khan was running thin, and this new breed of Sinicized Mongols, unfamiliar with the hard disciplines of the steppes, was a race of short-lived weaklings. Fevers and drunkenness carried them off. Chaos grew. Famine engulfed whole provinces; the currency became worthless; the Chinese frequently rebelled against their masters, and harried Mongol armies rushed to and fro in the vast realm in hopeless attempts at suppressing the uprisings. John of Monte Corvino labored on through this time of gathering chaos, aided by such friars as Odoric of Pordenone who came out from Europe to join him. The Archbishop of Cambaluc achieved a notable triumph one year when the emperor of the moment knelt before him to kiss the cross; but no wholesale conversion of the Mongols to Christianity followed, for soon that emperor was dead and the new one had no interest in the tenets the friars preached. Archbishop John himself died about 1328, and the Latin community in China began to disintegrate. For some years there was no archbishop there. Pope John XXII named a successor to John of Monte Corvino in 1333, but the archbishop-designate never reached Cathay, and in 1338 a delegation of sixteen Mongol Christians arrived in Avignon to petition the Pope for another legate. This time Pope Benedict XII chose a Franciscan, John de' Marignolli, to head a four-man mission.

Marignolli was a Florentine aristocrat, a member of an influential noble family. His eastward journey commenced at Naples, where the four papal envoys joined the Mongol ambassadors for the voyage from Italy to Constantinople; from the Byzantine capital he traveled overland to China, arriving finally at Khan-baliq in the spring of 1342. The Mongol emperor received Marignolli warmly, and for nearly four years he headed the Latin mission at the capital, converting a good many of the great khan's subjects and even staging Christian ceremonies within the imperial palace—which was next door to the cathedral—for the enlightenment of the emperor. About 1347 Marignolli left Khan-baliq for southern China, going thence to India for a visit to the shrine of St. Thomas, and returning to Europe by way of Ceylon, Persia, Syria, and Palestine. By 1353 he was back in Avignon to ask the Pope for an additional complement of priests for China, which had been requested by the great khan himself.

John de' Marignolli wrote an account of his Eastern travels which, in the words of his nineteenth-century translator Henry Yule, is to be found, "like unexpected fossils in a mud-bank, imbedded in a Chronicle of Bohemia" that he composed about 1355. This lengthy interpolation enters the chronicle on the flimsiest of pretenses: Marignolli chooses to begin his history of Bohemia with the Creation and the expulsion of Adam and Eve from Eden, and, having got as far as the statement that Eden is located "beyond India," is reminded that he himself once visited India, which leads him to say, "And now to insert some brief passages of what I have seen myself . . ." An anecdotal description of the Orient that runs to more than fifty printed pages follows. Marignolli tells of the route he took eastward, speaks of the opulence of the Mongol capital, discusses the things he saw in India, and, launching into a lengthy essay on the terrestrial paradise and the four rivers that flow from it, remarks that the river "Gyon" is "that which circleth the land of Ethiopia where are now the Negroes, and which is called the Land of Prester John. It is indeed believed to be the Nile, which descends into Egypt by a breach made in the place which is called Abasty. The Christians of St. Matthew the Apostle are there, and the Sultan pays them tribute on account of the river, because they have it in their power to shut off the water, and then Egypt would perish."

The tenor of Marignolli's phrase—"Ethiopia . . . which is called the Land of Prester John"—indicates that the process of transplantation was now complete; Europeans had come to look upon Ethiopia, and not the Central Asian steppes, as Prester John's habitat. No longer would he be sought in Asia. There would, in any case, be little further opportunity to seek him there, for the end of the Mongol empire was at hand. By 1356 a rebellious army of Chinese had captured Nanking and was rapidly pushing the Mongols northward; a steady retreat toward the Great Wall marked the last years of Mongol rule. They were driven from Khan-baliq—Peking, now—in 1368, and two years later the last Mongol emperor died at Genghis' old capital of Karakorum. A year later the Mongols were chased entirely out of China; the panicky descendants of the warriors of Genghis fled like sheep before the onrushing Chinese armies. For the first time in hundreds of years, all of China came under the rule of a man of Chinese birth, as the general of the rebels mounted the throne to proclaim the establishment of the new Ming Dynasty. Centuries of pent-up grievance exploded in a blazing hatred for all things foreign. The Catholic missionaries were expelled, as were all merchants doing business in China. The caravan routes linking East and West were closed. The eastern half of Asia disappeared behind a bamboo curtain, and not for two centuries would Europeans again be able to enter it. Popes continued to designate Archbishops of Cambaluc until 1426, but not one ever reached his see. Had Prester John not turned out to be an Ethiopian after all, it would have been impossible to make contact with him.

3

Ethiopia, where the quest for Prester John would be centered from the middle of the fourteenth century onward, was then and remains one of the most extraordinary and complex nations of Africa: a Christian land whose royal dynasty claims to trace its ancestry to King Solomon, and whose inhabitants are a proud, cultured, and vigorous people, a curious and fascinating mixture of barbarism and sophistication.

Bounded on one side by a burning desert and on the other by steaming tropical lowland jungles, Ethiopia stands on a lofty plateau, six to seven thousand feet above sea level; its climate is relatively cool and pleasant, and there is ample rainfall to stimulate agriculture. These natural advantages allowed a fairly advanced civilization to develop there at an early date. The nature of the plateau, however, kept the Ethiopians isolated. Mountains nearly three miles high in places border their territory, making it almost inaccessible from the outside. The center of the plateau slopes inward to form a basin, across which many strong rivers have cut deep channels, breaking it up into districts separated by plunging gorges that all but prevent communication. Cut off from the rich civilization of Egypt by the Nubian Desert, Ethiopia in ancient times was able to make contact with her neighbors only by way of her ports on the Red Sea. These harbors served as export stations for the gold, ivory, and spices of inland Africa—and the same commerce brought ideas and travelers from without.

The original Ethiopian population belonged to the racial stock sometimes called "Hamitic"—people who have brown skin, dark crinkly hair, lean, muscular bodies, thin lips, and sharp, straight noses. This racial group still is dominant in Ethiopia. But through the Red Sea ports several thousand years ago came Arab tribesmen from Yemen, who gradually occupied the northern highlands. One of these Arab tribes was known as the Habashat, which caused neighboring countries to call the land where they settled "Habesh." From this is derived "Abyssinia," the name by which the plateau has been known to outsiders. (The Ethiopians themselves prefer not to have their country named for a tribe of Arab invaders, and invariably speak of it as "Ethiopia," a name derived from Ethiops, the Greek form of the name of Noah's grandson Cush, from whom they believe they are descended.)

The Arabs, conquering and intermarrying with the native Hamitic population, imposed their language on the plateau: Ge'ez, a Semitic tongue akin to Hebrew and Arabic. This has long since given way to a dialect known as Amharic, which is the main language of Ethiopia today, but Ge'ez remains the classical literary and liturgical language, as Latin is for the Roman Catholic world. In the first century A.D. these mixed Hamitic and Semitic people founded a kingdom known by the name of its capital, Axum, the nucleus of the future Ethiopian empire. The Axumites were almost certainly pagan, but through a retroactive adjustment of history the Ethiopians came to assert that they were of the Jewish faith during this time.

According to a cherished Ethiopian legend, the Queen of Sheba who visited King Solomon in Jerusalem was actually Makeda, the Queen of Ethiopia. Learning of the magnificence of Solomon's kingdom and of the wisdom of Solomon himself, the queen set forth with a great caravan laden with gifts—"with camels that bore spices, and very much gold, and precious stones," the Bible declares. Impressed by the splendor of Solomon, the queen submitted to his embrace, and when she returned to her own land she bore a son named Menelik, who after some years was sent to Jerusalem to be anointed by his father. King Solomon instructed Menelik in Judaism and proclaimed that he and his heirs should be rulers of Ethiopia forever; when the young man went back to Ethiopia, he succeeded in carrying the Ark of the Covenant off with him, and deposited it in his mother's capital. Upon the death of the queen, in 986 B.C., Menelik became Ethiopia's king and converted his nation to the Jewish faith.

This legendary history of Ethiopia maintains that the kingdom practiced Judaism for thirteen hundred years, until about A.D. 300, when Christian missionaries arrived. We know in fact that the Ethiopian royal dynasty is not descended from King Solomon and that the Ethiopians were not Jews before they became Christians; but yet there are many Jewish elements in Ethiopian Christian practice. Ethiopians follow the laws of Moses on such matters as circumcision, the eating of "unclean" meat (that of animals which do not chew the cud and have cloven hooves), the Saturday Sabbath, and the sacramental impurity of those who have recently had sexual intercourse. The Ethiopian words for hell, idol, purification, and alms are of Hebrew origin. But it appears that all these Judaic elements came into Ethiopia from Arabia—then a center of Jewish life—early in the Christian Era, and do not indicate an Ethiopian allegiance to Judaism going back to the time of the Solomonic monarchy.

In any event, the Axumite kingdom by the beginning of the fourth century A.D. was a sturdy entity with a highly developed social organization, sophisticated architecture and art, and a system of writing, and for a few generations it functioned as a major international power, establishing control over the Red Sea, Arabia, and Nubia. The king known as Ella-'Amida, whose reign ended about the year 325, even dared to seize a number of Roman ships in reprisal for an attack on one of his North African vassals by the troops of Constantine the Great. Ezana, Ella-'Amida's son and successor, brought the Axumite empire to the peak of its greatness, subduing and assimilating the minor barbarian tribes of Ethiopia, encouraging the growth of commerce and the arts, furthering literacy, and commemorating his achievements in a series of monumental structures still capable of inspiring awe.

It was King Ezana who led Ethiopia to Christianity. There is an apocryphal European tradition to the effect that the Ethiopians were converted by St. Matthew, just as the Indians were by St. Thomas, but this appears to have no basis in fact. More reliable is the story told by an Italian ecclesiastical historian of the fourth century, Rufinus, and confirmed in its essential details by an independent Ethiopian version. Rufinus wrote that about the year 300 one Meropius, a philosopher of Tyre, embarked on a voyage to India "in order to view places and see the world." With him he took two small boys, Frumentius and Aedesius, who were of his family and whose education he had undertaken. On the voyage homeward from India the ship bearing Meropius and the boys put in for water and provisions at an Ethiopian port; but anti-Roman feelings were so strong then in Ethiopia that the natives put to death the philosopher and everyone else on board, save only the two boys, who, Rufinus said, "were found studying under a tree and preparing their lessons, and, preserved by the mercy of the barbarians, were taken to the king. He made one of them, Aedesius, his cupbearer. Frumentius, whom he had perceived to be sagacious and prudent, he made his treasurer and secretary. Thereafter they were held in great honor and affection by the king." The king—evidently Ella-'Amida—died, leaving the child Ezana as his heir, and the queen "besought them with tears, since she had no more faithful subjects in the whole kingdom, to share with her the cares of governing the kingdom until her son should grow up, especially Frumentius, whose ability was equal to guiding the kingdom—for the other, though loyal and honest of heart, was simple. While they lived there and Frumentius held the reins of government in his hands, God stirred up his heart and he began to search out with care those of the Roman merchants who were Christians and to give them great influence. . . ." Thus Frumentius nurtured Christianity in Ethiopia, founding churches and arousing the young king's sympathies. When Ezana had reached manhood, Frumentius and Aedesius sought his permission to leave the kingdom; Aedesius returned to Tyre, but Frumentius went to Alexandria, where the Christian patriarch consecrated him a bishop and sent him back to Ethiopia. "And when he had arrived in India [Ethiopia] as bishop," Rufinus concludes, "such grace is said to have been given him by God that apostolic miracles were wrought by him and a

countless number of barbarians were converted by him to the faith.
. . . These facts I know not from vulgar report but from the mouth of
Aedesius himself, who had been Frumentius' companion and was later
made a priest in Tyre."

The coinage of Ezana's reign indicates that he accepted Christianity himself and made it the official religion of the realm, for his early
coins bear pagan emblems and the later ones show the cross. Greek
was the original language of the Ethiopian Church, later supplanted by
Ge'ez. Because of Ethiopia's geographic isolation, the doctrines of Ethiopian Christianity rapidly diverged from those held by the Church in
the Roman Empire, and grew further apart with the passing of time.
Ethiopian religious practice was dominated neither by Rome nor by
Constantinople, but by Alexandria, whose Coptic Christian patriarch
held from earliest Christian times the privilege of appointing the *abuna*,
the Ethiopian chief primate. In doctrinal matters Ethiopia was also
under the authority of Coptic Egypt: since Alexandria was a stronghold of the Monophysite belief in the single divine nature of Christ,
Ethiopia likewise adhered to Monophysitism, remaining loyal to that
teaching after its condemnation in the fifth century by the Roman and
Byzantine branches of the Church. In ritual, calendar, and customs,
the Ethiopian Church also generally follows the Coptic; however, as
we have seen, certain Judaic features such as circumcision have been
preserved in Ethiopian Christianity, and the unique Ethiopian liturgical style, marked by vigorous dancing, chanting, and the beating of
drums, appears to owe much to ancient pagan practice.

Byzantine writers testify to the continued power of Axumite
Ethiopia in the fifth and sixth centuries. Ethiopian ambassadors were
in attendance at the courts of Constantinople, Persia, India, and Ceylon. Ethiopian caravans spanned the desert routes to Egypt and went
up from Yemen across Arabia to Mesopotamia; Ethiopian vessels were
active in the Red Sea. Kosmas Indicopleustes, who visited Ethiopia
about 525, set down a vivid account of the great expeditions of traders
sent from the Axumite capital every other year to the Ethiopian interior to bargain for gold, offering the primitive natives salt, iron, and
cattle in return. Kosmas also told of the king's palace at Axum, with
four great towers topped by four statues of unicorns, and marveled at
the tame elephants and giraffes in the palace courtyard. During his
visit he witnessed the mustering of a vast Ethiopian army under King
Ellesbaas, a champion of Christianity who was about to invade the

Yemenite kingdom of Himyar in order to end the persecution there of Christians by Jewish kings. Another Byzantine visitor to Ethiopia during the reign of Ellesbaas was one Julian, an ambassador sent by the Emperor Justinian to negotiate trade arrangements that would link India to Byzantium by way of Ethiopia's Red Sea ports. The scheme failed, but the ambassador did return with a remarkable description of the splendor of the Axumite court. The king, he reported, was clad in a linen loincloth embroidered with gold and a short cloak bedecked with pearls and precious stones; he wore a turban of linen interwoven with gold, golden bracelets, and a golden necklace. He was seated in a gold-plated chariot drawn by four elephants, and carried two gilded spears and a gilded shield. About him stood his courtiers, arrayed nearly as opulently.

The expansion of Persia in the latter half of the sixth century began the process of Axum's downfall. The Persians, entering by way of Aden, took control of southern Arabia and bottled up the Ethiopian shipping operating out of the ports on the opposite coast of the Red Sea. With her mercantile fleet thus crippled, Ethiopia attempted to extend her land routes to Egypt and beyond, into the other Byzantine provinces of the eastern Mediterranean world. But this was complicated by the rise of militaristic Islam. Arab armies stripped Byzantium of Egypt, Palestine, and Syria in the first half of the seventh century, cutting Ethiopia off from the rest of the Christian world. Relations between the Ethiopians and the Arabs were friendly at first; Mohammed himself had unusual respect for the Axumites, telling his followers, "If you go into Abyssinia, you will find there a king under whom no man is persecuted. It is a land of justice, where God will bring you rest from your afflictions." He said that God had enjoined the Moslems never to enter into any sort of strife with the Ethiopians, "for it has fallen to them to receive nine-tenths of the courage of mankind." But then Ethiopian pirates, with the tacit blessing of Axum, began raiding the towns on the Arabian side of the Red Sea, the raids reaching a climax with a heavy assault in 702 on Jidda, the port of Mecca. A prophecy had begun to circulate that the Ethiopians would sack Mecca itself and destroy the sacred black stone, the Ka'aba. Thus threatened, the Arabs occupied the Ethiopian coast in the early eighth century and put an end to the piracies. Stripped of her ports, Ethiopia became a desolate landlocked realm, wholly isolated from the civilized world, forced back entirely on her inner resources. The days of splendor now were over. Yet the old prophecy continued to give hope to Christians and alarm to Moslems: one day, it was said, the Emperor of Ethiopia would lead forth his armies and capture Mecca, and then, joining forces with the Emperor of Rome, he would drive Islam from the world. These apocalyptic predictions can be found in Byzantine literature of the seventh and eighth centuries, and in two later works ascribed to a pair of Coptic monks, Pisentios of Thebes and Samuel of Qalamun. Quite possibly this dream of deliverance at the hands of the Christian monarch of Ethiopia was one of the fantasies out of which the twelfth-century legend of Prester John was born.

4

During her first two centuries of isolation Ethiopia turned her attention southward, into the fertile but undeveloped pagan lands beyond the central plateau, which now underwent full assimilation into Ethiopian life. At the same time northern Ethiopia, the original Axumite heartland, came under severe pressure from warlike tribes entering out of southern Egypt. The effect of this was a general shift of power; in the late ninth century the old capital city of Axum was abandoned as the seat of government, and the southern districts emerged as the dominant sectors of the new Ethiopia. Late in the tenth century Ethiopia was disrupted by an uprising of the Agous, an indigenous pagan people of the central highlands, and this led to a prolonged period of internal chaos that resulted finally, in the middle of the twelfth century, in the downfall of the long-established royal dynasty. The new rulers, though Christian in religion and Semitic in language and culture, were of Agou stock and made their capital in the lofty, almost inaccessible Lasta Mountains, an Agou stronghold. Like the kings they had displaced, they claimed Israelite descent, but traced their ancestry to Moses rather than to Solomon.

These kings, regarded as usurpers in many parts of Ethiopia, seem to have taken pains to establish their legitimacy by gaining the blessing of foreign ecclesiastical authorities. It was one of the early kings of this line who sought an Ethiopian church in Jerusalem and who may have wished to transfer Ethiopia's religious allegiance from the Patriarch of Alexandria to the Pope; Pope Alexander III's letter of 1177 to Prester John, and the diplomatic mission to Prester John headed by the Pope's physician Master Philip, evidently were responses to these moves. No link with Rome was forged, though, and the traditional appointment of Coptic Egyptians as heads of the Ethiopian Church continued.

The usurping dynasty was overthrown about 1270 by a prince of the Solomonic line, leaving behind one enduring heritage: the astounding group of rock-hewn monumental churches built early in the thirteenth century by Lalibela, the most celebrated king of the dynasty, at the city that now bears his name. With the restoration of the Solomonic dynasty a period of consolidation and rebuilding began; much Ethiopian territory had been whittled away by the Arabs on the one hand and the pagans on the other, and the remainder of the country had become a cluster of tiny quasi-independent principalities. One Moslem writer of the period speaks of ninety-nine kings ruled by the Ethiopian emperor, which would be an impressive figure if one did not know how small the region was into which those ninety-nine kings and their emperor were packed. But a series of strong rulers restored order within Ethiopia and limited the power of the Islamic kingdoms that had become established on her borders. At the same time an artistic, literary, and religious renaissance began, and the Ethiopians devoted much effort to compilations—largely of an apocryphal nature—of their own early history.

Conflict with Egypt, where the Moslem rulers were persecuting Coptic Christians and destroying their churches, was frequent in this period. King 'Amda-Seyon (1314–44) put a temporary halt to this by reviving a threat that the Ethiopians had made to Egypt several times in previous centuries: that he would cut off the flow of the Nile, which is fed by the rivers of Ethiopia, and turn Egypt into a desert. As we have seen, reference to this incident found its way into the narrative of John de' Marignolli. It appears also in an inverted form in the journal of Simon Sigoli, a Florentine who visited Egypt and the Holy Land in 1384: "'Tis true that this sultan [of Egypt] is obliged to pay a yearly ransom or homage to Prester John. Now this potentate Prester John dwells in India, and is a Christian, and possesses many cities both of Christians and of infidels. And the reason why the sultan pays him homage is this, that whenever this Prester John chooses to open certain river sluices he can drown Cairo and Alexandria and all that country; and 'tis said that this river is the Nile itself which runs by Cairo. The said sluices stand but little open, and yet the river is enormous. And so it is for this reason, or rather from this apprehension, that the sultan sends him every year a ball of gold with a cross upon it, worth three thousand gold bezants. And the lands of the soldan do march with [that is, adjoin] those of this Prester John." It can be seen from this passage that Ethiopia was still considered a limb of India by Europeans of the late fourteenth century.

'Amda-Seyon did not actually interfere with the flow of the Nile, but he and his successors were able to end the persecution of the Copts and establish friendly relations with the Egyptian government. After a long period of hostility the caravan routes linking Ethiopia and Egypt were reopened, and contact between Ethiopia and the Mediterranean world by way of Alexandria again became possible. Thus we find Europeans visiting Ethiopia in the fourteenth century for the first time in seven or eight hundred years.

We know very little about the beginnings of this tourism. Merchants of Genoa and Venice maintained warehouses in Alexandria from the late thirteenth century onward, and some of the Genoese certainly ventured as far south as Dongola, the great emporium on the Nile in what is now the Sudan. Probably a few of them went on up the Nile into Ethiopia, but we have no direct evidence of this, only a secondhand account of a Venetian named Bragadino who claimed to have reached Ethiopia in the middle of the fourteenth century; he said it was ruled by a king he called "Prete Jane." It was long believed that eight Dominican missionaries had entered Ethiopia in 1316 and had made a number of converts to Catholicism, even enrolling some Ethiopians in their own monastic order; but recent historical research has shown that this enterprise did not in fact take place. In 1391 a Spanish priest announced to King John I of Aragon that he had lately spent several years at the court of Prester John in Ethiopia, and from what little is known of this story, it seems to have been true. A few years later a Florentine named Antonio Bartoli visited Ethiopia; when he returned to Italy in 1402 he was accompanied by a group of Ethiopian envoys. Another Italian saw them in Rome in 1404 and wrote of meeting them—"black Ethiopians, of India, good Christians."

A young Italian traveler, Pietro Rombulo, arrived in Ethiopa in 1407; his motive for making the journey appears to have been neither commercial nor religious, but one of curiosity alone. He settled there and enrolled in the service of King Yeshak (1414–29), whom he persuaded to seek an alliance with a European prince against Islam. In

1428, King Alfonso the Magnanimous of Aragon received two Ethiopian ambassadors at his court in Valencia, bearing a letter from Yeshak in which the Ethiopian monarch proposed not merely an alliance but a double royal marriage, with Alfonso's son to marry an Ethiopian princess. Alfonso sidestepped the marriage proposal, but he did send thirteen of his subjects to Ethiopia, including some artisans whom Yeshak had requested to decorate one of his palaces. All, however, perished en route.

The remarkable exploits of Nicolò de' Conti were being performed during this period. Conti, a Venetian of noble family, settled in Damascus about 1416 as a merchant. After acquiring a fluency in Arabic, the young man began an amazing series of journeys: across the Arabian Desert to the valley of the Euphrates, then through southern Mesopotamia to Baghdad, and by riverboat down the Tigris to Basrah on the Persian Gulf; then a long stay in Persia, followed by a voyage to India, where he lived for many years. He traveled through most parts of India, making a special point of visiting the shrine of St. Thomas at Mylapur. Then, accompanied by the wife he had acquired in India, he moved onward to the East Indies, spending a year in Sumatra. His next port of call lay in the Ganges Delta, after which he penetrated Burma as far as Mandalay, toured the Malayan Peninsula, and visited Java. After further adventures in Southeast Asia—four children now traveled with him—Conti returned to India by way of Ceylon, and after a tour of Malabar he began a leisurely journey back to Europe, some twenty years since his departure. On his way up the Red Sea he visited the coast of Ethiopia—the Ethiopians had by now regained their harbors from the Arabs—but did not enter the interior of that country. He called also at Aden and Jidda and traversed the Holy Land in 1436 and 1437, reaching his native Venice several years later.

Conti was nearly at the end of his wanderings in 1436 when, while staying at the Monastery of St. Catherine on Mount Sinai, he encountered a Spanish traveler named Pero Tafur, who was eager to hear all his tales of the wonders of the Orient. Tafur, a Castilian from Andalusia, had gone first to Italy, then to Palestine as a pilgrim touring the Christian shrines, then to Cyprus, where the king chose him as an ambassador to the Sultan of Egypt. Following an extensive sightseeing tour on the Nile, Tafur set out from Cairo to Mount Sinai. On his fourth day as a guest at the monastery Tafur suddenly conceived a desire to go to India, which he thought to be the land of Prester John.

While visiting Egypt Tafur had learned that the Patriarch of Alexandria has the privilege of naming the head of the Church in Prester John's land, for at that time the patriarch had just chosen a new *abuna* for Ethiopia and dispatched him thither; but what Tafur had not managed to find out, apparently, was that Prester John did not live in the true India, merely in Ethiopia, which was close at hand up the Nile.

Tafur conferred with the prior of the monastery about the feasibility of a journey to India. "He told me," Tafur wrote, "that a caravan, which was the means of communication with those parts, was due to arrive within two or three days, and that we could then obtain information as to the possibility of making the journey, but that he was altogether opposed to it. In four or five days the caravan duly arrived, bringing so many camels with it that I cannot give an account of them, as I do not wish to appear to speak extravagantly. This caravan carries all the spices, pearls, precious stones and gold, perfumes, and linen, and parrots, and cats from India, with many other things, which they distribute throughout the world." It was, actually, the regular caravan from Mecca, bearing merchandise from India for sale in Syria and Egypt. Tafur went out to meet the caravan, "and I found that a Venetian had come with it, called Nicolò de' Conti, a gentleman of good birth who brought with him his wife and two sons and a daughter, all of whom had been born in India. It appeared that he and they had become Moors, having been forced to renounce their faith in Mecca, which is the Moors' holy place."

Tafur and Conti struck up an immediate friendship, and soon Tafur—having heard a quick summary of the Venetian's decades of travel in Asia—was telling Conti of his intention to go to India. Conti, not realizing that what Tafur meant by India was only Prester John's nearby country of Ethiopia, replied that he hoped Tafur would not embark on "such madness, for the way is very long and troublesome and perilous; the country is inhabited by strange races without king or laws or rulers; how can you expect to pass without a safe-conduct, and whom shall he fear who is minded to kill you? Further, the air is strange, and food and drink are different from those in your country. You will meet with bestial people, unable to govern themselves, and although there are monstrous things to be seen they are not enough to give you satisfaction. You will see heaps of gold and pearls and precious stones, but what shall they profit you since the people are beasts who wear them?"

Such talk swiftly discouraged Tafur, and he gave up the project forthwith. He and Conti departed from Mount Sinai to go back to Cairo, where Conti obtained a position as an interpreter at the sultan's court and Tafur made final arrangements for his return to Europe. During the fortnight-long journey from Sinai to Cairo, Tafur drew from Conti a long account of his adventures, questioning the Venetian particularly on the subject of Prester John. Much of what Conti told him was incorporated in Tafur's account of his own travels. It is apparent that Tafur never did grasp the geographical distinction between Ethiopia and India, which was clear to Conti, who had visited both lands. For example, he quotes Conti as saying, "When I arrived in India I was taken to see Prester John, who received me very graciously and showed me many favors, and married me to the woman I now have with me, and she bore me these children." It was in the true India that Conti did meet his wife, if not Prester John. Yet in another passage Conti is made to speak of the Nile as flowing through Prester John's realm. The confusion is Tafur's, not Conti's; the Spaniard's head must have been so stuffed with fables about Prester John of India that he was incapable of getting straight what Conti told him, and, writing from memory several years later, made a piquant hash out of Conti's authentic tales of India and his own fantasies of Prester John.

According to Conti, Tafur says, Prester John "had twenty-five kings in his service, although they were not great rulers, and . . . many people who live without law, but follow heathen rites, are in subjection to him. They say that there is in India a very high mountain, the ascent of which is exceedingly difficult, so much so that in ancient times those below knew nothing about those above, and those above had no knowledge of those below, and a road was made, and a chain was stretched from the top to the bottom, to which those who ascended or descended could cling. On the top of the mountain is a great plain where they sow and reap corn, and keep cattle and grain, and where there are many orchards full of fruit, and much water; all things, in short, necessary to the life of man. On one side is a very notable monastery, to which it is the custom for those of fit rank to be Prester to send twelve ancient men, nobles by descent, and virtuous, to elect a new Prester John when the office is vacant, and they do it in this manner. The chief sons and daughters are sent there to serve, and they marry one with another and raise up children, and they provide there all that is necessary for their existence, and give them horses and arms, and bows and arrows, and they teach them warlike arts, and the art of governing men. The electors who are there take counsel daily, and observe that one which appears to them most fit to succeed to the government when Prester John vacates it, and are already agreed as to the person to be chosen. When the ruler is at last dead, his knights, as the custom is, carry him to that mountain on a bier, covered in mourning, and the electors, beholding them from the heights where they are, take the one who has been chosen, and give him to the knights in exchange for the dead ruler. They then take up the body and bury it in the mountain, with the honors due to it, while the others go with their lord and, amidst great feasts and rejoicings, make their submission to him."

Among the wonders which Tafur claims Conti saw in Prester John's India was "a sea coast where the crabs, on reaching land, and being exposed to the air, turn to stone," and a place where certain men, "in order to leave behind them a reputation for strength, and that their sons may be known to be the sons of good men, make an apparatus like shears, and putting their heads between the blades they force them to shut with their feet, and so cut off their heads." Suicides of this kind actually were known in India; one such incident is described by Friar Jordanus and another by the fourteenth-century Arab traveler Ibn Battuta. "Nicolò de' Conti told me also," Tafur goes on, "that he had seen people eating human flesh, the strangest thing he had ever seen. This, be it understood, is a heathen practice, but he had seen Christians eating the raw flesh of animals, after which it is necessary to eat of a very odoriferous herb within fifteen to twenty days, but if they delay longer they become lepers." Raw steak, many shocked European travelers later were to report, is a favorite Ethiopian delicacy, although the part about the odoriferous herb appears to be an invention of Tafur's.

"I learnt also," writes Tafur, "that Prester John, desiring to know whence the Nile had its beginnings, prepared boats and sent men and provided much food, and ordered them to bring back news of its source, and they set out and saw so many strange countries and peoples and unfamiliar animals that it was a great marvel, but as they had eaten all their victuals they had to return without having found what they sought, and Prester John was much cast down. He then took counsel as to whether it was possible to send men who would not perish for lack of food, and he ordered them to take young children, and, depriving them of milk, he reared them on raw fish. . . . After these children were grown up he prepared boats and nets, and ordered that they were in no wise to return without certain information concerning that which they sought. They departed and journeyed up the river, through divers countries, but they communicated with no one for fear of being prevented, and they came to a great lake like the sea, and they followed the shore, and went all round it to find out whence the water came which made that lake. They came at last to an opening where the water entered, and they proceeded until they came to a great mountain range which was very lofty and precipitous, and which seemed to be hewn out of the rock, and the top of it could not be seen. In it was a great opening through which the water poured, and close to that mountain range, and joined to it, was another as high as the former, and it could well be seen that the water came from it. The travelers decided to send up one of their party to report, but he that ascended, so they say, having beheld what was within, refused to come down or even to answer questions. Another of the party was then sent up, but it was with him as with the first. When the others saw this, and that there was no possibility of obtaining more information, they left those two on the mountain, being unable to recover them, and returned by the way they had come. They related to their Master all that had befallen them, telling him that nothing further could be discovered, since it was clear that God did not desire that mortals should know more, and that He had therefore locked up the secret in that wise."

Tafur declares that Conti told him of "the preparations made by Prester John to come with his hosts to Jerusalem, which is much farther than the journey to Europe." For, Tafur reports, "Prester John and his people are said to be as good Catholics and Christians as could be found anywhere, but they are not in touch with, nor are they governed by, our Church of Rome." Yet the fabled prince showed a lively interest in Western affairs: "I learnt from Nicolò de' Conti that Prester John kept him continuously at his court, enquiring of him as to the Christian world, and concerning the princes and their estates, and the wars they were waging, and while he was there he saw Prester John on two occasions dispatch ambassadors to Christian princes, but he did not hear whether any news of them had been received."

5

The Prester John of Pero Tafur's book is an odd and elusive composite figure, existing simultaneously in Ethiopia and in India and in the never-never land of myth. The land of Prester John, as Conti describes it in Tafur's account, is clearly India; he speaks of elephants and howdahs, of the ceremonial burning of widows on their husbands' funeral pyre, and much else that he could have seen only in India. Yet there was certainly no Christian monarch on the Indian subcontinent in the fifteenth century who could have been the prototype of this Prester John, and it would not have been an Indian king who sent expeditions out to trace the Nile to its source. The transpositions and fusions of fact that Tafur employed in combining authentic Indian background and authentic (if secondhand) stories of the Ethiopian king into an image of Prester John are of the sort that produce enthralling fiction, but they make his work less useful as a documentary source.

About the time that Conti paid his brief call on Ethiopia, a vigorous new king was coming to power who perhaps served as the model for Tafur's Prester John. He was Zar'a Yakob ("Seed of Jacob"), a formidable warrior and reformer, who ruled from 1434 to 1468. He imposed Christianity by force on the pagan peoples of the Ethiopian borderlands, and organized a campaign to extinguish the last vestiges of paganism among his already Christian subjects. All Ethiopians were ordered to wear upon their foreheads amulets inscribed, "I belong to the Father, the Son, and the Holy Ghost," and upon their arms amulets which said, "I deny the devil in Christ the God," and "I deny Dasek the accursed. I am the servant of Mary, the mother of the Creator of the World." Those who refused were executed and their estates seized. A grand inquisitor, the Keeper of the Hour, headed a governmental department charged with the responsibility of detecting idolators. Zar'a Yakob codified and reorganized church practice, and crushed the heresy of "the Sons of Stephen," who would not kneel to the Virgin and the cross. Like many Ethiopian kings, he was adept in theology, and not only took part zealously in religious disputes but himself wrote several volumes dealing with fine points of the faith. In secular matters he was equally forceful, reconstituting the system of provincial governments and expanding Ethiopia southward until it attained much the same dimensions it has today.

One of his goals was to bring the Ethiopian Church into harmony with the Church of Rome. An ecumenical movement was then gathering strength in the Christian world, largely as a result of the efforts of Pope Eugenius IV. The Council of Constance (1414–18) had healed the schism in the Roman Catholic Church that had produced rival popes in Rome and Avignon; representatives of the Greek Orthodox and Ethiopian churches had been present at these sessions, though only in the capacity of private observers. Negotiations between the Greek and Roman churches had followed, culminating in the decree of union between the two churches that was proclaimed at the Council of Florence on July 6, 1439. (The Byzantines rejected the decree their emperor had negotiated, and it never became effective.) Pope Eugenius hoped also to bring about unions with the various Christian churches of the Near East and Asia, and later in the summer of 1439 he appointed a Franciscan friar, Alberto da Sarteano, as his commissioner for India proper, Ethiopia, Egypt, and Jerusalem. Fra Alberto was fluent in Greek and was familiar with the Near East, having made the pilgrimage to the Holy Land in 1436–37. As Fra Alberto prepared to set out again for the Eastern lands, the Pope provided him with a series of letters inviting various Oriental Christian potentates to affiliate their churches with that of Rome. One was addressed to the Coptic Patriarch of Alexandria; one was addressed to Emperor Prester John of the Ethiopians; and one was addressed to "Emperor Thomas of the Indians," a figure otherwise unknown to history, and evidently conjured up out of some distortion of the legends of St. Thomas. The papal letters to Prester John and Emperor Thomas were identical except for their salutations; each began with the phrase, "There has often reached us a constant rumor that Your Serenity and all who are subjects of your kingdom are true Christians."

Fra Alberto and several other friars departed from Venice early in 1440, going first to Jerusalem, where they conferred with Nicodemus, the abbot of the Ethiopian community in the Holy City. Fra Alberto explained the Pope's wishes for a union of all Christian churches, and, since Nicodemus was aware that this would be of interest to his sovereign Zar'a Yakob, the abbot sent word of the mission to Ethiopia at once. Meanwhile Fra Alberto proceeded to Egypt and met with the Coptic patriarch, as well as the Orthodox one. He intended to continue southward into Ethiopia, but the Sultan of Egypt, foreseeing the dangers for himself in a possible alliance between Christian Europe and Christian Ethiopia, refused to let the papal emissaries cross his territory. It therefore became necessary for Fra Alberto to dispatch one of his colleagues, Fra Tommaso Bellacci, on a dangerous roundabout route through Mesopotamia and the Persian Gulf in order to deliver Pope Eugenius' letter to Prester John. This adventure ended disastrously; Fra Tommaso fell into the hands of enemies of Christianity, endured several years of enslavement, and never reached Ethiopia. We do not have any idea what means Fra Alberto planned to employ for delivering the Pope's other letter, to Emperor Thomas of India, but we may be sure that this, too, failed to get to its addressee.

On the basis of what Abbot Nicodemus told him about Pope Eugenius and his ecumenical scheme, King Zar'a Yakob ordered the abbot to nominate two monks from the Ethiopian monastery at Jerusalem as delegates to the Council of Florence. The Ethiopian delegates sailed to Rhodes in October 1440, waiting there with Fra Alberto until the arrival of a Coptic delegation the following spring. In August 1441 the party of Italian friars, Egyptians, and Ethiopians reached Florence, and on September 2 the Ethiopians addressed the ecumenical conference. Later that year Zar'a Yakob's envoys signed a decree formally acknowledging the submission of the Coptic Church (including its Ethiopian branch) to the Church of Rome. But this agreement, so laboriously arrived at, went the way of the one two years earlier that had united the Greek and Roman churches: the Ethiopians, like the Byzantines, simply paid no attention to it, the Pope and his whole Church being as remote to them as the valleys of the moon, and the priests of Prester John's land continued to practice their rites heedless of the doctrines promulgated in Rome.

In 1450 another ambassador from Zar'a Yakob came to Europe. The only surviving account of his visit is the work of a Dominican monk named Pietro Ranzano, who encountered the Ethiopian emissary in Naples. Fra Pietro had expected to meet a dark-skinned man who spoke a strange language, and so he brought with him an interpreter. He was surprised to find that the "Ethiopian" was quite European in complexion and dressed in Italian style. The monk addressed him through the interpreter, but the envoy replied that that was unnecessary, for he spoke Italian. He was, indeed, Pietro Rombulo, who had gone to Ethiopia in 1407. After residing there for thirty-seven years, Rombulo said, he had been sent on diplomatic missions to India and China by Zar'a Yakob, and now had come to Europe to revive a project that had miscarried in 1428—an alliance between Ethiopia and King Alfonso the Magnanimous of Aragon. Rombulo had brought with him a manuscript about his travels, which has not survived to our time except in the form of the extracts taken from it by Fra Pietro for a book of his own. Unfortunately, Fra Pietro mixed into Rombulo's factual account a number of current geographical fantasies drawn from less trustworthy sources, so what might have been the first reliable firsthand description by a European of Prester John's court became badly diluted by imaginary wonders. Fra Pietro says that Prester John is a Christian but that many of his subjects are Moslems or pagans, which was the case; and the information given on Ethiopian geography and natural history is accurate. However, the depiction of Prester John's vast army, his elephants and his jewels, could not have come from anything Rombulo had said, and the details of the African kingdoms west and south of Ethiopia bear no resemblance to those in any other contemporary account.

Rombulo, accompanied by an Ethiopian envoy known as Fra Michele, went on to have an audience with Alfonso of Aragon, who had transferred his court from Spain to Naples. This energetic and intelligent prince remembered the exchange of letters he had had with King Yeshak of Ethiopia twenty-two years before, and at Rombulo's urging now sent a new message to Zar'a Yakob, offering to open diplomatic relations and expressing a willingness to send artisans to the Ethiopian court—provided Zar'a Yakob could guarantee their safe arrival, Alfonso added, recalling the death of the thirteen craftsmen he had dispatched to Ethiopia in 1428.

Again, nothing came of this endeavor. But it was now firmly established in Europe that the ruler of Ethiopia was that very same Prester John of fable and legend whose realm had been sought since the middle of the twelfth century. A Genoese traveler, Antonio Uso di Mare, provided a handy explanation in 1455 of how Prester John, once thought to be an Asian monarch, happened to live in Africa: "The Emperor and Christian Patriarch of Nubia and Ethiopia, Prester John, is called *Abet Selip*, that is, 'hundred men.'" (A corruption of *Abd-es-Salib*, the Arabic translation of one of the king's actual titles of honor, "servant of the cross.") Uso di Mare goes on, "These countries are all that is left to Prester John, since the great Khan of Cathay, named Castigan, gave battle to him in 1187 in the beautiful plain of Tenduch in Cathay. Crushed by the innumerable multitude of his adversaries,

Prester John lost all the territories he possessed in Asia. He only kept the provinces of Ethiopia and Nubia, which abound in gold and silver."

The wondrous map of the world completed in 1460 by the Venetian monk Fra Mauro demonstrates in a single sentence of seven words how complete the shift in Europe's theories about Prester John had been. This masterpiece of medieval cartography, richly ornamented with many-towered castles and pictures of walled cities, embodied the latest and most accurate geographical information available in Europe in the middle of the fifteenth century. The section of the map that shows "Abassia"—Ethiopia—bears the simple legend, *"Qui il Presto Janni fa residentia principal"*: "Here Prester John makes his principal residence."

6

Now that Prester John had been tracked to Ethiopia, one matter was in need of settlement: was this Prester John who ruled there the same man, preserved by the Fountain of Youth, of whom tales had been told for three hundred years, or was "Prester John" merely the title by which all Ethiopian kings were known? That was easy to deal with; obviously the Ethiopian monarchs were mortal men, for in 1428 Yeshak had occupied the throne, and in 1441 envoys from a king named Zar'a Yakob had attended the Council of Florence. Therefore "Prester John" must be some sort of generic title, passed along from king to king; Zar'a Yakob was the current Prester John, and Yeshak had been Prester John before him. This simple explanation was deemed satisfactory by Europeans, although it baffled the Ethiopian delegates of 1441, who wholly failed to recognize "Prester John" as any name, title, or appurtenance of their king. When the prelates of the Council of Florence referred to their master as "Prester John," the Ethiopians replied in some indignation that his name was actually Zar'a Yakob. But did he have some other name by which he was known? Oh, yes, they said, his throne name was Kuestantinos, or Constantine. He had an assortment of regnal names and titles besides; but none of them, the puzzled Ethiopians said, was Prester John.

No matter. Prester John was what Europe wanted to call the King of Ethiopia, and Prester John was what Europe called him.

Europeans now were going to Prester John's land in increasing

numbers. Most of them are shadowy figures to us, known only by passing references in fifteenth- and sixteenth-century documents. Some
were merchants, some were priests, some were curiosity-seekers, and
nearly all of them spent much more time in Ethiopia than they had
planned, for it had become the custom of Prester John to detain his
guests from overseas for indefinite stays; to go to Ethiopia was to risk
having to remain there the rest of one's life. Some indication of how
many such permanent guests Prester John came to have may be found in
a document known as *Iter S*, written in 1482 by Francesco Suriano, a
member of a group of Franciscan missionaries who successfully visited
Ethiopia and returned from it between 1480 and 1483. Suriano and
his companions, setting out from Cairo, sailed up the Nile for thirty
days, went by camel caravan to the shore of the Red Sea, and journeyed
by ship to the port of Suakin in what is now the Sudan, where they
bought camels and rode into Ethiopia. Suriano writes, "Having crossed
the river [the Nile] we traveled for ten days and reached the court of
the great king Prester John, which was in a place called Barar. In which
court we found ten Italians, men of good repute, viz. Master Gabriel,
a Neapolitan, Master Jacomo di Garzoni, a Venetian, Master Pietro da
Monte from Venice, Master Philyppo, a Burgundian, Master Consalvo,
a Catalan, Master Ioane da Fiesco, a Genoese, and Master Lyas of Beirut
[?], who went there with papal letters. All these had been there for
twenty-five years. But since 1480 there had gone there Master Zuan
Darduino, nephew of Nicolò da le Carte, a Venetian, my dear friend
and an honest man of good repute, Cola di Rosi, a Roman, who had
changed his name to Zorzi, Matheo of Piedmont, Nicolò, a Mantuan,
Master Nicolò Branchalion, a Venetian, Brother Ioane aforesaid from
Calabria and Batista da Imola. I asked these men what they had gone
to do in this strange land. They replied saying that their intention was
to seek jewels and precious stones. But since the king did not allow them
to return they were all ill content, although they were all well rewarded
and provided for by the king, each in accordance with his rank."

Of this group only one is known from other sources: the Venetian Nicolò Branchalion, or Brancaleone. He was a painter who had
come to Ethiopia for reasons unknown during the reign of Zar'a Yakob's
successor, Ba'eda-Maryam (1468–78). Impressed by Brancaleone's
artistic skills, the king commissioned him to paint murals in a great
many churches. One of his paintings caused a furor because the artist,
following European conventions, had painted the infant Jesus in the left

arm of the Virgin; the left arm was considered less honorable than the right in Ethiopia, and the clergy demanded that the sacrilegious work be destroyed. Ba'eda-Maryam defended his artist, though, and the mural remained. Brancaleone's most important task was to decorate the church in which the king planned to be buried; Suriano visited it a few years after Ba'eda-Maryam's death and was amazed to find in it "a large and ornate organ in the Italian style," which Brancaleone apparently had constructed. The artist, who was never able to gain permission to leave Ethiopia, lived there more than forty years and exerted a profound influence on the style of native Ethiopian painting. A Portuguese ambassador who met him in the 1520s described him as "a very honorable person and a great gentleman, though a painter."

Suriano's manuscript, which went unpublished until 1900, might have served well to deflate the myth of Prester John's splendor if it had been published in his own time. This is what he learned from the Italians at the Ethiopian court:

"They told me that their houses and dwellings were made of reeds plastered with mud within and without. And in the said country there is no house of dressed stone, nor any other buildings, except that each king on reaching the throne builds a church in which he should be buried. The king keeps his treasure in caves under a strong guard. This country has much gold, little grain, and lacks wine; it has a very large population, a brutish people, rough and uncultured. They have no steel weapons for combat. Their arrows and spears are of cane. The king would not take the field with a force of less than two hundred thousand or three hundred thousand people. Each year he fights for the faith. He does not pay any of those who take the field, but he provides their living and exempts these warriors from every royal taxation. And all these warriors are chosen, inscribed and branded on the arm with the royal seal. No one wears woolen cloth because they have none, but instead they wear linen. All, both men and women, go naked from the waist upwards and barefoot; they are always full of lice. They are a weak people with little energy or application, but proud. They are zealots for the faith, and of a fervent spirit above all other Christians."

These are harsh words, and to some extent unjust, for Ethiopia, whatever its cultural shortcomings, was at that time the most advanced nation in Africa other than Egypt, even if it seemed primitive by the standards of a fifteenth-century Italian. But it was inevitable that a process of demythologizing would set in now that Europeans were at last able to take a close look at the land of Prester John. Shortly the scrutiny would become more intense and the last traces of fantasy would be pared away; for the Portuguese were about to launch their remarkable century of imperial expansion, and the realm of Prester John was to be one of their most urgently desired goals.

SIX

The Portuguese and Prester John

Until the fifteenth century Portugal had been nothing but an unimportant strip of rocky coast on the Iberian Peninsula, an insignificant appendage to Spain. The Romans had given that coastal strip its name when they anchored their ships in its one good harbor at the mouth of the Douro River; they called their anchorage *Portus Cale*, "the hot harbor," and the name came to include the entire coast. (The settlement at that harbor is known today as Oporto.) Before the Romans penetrated the Iberian Peninsula, the Carthaginians were there; if there is a genetic predisposition to the maritime life, those heirs of the Phoenicians must have transmitted it, making the Portuguese seafarers by first nature. Their small, poor country looks toward the sea anyway, with nothing behind it but bleak Spain, hostile to Portugal through most of history and walling her off from Europe. So the Portuguese went to sea, first as fishermen, then as merchants plying familiar routes to Brittany, Flanders, and England.

The country's progress was hampered by war. For centuries there was the struggle against the Moors, who came out of North Africa in

A.D. 711 to seize most of Spain and all of Portugal. Gradually the Moors were pushed out, but still Portugal had no independent existence, being merely a district of the Spanish Kingdom of León, distinct only in its dialect. Through a long and intricate struggle the Portuguese detached themselves from León in the twelfth century and preserved their independence by means of a series of shifting alliances with the numerous kingdoms and principalities of which Spain was then composed.

In the fourteenth century Portugal, with English help, succeeded in resisting several attempts to absorb her made by the Kingdom of Castile, the leading power of medieval Spain. When the Portuguese dynasty became extinct in 1383, the throne was claimed both by the King of Castile and by João of Avis, the illegitimate half brother of the late king; war followed, in which the outnumbered Portuguese withstood a Castilian thrust and whipped the Spaniards decisively, and in 1385 João of Avis became King João I of Portugal. The accession of the House of Avis marked the birth of Portugal as a modern nation. With external enemies at last neutralized, the new dynasty was able to commence an expansionist policy. The Portuguese shipyards flourished; from Portugal's harbors sailed flotillas of the squat, heavy, single-masted, square-rigged ships called *naos*, bringing cork, sardines, port wine, salt cod, and hides to England, and returning with wool, tin, and manufactured goods. The *naos* were awkward, stolid vessels that could take a great deal of punishment, but their usefulness was limited by their inability to tack—to move forward in a side wind or to sail into the wind. In favorable weather a *nao* went forward; with the wind against it, it was helpless. But for the purpose of the trade with England the *naos* served Portugal well.

In 1411, when Portugal had arrived at an unaccustomed state of complete peace, João of Avis adopted a suggestion of his English-born queen, Philippa: to maintain the momentum of the national economy, he would send an armed expedition to North Africa. João and Philippa envisioned a conquest of the Moorish kingdom of Fez, thus opening the way for a Portuguese penetration, by land, of Prester John's kingdom, somewhere in the heart of Africa. With Prester John's cooperation, perhaps, a new spice route could be established, with caravans crossing Africa from Morocco to the Red Sea and bringing pepper and cloves to Lisbon.

Philippa herself organized the expedition, devoting three years to arranging the financing and assembling the arms, ships, and men. Three of her five sons took part: Duarte, Pedro, and Henrique, the last of whom is better known to us as Prince Henry the Navigator. Prince Henry, born in 1394, was three years younger than Duarte, two years younger than Pedro. All three were coming to manhood almost at once, and welcomed the opportunity to meet the test of war. The expedition was ready by the summer of 1415: forty-five thousand men aboard two hundred ships waited in harbor at Lisbon. The fleet sailed on July 25; the inadequacies of the clumsy *naos* were immediately revealed, for, as they headed south in the Atlantic, bound for the Moorish port of Ceuta, they were caught by a contrary wind and swept through the Straits of Gibraltar into the Mediterranean. This mishap had unexpectedly favorable consequences, for the defenders of Ceuta, seeing the Portuguese ships disappearing eastward, relaxed their vigilance and dismissed the reinforcements they had called up upon first learning of their peril. The Portuguese managed to swing a few of their heavy ships around by night when the wind changed, and, aided by oar-propelled galleys, descended on Ceuta in a surprise attack. By nightfall the Portuguese flag flew over Ceuta's citadel; Prince Henry had distinguished himself by his valor, being wounded in the invasion. Portugal had taken the town known as "the key to the Mediterranean" and had begun her advance into Africa.

Queen Philippa's plan for gaining access to the spices of the East Indies by way of caravan routes across Africa came to nothing. Dislodging the Moors proved impossible, and, even if it had not, beyond Morocco lay the desert, and then the dark, unknown heart of the continent. Prince Henry swiftly grasped the truth: the way to the Indies lay around Africa, not across it. Though he went on several further military expeditions in North Africa, he gradually withdrew from active campaigning to concentrate on geographical study that would lead toward attainment of that goal. In 1419 his father named him governor of the Algarve, Portugal's southwestern province, and the ascetic prince, who remained celibate and wore a hair shirt, established a center for research in that isolated region. On the promontory known as Cape Sagres he built a small town where he dwelled as a recluse, collecting information about the shape of the world and especially about the eastern Atlantic. He read the works of Arab geographers, he conferred with travelers and merchants, he purchased maps and astronomical instruments—and he sent out expeditions of discovery.

Within a year Portugal had occupied the island of Madeira at

Henry's urging. From a map brought back from Venice by his brother Pedro, he learned of the existence of the Azores and directed the rediscovery of those islands in the early 1430s. For these explorations Henry scorned the lumbering *naos* in favor of lighter ships called *barcas*, which were nothing more than fishing boats with one big mast and a square sail, requiring a crew of about fourteen men. Later he used *barinels*, larger and longer vessels equipped with oars as well as sails, but even these did not give him the capabilities he sought. From 1440 on Henry's expeditions were usually made in *caravels*, ships carefully designed to meet the needs of explorers. The early Portuguese caravels were vessels of fifty to a hundred tons, with two or three masts and triangular lateen sails. They were capable of advancing in a side wind and, to some extent, of tacking into the wind, and so were not compelled to await fair breezes at sea.

Prince Henry himself never sailed with his caravels. His task was to learn and to impart, not to explore, and he remained at his observatory at Cape Sagres, directing his grand enterprise from a distance. In his person was focused all the accumulated navigational wisdom of the centuries. He surrounded himself with astronomers and geographers from abroad; he pumped his returning captains for details of latitudes, currents, winds, coastlines; he worked to perfect the astrolabe, the quadrant, the compass, and other navigational instruments; and he added each newly gathered bit of information to his charts. Systematically he sent his ships farther and farther, from Madeira to the Azores, from the Azores south along the bulging hump of Africa's western coast. His hardy little vessels underwent continual tinkering of design, and new combinations of sails, both lateen and square-rigged, came into use. The mariners grew bolder as they pierced deeper into the unknown. The dreaded zone of fire feared by medieval sailors did not materialize even as they neared the Equator, for the heat, while intense, was tolerable; but, discouragingly, there seemed to be no end to Africa. The interminable continent bulged farther to the west as Henry's explorers continued their southerly cruises. Looking shoreward, they saw only the desert wastes of the Sahara; but then the terrain improved, and in 1441 inhabited lands were spied. Two of the Portuguese captains celebrated by inaugurating the European slave trade, coming home with a cargo of blacks that would provide an economic basis for Henry's costly researches. Henceforth Portuguese caravels called frequently at the West African ports, where obliging native chiefs were ready to do business, offering elephant tusks, sacks of gold dust, hides, and slaves from villages in the interior.

Gomes Eannes de Azurara, the Portuguese historian who wrote an account of Prince Henry's African explorations in 1453, tells us that the Navigator had five main purposes. One was purely geographical: to obtain knowledge of the lands beyond Africa's western curve. One was commercial: to enter into profitable trading relations with any Christians who might dwell in those lands. Two were political: to learn the extent of the Moslem domains in Africa, and to discover "if there were in those parts any Christian princes, in whom the charity and the love of Christ was so ingrained that they would aid him against those enemies of the faith." And the fifth was spiritual: his desire to bring about the conversion of Africa's heathens, "to make increase in the faith of our Lord Jesus Christ and to bring to him all the souls that should be saved." He hoped to send his ships ever southward, until at last they came to Africa's tip and could round it, going into the Indian Ocean and making sail for the ports of India and the isles of spices even farther to the east. But, as he told one of his companions in 1442, he desired to have knowledge not only of Africa and the Indies but "of the land of Prester John as well, if he could."

In 1444 a landmark was reached: Cape Verde, Africa's westernmost point. Now the continent trended eastward, and the green and fertile lands south of Africa's bulging hump were open to the Portuguese. On past the mouth of the Senegal, on past Sierra Leone and the Ivory Coast, on to Guinea the caravels sailed—and still more of the African coast lay ahead. In dark moments Prince Henry may well have felt that the guess of the ancient geographer Ptolemy had been correct, and that the land stretched unbroken to the South Pole, permitting no access by sea to the Indian Ocean.

Still the geographer-prince sought his goal. The eastward trend of the land inspired hope. His researches produced a better southward route: instead of clinging to the North African shore, with its reefs and sandbars, the caravels now swung wide of the coast, far out into the Atlantic to catch favorable winds that sped them toward the slave ports. But the love of exploration for its own sake seemed to fade among the Portuguese; most of the voyages now halted in known lands, and the southward impetus faltered. When Prince Henry the Navigator died in 1460, Africa's southern tip was yet to be found, the sea route to the Indies still unknown.

For nearly a decade Portuguese exploration halted altogether. Only the slaving voyages to Africa's by now familiar western coast continued. But, though the profits of West Africa were immense enough, they were nothing compared with the yield to be had by reaching the Indies. In 1469, King Afonso V—the son of Henry's brother Duarte—awarded African trading rights to one Fernão Gomes of Lisbon, in return for Gomes' agreement to discover a hundred leagues of coast a year. The details of Gomes' voyages were kept secret, to discourage the ships of other nations, but their results were notable in both gold and geography. By 1472 the Portuguese were in the Cameroons; the following year they crossed the Equator for the first time. When the Gomes concession expired in 1474, King Afonso awarded exploration rights to his own son João, a man who had some of the questing spirit of his great-uncle Henry the Navigator. The young prince's plans were curtailed between 1475 and 1479 by war between Portugal and Castile, but he was able to pursue an energetic expansionist policy when he came to the Portuguese throne as João II in 1481.

King João founded Portuguese fortresses on the Guinea coast, sent new caravels southward into the unknown lands beyond, and revived Prince Henry's practice of encouraging advances in the science and art of navigation. A pair of Jewish astronomers, Joseph Vizinho and Abraham Zacuto, calculated elaborate and extremely valuable tables for determining positions at sea; improvements were made in the design of ships; new charts were drawn. In 1483 an expedition commanded by Diogo Cão reached the mouth of the Congo, explored the river to some extent, and continued along the coast to 13°S. before turning back. When Cão reached Portugal in 1484, King João knighted him, awarded him a pension, and almost immediately sent him on a second voyage. The following year, as Cão's caravels headed once more toward Africa, Portugal made her first public announcement of her new discoveries. King João sent a party of ambassadors to render homage to the newly elected Pope Innocent VIII, and at this audience a Portuguese orator told the Pope that "by far the greatest part of the circuit of Africa" had then been completed by his nation's mariners. If the geographers were correct, he said, the ships of Portugal had reached a point only a few days' journey short of the Barbarian Gulf, as the indentation on the East African coast with Zanzibar at its center then was known; and here, so it was thought, the kingdom of Prester John began. Thus the Portuguese now boasted of "the by no means uncertain hope of exploring the Barbarian Gulf, where kingdoms and nations of Asiatics, barely known among us and then only by the most meager of information, practice very devoutly the most holy faith of the Savior."

2

Diogo Cão's second voyage did not bring the caravels of Portugal to the land of Prester John. He did get nearly to the Tropic of Capricorn, attaining 22°S. without finding the desired eastward turning. The king was keenly disappointed when the Cão expedition returned to Lisbon in 1487 with no news of success; Cão, who had explored 1450 miles of unknown coast, working against the current and the winds much of the time, fell from grace, his career broken by his failure to find India. His successor, Bartolomeu Dias, brought the king happier tidings. Setting out in 1487, Dias traveled down the coast far beyond the most southerly point visited by Cão. After provisioning at Lüderitz in what is now Southwest Africa, Dias' caravels were beset by storms and driven far into the Atlantic. On a great arc they swept around the Cape of Good Hope without sighting it, and by the time they could regain the coast, in the vicinity of Mossel Bay in the Republic of South Africa, they had unwittingly crossed from the Atlantic to the Indian Ocean. The land trended eastward; the gateway to the Indies was open, for they had attained Africa's terminal point and found clear water. But provisions were low and Dias' men were exhausted by the rough weather; reluctantly he agreed to turn back. On the return voyage the great southern cape came into view. He named it *Cabo Tormentoso*, the Cape of Storms; but after Dias' arrival in Portugal at the end of 1488, King João rechristened it optimistically the Cape of Good Hope.

Meanwhile the Portuguese stationed in the new permanent outposts on the West African coast were attempting to penetrate the mysteries of the interior. In 1486 one Afonso de Aveiro founded a trading depot at Benin, in what is now Nigeria. From a local chieftain he learned that twenty moons' march from the coast there lived a mighty monarch known as King Ogané, who was revered as deeply by his subjects as the Pope was by Catholics. Whenever a chief came to power in the Benin region, he was obliged to send ambassadors to Ogané to have his accession confirmed; Ogané would provide a brass helmet, scepter, and cross as tokens of his approval, and without these emblems the people of Benin would not accept a chief as a legitimate ruler. None of the Benin envoys had ever seen Ogané; invariably he received them screened by curtains of silk, and he revealed to them only one foot, thrust tantalizingly out of the curtains for a moment at the conclusion of an audience.

King João's geographers analyzed Aveiro's report with care. A march of twenty moons, they calculated, would cover some three hundred leagues, that is, about nine hundred miles. Studying their maps, they concluded that a three-hundred-league journey eastward from Benin would bring one to Ethiopia. Travelers who had already been to that land had reported that Prester John never showed himself to his subjects but always was veiled in silken curtains. This Ogané, who hid himself the same way, and gave out crosses as tokens of approval, and was held in such awe throughout so much of Africa, and who lived three hundred leagues east of Benin, must surely be none other than Prester John, the great Christian monarch!

Seventy years before, Queen Philippa had urged the quest for a land route across Africa from west to east, thus bringing Portugal to Prester John's kingdom, which could perhaps be made to serve as a half-way house for Portuguese merchants en route to the Indies. That scheme was deemed impractical, and her son Prince Henry the Navigator devoted his life to finding a sea route around Africa that would lead both to Prester John's land and to the Indies. Discovering that route had proven unexpectedly difficult; but now these tales of Ogané revived the possibility that Prester John might be reached after all by land, from the Portuguese bases in West Africa. Certainly the idea was worth investigation. In 1487, King João chose two of his courtiers, Pero da Covilhã and Afonso de Paiva, as ambassadors to Prester John—sending them, however, not by the untraveled and undoubtedly hazardous route across Africa's heartland, but by the more usual route for Europeans going to Ethiopia, by way of the Mediterranean and Egypt.

Covilhã, who was about forty, was a man of humble birth who had spent much of his youth in Spain in the service of the Duke of Seville, and then, returning to Portugal, had been made a "groom of the spurs" in the court of King Afonso V. Rising swiftly, Covilhã had become the king's squire and close companion, a position he retained when Afonso was succeeded in 1481 by his son João II. Covilhã showed himself to be a gifted linguist and a subtle negotiator, and João used him in many delicate tasks, sending him as a spy to Spain and as an ambassador to Morocco. Of Paiva less is known, but his family came from the Canary Islands, and so it is probable that he had some familiarity with the African mainland.

The emissaries conferred with the royal geographers, who supplied them with maps and charts and descriptions of their route, and with the king, who underscored the importance of their reaching Prester John and entering into a commercial treaty with him. Control of the spice trade seemed essential to the growth of Portuguese prosperity. "Spice," to the medievals, meant many things: not merely condiments for seasoning and preserving foods, but also dyes, drugs, perfumes, cosmetics, and other exotic goods. Francesco Pegolotti, a Florentine merchant of the fourteenth century, compiled a list of 288 "spices" that included eleven kinds of sugar, a variety of waxes and gums, and even glue. The core of the spice trade, however, lay in true spices: pepper, nutmeg, mace, cinnamon, and cloves.

Europe depended wholly on the fertile tropics for these commodities, which were valued not merely as adjuncts to flavor. Spices were necessities for medieval Europe. Lacking fodder to see their livestock through the winter, European farmers slaughtered most meat animals as the cold weather approached; this produced a great surplus of meat in autumn, which had to be consumed gradually over the long winter months. The rich could experiment with ice cellars, but most people made do with smoked or pickled meat for seven or eight months of the year. Spices were essential to cure and preserve the stored meat; spices also tended to disguise the effects as the meat spoiled. Pepper, the master spice, was most useful, and Europe's appetite for pepper was insatiable, but the other spices also were highly prized.

An elaborate mercantile chain brought these goods to Europe in the fourteenth and fifteenth centuries, after the collapse of the Mongol empire had ended easy contact between East and West. The raw materials came from countries at the eastern edge of the known world—that is to say, from countries bordering on the Pacific Ocean. Cloves, nutmeg, and mace grew only in a few islands of what is now the Republic of Indonesia; the source of cinnamon was Ceylon; pepper grew in western India, but the choicest came from the Indonesian island of Sumatra. Chinese and Malayan merchants made regular tours of the spice islands, collecting the baled produce and carrying it to the great port of Malacca near the tip of the Malay Peninsula. Here it was sold to Hindu traders from India, who shipped their purchases across the Bay of Bengal for sale in the ports of India's Malabar Coast—Calicut, Cochin, Cananor, and Goa. Arab merchants were the next purchasers. Loading their vessels with precious cargoes, they set sail for Persia, Arabia, or East Africa. From the Indian Ocean to the Mediterranean there were many possible access routes. One was via the Red Sea; the cargo could be landed at the Ethiopian port of Massawa and fetched inland by caravan to Egypt, thence up the Nile to Alexandria. Another Red Sea route necessitated transferring the cargo at the Gulf of Aden; the spices were taken from the big oceangoing ships and placed aboard small Egyptian coasting vessels that threaded the hazardous path to Suez, the harbor for Cairo and the Nile Delta. An alternate route, via Jidda in Arabia, required a lengthy desert trek to Syria. One way or another, the valuable goods at last reached the ports of the eastern Mediterranean. Now for the first time they passed into European hands. Italians, mainly Venetians and Genoese, collected the spices from Alexandria, Antioch, Tripoli, Beirut, or Constantinople. Though relations between Christians and Moslems were bitter in the late Middle Ages, these pragmatic Italian merchants were able to maintain their trading concessions in hostile cities through shrewdness and determination. They paid for the spices with Europe's woolen and linen textiles, with arms and armor, with copper, lead, and tin from European mines, with amber, and with gold and silver bullion; they also did a retail trade in slaves from the Caucasus and coral from the depths of their own Mediterranean.

To Venice and Genoa, at last, came the harvest of Asia—mainly to Venice. Dealers crowded the Rialto to buy what the spice fleets brought, and passed the spices along, at enormous markups, to the ultimate recipients all over Europe. The profits were vast; but until the rise of Portugal, there was no European nation hungry enough to want to steal the spice trade from the Italians and determined enough to accept the risks and costs of developing its own routes. Portugal, though, needy and ambitious, hoped to insinuate herself into the spice trade at one of its early stages—preferably by setting up trading depots in India, thus eliminating the Arab middlemen as well as the Italians, or else by establishing commercial outposts on Ethiopia's Red Sea coast. Winning the friendship of Prester John was essential for that.

In May 1487, Covilhã and Paiva bade their sovereign farewell, receiving from him four hundred golden *cruzados* and a letter of credit that would be honored by any European banker. They went by way of

Barcelona to Naples, thence to Rhodes, where, advised by some Portuguese who lived there to disguise themselves as merchants, they bought a cargo of honey. Then they sailed to Alexandria, where they both fell ill of fever; they seemed so close to death that the governor of the city, who was entitled to attach the property of foreigners who died in Alexandria, confiscated their honey. Upon their unexpected recovery, they sued the overeager official for an indemnity, and, after a long delay, received some money with which they bought new goods. Going on to Cairo, they joined a party of Moorish merchants and in the spring of 1488 sailed with them down the Red Sea in an Arab dhow as far as Aden. There they parted, Paiva to go to Ethiopia while Covilhã took passage for India in order to study the spice trade closer to its source. They agreed to meet eventually in Cairo.

Covilhã, boarding an Arab ship, reached India after a month's voyage, landing at the port of Cananor. Journeying up and down the Malabar Coast, the resourceful Portuguese observed the activities of the Arab and Hindu spice merchants, learning of commodity prices, sources of supply, the prevailing winds governing the shipping seasons, and much else. (Among his discoveries was the information that there was open sea beyond the southern tip of Africa, a fact that Bartolomeu Dias was independently learning about the same time.) To confirm this news of a sea route around Africa, Covilhã left India for Ormuz, the great mart on the Persian Gulf, and in 1489 headed by ship along the Arabian coast to East Africa. Reaching it well south of Ethiopia, he ventured as far as Sofala at 21°S., some two thirds of the way down Africa's eastern shore; Arab traders were busy there, and he gained from them more details of the seaway around Africa, by which, he saw, Europe and the Orient could readily be linked. After collecting a wealth of data about harbors and sailing conditions in this part of Africa that would later be of immense value to Portugal, Covilhã returned to Cairo, reaching it in 1490.

There was no sign of Paiva. A lengthy investigation revealed that Covilhã's companion had lately arrived in Cairo from parts unknown in the last stages of a grave illness, and had died without telling anyone where he had been. At this news Covilhã decided to go back to Portugal; but then he encountered two Portuguese Jews whom King João had sent to find him. They bore letters from the king reaffirming the importance of visiting the court of Prester John, and, since Covilhã had no way of knowing whether Paiva had succeeded in reaching Ethiopia, he realized it was necessary for him to go there himself. One of the Jews agreed to accompany him part of the way; the other received from Covilhã a detailed account of his discoveries on the coasts of India and Africa, and carried it back to Portugal. Thus the information Covilhã had gathered was made available to the coming generation of Portuguese explorers, who would make use of it in opening the hoped-for route to the Indies.

Covilhã and his new companion, Rabbi Abraham, sailed to Aden; then, because the rabbi had business in Ormuz, Covilhã escorted him there before turning toward Ethiopia. His progress toward Prester John was leisurely and indirect: he sailed to Jidda and then, disguised as a Moslem pilgrim, dressed in white and with his head shaved, he made the perilous journey to Mecca apparently just to satisfy his own curiosity; he went on even to Medina, and then to Sinai, where at the Monastery of St. Catherine he heard Mass for the first time since his departure from the Christian world four years before. At last, in 1493, he penetrated Ethiopia and presented himself to King Eskender (1478–94), who greeted the ambassador from João of Portugal with great warmth. Flattered by the attention of an envoy from a brother Christian monarch of a distant land, Eskender promised to send Covilhã back to his homeland laden with gifts and honors.

But Eskender died before Covilhã was able to leave, and his brother Na'od (1494–1508) ascended the throne. Na'od treated Covilhã graciously, but when the Portuguese ambassador reminded the king of his wish to go home, Na'od replied that it was not the custom of his land to allow foreign visitors to leave. And so Pero da Covilhã's travels came to their end: he was marooned in the land of Prester John, like the painter Nicolò Brancaleone and a few dozen other Europeans who had happened to go to Ethiopia, and, like old Brancaleone, he was still there when the next ambassador from Portugal arrived at Prester John's court in 1520. Francisco Alvares, a member of that ambassador's retinue, met Covilhã and took down a full account of his adventures and of his quarter of a century in Ethiopia. According to Alvares, Covilhã had applied to Na'od's son and successor, King Lebna Dengel, for permission to depart, but this king also "would not give it, saying that he [Covilhã] had not come in his time, and his predecessors had given him lands and lordships to rule and enjoy, and that leave he could not give him, and so he remains." Alvares relates that Covilhã had been given "a wife with very great riches and possessions. He had sons by her

10. Title page of the first edition of Giuliano Dati's *Treatise on the Supreme Prester John*, c. 1495.

11. Title page of the Portuguese first edition of Alvares' *The Prester John of the Indies*, Lisbon, 1540.

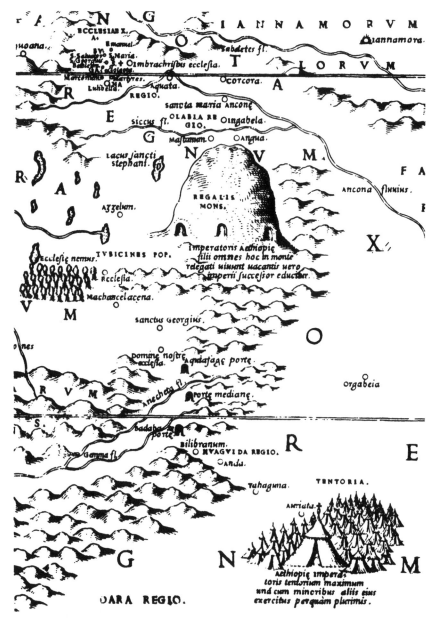

12. The Ethiopian provinces of Amhara and Shoa, as depicted in the *Geografia* of Livio Sanuto, Venice, 1588. The churches of Lalibela are at top left, the royal amba in the center ("regalis mons"), and the traveling court of the king at lower right.

13. An ancient granite obelisk at Axum, Ethiopia's first capital. WIDE WORLD PHOTO.

14. A modern-day priest of Axum, wearing an old crown of decorated gold. WIDE WORLD PHOTO.

and we saw them. . . . This Pero da Covilhã is a man of great wit and intelligence and there is no one else like him at court; he is one who knows all the languages that can be spoken, both of Christians, Moors, Ethiopians, and heathens, and who got to know all the things for which he was sent; he gives an account of them as though he had them present before him. For this reason he is much liked by the Prester and all the court." When the new Portuguese envoys arrived, Alvares says, "a passionate desire to return to his country came upon him. He went to ask leave of the Prester and we went with him and we urged it with great insistence and begged it of him. Yet no order for it was ever given." Eventually the emissaries of 1520 were able to arrange their own departure from Ethiopia, but Covilhã stayed behind, and remained in Prester John's land to the end of his life.

3

Before Portugal could capitalize on the discoveries of Bartolomeu Dias and Pero da Covilhã in Africa, the quest for a sea route from Europe to the Indies took an unexpected turn: Spain sent an expedition *westward* into the Atlantic under the command of a certain Italian named Columbus, and in March 1493 he returned to Europe with the news that he had succeeded in reaching Asia. He had not actually come upon India or Cathay, he admitted, but only the isles of the Indies; yet he had no doubt that the Asian mainland lay nearby.

Neither Columbus nor anyone else realized, at this point, that two huge unknown continents and an incredible expanse of ocean lay between Spain and the isles of spices; and the Portuguese, troubled by visions of Spanish caravels sailing west into the Atlantic and returning with bales of pepper and cloves, hastened to resume their own quest for an eastward sea route to the Indies by way of Africa. King João II ordered Bartolomeu Dias to construct two new ships, take them on the route he had discovered around the Cape of Good Hope, and, if possible, to sail from Africa to India in accordance with the instructions Pero da Covilhã had sent back.

João died in 1495, only forty years old. To the throne came his cousin Manoel the Fortunate, twenty-six years of age, handsome, ambitious, a good administrator, something of a miser, who would be the beneficiary of all the labors of the House of Avis. In his reign Portugal would finally attain the empire in the Orient of which his ancestors had dreamed. Dias was still building his ships when Manoel became king: not caravels, which had given him trouble near Africa's windy tip, but two large old-fashioned square-rigged *naos* for the long voyage to India. In 1496, Manoel added two smaller lateen-rigged caravels to the fleet anyway, and, surprisingly, gave supreme command of the expedition not to Dias (who accompanied it only as far as Guinea) but to a twenty-eight-year-old nobleman and diplomat, Vasco da Gama. Gama's prior naval experience is unknown, but evidently he had already won some reputation at sea; and Manoel's faith in him was justified, for Gama successfully carried out the finest feat of navigation ever achieved up to that time, Columbus' voyage included.

The four Portuguese vessels left Lisbon on July 8, 1497. They followed the familiar route past the Canary Islands and around the bulge of Guinea, and, swinging far out into the South Atlantic as he had learned from Dias to do, Gama spent thirteen weeks in the open sea, the longest passage European seamen had ever made out of sight of land. (Columbus took five weeks sailing between the Canaries and the Bahamas.) At last turning east—a little too soon—the Portuguese made land on November 8 about 130 miles north of the Cape of Good Hope; after a short halt for reprovisioning, they went on, and, despite storms, contrary currents, and an attempted mutiny, Gama pushed onward beyond Dias' farthest point, into the unknown.

Now they sailed northward up Africa's eastern coast, calling at various ports. In March 1498 they reached Mozambique, the southern limit of the Moslem coastal domain. Gama questioned the local merchants about Prester John, for Manoel had told him to gain what information he could on that subject. "We were told," the journal of an anonymous member of Gama's crew reports, "that Prester John resided not far from this place; that he held many cities along the coast, and that the inhabitants of those cities were great merchants and owned big ships. The residence of Prester John was said to be far in the interior, and could be reached only on the back of camels." But it was not Vasco da Gama's purpose to make a trek into the Ethiopian hinterlands; leaving Prester John unvisited (and the hapless Covilhã unrescued), he continued on up the African coast, seeking an experienced pilot who would guide him to India.

Gama found his pilot at Malindi in Kenya, twenty-five hundred miles north of Dias' stopping point of 1488. He was a famed Moslem geographer and navigator, Ahmed ibn Majid, who guided the Portuguese fleet safely across the Indian Ocean. On May 20, 1498, European ships at last appeared in the harbor of Calicut. The long quest was over; the sea route to the Indies had been found. With great difficulty—for he was opposed by the Moslem merchants, trying to protect their monopoly—Gama managed to purchase a cargo of spices, and, after a harrowing return voyage, he arrived in Lisbon in September 1499, having lost two of his four ships en route and more than 100 of his 170 men. Yet the expedition was a triumph despite these losses. In two years and two months he had covered 28,000 miles, he had found India, and he had come home with spices worth sixty times the cost of the whole enterprise. Within six months of Gama's return, King Manoel was ready to send out a second and far larger fleet: thirteen ships, 1200 men.

This great expedition sailed in March 1500, commanded by Pedro Alvares Cabral. Swinging a little too far to the west in the Atlantic, Cabral managed to discover the coast of Brazil before starting his run for the Cape of Good Hope; thus he gave Portugal a foothold in the New World. Then he went on to India, where he blundered into war with a native ruler, the Zamorin of Calicut, and had to buy his spices at a rival city, Cochin. In 1501, Vasco da Gama led the next expedition, twenty-five ships; he won permission to set up Portuguese factories at Cochin and Cananor, and arrived at treaties with the local rulers fixing weights, measures, and prices. Portugal's grip on the Malabar Coast tightened in 1503 when another fleet arrived, commanded by Afonso de Albuquerque. He reached Cochin just in time to save that friendly port from an invasion by Calicut, and its grateful ruler allowed the Portuguese to station a permanent garrison in his city. Over the next few years the Portuguese sent fleet after fleet to India, until Lisbon replaced Venice as the chief spice market of Europe, and Portugal experienced unparalleled prosperity as a result.

Of course, the Moslem merchants who had for so many centuries dominated commerce on both the Indian and the African sides of the Indian Ocean resented the Portuguese intrusion and resorted to warfare to put an end to it. So Portugal's quest for spices shortly involved her in strife on two fronts. It was necessary for her to break the Moslem hold on the East African ports, which were vital as halfway houses on the route from Portugal to India, and, in India itself, the Portuguese had to extend their control beyond Cochin and Cananor to such rich and hostile cities as Calicut and Goa. Only by conquering substantial strips of the Indian and African coasts, and by building a chain of forts along them, could Portugal be certain of maintaining her new and lucrative trade route.

In 1505, King Manoel appointed Francisco d'Almeida as his first Viceroy of India. Almeida sailed east at the head of a fleet of twenty-two vessels; among the 1500 sailors, soldiers, and laborers in the armada was a young man making his first major voyage, one Fernão de Magalhães—Magellan, the future circumnavigator. The Portuguese called first at Kilwa, an important city on the East African coast, controlled by a Moslem sheikh. Vasco da Gama had forced the Sheikh of Kilwa to swear allegiance to King Manoel three years earlier, but the sheikh's stipulated annual tribute of gold had not been forthcoming. Almeida stormed the town, drove out the sheikh, established an obliging Arab puppet as the new ruler, and built a sturdy fortress overlooking the harbor. Leaving a garrison of 550 men, he sailed north to the great port of Mombasa, which he captured and sacked in August 1505. Almeida then went across to India with most of his fleet, while the men who had been left behind seized the major port of Mozambique—giving the Portuguese control of a thousand-mile stretch of the African shore, from Sofala to Mombasa.

On the Indian side, Almeida set about breaking the power of the independent principalities of the Malabar Coast. This task was complicated by the fact that Venice and Egypt, who had both lost heavily through the Portuguese takeover of the spice trade, had formed an alliance and had sent a fleet to help the Malabar princes drive the Portuguese out. Early in 1508 the Portuguese ships were surprised by this Venetian-Egyptian fleet, reinforced by more than a hundred Indian and Arabian vessels; the Portuguese suffered heavy casualties, and their campaign of conquest was momentarily halted. They did not regain their impetus until the end of the year, when Almeida seized and sacked the city of Dabul; then, in February 1509, a rebuilt Portuguese fleet came to the port of Diu, where the navies of Goa, Calicut, and Cambaya had made rendezvous with the Venetian-Egyptian forces. Almeida led his ships into the midst of this much larger armada and shattered it. It was the decisive battle of Portugal's war for India. Egypt was eliminated as an Indian Ocean power; Venice lost her last hope of maintaining the spice trade; the native princes of the Malabar Coast waited in terror for the mopping-up operation to begin.

Meanwhile still another Portuguese force was at work in a third corner of the Indian Ocean: the upper end of the Arabian Sea. If the key ports of Ormuz and Aden could be captured, Portugal could close the Indian Ocean to Moslem shipping entirely. The leader of this squadron was the veteran warrior Afonso de Albuquerque, one of Portugal's greatest heroes. In 1506 he and his lieutenant, Tristão da Cunha, captured the coastal towns of southern Somaliland and the strategically located island of Socotra. This gave them easy access to the Oman Coast of southern Arabia, which was the next to fall. Aden, at the mouth of the Red Sea, was too well fortified for the Portuguese to attempt at this point, but Albuquerque did succeed in capturing Ormuz, the gateway to the Persian Gulf and the valley of the Euphrates. However, he was called away to India in 1509 to replace Almeida—who had been abruptly dismissed by King Manoel—as viceroy, and in his absence Ormuz soon regained its freedom; the Portuguese did not recapture it for several years.

Albuquerque's operations of 1506–09 along the Arabian coastline, conducted almost within hailing distance of Ethiopia, brought Prester John back into Portugal's plans. The original scheme of forming an alliance with Ethiopia so that Portugal might make use of the Ethiopian ports in reaching the Indian Ocean had been discarded, now that Manoel's grandiose imperial design had given Portugal possession of most of Africa's Indian Ocean coastline. But Prester John still could be useful to Portugal. Albuquerque had nothing less than a holy war in mind. The Ethiopians, after all, were Christians, and would surely join forces with the Portuguese to smash the Moslem nations who surrounded them. Albuquerque dreamed of using the Ethiopian port of Massawa, on the Red Sea, as a staging base for an invasion of Arabia: aided by the legions of Prester John, he would capture Mecca, carry off the coffin of Mohammed, and use it to ransom the Holy Land. Then, too, he wanted to revive an age-old scheme and dig a canal across Ethiopia from the Nile to the Red Sea, thus diverting the great river and making a wasteland out of Egypt.

To do all this, of course, Albuquerque first had to make contact with Prester John. Nothing had been heard out of Ethiopia since the disappearance of Covilhã in 1493. When Albuquerque reached Africa in 1506, therefore, he picked two men, João Gomes and João Sanches, gave them a Tunisian Moor named Sidi Mohammed as their guide, and instructed them to make their way to Prester John.

Gomes and Sanches went ashore at Malindi, just north of Mombasa in what is now southern Kenya. They planned to march northward across Kenya until they reached Ethiopia, but before they had gone very far they discovered that the natives of the interior were savage and fierce, and they decided it would be better to make their entry from a higher part of the coast. So the two emissaries and their guides returned to Malindi and waited there until March 1508, when a unit of the Portuguese fleet dropped anchor there. The astonished commander took them with him to Albuquerque, who was in the midst of his Arabian campaign and cruising off Cape Guardafui at the tip of Somaliland. Sidi Mohammed explained that it had proven unwise to try to go to Ethiopia by way of Malindi, and that he would much rather make the attempt by following the Somali coast to Berbera or Zeila on the Gulf of Aden and striking southward into Prester John's land. This was, indeed, a far more sensible route, and Albuquerque, giving the three men letters of introduction in Arabic for Prester John and some money for their traveling expenses, landed them in Somaliland.

Posing as Moslem merchants whom the Portuguese had robbed, they walked off toward Berbera, and their subsequent path is difficult to trace. Two Spanish Jews reported meeting João Gomes and Sidi Mohammed at the Sudanese port of Suakin in 1510; Sanches, they said, was dead. Gomes and the Moor were then on the verge of departing for Cairo, but quarreled and separated, Sidi Mohammed disappearing into the desert and Gomes taking ship for Jidda. He was not heard from again.

There is no doubt, though, that Albuquerque's envoys did reach the court of Prester John, for their arrival is mentioned in a letter from Queen Eleni of Ethiopia to King Manoel of Portugal written not long afterward. King Na'od had died in 1508, and the throne had gone to his son Lebna Dengel, who was only twelve years old. Eleni, whom the Portuguese called Helena, took power as regent. This remarkable woman was Lebna Dengel's step-grandmother, and his step-great-grandmother as well; the daughter of a Moslem prince who was an Ethiopian vassal, she had been married to King Zar'a Yakob, and after his death in 1468 she became the second wife of his successor Ba'eda-Maryam, Zar'a Yakob's son by another woman. During the reign of the next king, Ba'eda-Maryam's elder son Eskender, she seems to have gone into retirement, but she played an important role in the time of Eskender's brother Na'od, and after Na'od's death emerged as the dominant figure of the country. Lebna Dengel's actual mother, Na'od Mogasa, appears not to have had much voice in the conduct of the regency, for the formidable Eleni—then about seventy years old—was quite capable of governing alone. She was skilled in the arts of diplomacy and administration, and, having become a Christian at the time of her marriage to Zar'a Yakob, was adept in theological matters, as an Ethiopian ruler of that era was required to be.

Queen Eleni's letter to Manoel was written both in Arabic and in Persian. It is odd that no Portuguese version was sent, since Pero da Covilhã's services as a translator presumably were available to her, but no such version ever reached Lisbon. She wrote:

"In the name of the Father, the Son, and of the Holy Ghost, Three Persons, and One God, grace and blessing rest upon our beloved brother King Manoel, Rider of the Seas, Subjugator and Oppressor of infidels and Moslem unbelievers—may the Lord Christ prosper you and give you victory over your foes. May He enlarge and extend your dominions through the intercession of those messengers of Christ, the four evangelists, John, Luke, Mark, Matthew, may their sanctity and prayers preserve you!

"We would inform our beloved brother how two messengers arrived here from your great and lofty house. One was named João, who said he was a priest, and the other João Gomes. They said: we require provisions and men. We are therefore sending Matthew, our ambassador, with orders to reach one of your Indian ports and tell you that we can supply you with mountains of provisions, and men like unto the sands of the sea!

"We have news that the Lord of Cairo is building ships to fight your fleet, and we shall give you so many men . . . as to wipe the Moors from the face of the earth! We by land, and you, brothers, on the sea! . . .

"Now is the moment come for the fulfillment of the promise made by Christ and Holy Mary, His Mother, that in the last time there would arise a king among the Franks who would make an end of all the Moors!

"Everything that Matthew, our ambassador, may tell you, believe as from ourselves, for he is the best man that we have, and if we had another who knew or understood more than he we should have sent him. We would have entrusted our message to those of your subjects who came here, but we feared that they might not represent our case as we desire.

"With this ambassador, Matthew, we are sending a cross made of the wood of that on which Our Lord was crucified. It was brought me from Jerusalem, and I had two crosses made out of it, one for us, and the other one for you. The said wood is black and has a little silver ring attached to it. We could have sent you much gold, but we feared that the Moors might steal it on the way.

"If you are willing, we should be very glad to have your daughters in marriage for our sons, or—better still—if you would marry your sons to our daughters. With which no more, save that salvation and grace of Our Redeemer Christ and Our Lady the Holy Virgin rest on your estate, upon your sons and daughters, and on all your house! Amen. We moreover add that were we to muster all our people we could fill the world, but we have no power on the sea. May Christ Jesus help you, for certainly the things that you have done in India are miraculous!"

4

This Matthew, Queen Eleni's ambassador, is a figure of some mystery. According to one report, he was a Christian merchant from Armenia; according to another, the brother of the Coptic Patriarch of Egypt, and the husband of a kinswoman of Prester John; a third story had it that he was a recent convert from Islam. Much of this may have been true. All that is certain is that he was lighter in color than an Ethiopian, middle-aged, and of distinguished bearing. In 1510 or 1511 he set out from Ethiopia accompanied by a boy whom he introduced as his brother-in-law, two women who were both his wives according to one account and a wife and a serving-maid according to another, and eight servants. All were disguised as Moslems and the piece of the True Cross was carefully hidden in their baggage. Matthew's destination was India, where he would present Queen Eleni's letter to Albuquerque, the Portuguese viceroy.

The mission nearly foundered at the outset. At Zeila, on the Gulf of Aden, Matthew and his party suffered imprisonment and the loss of most of their possessions. Finally managing to escape, they took ship for India, and in 1512 reached the Indian port of Dabul, ruled by a Moslem prince. Matthew promptly got in trouble with the local authorities and landed in jail again, whereupon he announced that he was a Christian and an ambassador from the King of Ethiopia to the King of Portugal. He raised such a clamor that the ruler of Dabul, fearing the wrath of the Portuguese forces that now occupied much of the Malabar Coast, decided that it was wisest to rid himself of this self-proclaimed ambassador, be he genuine or false; and so in December of 1512 Matthew was released and escorted to the nearby city of Goa, where he was brought before Albuquerque.

Albuquerque, in the four years since he had for the second time dispatched Gomes and Sanches to Prester John, had labored mightily and with great success at the task of turning the Indian Ocean into King Manoel's lake. The East African shoreline was already controlled by Portugal from Sofala to Somaliland, and, since replacing Almeida as viceroy, Albuquerque had regained command of southern Arabia by reconquering Ormuz and the island of Socotra. On the Malabar Coast, having found Almeida's stronghold of Cochin unsatisfactory because its harbor was difficult of entry during the monsoon seasons, he had chosen the island city of Goa in the middle of the coast to be the new capital of Portuguese India, and had conquered it in November 1510. With Goa as his base he was rapidly bringing the remaining Malabar principalities into submission. This vigorous empire-builder had even reached east of India to Malacca, the superbly located Malayan port that flanks the strait connecting the Indian Ocean and the South China Sea. The spices of Indonesia and all other westward-bound commodities of the exotic Orient passed through Malacca for shipment to India, and, in line with Portugal's policy of eliminating middlemen wherever possible, Albuquerque sent a powerful armada in 1511 that bombarded the well-defended city, broke through its defenses, and converted it into the easternmost outpost of the Portuguese Empire. Now, when Matthew was presented to him at the end of 1512, Albuquerque was planning the next phase in his grand scheme: the conquest of Aden, which would open the Red Sea to Portugal and place the Moslem realms of Egypt and Arabia at his mercy. The arrival of an ambassador from Prester John was thus more than timely, for Ethiopian cooperation would be invaluable in any penetration of the Red Sea. No European vessel had ever entered that narrow waterway, nor had the Ethiopians had much benefit from their Red Sea ports since the rise of Islam; Moslem shipping alone enjoyed the use of this con-

venient maritime link between the Indian Ocean and the Mediterranean.

"We received the ambassador with a procession," Albuquerque
declares in his account of his career in India, "and went with him to
church. There, a sermon was delivered by a preaching friar who showed
us the True Cross and held it out for us to kiss, and we touched many
jewels with it. Afterwards I accompanied the ambassador to his lodging,
where I ordered that he should be well provided for and served. I gave
him two slave girls, his countrywomen, for his service and that of his
wife, and I also gave him two boys from his country who could speak
our language." In a buoyant letter to King Manoel, Albuquerque declared, "If Your Highness could but see what is going on in India since
it became known that this was an ambassador from Prester John, it
would seem to you as the portent of some great change, so dismayed
are the people of India. May it please Our Lord that this should be
the beginning of the ruin of the house of Mecca."

After entertaining Matthew at Goa in a style that would have
been fitting for Prester John himself, Albuquerque ordered that the
ambassador be conveyed to Portugal with every honor. Unfortunately,
the three captains charged with this assignment held real or fancied
grievances against Albuquerque, and once they were at sea they vented
their hatred of the viceroy on the handiest scapegoat—Matthew. Ac-
cusing him of being a Moslem spy in the pay of Egypt—for Ethiopians
were said to be black, and his skin was as fair as theirs—they put him
in irons, boxed his ears, plucked his beard, appropriated for themselves
the lavish gifts Albuquerque had given him, and made free with his
women. But Matthew's ordeal ended when he reached Lisbon in February 1514 after a disagreeable thirteen-month voyage. King Manoel's
advisers accepted Queen Eleni's letter as genuine and the king greeted
Matthew as a heaven-sent messenger; Manoel broke into tears and fell
to his knees when the envoy gave him the queen's cross. The Portuguese monarch sent a jubilant letter to the Pope, informing him that
Prester John's ambassador was "offering in the name of his monarch, as
one Christian to another, all possible aid and everything necessary for
a war against the enemies of the Catholic faith, such as soldiers, arms,
and supplies, especially if our fleet should penetrate the Red Sea, on
which his domains border and where the forces of both can be most
conveniently joined." Manoel resolved to send Matthew back to Ethiopia accompanied by a Portuguese ambassador, who would bestow gifts

of the most costly kind on Prester John and negotiate with him the terms of the proposed alliance. Fleets bound for India always sailed from Portugal in the spring; it was too late for the envoys to go with the 1514 voyage, but, Manoel decreed, they would travel with the fleet of 1515.

Albuquerque had begun his Red Sea campaign while Matthew was en route to Portugal, but it had not gone well. An attack on Aden early in 1513 failed. The Portuguese ships then went on past that city into the Red Sea, the intent being to mount an assault against Jidda or even Suez; but the wind was too sluggish to permit the fleet to advance more than a short distance northward, and when they reached the isle of Kamaran, off the coast of Yemen, it died altogether. There they sat for eight stifling weeks, from May to July of 1513, unable to go forward, unable to go back. By the time the winds did relent, it was too late in the season for further campaigning. Albuquerque had taken advantage of this dismal period of enforced idleness, though, to learn as much as he could about the Red Sea from a local sheikh, and he concluded that Portuguese control over just two ports would provide complete mastery of the waterway. On the Arabian side, it was necessary to take Aden, just outside the Red Sea's mouth; and on the Ethiopian side, the strategic spot was the island of Massawa, close to the shore in the southern reaches of the sea. Given these two, the Egyptian and Arabian navies would be bottled up and wholly cut off from Indian Ocean trade.

Massawa once had belonged to Ethiopia, but had been lost to the Moslems in the eighth century, and had been ruled ever since by independent Islamic princes. Despite its proximity to the mainland, it had never been reconquered even through the efforts of some of Ethiopia's mightiest kings, although from time to time the ruler of Massawa had been forced to accept Ethiopian suzerainty and pay tribute. Albuquerque reported to King Manoel that the friendly sheikh "told me that Prester John had often tried to gain the island of Massawa, but had no means of crossing over. He had already attempted to fill up the arm of the sea between the island and the mainland, but could not. Moreover, he told me that Prester John greatly desired to see us and have intercourse with us and he believed that if a captain of Your Highness went there with the fleet, Prester John would come to visit him in person, and to see Your Highness' ships."

If Massawa became a Portuguese base, Albuquerque informed the king, it would be impossible for Egypt ever again to threaten Portuguese ships in the Indian Ocean, for a small Portuguese force would suffice to go up the Red Sea to Suez and, "if anything is breeding there, [we] can burn as many ships as they [the Egyptians] can launch before they are armed or equipped." Jidda, the port of Mecca, would also be at the mercy of Portugal, "for neither spice, nor merchandise, nor food could reach it from outside, and if the sultan would maintain a garrison, he could not feed the men, for he would have no source of supply; whereas Your Highness can hold the place and draw provisions from the land of Prester John, just opposite." Prester John also could furnish horses—"there are many good horses in the land of Prester John"— which could be shipped across to Jidda and used by the Portuguese in a raid on Mecca. That city was full of pilgrims, not of soldiers, Albuquerque said, and could be burned to the ground in a single strike. Then, too, the viceroy wrote, "If the King our Lord would send out some of those engineers who make cuttings through the mountains of Madeira, they could divert the flood of the Nile and turn it aside from watering the lands of Cairo—thus in two years Cairo would be undone, and the whole country ruined. . . ."

But all this depended on taking Massawa; and the Portuguese fleet, still stranded at Kamaran, looked longingly across the Red Sea at the island opposite with no way of reaching it. One night a brightly gleaming cross rose in the sky over Ethiopia, a heartening omen, yet even so the sails remained limp. The only winds that came were those that could carry the fleet out of the Red Sea. Albuquerque's viceregal duties now were calling him back to India, and he was forced to give up the campaign. By September of 1513 he was back in Goa. He hoped to make another attempt to break into the Red Sea the following spring, but the merciless sun over Kamaran had so warped and split the hulls of his vessels that they had to be put up for repair and the invasion postponed. In 1515, too, the Red Sea project remained in abeyance when circumstances compelled Albuquerque to defend the base at Ormuz. But it was foremost in his mind. "We have no unsettled question left in India now but that of Aden and the Red Sea," he wrote King Manoel from Ormuz in September 22 of that year. "May it please Our Lord," he says in another section of that letter, "that we should fix ourselves at Massawa—the port of Prester John." Then the great old conqueror fell ill, and in November 1515 he sailed back to India, leaving instructions with the captain of the Ormuz garrison to prepare for an attack on the Red Sea in January. But Albuquerque did not live to see the coming of the new year, and with his death the project collapsed. He had given Portugal command of three coasts of the Indian Ocean—the African, the Indian, and the Arabian—and had reached even to far-off Malaya; but he had not quite succeeded in forging the vital link with Prester John that could give Portugal an absolute monopoly of the spice trade.

5

Matthew the Armenian, who had left Ethiopia about 1510 to carry the greetings and good wishes of Prester John's step-grandmother to the King of Portugal, did not return to Ethiopia until a full decade had passed. When he came back, he brought an official Portuguese embassy with him, inaugurating the era of regular contact between the governments of Portugal and Ethiopia. In the years between Matthew's departure and his return, however, a good deal of information about the land of Prester John did reach Europe through other channels.

In 1513, for example, while stranded with his fleet in the Red Sea, Albuquerque managed to land a scout on the Ethiopian shore. He was an Arabic-speaking Moor from Azemmour in Morocco who had been enrolled in the service of Portugal, and who had volunteered to enter Ethiopia, make his way overland to Cairo, and go thence to Portugal to report to King Manoel. For his own safety he was put ashore with his ankles fettered, so that he could pose as a fugitive from Albuquerque's fleet while traveling among the Moslems of the coast. He did eventually reach Portugal, and provided Manoel with a description of Ethiopia that confirmed much of what Matthew had been telling him.

Another important source of information was a Venetian, Alessandro Zorzi, who never visited Ethiopia himself but who made it his business to interview everyone he could find who had been there. The first of these interviews was conducted about 1470; Zorzi's informant was an Italian monk who claimed to have traveled between Axum and Cairo. Nearly fifty years later, in 1519, Zorzi spoke with an Ethiopian monk, Brother Zorgi, who had lately come to Italy from Jerusalem. Next he received data from an Ethiopian Franciscan who had come to Italy in 1518, Brother Raphael; in 1523 he interrogated another Ethiopian Franciscan, Brother Thomas, and in 1524 he spoke with a different

Brother Thomas, also an Ethiopian. Zorzi seems still to have been compiling facts about Ethiopia as late as 1538, when he was at least eighty years old.

Zorzi's writings show how confused even an expert could be about the proper name and title of the Ethiopian king. Frequently he refers to him as "Prete Jani"—that is, Prester John—or as "Presta Jani" or simply as "the Presta." But Zorzi often speaks of the king as "Davit," as when he quotes Brother Zorgi on the subject of "Prete Jani, who has the name of Davit." The king he means is Lebna Dengel (1508–40). Ethiopian kings had at least two names, one a baptismal name and the other a "throne name" that they assumed upon commencing their reigns. Thus in the fourteenth century 'Amda-Seyon took the throne name of Gabra Maskal, "Servant of the Cross," when he came to power, and the same throne name was used about a century later by the king whose baptismal name was Yeshak. Zar'a Yakob's throne name was Kuestantinos, which was understood as "Constantine" by the prelates at the Council of Florence in 1441 who questioned the Ethiopian delegates about their master's name. Lebna Dengel used the throne name of Wanag Sawad, "Revered by Lions," but he seems also to have had a second baptismal name: Dawit or Davit, the Ethiopian form of David. These three names were used fairly indiscriminately by the Ethiopians themselves, judging by a group of royal charters dating from the early sixteenth century; one speaks of "Lebna Dengel whose throne name is Dawit," one of "Lebna Dengel whose throne name is Wanag Sagad," one of "Wanag Sagad whose throne name is Dawit," and one of "Wanag Sagad whose throne name is Lebna Dengel." It is not surprising, then, that Zorzi talks in some places of "Presta Davit" and says in another, "Presta Davit, which means Emperor, King, and Lord; Davit is not his proper name."

Under whatever name, this king ruled a fruitful and prosperous land, according to Zorzi. Brother Raphael the Franciscan, who had been a member of the Ethiopian community at Jerusalem until the conquest of the Holy Land by Turks in 1517 forced him to flee to Italy, told Zorzi that "the land abounds in all fertility; the air is good, and he [Brother Raphael] has seen many men who lived for 130 to 150 years." There were in Ethiopia "many monks of every order and priests, canons, bishops and archbishops and excellent Christians; they do not commit perjury or blaspheme, but always bless God." Brother Raphael's account of the wildlife of Ethiopia stirs echoes of the fabulous old letter of Prester John: "Buffaloes, oxen, cows, sheep, goats, dromedaries, great store of fair horses, mules, asses, and very great dogs, stags, roebucks, hares, gazelles, countless elephants, lions, panthers, giraffes, lynxes. Item, many other forest animals, amongst which one that they call Aris, which is great as a cow but very bulky, of a tawny hue, with two horns on the head of one branch and curved, the one on the forehead curved backwards, the other between the ears curved forwards, with which it kills many men; it runs fast, and while running it breaks wind."

One of the Ethiopian Franciscans told Zorzi of a certain Gregorio or Hieronimo Bicini, of Venice, who lived at the court of "Presta Davit." Zorzi knew of the Bicini family, to which his wife was related; and, calling at the Bicini house in Venice in 1524, he spoke with Maria, Bicini's daughter. She told him that her father had gone as a merchant to Ethiopia in 1482 and had never returned, though he had somehow sent home an account of his life there. "Presta Davit gave the said Venetian Bicini an estate with castles and a city under him," Zorzi reported, "and he is married and has several children and rides with 70 horse, and is secretary of the said Presta; and he has painted for the said Presta many things, and he often resides with him and plays chess and cards with him night and day." From Bicini's daughter Zorzi learned that "the said Presta, when he gives audience, is behind a curtain, and none see him, and they speak through an interpreter with eyes lowered; and when he rides abroad, they all look towards the ground, and woe to them who look in his face, for they die at once, excepting all the foreigners from here, who speak face to face." And from Brother Raphael came this other piece of information about the "Presta": "They say that Presta Jani could take the water of the Nile from the Moors, so that it did not reach Cairo; but that he will not because he fears that the Moors would ruin the churches and the Christian monks who are in Jerusalem and those in Egypt of whom there are so many."

6

Most sophisticated Portuguese were aware by this time that the Ethiopian king they liked to call "Prester John" was entirely unrelated to the legendary monarch of that designation over whom there had been so much excitement in Europe since the twelfth century. Later, some

Portuguese historians would work up a specious etymology designed to show that "Prester John" had in fact always been one of the titles of the Ethiopian sovereign; but in the early sixteenth century it was clearly understood that it was merely a conventional epithet that the Portuguese were pleased to apply to this Christian king in Africa, not because he *was* Prester John but because it satisfied some indefinable need to call him that. This was made quite plain as early as 1502 by the Portuguese scholar Valentim Fernandes, who in that year published a translation into Portuguese of the narratives of Marco Polo and several other travelers. In his preface, Fernandes declared, referring to the ruler of Ethiopia, "And this is the king whom we consider to be Prester John, and he is not Prester John. For Prester John is out there in Cathay. Even though the Great Khan killed him and took his lands, there is still a descendant of his who pays tribute to the Great Khan. And this ruler is a Nestorian Christian connected with St. Thomas. And that other one is a Jacobite [Monophysite] Christian, not an Indian but an Ethiopian, not Prester John but the King of Ethiopia."

Nevertheless, though the myth of the Asian Prester John had been exploded and the Ethiopian Prester John had been revealed as a mere mortal prince, the old fantasies continued to circulate in Europe: Prester John had become a permanent part of the body of legend on which imaginative writers drew. He was a familiar figure in the popular literature of the fifteenth and sixteenth centuries, when the development of printing with movable type first made possible the wide distribution of books.

In particular Prester John figured in many *chapbooks*—slender, cheaply printed pamphlets sold by street peddlers and occupying roughly the same cultural niche in late medieval times that dime novels did in the nineteenth century and paperback books do in our own. The chapbooks, dealing with themes of great popular interest and illustrated by crude woodcuts, found surprisingly large audiences, although, because of their flimsiness and the eagerness with which the mass market consumed them, very few have survived to the present day.

One of the earliest of the Prester John tales to see print was *Guerino il Meschino*, composed by the Italian poet Andrea da Barberino about 1409, and first published in a printed edition at Padua in 1473. It tells of Meschino, a young man living at the imperial court of Byzantium, who set out about 820 on a world-wide journey in order to discover the identity of his parents. His adventures in Mecca, Jerusalem, Sheba, and many other celebrated places are described; then the story brings him to the court of Prester John. The throne room is an opulent one, "a marvelous room sixty braces long and forty wide, and in its middle two columns of solid gold. The four walls were of alabaster, and also where one walked. And on the side whence blew the cold north wind there were four or five windows all decorated in gold, and in the middle of each window a crystal column. At the end of the room was a chair all of gold completely decorated with precious stones. The dais consisted of seven steps, and each step bore the name of a deadly sin inscribed in black letters. . . . The first was Covetousness, and its step was of gold. The second step was of silver, and it said: 'Flee Sloth.' The third, of copper, spelled out Envy. The fourth, of iron, said Anger. The fifth, of lead, said Gluttony. The sixth, of wood interspersed with flames such that it appeared to be on fire, was Lust. The seventh step was of earth, and its letters spelled Pride." After an audience with the Prester— an ancient man, who had been alive in the days of Alexander and Caesar —Meschino goes on to Rome and then to the shrine of Santiago de Compostela in Spain, where he meets an Irish monk who leads him to his parents, the King and Queen of Durazzo.

The so-called letter of Prester John appeared in printed form for the first time in 1478, in Venice; this was an Italian translation of the expanded text, full of late interpolations. The first Latin printed edition was published in Germany two or three years later, as part of a chapbook entitled *De Ritu et Moribus Indorum*, "On the Rites and Customs of the Indians." Accompanying the Prester John letter in this was the twelfth-century document known as *De adventu*, describing the visit of "Patriarch John of the Indians" to Rome and telling of the miracles credited to St. Thomas. Even now, it was impossible to separate Prester John and St. Thomas in the popular mind.

De adventu and the letter of Prester John again appeared side by side in a chapbook issued about 1490 in the Dutch city of Deventer; bound with them were two short pieces by Pope Pius II, unconnected to the Prester John legend. Another chapbook published about the same year in Cologne exploited the public interest in Prester John in a different fashion. The first of the four items it contained was an account of the travels of John de Hese, originally written about 1389: a spurious document patterned after Mandeville's book, but in at least one respect out-Mandevilling Mandeville, since John de Hese claimed to have reached the terrestrial paradise and to have seen Eden's walls shining like stars. Among the places he allegedly visited en route was, naturally, India, where he attended Prester John's court and worshiped at the shrine of St. Thomas. Prester John, Hese declared, "passes you by like a Pope, with a very precious long red cape, but after dinner he struts around just like a king, riding and ruling his land." St. Thomas' body lay at Hulna in India, four days' journey from the city of Edissa (sic); Hese was there for the ceremonies of the apostle's feast day, and Prester John attended also, accompanied by his patriarchs, archbishops, and other prelates; Prester John received communion from St. Thomas, assisted by the chief patriarch. Following this item, the Cologne chapbook offered a much more sober piece, the *Treatise on the Ten Nations and Sects of Christians.* This gave a brief account of each Christian faction: the Latins, the Greeks, the Nestorians, the Jacobites or Monophysites, the Syrian Orthodox, and so on. A separate category was reserved for the Indians, whose prince is Prester John and in whose land the shrine of St. Thomas the Apostle is to be found. The remaining sections of the chapbook are a fictitious letter from one "Sultan John of Babylon" to Pope Pius II, expressing an unwillingness to embrace Christianity, and a fabricated reply attributed to the Pope.

The next chapbook of significance here also appeared in Cologne, about 1499, the work of a printer named Cornelis de Zierikzee. Here again the Latin texts of *De adventu* and the Prester John letter were offered. Accompanying them was the *Treatise on the Pontificate of Prester John,* a work which the printer borrowed without acknowledgment from the huge *Supplementum Chronicarum,* "Supplement to the Chronicles," of an Italian monk, Jacopo Filippo Foresti of Bergamo. Foresti's *Supplementum,* published in 1483, was a vast general history of the world in fifteen books; it includes an abstract from the Italian geographer of the early fourteenth century, Giovanni da Carignano, previously noted, which is the oldest known reference to Ethiopia as the seat of Prester John. In the second edition of his chronicle, issued in 1485, Foresti inserted the *Treatise,* an account of the life, customs, and times of Prester John, "Most High Pope of the Christian Indians and Ethiopians." This was based—with full credit given—mainly on a work by Poggio Bracciolini, secretary to Pope Eugenius IV, whose chief source in turn had been the indefatigable traveler Nicolò de' Conti. It blended Ethiopia and India into one vast Christian realm whose king and "pope" was Prester John. The *Treatise,* lifted intact out of Foresti's book, was joined in the 1499 Cologne chapbook by an original text,

Another Treatise on India, studded with references to fabulous beasts borrowed largely from Pliny.

This combination of texts was so successful that it was at once appropriated by Richardus Pafraet, the Dutch printer who had issued one of the two 1490 chapbooks. Dropping the two works by Pope Pius II from his book, Pafraet added the Foresti treatise and *Another Treatise on India* to *De adventu* and the Prester John letter; for good measure he included the narrative of John de Hese and the other three items from the 1490 Cologne chapbook. The second Cologne printer, Cornelis de Zierikzee, retaliated by assembling the identical eight-item collection and issuing three different editions of it in 1500. That year an Antwerp printer put out his own edition of the eight, and further Dutch and French issues followed.

Among those who drew inspiration from these chapbooks was an Italian poet, Giulano Dati (1445–1524), a priest who near the close of his life became a bishop. Dati's first important work, published at Rome in June 1493, was an adaptation into Italian *ottava rima* verse of Christopher Columbus' account of his recent voyage across the Atlantic. Columbus, who was keenly interested in Prester John, had hoped to find his kingdom on that voyage, and it was one of his great disappointments that he did not. Dati, also disappointed that he could make no reference to Prester John in his Columbus poem, remedied the lack with two further works composed between 1493 and 1495: *Treatise on the Supreme Prester John, Pope and Emperor of India and of Ethiopia,* and *Second Song of India.* The first of these went into four printed editions; the *Second Song* was printed only once, in 1494 or 1495.

As its title indicates, Dati's *Treatise on the Supreme Prester John* was derived from Jacopo Filippo Foresti's *Treatise on the Pontificate of Prester John;* since the chapbook plagiarisms of that work had not yet begun to appear when Dati wrote his poem, he must have made use of Foresti's own text. However, Dati's poem also leans heavily on the *Treatise on the Ten Nations and Sects of Christians,* an item from the early chapbooks, and on such texts as Prester John's letter and Andrea da Barberino's *Guerino il Meschino.* The Dati *Treatise* consists of fifty-nine eight-line stanzas. It opens with the catalogue of the ten "nations" of Christians—Latins, Greeks, Indians, Jacobites, Nestorians, Maronites, Armenians, Georgians, Syrians, and Mozarabs, who were Spaniards practicing a distinctive rite in the centuries when Spain was under Moslem rule. Dati counsels tolerance for the various exotic breeds of Christians, though they may err in some theological matters:

> Although a few profess erroneous creeds,
> Nevertheless from Christ their faith proceeds.

Then, passing over the Latins and the Greeks, he turns his attention to the third group, the Indians, and their mighty ruler, Prester John. As in Foresti (and Poggio Braciolini before him) authentic information about Ethiopia and India is fused; Dati speaks of the conversion of the Ethiopians by St. Matthew and of the tomb of St. Thomas at Mylapur as though both apostles had preached in the same land. The description of Prester John's court, including the throne atop the steps named for the Seven Deadly Sins, is taken (with credit given) from Barberino's *Meschino*. In the first three editions of Dati's poem the title page displays a woodcut of the venerable Prester, adorned with a lofty papal tiara and surrounded by his courtiers, seated on this structure; the steps are labeled, in Latin, FLEE PRIDE OF EARTH, FLEE LUST OF WOOD, FLEE GLUTTONY OF LEAD, and so on down to FLEE COVETOUSNESS OF GOLD. The poem ends with the promise of a second song, and the sequel, which shortly followed, offers another fifty-nine stanzas devoted mainly to a description of the monsters and other natural wonders of Prester John's realm.

A much greater Italian poet, Ariosto, embedded a visit to Prester John's kingdom in his *Orlando Furioso* (1516), which relates the adventures of Charlemagne's paladins in their wars against the Saracens. Astolfo, an English duke, one of the Twelve Paladins, rides across North Africa from west to east on a hippogriff, coming at last to the wealthy and populous land of Ethiopia, ruled by a Christian king whose name is Senapus. (This is derived from Senap, another of the fourteenth-century corruptions of the Ethiopian king's Arabic title *Abd-es-Salib*, "Servant of the Cross.") Ariosto offers this familiar information about this monarch (in the sixteenth-century English translation of William Stewart Rose):

> The soldan, king of the Egyptian land,
> Pays tribute to this sovereign, as his head,
> They say, since having Nile at his command
> He may divert the stream to other bed.
> Hence, with its district upon either hand
> Forthwith might Cairo lack its daily bread.

Senapus him his Nubian tribes proclaim;
We Priest and Prester John the sovereign name.

We find Prester John again in much other European literature of the early and middle sixteenth century, particularly that of Italy and Spain; one of his last appearances was in the *Gerusalemme Liberata* (1581) of Torquato Tasso, an epic of the Crusades, in which Senapus makes a peripheral entrance:

Senapo once filled Ethiopia's throne,
    And still, perhaps, endures his prosperous reign;
This potentate the laws of Mary's Son
    Observes, and these observe the swarthy men
He rules. . . .

Of all the Prester John fictions current in the sixteenth century, though, by far the most popular was the *Book of the Infante Dom Pedro of Portugal, Who Traveled Over the Four Parts of the World*, a Spanish work first published in printed form at Seville in 1515. Dom Pedro, Infante (that is, Prince) of Portugal, was one of the sons of King João I, and an elder brother of Prince Henry the Navigator. He was a man of considerable culture and intelligence, who sponsored translations of Latin classics into the Portuguese and wrote at least one complex philosophical treatise himself; in 1425, at the age of thirty-two, he set out on an extensive course of travels to increase his knowledge and to gain experience in international affairs. His plan was to tour Europe, then to make the Holy Land pilgrimage, and, if possible, to reach Mount Sinai and Cairo. He went first to England, his mother's native land, went on to Flanders and Germany, then to Hungary and Rumania. There, in 1428, he learned of the impending marriage of his brother, the Infante Duarte, heir to the Portuguese throne; and, canceling the rest of his trip, he returned home by way of Italy—acquiring in Venice a manuscript copy of Marco Polo's book and several other important geographical works that gave great delight to his brother the Navigator. He had been absent about three years and four months.

Dom Pedro's itinerary, while wide-ranging, was thus nothing extraordinary. Pedro himself, however, acquired a remarkable reputation in the later years of his life and afterward, becoming a symbol in Europe of fifteenth-century Portuguese dynamism and brilliance. He was an active internationalist, maintaining contacts in many lands and serving, in a sense, as Portugal's foreign minister during the closing years of his father's reign and in the reign of King Duarte, who succeeded in 1433. He provided encouragement and financial support for Prince Henry's explorations, and worked with the Navigator toward the great Portuguese goals of attaining the Indies and making contact with the legendary Christian monarch in Africa. Upon Duarte's death in 1438, Pedro took power as regent for his young nephew Afonso V; the regency was an unhappy one, though, for many powerful Portuguese resented Pedro's ambitions and imperious ways, and after Afonso came of age in 1446 there was bitter friction between uncle and nephew. This culminated in civil war: Pedro, faced with a choice between exile and insurrection, attempted to overthrow Afonso, and was slain in battle in 1449.

Pedro's active career and tragic end stirred the European imagination: to those outside Portugal, knowing no details of the domestic political struggle, his downfall seemed like the toppling of a mythic hero, and swiftly the mythmaking began. His deeds were rehearsed by historians, they were dramatized by poets, and they passed into the oral tradition as folk legends. The aspect of Dom Pedro's life that received the greatest embellishment was his grand tour of 1425–28, which became not merely a conventional trot through the capitals of Europe but, in some retellings, a splendid journey to the ends of the earth. The *Book of the Infante Dom Pedro* was the climactic work of this group.

Its author is unknown, though there is some internal evidence that he was a priest. The book purports to be "written by Garci Ramírez de Santisteban, one of the twelve who traveled with the said prince," but since Dom Pedro did not in fact visit most of the places described by Garci Ramírez, it is clear that this ascription is merely a literary device. Though the publication of the work in printed form can be dated to 1515, it evidently circulated widely in manuscript for some time prior to that, perhaps for ten or even twenty years.

The world of the *Book of the Infante Dom Pedro* is the familiar medieval fantasy world already well explored in the fancies of such writers as Mandeville. Beyond Christendom lies the Moslem world, and on the far side of that is a world of fables, inhabited by Amazons, the Lost Tribes of Israel, and Prester John; east of the domain of Prester John is the terrestrial paradise. All the remote lands save Eden itself are under the sovereignty of Prester John, who here is as much a figure of legend as he ever was in the twelfth or thirteenth century. The author's intent seems utopian and ecumenical; he implicitly criticizes the disunified world of Latin Christendom by showing the ideal community of Prester John's land, where command of church and state is united in the person of the same benevolent autarch, and Christian justice and harmony are universally prevalent.

The book opens with Dom Pedro, desirous of seeing the world even unto the land of Prester John, assembling a fellowship of twelve sturdy companions "in remembrance of the Twelve Apostles," and seeking the permission of his father, the King of Portugal, to go abroad. He visits first his cousin, King Juan II of Castile, from whom he acquires the services of Garci Ramírez—an interpreter who claims a knowledge of many languages, including not only the usual European and Near Eastern ones but also Hungarian, Armenian, Babylonian, Rhodanese, Tritonish, and Pilean. Their route takes them next to Venice, Cyprus, and Greece, from which they make a side trip on camelback (!) to Norway, a journey of three days; onward then to Babylonia and the Holy Land, into Armenia to peer at Noah's ark in its mountaintop resting place, then to Egypt, Cappadocia, Arabia, and Sinai; a visit to Mecca follows, and they observe Mohammed's steel coffin floating in the air, held aloft by six lodestones. But the real wonders are only beginning. "Afterward," the narrator Garci Ramírez declares, "we went to the Amazons, which is a province exclusively inhabited by Christian women subject to Prester John of the Indies." The warrior women, he says, suffer men to enter their realm only between March and May, when males from Prester John's kingdom come to them for purposes of increasing the population. The Amazons are friendly to Dom Pedro even though he has arrived out of season, and give him gold to aid him in his journey to Prester John.

From the Amazons, says Garci Ramírez, they went to the home of the Lost Tribes of Israel, "and reached the River of Stones, which is near Judea, and it is called a river by everyone. And what are called stones are not stones, for, in order to be a real river, it must have three things, namely, source, and water, and a means of escape, and if it has these, it is called a real river. For a real river is not like the River of Stones, which is comparable to a mill wheel, for, from the moment you set the water in motion, you find no beginning nor end to it. The River of Stones encloses all of Judea, and has neither water nor stones but only a material which is said to be coarse sand, and as soon as air strikes it, it moves." Crossing the river, Dom Pedro and his companions are met by Jews of the tribe of Benjamin, who inform them that they are the first Western Christians to enter their province since the Crucifixion. These Jews, vassals to Prester John, detain the travelers for nine weeks but eventually release them and send them on their way.

They pass through the city of Luca, inhabited by long-lived giants nine cubits tall, and enter the Indies, going from city to city in search of Prester John until they come upon him in a place called Alves: "This city of Alves is the best and noblest city that there is in the world, and in it there are more than nine hundred thousand inhabitants, and it is completely walled in with mortar on all sides, and within the outer walls there are six hundred additional walls and as many streets." The chamber of Prester John is guarded by thirteen doormen, "twelve of them like bishops and the other like an archbishop," but when Dom Pedro reveals that he is the cousin of the King of Castile he wins immediate entry. (The Spanish author finds it unnecessary to have Dom Pedro announce also that he is the son of the King of Portugal.)

Dom Pedro kneels before Prester John and kisses him, and kisses his wife's hand as well, and that of his son, "who was emperor of the land of Galdras." Then he presents letters from the King of Castile, which one of the lesser kings in attendance on Prester John reads. Dinner comes next: "Fourteen kings ate at his table and seven kings served his board. Prester John had them set another table for us. This room in which Prester John ate was very rich, for the walls were Acre blue and the roof was of gold clusters and the floor was all of precious stones and the surface of the table was all diamonds." The wanderers spent fourteen weeks with Prester John. Each day his attendants placed four gold urns before him; one contained the head of a dead man, "so that he might take note that thus he himself would one day be," one was full of earth, one full of ashes, "so that he might be reminded of the pains of Hell," and the last held pears from the land between the Tigris and the Euphrates, of a miraculous nature, for no matter how they were sliced, the image of the crucifix was found in them.

The details of Christianity in Prester John's land that Garci Ramírez gives are highly imaginative ones. The Mass is an upside-down affair, beginning with "*Ite, missa est*," and ending with the *Confiteor*. Each church has two priests, two altars, and an image of the Virgin as well as a crucifix. Priests are allowed to marry, but "if the wife dies, the cleric may never again leave the temple, even though he lives for two hundred years. If he is found outside the church, he is incarcerated at once." Owning property is forbidden to the clergy: they may have neither camels nor any other beasts of burden, and must not possess anything made of iron or brass or copper or steel, which are valued there as gold and silver are in Europe.

From the Prester John letter comes the next piece of information: "When Prester John rides out, he does not have a banner in front of him nor a standard, but rather thirteen crosses, twelve in remembrance of the Twelve Apostles, and the other with the crucifix, which signifies Jesus Christ." Then the author remembers to tell of a few monsters of a familiar sort that had been met just before entering Prester John's capital: "We came to a part of the Indies which is called the mountains of Aducen, and there we found an unnatural race called Ponces, and these are the most Catholic Christians in the world, and they have but a single leg and a single foot, and, in the middle of the men's bodies, the reproductive organ. They have their leg continuing right down below, and a foot like that of a horse, and two palms in width and two palms in length. The women as well as the men have reproductive organs. In that land we found very small sheep that have eight feet and six horns each." This afterthought of a passage is followed by another: the city of Alves is also known as "Edicia," it seems, and the shrine of St. Thomas is to be found in it, holding the body of the apostle, "and the arm and hand that St. Thomas placed in Our Lord's side never died and is as fresh as if it were yet living." Several miracles of St. Thomas are related; this leads to a discussion of how a new Prester is chosen upon the death of the old one: "No one can become the new Prester through inheritance or through personal power, but only through the grace of God and through the intervention of the holy Apostle. . . ." All ordained priests in Alves/Edicia go in procession around St. Thomas' body, "and as for the one whom it pleases God to be Prester and lord of all the others, the Apostle extends his arm toward him and opens his hand. Then all the others take him with great solemnity and lead him to the Apostle, and the one who is to be Prester John kisses the hand of St. Thomas, and all the others kiss that of Prester John. He thus becomes lord for his lifetime. . . ."

At length Dom Pedro asks Prester John for leave to proceed eastward. The Prester tries to discourage this, saying that the travelers "might reach a land where we would find that the sons are the tombs of their fathers, and the fathers of their sons, and the ones eat the others"—a baroque figure of speech implying cannibalism. But when he sees that they are determined to go on, he gives them interpreters and dromedaries, and after a seventeen-day desert crossing they come to the four rivers of Eden, where they see the wondrous pears that contain the image of the crucifix, after which they return to Prester John for another thirty days' stay. When they depart for Europe, he gives them nine thousand pieces of gold and also a letter, addressed to the people of Latin Christendom, which is essentially just another version of the old Prester John letter of the twelfth century:

"Prester John of the Indies, greatest king of the Christians, we have you know that all our belief is in God, Father and Son and Holy Ghost, three persons and one true God. To all those who wish to see and learn what things are in our dominions, we declare that we have sixty kings as our vassals; and as for the poor of our land, we have them supported from our own income out of love for God. You should know that our parts consist of three Indies: India Major and Middle India and India Minor. The one in which we dwell is India Major, and the body of St. Thomas the Apostle is in this one. And know also that ours is the land of elephants and camels and lions and griffins, which griffins have such great strength that they can fly and at the same time carry an ox for their young to eat. . . . In some parts we have people who have only one eye, and likewise in other parts people who have four eyes in front and behind." The letter goes on to speak of the cannibalistic tribes of "Got and Magot," of centaurs, of pygmies who make war against birds, and many other standard items of medieval mythlore; there is also an account of Prester John's annual visits to the shrine of the prophet Daniel in Babylonia, of the splendors of his palace, and of the religious customs of his court, all of it taken more or less directly from the text of the earlier letter. As if to excuse these borrowings, Prester John is made to conclude the present letter by saying, "Concerning these above-mentioned things I sent word to your parts on another occasion, and I now confirm them. . . ." Parting sorrowfully from the great Prester, Dom Pedro and his companions make their way home by way of the Red Sea and Morocco.

The *Book of the Infante Dom Pedro* can readily be seen to be a bouillabaisse of conventional legends, some of them three or four hundred years old, brought together partly for entertainment and partly to make some satiric points about the state of political and churchly

harmony in Europe of the late fifteenth century. It could never have
been intended to be taken seriously as a geographical treatise, since
even the sections dealing with known parts of the world are in a hopeless jumble, as the three-day camel trip from Greece to Norway
shows. The reading public, of course, loved it, and it went into hundreds of editions in the sixteenth, seventeenth, and eighteenth centuries, continuing to emerge from Spanish and Portuguese presses every
few years even in the nineteenth. As the last of the great Prester John
tales, it enjoyed a strong following long after Prester John himself had
ceased to preoccupy Europe. Its great popularity earned it the hostility
of scholars, who, ignoring the subtle political satire running through it,
chose generally to view it as a clumsy hodgepodge of fable, a Spanish
Mandeville, an unworthy plagiarism: one early critic denounced its
author as an *"ignorante falsario,"* another called his book a work of
"mendacísimo." When it did receive praise from one sixteenth-century
Spanish scholar, Fray Jerónimo Román, it was not for its utopianist political content but merely because its author had not placed Prester
John's kingdom in Ethiopia. Fray Jerónimo, examining the entire legend of Prester John in his *Republics of the World*, had concluded, after
a study of Marco Polo, Otto of Freising, the various St. Thomas tales,
and other documents, that the true Prester John had been, as once was
thought, a Tartar chieftain. By locating Prester John in Asia rather than
Ethiopia, therefore, the author of *Dom Pedro* had in Fray Jerónimo's
estimation given his book a certain basis in truth—although the text as
a whole was riddled with lies. In Portuguese translations of the book,
however, Prester John's "Middle India" was always explicitly identified
as Ethiopia; even in fantasies, the Portuguese wanted it known that they
had found Prester John.

7

In the same year, perhaps the same month, that the first edition of the
Book of the Infante Dom Pedro was coming off the presses in Seville,
King Manoel of Portugal was readying an embassy to Ethiopia, in re-
sponse to the letter brought by Prester John's envoy, Matthew the
Armenian. As head of the Ethiopian mission the king chose Duarte
Galvão, a learned and tactful diplomat, seventy years of age. Galvão
would have three companions: Lopo de Vilalobos, secretary to the mis-

sion, Padre Francisco Alvares, its chaplain, and Lourenço de Cosmo, in charge of Portugal's gifts to Prester John.

Those gifts were indeed princely. King Manoel offered his royal brother of Ethiopia two complete suits of clothes, one in silk and one in damask. There were suits of armor inlaid with gold and silver, costly shields, swords of the most supple steel. For Prester John's repose Manoel sent a magnificent canopied bed, with four fine linen sheets nearly five yards in length, six bulky mattresses stuffed with merino wool, bolsters and pillows embroidered in gold, a woolen blanket embellished with Manoel's armorial bearings. A splendid dining table, a tablecloth of silk and gold, a gleaming dinner service, a brocaded chair stuffed with silver nails, Flemish draperies of silk and gold—there was no end to Manoel's generosity. Nor were the spiritual needs of Ethiopia neglected: the ambassadors were to bring altarpieces, organs, bells, devotional pictures, illuminated missals, thirty books of catechism, a thousand volumes of pious works suitable for the young, candles, vestments, and other religious items. And there was much more, to a total value of some 30,000 *cruzados* of gold.

In the spring of 1515 Matthew and the ambassadors set forth, traveling with Portugal's annual India-bound fleet. This year the fleet was under the command of Lopo Soares de Albergaria, a petty and incompetent man who through political intrigue had arranged to have himself named as Viceroy of India in place of the great Albuquerque. Some gnawing sense of guilt and inferiority, perhaps, caused Lopo Soares to detest everything originated by his formidable predecessor, and, since the exchange of ambassadors between Ethiopia and Portugal had been one of Albuquerque's most cherished projects, Lopo Soares regarded the whole enterprise with disdain, treating both Matthew and the Portuguese envoys in a contemptuous, offhand manner.

The fleet called first at Goa, late in 1515. Albuquerque was still in Ormuz, unaware that he had been dismissed from office and already suffering from the disease that would shortly end his life. Slyly, Lopo Soares slipped into Goa in Albuquerque's absence, showed the Portuguese officials the documents confirming his appointment as viceroy, and slipped quickly out again lest Albuquerque arrive and cause an embarrassing face-to-face confrontation. During this episode Jacob, the boy who had accompanied Matthew from Ethiopia, fell ill aboard ship; but Lopo Soares paid no heed to Matthew's request for a physician, and the boy died while the fleet was sailing from Goa to its next stop,

Cochin. This led to a bitter dispute between Matthew and the new viceroy.

The ambassadors could not go on to Ethiopia until Lopo Soares was ready to provide transportation; and Lopo Soares, who planned to take them there in the course of an intended invasion of the Red Sea, told them that the fleet was not going to sail until January 1517. This compelled the envoys to spend a sour, restless year in India; they passed the time by quarreling with Lopo Soares and one another, and by studying the Ethiopian language and alphabet.

The fleet, when it finally embarked, was a huge one—thirty-eight ships—but the outlook for a successful campaign against the Moslems was poor, for the officers and seamen had no respect for the authority of their arrogant and foolish commander, Lopo Soares. Most of them were still devoted to Albuquerque, who had died in December 1515 without ever meeting his successor, and even those who had disliked the late viceroy came to love him posthumously after a taste of Lopo Soares' leadership. Morale thus was not high to begin with, and matters grew much worse after the fleet's visit to Aden. Several times Albuquerque had tried to capture this strategic port, without success; but now its sheikh, appalled by the size of the force under Lopo Soares, hastily offered to surrender without a battle. To the astonishment of his men, the viceroy blandly replied that he had no time to accept the town just then, for he was on his way up the Red Sea to exterminate the Turks who had lately occupied many of its ports; he wanted only pilots and provisions from Aden at the moment, and would see to the formal ceremonies of surrender on the way back. The amazed sheikh supplied Lopo Soares' modest needs, and, as soon as the Portuguese fleet had gone on, set about fortifying his city against the return of this incredible commander.

Upon entering the Red Sea the fleet found itself in immediate difficulties. Ignoring his pilots, Lopo Soares insisted on sailing by night; they ran into reefs and shallows, and one ship sank with all hands. Among the men lost was the son of the ambassador Duarte Galvão, who had volunteered for service in India. Another ship, bearing Matthew and the Portuguese chaplain, Francisco Alvares, went astray in the Dahlak Islands, near Massawa, and, its captain having no idea where the rest of the fleet had gone, it remained at anchor there for three weeks. Eventually two caravels came looking for it, commanded by Lourenço de Cosmo, the keeper of the gifts for Prester John. The fleet, he said, had gathered at the island of Kamaran. The ship that had been anchored off Dahlak went off to join the others, but Lourenço de Cosmo, who was trying to find a native pilot to guide him to the Ethiopian shore, disembarked at Dahlak against Matthew's advice. The natives, who were Moslems, promptly seized and slew him; the survivors escaped and hurried to Kamaran.

Lopo Soares had brought his ships to this parched island on the Yemen coast after another baffling exploit: he had gone up to the Arabian port of Jidda, entered it under heavy bombardment from the shore, anchored his ships and defied the Turks to come out and fight, which the Turks declined to do—and then, after three days without action, had sailed away again without even attempting a landing. On the retreat to Kamaran the water supply almost gave out, and now, under a blazing summer sky, the Portuguese fried as they had in 1513, glowering at their commander and openly expressing their contempt for his absurd leadership. There was nothing to eat but a meager ration of boiled rice. Men were dying daily. Old Duarte Galvão, staring across the sea at Ethiopia, begged to be landed at Massawa, but Lopo Soares refused. He was waiting for Lourenço de Cosmo to return from his explorations around Dahlak: the ambassadors would go to Ethiopia together, he said, or not at all.

Cosmo, though, was dead; and, early in June 1517, so was Duarte Galvão, killed by grief for his lost son and the rigors of the stay on Kamaran. Padre Alvares conducted a funeral service for King Manoel's envoy and his body was committed to Kamaran's fiery sands. Since there now was no point in landing on Prester John's shore, the fleet began its return voyage to India, stopping on the Somali coast to sack the town of Zeila—Lopo Soares' one military accomplishment. Then he went across to Aden, but the sheikh was less eager to surrender than he had been five months earlier, and Lopo Soares no longer had much control over his weary, mutinous seamen, so there was no attack. The fleet dispersed, some of the ships going back to India by way of Ormuz, some choosing individual routes, some simply cruising off to take up piracy. Late in 1517, Lopo de Vilalobos and Padre Alvares, the only survivors of the embassy, found themselves back in Cochin, along with Matthew the Armenian. They were without the sumptuous gifts intended for Prester John, since everything had rotted or rusted or other-wise perished in the heat of the Red Sea region—the fine table, the great bed, the costly armor, the clothes of silk and damask, and the rest.

"All was lost through the fault of Lopo Soares," wrote the sixteenth-century Portuguese historian Gaspar Correa, "and Lopo Soares never paid for it."

8

The wretched Lopo Soares was replaced as viceroy at the end of 1518 by Diogo Lopes de Sequeira, a much more capable man. Among the problems he inherited was what to do with the ambassador Matthew, who had been stranded in India since the collapse of the Galvão mission and was eager to get home to Ethiopia. Diogo Lopes was planning to make yet another attempt at gaining control of the Red Sea, and, when his expedition set out from Cochin in January 1520, he took Matthew along, hoping to find some way of landing him on the Ethiopian shore. Also aboard were Padre Alvares and some carpenters and musicians who had been part of the original Galvão party; its remaining high officer, the secretary Lopo de Vilalobos, had returned to Portugal in 1517.

The winds of the Red Sea were contrary, as usual: Diogo Lopes' flagship ran aground and broke up near Aden, and then, when he tried to sail up to Jidda, the breeze took his fleet to Massawa instead. Seeing a chance at last to get to Ethiopia, Matthew asked to be put ashore there, and requested that Alvares be landed with him. The viceroy asked the chaplain how he felt about this. "I answered his lordship," Alvares later wrote, "that by the said Saturday it had been five years since I had left Lisbon by order of the king our lord, with the intention of making this journey and that this desire of mine had not changed, for it seemed to me that I was serving God and the king." Diogo Lopes was uneasy though, for, like many of the Portuguese officials in India, he suspected that Matthew was a Moslem and an impostor; Massawa being under Moslem rule, Alvares might perhaps be put to death there as Cosmo had been on neighboring Dahlak. While he hesitated over putting the priest ashore, "there was a great tumult among the whole galleon's company," Alvares wrote, "and they called me to get up and come to see a great sign which was appearing in the sky. And when I went above there was nothing to be seen, and in this uproar, some giving thanks to God and others weeping for joy, everyone told me how for a good while they had seen a big red cross in the sky, which I for my sins did not see." This miracle—a replay of the one experienced by Al-buquerque and his men at Kamaran in 1513—convinced the viceroy not only that he should let Alvares land, but that he should make a landing himself, and on Monday, April 9, 1520, the Portuguese entered Massawa's harbor.

They found the town empty; its inhabitants, frightened by the arrival of the Portuguese, had taken to the hills with all their belongings. After a few days two men came to them from the town of Arkiko, on the Ethiopian mainland, and invited the Portuguese to cross the strait to meet the *bahr nagash*, as the governor of Prester John's coastal province was known.

On April 17—after having consecrated Massawa's abandoned mosque as a church, and celebrating a Mass of thanksgiving in it—the Portuguese met with the *bahr nagash* in a plain outside Arkiko. There was some problem at first over whether Diogo Lopes would go to the Ethiopian's tent or the *bahr nagash* to the tent of Diogo Lopes, but eventually they compromised, holding their talk on carpets midway between their two tents, and everything thereafter went well. Our chief informant on these events is Padre Alvares, who after his return to Portugal wrote a memoir, *Verdadera Informaçam das Terras do Preste Joam das Indias* ("Truthful Information about the Countries of Prester John of the Indies"), that was published in 1540. This sturdy, straightforward priest, about whom little is known other than his great adventure in Ethiopia, tells us that Diogo Lopes and the "Barnagais," as he calls him, "both gave thanks to God for their meeting, the Barnagais saying that they had it written in their books, that Christians from distant lands were to come to that port to join with the people of the Prester John,[1] and . . . that there would be no more Moors there: and since God had fulfilled this, that they should affirm and swear friendship." Producing a cross, the *bahr nagash* vowed on it that he would always give all possible aid to the men of Portugal and would assist any ambassadors who came from that land to see his master, Prester John. Diogo Lopes swore a reciprocal oath, and there was an exchange of gifts, and, says Alvares, "they took leave of each other very joyful and contented."

[1] It should be noted that the *bahr nagash* surely did not refer to his overlord as "Prester John," the usage here being Alvares'. As in earlier meetings, the Ethiopians found it hard to understand why the Portuguese insisted on applying that name to their king.

Having made contact in such an encouraging way with the Ethiopians, Diogo Lopes decided on the spot to reconstitute the Portuguese embassy to Prester John and called for volunteers. Nearly all his men clamored to be allowed to go. The viceroy chose Dom Rodrigo de Lima, a man of high birth, as the head of the mission, and Jorge d'Abreu as his deputy. João Escolar was named secretary of the expedition, Padre Alvares was again the chaplain, and João Gonçalves held the posts of interpreter and factor. A dozen others were included, among them an organist, a painter, and an odd individual named João Bermudes, a former barber now serving as a physician, who many years later was to claim that he was the legitimate successor to the late *abuna*, the head of the Ethiopian Church.

The envoys assembled new gifts for Prester John, hardly as impressive as the ones that had been lost through the foolishness of Lopo Soares: "A rich sword," writes Alvares, "a rich dagger, four pieces of tapestry, some rich cuirasses, a richly gilded helmet and two short cannons, four gun chambers, some balls, two barrels of powder, a map of the world, some organs." On April 30 they started inland from Arkiko. The *bahr nagash* himself was to have been their guide, but Matthew insisted that he knew a route more direct than the one the *bahr nagash* had chosen; he was so stubborn about it that the *bahr nagash*, shrugging, went off and left the others to follow Matthew. Soon they were struggling through a dry river bed, and as they rested there a young man came to them who introduced himself as the *bahr nagash*'s brother-in-law and offered to put them back on the right road. "In spite of his blackness he was a gentleman," Alvares says, but Matthew claimed that he planned to lead them into a den of brigands, and, disdaining the offer, marched the envoys onward through rough country, a roadless wilderness of thickets. "We were traveling where the wolves went," Alvares declares, but finally Matthew was induced to be more reasonable, and in a few hours they returned to the main highway. Shortly, though, Matthew was dragging them off on an impossible route again, "through mountains and devilish jungle." It developed that he intended to make a detour, for some reason, to a monastery at the town of Bizan, and since it seemed to be of such importance to him to get there, the emissaries let him have his way. They reached the monastery, exhausted, on May 4, and took up lodgings there, intending to rest a few days. But then the Portuguese began to fall ill, the first victim being the physician Bermudes and the others soon following. Bermudes made a quick recovery and treated the rest with purges and bloodletting; Matthew, who was also sick, rose too quickly from his bed in the belief that he was well, traveled on to the next village alone, and suffered a relapse. Alvares hurried to him to administer the last rites, and on May 23, 1520, the ambassador from Prester John died, having been absent from Ethiopia about ten years on his mission of diplomacy.

The envoys resumed their trek on June 18, going on to Debarwa, the capital of the *bahr nagash*'s province. En route Alvares attended an Ethiopian church service and was much amazed at the shouting, the chanting, the drumming, and the dancing, while the Ethiopians were equally astonished that the Portuguese entered a church with their shoes on and did not hesitate to spit inside it. ("We excused ourselves, saying it was our custom.") In a town close by Debarwa they caught up with the *bahr nagash*, who, this far inland from the guns of the Portuguese fleet, was very much less genial than he had been at Arkiko. He kept the emissaries waiting about interminably when they sought an audience with him; his doorkeepers demanded bribes of pepper before they would admit anyone; and he was cool and aloof when the meeting at last took place. Dom Rodrigo de Lima asked for oxen and asses to carry their baggage, and mules to ride themselves. "To this the Barnagais replied," says Alvares, "that he could not give any mules, and that we might buy them ourselves; that he would give orders for the rest, and would send a son of his with us to the court of the Prester John, and with that he gave us our dismissal."

The *bahr nagash*, preoccupied with a war he was waging against some neighboring tribes, put the envoys out of his mind the moment they left his presence and avoided them when they sought to see him again. The coming of the rainy season further complicated the journey of the Portuguese. When they did manage to round up porters and beasts of burden, they found themselves escorted only a few miles; the natives then abandoned them, "saying that their boundary went no further, and that another town had to take us further on. As I said, it was in June, in the full force of the winter of this country, and they set us down, with our goods, in a plain, and very heavy rain." By complaining to the *bahr nagash*, they finally obtained mules and camels and began to ascend into the mountainous province of Tigré.

Here they had their first view of Ethiopia's strangest and most characteristic geographical features: the lofty peaks called *ambas*, solitary needles of rock rising almost vertically, like spires or obelisks, to improbable heights. The *ambas,* flat on top with sheer sides, sprang up everywhere here in Tigré, and perched precariously atop nearly every one was a chapel or a monastery; Alvares could not imagine how the Ethiopians could possibly climb such peaks, let alone erect buildings at their summits. Alvares was bothered by another typical feature of this province: "The married women wear very little covering, and the single women, who have neither husbands nor lovers, have less shame. The beads which other women wear round their necks these wear round their bodies, and a large quantity of bells over their private parts. . . . At every little movement one can see from one side of the body to the other what man wishes." However, he adds, "They wash once and sometimes two or three times a day and are therefore quite clean."

The governor of Tigré provided them with transportation through his province. Their route took them to the ancient capital city, Axum, where they observed in considerable awe the mighty stone churches and palaces, then at least a thousand years old, that had been built in Ethiopia's greatest era. These seemed more impressive to the travelers than the Pyramids of Egypt. Beyond Axum, their baggage became mired in the mud of a flooded field, and "it grieved us to see our goods thus," Alvares remarks. While they considered ways of extricating their belongings, four or five men on mules and about a dozen on foot rushed up to them, and one, seizing the official of Tigré who was in charge of the baggage train, began to beat him severely. Dom Rodrigo de Lima, thinking they were beset by brigands, hastened to the rescue, and the other Portuguese drew their weapons; but then the attacker cried out some phrases in broken Italian, which Jorge d'Abreu understood, and the mystery of the onslaught was solved. These were no bandits, but rather an escort sent by Prester John himself to convey the Portuguese emissaries to his court. The one who had launched the attack was a monk, Saga za Ab, who was thus expressing his fury over the carelessness of the official's handling of the envoys' baggage.

Peace was restored, and Saga za Ab promised to meet them at a town close by where he would supply mules and camels. On their way there they passed through rough countryside broken by deep valleys, where, as night was coming on, "so many tigers followed us that it was a thing not to be believed, and if we approached near any thickets they came so close to us that at arm's length one might have struck them with a lance," Alvares asserts. "In all our company there was not more

than one lance; all the others carried their swords drawn, and I, who
did not bear any, went in the middle." There are, of course, no tigers
to be found anywhere in Africa except in zoos, and what the Portuguese
may have seen were leopards, although it is more likely that they were
only hyenas. The travelers passed a frightening night huddled together
with swords ready, and went on, unharmed, in the morning.

There were other perils and hardships as they proceeded southward
across Ethiopia. Cold rain accompanied them daily. The road was often
close to impassable from mud, thickets, or hills. Some regions were in-
fertile and famine-stricken and could provide no food. In other places
the food was strange, and troubled the palates and stomachs of the
Portuguese: Alvares tells of being given some bread of unfamiliar and
and inedible grain, and raw meat—a favorite Ethiopian delicacy—the
sauce for which was "cow dung." (In fact it was the bile or gall of the
cow, not its dung, that was used for the sauce.) Then they passed into
a hot, dry, thorny area, but here too there were unexpected dangers:
as they camped one morning beside a puny stream, thunder sounded
in the distance, and then Bermudes, who had gone upstream to relieve
himself, came running wildly back, calling, "Look out! Look out!" A
flash flood was sweeping toward them; it carried away some of their
goods and would have swept them away as well if they had still been
in the tent by the stream where they had taken their lunch. Alvares
lost his breviary and a full bottle of sacramental wine but managed to
save his chalice.

On they went despite everything, the countryside displaying un-
ending and baffling variety: now fertile, now barren, now hot, now
cold, now dry, now rainy, now jungle, now desert, now flatland, now
spire-sharp mountains. In early September they stopped at the monumental rock-cut tombs of Lalibela, of which Alvares offers an extensive and respectful description. A week later, in the province of Angote,
they were stoned without warning by hostile villagers; they all were
well battered, and Bermudes suffered serious injuries. But the episode
ended with apologies and an invitation to Sunday dinner at the local
governor's house. Prudently, the Portuguese took their own meal
along—roast fowls and beef boiled with cabbage—"because we could
not eat their dishes, neither did they eat ours." The Ethiopians dined
on raw beef and a sort of soup made of half-digested cud, "which in
this country they consider an esteemed food; and only great personages
eat it." An excellent honey wine passed freely, but otherwise the meal

was not a pleasant one for the envoys: "So we came to the end of the dinner," Alvares comments, "and thanks be to God."

Ethiopia did not then have a fixed capital. For tradition's sake a new king went to Axum to be crowned, but for the rest of his reign he continually marched from province to province, traveling in a vast cavalcade of servants, soldiers, and priests, of palatial tents and portable churches. At the moment the king was in one of his southern provinces, Shoa, a land of marshes punctuated by mountains. The Portuguese entered it at the beginning of October. The first night Saga za Ab, the monk who was their guide, tried to get them to make their camp atop one of the steepest of the mountains, but the tired Portuguese refused to go with him, and Saga za Ab left them to spend the night in the lowlands, where the mosquitoes harried them greatly. He did not rejoin them for several days. But soon afterward the quality of the land improved—all about them now were fields sown with wheat and barley—and, Alvares relates, on Wednesday, October 10, 1520, "We saw in the distance, to our great joy, the tents and camp of the Prester John, which seemed endless, and covered the whole countryside."

9

Another week passed before they reached the royal encampment, and not until October 20 were they summoned to the tent of Prester John. "We dressed ourselves and arranged ourselves very well, God be praised," says Alvares, "and many people came to accompany us on foot and on horseback. So we went in order from the place we started from as far as a great portal, where we saw innumerable pavilions and tents pitched like a city in a great plain. . . . There were many people collected together here; so many that they would be over 20,000 persons." This great throng was arrayed in rows, everyone standing motionless; Alvares noted "many canons and ecclesiastics with caps like mitres, but with pointed peaks of silk, and some of them dyed crimson: and there were other people very well dressed." A hundred men with whips marched about, keeping order. Four lions, traditional Ethiopian symbols of royalty, were chained to free-standing arches. Dismounting, the Portuguese were escorted to the middle of the plain, where four high officials of the government awaited them. One of these asked

Dom Rodrigo who he was and why he had come. He replied that he had come from India as the King of Portugal's emissary to Prester John. The official questioned Dom Rodrigo at length, several times going into the king's great tent for instructions; but the ambassador refused to reveal the specific details of his embassy to anyone but the king himself. At length the king sent word that he consented to receive whatever gifts the envoys might have brought for him. Thereupon Dom Rodrigo handed over the modest offerings that perforce had to substitute for the splendid things King Manoel had originally sent; the present looked so modest, indeed, amid the magnificence of the royal gathering, that the Portuguese added to it four bales of pepper that had been intended for their own use. One of the court officials called out an inventory of the gifts, piece by piece, in a loud voice, and then the Portuguese were allowed to retire to a tent the Ethiopians had pitched for them.

As soon as they were lodged, Prester John sent them three hundred great white loaves, many jars of mead, and a cow. The next day, the twenty-first, he again sent gifts of food: "An infinite quantity of bread and wine, and many dainties of meat of various kinds, and very well prepared." The same happened on Sunday, "when, among other dainties, he sent us a heifer calf whole in bread, that is to say in a pie, so well dressed (being stuffed with spices and fruits) that we could not have too much of it." But they were not called to an audience with the king, and on Monday no food arrived. Instead Saga za Ab came and told them that he understood the ambassadors had kept back many bales of pepper that they were supposed to give to the king. Until they handed over the pepper, said the monk, no food would be given them, nor would they be permitted to leave their tent.

The next day the dismayed Portuguese found that Prester John had broken camp and moved on. Saga za Ab informed them that the king had taken his court to another place two leagues away; if the Portuguese wished to follow him, the monk added, they should buy mules on which to carry their baggage. He also told Dom Rodrigo "that if he wished to buy and sell he might do so."

The Portuguese realized now that their gifts had been weighed in the balance and found wanting; perhaps the king had heard descriptions of the opulence of the original presents from Manoel and was displeased by the gulf between expectation and reality. That was, in truth, part of the problem. But it was also the case that Lebna Dengel had lately come to experience the full power of his office and was choosing, in the pride of his kingship, to treat the strangers coolly. They had, after all, been summoned not by him but by his step-grandmother, Queen Eleni. It has already been noted that this king came to the throne in 1508, when he was twelve. The early years of his reign had been dominated by the old matriarch-regent, but he had emerged from the dowager's tutelage in 1517, when the Emir of Harar, ruler of one of the independent Moslem principalities on Ethiopia's eastern frontier, had invaded the Ethiopian province of Fatigar. Lebna Dengel, leading an army for the first time, had ambushed the invaders, destroyed their army, and beheaded the emir; then he carried the war into the Moslem realms, entering the kingdom of Adel on the Gulf of Aden and burning the palace of its sultan. That had established him as a vigorous warrior-king in the proper Ethiopian tradition, and old Queen Eleni was living in retirement.

On October 25 Dom Rodrigo sent Padre Alvares and João Gonçalvez, the interpreter, to the new site of the royal court. They met with the *behtwadad,* or prime minister—whom Alvares calls the "Betudete"—and bitterly protested the implied insult in the king's permission for Dom Rodrigo to engage in trade, saying "that the ambassador was much amazed at this, because neither he nor his father, nor his mother, nor ancestors bought or sold, or had such an occupation; and the same was the case with the gentlemen and persons who came with him, and who had never been so accustomed. . . ." They complained also of the decree that they must buy mules if they wished to travel to the king. "To this the Betudete answered," Alvares says, "that the Prester had already ordered ten mules to be given, and asked if they had not given them. We replied that we had not seen any such mules, only that on the journey this monk had given three tired mules to three men that came on foot. To the other matters he gave us no answer, but spoke of things that were irrelevant, as, for instance, whether the King of Portugal was married, and how many wives he had, and how many fortresses he had in India, with many other questions beside the purpose. . . . So we returned without any conclusion."

The Portuguese now were visited by two fellow Europeans who said they were members of a group of about sixteen—some Genoese, two Catalans, a Basque, a Greek, a German—who were stranded at the Ethiopian court. This group did not include such long-time residents of Ethiopia as Pero da Covilhã and the painter Brancaleone, who were still off on their distant country estates, unaware that a Portuguese embassy had arrived; rather, they were men who had been held captive by the Turks in Arabia for as much as forty years, and, escaping from Jidda in 1517, had fled as far as Ethiopia, taking refuge with Lebna Dengel and thus falling into a kindlier captivity. They told the Portuguese that the king and his court were indeed upset at the alleged holding back of gifts by the envoys, "and they were of opinion that it would be well to give this pepper that we had brought and all the other cloth, because otherwise we should not have leave to return, because this was their custom, never to allow anyone to return who came to their kingdoms. . . ." Dom Rodrigo, therefore, decided to give the king four of their remaining five bales of pepper, and to turn over to him four leather-covered chests containing clothing. On Monday, October 29, assisted by the other Europeans, the Portuguese carried these goods toward Lebna Dengel's camp. On the road they were met by a messenger who said he had come to fetch them to that same place. Once more they came into a grand tent-filled encampment; once more they encountered several echelons of officials, but not the king himself; once more they were given a tent and told to await Lebna Dengel's pleasure.

The next evening, Alvares relates, "came a message from the Prester asking whether the ambassador or any of his suite had a gold or silver cross, to send it to him to see it. The ambassador said that he had not got one, neither was there one in his company, and that one he wore he had given to the Barnagais; and with this the page went away. He returned at once saying that we should send any we had got. We sent one of mine of wood, with a crucifix painted on it, which I always carried in my hand on the road, as is the custom of the country. He sent it back at once saying that he rejoiced much that we were Christians." Several further messages passed back and forth, and then, about three hours after sundown, another messenger arrived bearing word that the king wished to see the ambassador and all his companions at once. "We all began quickly to dress ourselves in our good clothes to go whither we were summoned," Alvares declares. "When we were dressed, another message came that we were not to go: so we all remained like the peacock when he spreads his tail and is gay, and when he looks at his feet becomes sad: so pleased we were at going, so sad at stopping behind."

They were summoned again late Wednesday night. Doorkeepers

made them wait outside the royal enclosure for more than an hour in a cold, sharp wind; then they were led into the king's tent, with much courtly ritual along the way, and, passing through rows of resplendently garbed attendants holding lighted candles, they came at last before Lebna Dengel—who was, however, hidden within an inner sanctuary of wood, completely covered by curtains of fine silk and gold brocade. "When we were standing still like this," Alvares writes, "from within the curtains there came a message from the Prester John, saying, without any other preliminary, that he had not sent Matthew to Portugal, and, although he had gone without his permission, the King of Portugal had sent by him many things for him, and what had become of them, and why did they not bring them as the King of Portugal had sent them. . . ." Dom Rodrigo then spoke at length, telling Lebna Dengel of the death of Duarte Galvão and saying that he himself had not come as a full-fledged ambassador, but only to make a short visit and ascertain the route; he added, bending the truth a bit, that once he had succeeded in opening friendly relations with Ethiopia the original gift of King Manoel would be shipped from India, where it now was stored. To this the king replied that he wished a written report from Dom Rodrigo on the wishes of the King of Portugal, and dismissed the group.

On Saturday, November 3, the king called them to another night audience. He questioned them carefully about their firearms and other weapons, and asked for a demonstration of swordplay; Dom Rodrigo and Jorge d'Abreu thereupon staged an elegant fencing match. The ambassador then begged Lebna Dengel to get down to the business of diplomatic negotiations, but the king (still concealed by his curtains) airily answered that there was plenty of time for that later. The letters Dom Rodrigo had brought would first have to be translated into Ethiopian. He demanded next that the Portuguese entertain him with some music; a portable organ that they had brought with them was produced, and the ambassadors obligingly sang and danced for the amusement of Prester John.

On Sunday the king had more questions. How were muskets used? Were the Portuguese capable of making gunpowder? What was the proper way of wearing a suit of armor? How did the Portuguese produce the wafers used in Holy Communion? Lebna Dengel's curiosity concerning the wafers was particularly intense; in Ethiopia, it seemed, a simple roll served the purpose, whereas the Portuguese used a wafering iron that yielded a handsome wafer imprinted with a crucifix. Monday morning saw Padre Alvares subjected to an intense examination on religious matters: he was asked to show the king first some wafers, then a wafering iron, then all the other implements of the Mass. "I brought to him the full vestments, the chalice, corporals, altar stone, and cruets. He saw all, piece by piece, and ordered me to take it and unsew the altar stone, which was sewn up in a clean cloth, and I unsewed half of it, and had it again covered up." Nightfall saw the weary priest still offering edification to the king. Standing in front of Lebna Dengel's curtained sanctuary, Alvares obediently garbed himself in all the vestments proper to the Mass, then disrobed again, explaining the symbolism of each garment, and dressed and disrobed a second time. The king seemed fascinated by the rites and appurtenances of a church that, although indubitably Christian was so different from his own. Alvares now turned to a potentially explosive point: the Catholic belief in the supremacy of the Pope. The king, who, like most Ethiopian monarchs, was deeply interested in theological matters and well versed in them, said that he understood there were two churches in the Western world, one with its head in Constantinople and one with its head in Rome, each claiming to be the authentic church in apostolic succession to Jesus. How could there be two churches? Alvares replied that "there was only one Church, and although at the beginning Constantinople had been the head, it had ceased to be so, because the head of the Church was where St. Peter was, by reason of what Jesus Christ had said: *Tu es Petrus, et super hanc petram edificabo ecclesiam meam* ('Thou art Peter, and upon this rock I will build my church')." Then, marshaling a host of traditional Catholic arguments, Alvares attempted to persuade the king that the Church of Rome was pre-eminent in Christianity because its head, the Pope, derived his authority from Peter. The king, who accepted the spiritual leadership of Egypt's Coptic Church—which was not in communion with Rome—did not at this point enter into a dispute with Alvares but merely questioned the priest about points of Catholic doctrine and ritual. At the end, after Alvares had sung some sections of the Mass, "the Prester showed the greatest pleasure and said that we had got everything of the Passion, and that we were Christians, as though still he had doubted it." It was past midnight when he let Alvares rest.

10

The routine of nightly interrogations continued; Lebna Dengel seemed more and more pleased with the company of his guests and bestowed frequent gifts of food and drink upon them, although the royal servants sometimes forgot to deliver these or diverted them to their own use. At one point the king asked the Portuguese to give him their swords as keepsakes, which they did after several times explaining that they were uneasy about parting with their only reliable weapons. Lebna Dengel kept the swords only a short while and returned them. Another time a royal messenger reported that the king yearned for a pair of breeches; Dom Rodrigo gave him some of his own and others belonging to one Lopo da Gama. A different whim led the king to send five beautiful horses late one night to Dom Rodrigo, with instructions that he and four companions should ride those mounts to the royal tent and stage a tourney for him; the ambassador grumbled somewhat at the lateness of the hour but obeyed the command and put on a passage at arms by torchlight. The king rewarded him the next day with the gift of a splendid silver chalice and three jars of wine of the highest quality. Later came a small reading desk of gilded wood, a lovely wooden ewer, and a massive, badly made saddle worked with carnelians. Lebna Dengel asked also if the King of Portugal would be interested in having some eunuchs, but Dom Rodrigo tactfully declined the offer.

The Ethiopian king continued to show the greatest interest in the religious practices of his guests. He sent all the lords and grandees of his court twice to watch the Portuguese at their Mass, and afterward there was a discussion of the differences between the Portuguese and the Ethiopian ceremony. Then, on November 19, Padre Alvares underwent another interrogation on theological subjects. In these sessions with the king he was traveling in difficult waters, for Lebna Dengel was a subtle master of the Christian mysteries, and poor Alvares was only a rough-and-ready priest who, moreover, tells us, "For six years I had been sailing about, and had no books with me, and my memory would break down." Therefore, he says, "I answered him as God helped me, to some of them, 'I do not know,' and to some of them, 'It is so.'" The king asked Alvares how many prophets had prophesied the coming of Christ. All of them, Alvares replied. How many prophets were there? I do not know, said Alvares. How many books had each prophet written? "I replied that it seemed to me each prophet had made one book in chapters." How many books were there all told in the Old and New Testaments? Alvares had heard one of the Ethiopian priests speak of "the eighty-one books," and so he said there were eighty-one, hoping he was at least close. "The answer came that I had a good memory, and that my replies were the truth, though I had given them as opinions."

The king had not yet shown his face to the Portuguese. Royal invisibility was essential to an Ethiopian king's prestige; he revealed himself to his subjects only three times a year, at Easter, Pentecost, and Christmas, and at other times was hidden except from his closest advisers and his immediate family. But on November 20 he granted the Portuguese the privilege of beholding him. The summons came, as usual, late at night, and they were left standing at the gate for three chilly hours. Then they were led in, past an immense throng of courtiers, some with lighted candles, many with weapons, and through a number of curtains, each richer than the one before, until they came to "a large and rich dais with very splendid carpets. In front of this dais were other curtains of much greater splendor, and while we were standing before them they opened them, for they were drawn together, and there we saw the Prester John sitting on a platform of six steps very richly adorned. He had on his head a high crown of gold and silver, that is to say, one piece of gold and another of silver from the top downwards, and a silver cross in his hand; there was a piece of blue taffeta before his face which covered his mouth and beard, and from time to time they lowered it and the whole of his face appeared, and again they raised it." It was one of the great climactic moments of the search for Prester John, ten European envoys entering the physical presence of the fabled Christian monarch of the East. "In age, complexion, and stature," Alvares asserts, "he is a young man, not very black. His complexion might be chestnut and bay, not very dark in color; he is very much a man of breeding, of middling stature; they said that he was twenty-three years of age, and he looks like that, his face is round, the eyes large, the nose high in the middle, and his beard is beginning to grow. In presence and state he fully looks like the great lord he is. We were about two lances distant from him."

Dom Rodrigo offered the king the Ethiopian translations that had recently been prepared of the letters he bore. Lebna Dengel, reading them swiftly, saw that there was no letter from King Manoel, but merely one from his viceroy in India, Diogo Lopes de Sequeira.

Dom Rodrigo glibly explained that the viceroy spoke for the king, and thereafter all went well. Lebna Dengel, thanking God that he had been allowed to see "those whom his predecessors had not seen, and he had not thought he should see," let it be known that it would please him if the Portuguese established fortresses on the island of Massawa and at the port of Suakin, and that he would gladly supply provisions and laborers for this work. He suggested also that the Portuguese capture the town of Zeila, just outside the mouth of the Red Sea, for better control of that waterway. A happy discussion ensued as the king and Dom Rodrigo envisioned the conquest of Jidda and Mecca, and everything else as far as Cairo, through the combined might of Portugal and Ethiopia. "This seemed good to the Prester," Alvares notes, "and he again said he would give the provisions, gold, and men, and all that was necessary for this expenditure and fleet, and that he would not spare anything he had in the world in order to find a way of opening up some road by which he could join up with the Christian princes." The interpreter for all this, as for several previous sessions, was Pero da Covilhã, whom King João II of Portugal had sent to Ethiopia in 1487 and who had been living there more than twenty-five years as an involuntary guest. Alvares tells us nothing of Covilhã's first meeting with his countrymen after so much time, describing neither the old man's show of emotion nor the difficulties he must have had in speaking Portuguese again; he merely mentions Covilhã's happiness at being once again able to make confession to a Catholic priest.

By way of Covilhã, Dom Rodrigo and Lebna Dengel had rapidly come to an agreement on the terms of the Ethiopian-Portuguese military alliance. "And so we took leave with good words," says Alvares, "and we went away pleased, chiefly with having seen and spoken to him." Presumably all that remained was for Lebna Dengel to prepare a letter for King Manoel, stating the agreement formally, and then Dom Rodrigo and his colleagues could set out for Massawa and the journey back to India. Dom Rodrigo hoped that the letter would be made ready speedily, for he had arranged for the Portuguese fleet to wait at Massawa for the envoys from February to April 1521; if the delegation did not show up by the end of that period, the ships would have to leave, for otherwise they would be trapped in the Red Sea by the unfavorable summer winds. It was now late November 1520; if the emissaries hoped to make their rendezvous successfully, they would have to be on their way to the coast quite soon.

Shortly it became apparent that Lebna Dengel's letter would not be quick in coming. It had to be composed with the greatest care, as befitted a message from one high prince to another, and the most learned Ethiopian doctors of theology and diplomatic protocol would have to be consulted on the proper phrasing. Then the text must be inscribed in gold lettering. Such things, the king remarked, could not be hurried. The Portuguese began to reconcile themselves to missing the fleet. Tension of another kind was growing among them: Jorge d'Abreu, the deputy ambassador, felt that the king had been paying too much attention to Dom Rodrigo and not enough to him. He had stirred a faction of the group against Dom Rodrigo, and each new gift from the king to the ambassador, each sign of royal preferment, increased the resentment of d'Abreu and his followers.

Further questioning of Padre Alvares took place in the final days of November. The king had seen references to St. Jerome, St. Dominic, and St. Francis in the viceroy's letter, and he wanted to know who they were, what countries they came from, and why they were so celebrated. Alvares answered as well as he could, describing the Dominican and Franciscan orders and cobbling together from memory biographies of the saints. Then came further discussion of the Church of Rome and its claim to supremacy; Alvares repeated his earlier lecture on the primacy of St. Peter. Did Catholics do everything the Pope commanded? asked the king. "I told them we did, and that so we were obliged to do by the article of our own holy faith in which we confess that we believe in the Holy Mother the Church, which is the Catholic Faith." But the king replied that if the Pope ordered anything contrary to the teachings of the apostles the people of Ethiopia would pay no heed. Even if their own patriarch, the *abuna*, were to ordain something unscriptural, they would throw his edict in the fire! This led Alvares to a rambling and faltering defense of papal authority. Since the Pope was the Holy Father, he said, his decrees could never, by definition, contravene the Scriptures. Off he went once more on an explanation of how the keys of the kingdom of heaven had passed from Antioch and Constantinople to Rome. The king, surprisingly, seemed attracted by Roman Catholicism and told Alvares to send him, the next day, a book that he had on the lives of the saints. The king studied this closely and asked that extracts from it be translated into Ethiopian. It seemed to Alvares that he had a good chance of winning Prester John's spiritual allegiance over to Rome. However, in all his theological discussions with Lebna Dengel, they had not touched at all on the topic of the definition of the Trinity; Alvares appears not to have been aware that his hosts were Monophysite heretics, and that any communion between Ethiopia and Rome would require a transformation of Ethiopia's most fundamental ideas about the nature of Christ.

11

On Monday, November 26, Lebna Dengel unexpectedly broke camp. "It was like this," Alvares tells us. "He mounted a horse and set out with two pages, and no other people; he passed in sight of our tent maneuvering his horse. There was a great tumult in our quarter, and cries of: 'The Neguz is gone, the Neguz is gone,' and this throughout all the camp: everybody started off after him as hurriedly as he could." (*Negus*, or "king," was the title by which the Ethiopians called their monarch, and also *negusa nagast*, "king of kings.") The astonished Portuguese soon found themselves almost alone in the abandoned camp. But an official named Rufa'el appeared and told them that the king had set aside fifty mules and some slaves for their use; and on Tuesday they set out after the peripatetic court, reaching it the following day. Alvares provides an interesting picture of the *negus'* travels through his kingdom, with some curious echoes of the old Prester John letter:

"It is unbelievable how many people always travel with the court; for certainly for a distance of three or four leagues from each place at which they break camp the people are so numerous and so close together that they look like a procession of Corpus Domini in a great city, without getting fewer in any part of the road, and the people are like this. The tenth part of them may be well-dressed people, and nine parts common people, both men and women, young people, and poor, some of them in skins, others in poor cloths, and all these common people carry with them their property, which all consists of pots for making wine, and porringers for drinking. If they move short distances, these poor people carry with them their poor dwellings, made and thatched as they had them; and if they go further they carry the wood, that is, some poles. Rich men bring very fine tents. I do not speak of the great lords and great gentlemen, because each of these moves a city or a good town of tents, and loads, and people on mules, a matter without number or reckoning. . . .

"The Prester John rarely travels straight, nor does anyone know where he is going. This multitude of people travels along the road until they find a white tent pitched, and there they settle down each in his own place. Often the Prester does not come to this tent, but sleeps in the monasteries and large churches which are in the country. In the tent which is thus pitched they do not fail to make solemn instrumental music and singing, yet not so perfectly as when the lord is there: moreover, the churches always travel with the court* and there are thirteen of them. They travel straight, although the Prester John goes off the road. The altar stone or stones of all the churches are treated with much reverence on the way, and are carried only by Mass priests, and always four priests go with each stone, and four others to take turns with them; they carry these stones as if on a stretcher raised on their shoulders, and covered with rich cloths of brocade and silk. In front of each altar or stone, for all go together, walk two *zagonaes* [deacons], with thurible and cross, and another with a bell ringing it. And every man or woman who is going on the road, as soon as he hears the bell goes off the road, and makes room for the church; and if he is riding a mule he dismounts and lets the church go by. Also, whenever the Prester travels with his court, four lions always go before him; these too travel by the straight road, and they go bound with strong chains, one behind and one before, and many men take them; to these also people give up the road, but it is from fear."

When the Portuguese arrived at the new camp of the *negus*, a monk came to them to find out if all was in order. Dom Rodrigo gave effusive thanks for the mules and the slaves, but the fiery d'Abreu burst out, according to Alvares, that the Ethiopians "had not given all the mules, and those that they had given were one-eyed or blind, and the slaves were old and worth nothing. . . . The ambassador answered that he should not say so, that all the mules and slaves and other things were perfect." The quarrel grew louder, with the abashed monk an unhappy witness, and in a moment the ambassador and his deputy were slashing away with swords and lances. Padre Alvares got between them and forced them to halt, though not before d'Abreu had suffered a minor wound; he and his friend Lopo da Gama then stalked away and spent the night outside the envoys' tent. News of this imbroglio reached the king, who asked the Portuguese why they fought with one another

* These "churches" were tents also.

and begged them to be friends. Dom Rodrigo, who understood d'-Abreu's status as deputy merely to mean that he should take charge of the embassy in case of Dom Rodrigo's death, and not that he should have any special privileges before then, told the king that d'Abreu and Lopo da Gama were troublemakers, and requested that they be housed in some other tent from him. Lebna Dengel continued to ask a reconciliation, and Dom Rodrigo—who would have killed d'Abreu had Alvares not intervened—stonily refused to consider one. Although it is clear that the imperious and touchy d'Abreu was more to blame for the dispute than was Dom Rodrigo, the king was displeased with the ambassador's reluctance to make peace, and, taking a fancy to d'Abreu, sent him some fine mules and showed him other signs of affection. "He is like an unbridled horse," Lebna Dengel is said to have remarked of him.

All through December the court was on the move, the Portuguese traveling with it. There were many events. Lazaro d'Andrade, the embassy's painter, was invited to wrestle with one of the king's pages, and came away with a broken leg. The king asked Dom Rodrigo if any of his other men cared to wrestle, and the ambassador sent two skilled wrestlers, Estevam Palharte and Ayras Diz, both servants. Diz wrestled with the same page and received a broken arm; Palharte, losing his courage, did not wrestle at all. Then the Ethiopian wife of one of the Genoese at the court gave birth, and the father asked Alvares to baptize the child. The priest, uneasy at performing the Catholic rite of baptism without the king's permission, tactfully sought leave to do so; the king not only encouraged the baptism but sent oil for it and ordered many of his highest courtiers to attend the ceremony. "They went away as much comforted as if they had eaten good food," Alvares reports, "and they praised our services very much, both baptism and the Mass, because we officiated very slowly, and they seemed to them more perfect than their own."

On Christmas Day the king ordered the tent that was serving as the Portuguese envoys' church to be pitched at the door of his own, so that he could listen to the Christmas service. Alvares assembled an improvised choir of six, and they sang for hours, "and in all this office as long as it lasted, the Prester John never moved from the edge of his tent. . . . Two messengers never ceased coming and going to ask what we were singing, whenever they heard a change in the sound of psalms, hymns, responses, proses, or canticles. I pretended what I did not know, and told them they were books of Jeremiah, which spoke of the birth of Christ; and so of the Psalms of David, and other prophets. He was pleased and praised the books. When our service, which was rather long, was finished, there came an old priest who had been and they say still is the Prester John's chaplain, and asked us if we had finished, or why we were silent. I told him we had finished. He replied that he would have rejoiced if the service had lasted till next morning, and it had seemed to him that he had been in Paradise with the angels." That night Alvares said Mass before Lebna Dengel, his queen, the queen mother, and Queen Eleni, and sprinkled the royal party with holy water. Afterward, Alvares was asked to remain for a private conversation with the king, attended only by an interpreter and the old chaplain, and yet another theological discussion took place, this one concerning the use of incense and other fine points of the Mass. The king questioned Alvares once more, also, about the number of books in the Bible, suspecting that Catholics had some books not known in Ethiopia, and though the priest insisted again and again that he knew only the canonical eighty-one, using the figure he had picked up from the Ethiopians, Lebna Dengel persisted far into the night. Finally Alvares had to ask the king "to have pity on an old man, who had neither eaten nor drunk since yesterday at midday, nor had slept, and could not stand for weakness." The king, who had dozens of further questions to ask, reluctantly let the priest go, and he staggered off to his tent, chilled and hungry and suffering from vertigo. In an hour and a half he was summoned back to sing compline, the last service of the day; it was now the middle of the night, but no sleep lay ahead, for the king had decided to move his camp before dawn, and the Portuguese, fearing to be left behind, packed hastily and went along.

As they traveled Lebna Dengel took pleasure in displaying the wonders of his realm, particularly its fine churches, including the ones for which the Venetian, Brancaleone, had done murals. He asked Alvares how Ethiopian churches compared with those of Europe, and though Alvares found the Ethiopian churches quite fine in their way, he was forced to admit that they were inferior to the great cathedrals of his native continent. At one of these churches the king produced four huge and splendid silk umbrellas, treasures of the state, under each of which ten men could take shelter, and demanded to know if King Manoel had any such magnificent parasols. No, the priest replied, adding, however, that when the King of Portugal wished to shade himself from the sun he could avail himself of one of his many hats, "trimmed with brocade or velvet, or satin or other silk, with braid and tassels of gold." In this and many other interchanges the Portuguese gently tried to defend their homeland against the self-esteem of the Ethiopians; once, when they had spoken too strongly of Portugal's wealth, the king reminded Dom Rodrigo of the meagerness of the presents he had had from King Manoel, and the ambassador, no doubt tired by now of having those presents flung back at him, found it necessary to point out that it was not his king's custom to send such gifts at all. If he had chosen to send some to Lebna Dengel, it had been as a special mark of favor; it was unfortunate that it had not been possible to deliver the original gifts, but that could not have been helped, and it really should not have been necessary for King Manoel to send anything whatever to a brother monarch. Dom Rodrigo went on to point out that he had accomplished his mission and was ready to go home. Alvares gives us the king's reply: "That we should not be angry, and we should soon be dispatched, with much satisfaction to ourselves, and that we should go in peace to dine."

12

It was now January 1521 and the envoys saw little hope of getting to Massawa in time to meet the fleet, for it had taken them from June to October to get from Massawa to the court of the *negus*, and their return journey might be even longer. There was no choice but to put a good face on things and await Prester John's pleasure. On January 4 the king invited them to attend his baptism and those of his family and courtiers, and suggested that the Portuguese might wish to be baptized also. They were baffled by this until Alvares discovered that annual baptism on the day of the festival of the Epiphany, January 6, was a cherished Ethiopian custom. (Although he did not realize it, the rite was not a true rebaptism but only a ritual bath in commemoration of the baptism of Christ.) On behalf of his countrymen Alvares declined the offer of baptism, saying it was not the habit of Europeans to be baptized more than once, when they were infants, but they agreed to attend the ceremony.

It began at midnight in a deep plank-lined tank, fed by water from a mountain brook. Temperatures were low at night in the lofty plateau where the king now was camped, and there was frost upon the ground; yet both baptizer and baptized took part in the rite entirely nude, which greatly scandalized Padre Alvares. The priest in charge was the king's aged chaplain. In this freezing weather the venerable cleric stood naked and shivering in the baptismal tank, the water almost to his shoulders, and as the worshipers one by one came forth, the old man touched their heads and immersed them three times, saying, "I baptize thee in the name of the Father, of the Son, and of the Holy Spirit." The first to enter the tank was Lebna Dengel, followed by the Abuna Marcos, head of the Ethiopian Church, and then the king's wife. These three wore loincloths and had the privilege of privacy as they participated. But after them came a procession of naked Ethiopians, first priests, then deacons, then the gentlemen and ladies of the court, then those of lesser rank, while Lebna Dengel watched from a curtained box on one side of the tank and Alvares and the other Portuguese looked on, shocked, from the other: "Those who were to be baptized entered by the steps, naked, with their backs to the Prester, and when they came out again they showed him their fronts, the women as well as the men."

When some hours of this had passed, the king called Alvares to his side and asked him what he thought of the ceremony. "I answered him that the things of God's service which were done in good faith and without evil deceit, and for His praise, were good, but that there was no such rite as this in our Church, rather it forbade us baptizing without necessity on that day, because on that day Christ was baptized, so that we should not think of saying of ourselves that we were baptized on the same day as Christ." This led to a long discussion of the theory of baptism, in which the king revealed that the present rite had been invented by his grandfather, who felt that, since men would not leave off sinning, they should undergo these annual immersions to cleanse their souls of the year's evil deeds.

After the ceremony Lebna Dengel invited the Portuguese to go swimming in the baptismal tank, and two of them at once jumped in. Meanwhile Alvares went over to talk with the Abuna Marcos, whom he had not met before, and who was "half dead with the cold" following his immersion. Like every *abuna*, Marcos was a Coptic Egyptian, whom Alvares describes as a small, withered old man, bald and white-bearded, said to be a hundred and twenty years of age. At once the *abuna* declared that Alvares was quite right about this annual baptism:

it was wholly unscriptural and much to be deplored; but he said that he had no support in this view, "and that if he had an associate or two, who would help him in speaking the truth, he would free the Prester from many things and errors, in which he and his people were." Then they spoke of such matters as circumcision, and Alvares expounded the Catholic position with such cleverness that the *abuna* laughed merrily; "and this priest, from this time forward became my great friend, and came every day to our Mass and was very friendly with the Portuguese."

A few days later the *abuna* invited Padre Alvares to witness the ordination of new priests. They rode out together to a broad meadow where, to Alvares' consternation, there seemed to be some five or six thousand candidates for holy orders waiting. Many of them were scantily clad or even virtually naked, and Alvares was further startled to find that some of the candidates were maimed or crippled or blind, whereas one had to be wholly sound of body to enter the Catholic priesthood. The *abuna* began the ceremony with a speech in Arabic, translated into Ethiopian by another priest, to the effect that anyone who either had or had had two wives or more must depart, upon pain of excommunication, even if one of the wives was dead. This too dismayed Alvares, to whom even one wife seemed at least one too many for a priest. The candidates now formed three long queues and advanced toward three priests-examiner, who had each one read a few words out of a book and, if he passed this trifling examination, stamped a seal of approval on his right arm. There were very few who did not pass. The successful candidates proceeded to the *abuna*, who pronounced a benediction on them; at the end of the day he gave communion to all the new priests. Alvares asked how many had been ordained that day, and was told there were 2357, all priests; deacons would be ordained two days later.

Speaking of what he had seen with the king soon afterward, Alvares said that "the rite seemed to me very good," but could not help commenting that "it seemed to me very indecent and a very shameful thing for priests who were ordained for the Mass, and were to receive the body of the Lord, to come almost naked and showing their private parts." Nor could he approve of ordaining blind men or cripples: how could a blind man have read the Scriptures, and how could a cripple administer the sacraments? The answer came that the king "was very pleased that I looked at all things and told him of what did not seem to me right, so that they could correct them." On January 10, when Alvares went back to see the deacons ordained, he encountered more surprises: most of the candidates were boys under fifteen, and some were babes in arms. "The children who can neither speak nor walk are carried by men in their arms," Alvares reports, "because women cannot enter into the church, and their wailing is like kids in a yard without the mothers, when they are taken away and are dying of hunger." Each deacon-to-be passed before the *abuna*, who said a short prayer and cut a lock of hair from him; the rest of the ceremony was equally simple. At the end, again, came communion, which to Alvares seemed perilous for some of the infants, who nearly choked on the sacramental wafers forced into their mouths. That evening Alvares asked the *abuna* for an explanation, telling him "that his services seemed to me very good, but that to ordain children newly born, and great ignorant boys, did not seem to me well." The *abuna* replied that he did as he was told, and the king had ordered him to make deacons of children, who could learn the niceties of their calling later: it seemed that the *abuna* was the only one in Ethiopia who could perform ordinations, and, since he was so old, the king feared he might die before he had created a sufficiency of clerics. Because of political disruptions Ethiopia had gone twenty-three years without an *abuna* in the time of Zar'a Yakob, and Lebna Dengel wanted to be certain he had an adequate supply of priests and deacons in the event of another such interregnum. Therefore thousands of ordinations were performed every week, all of them done by the *abuna*, and nearly every Christian male in the kingdom would soon have become a priest or a deacon.

Such things made Alvares increasingly aware of the great cultural chasm separating these people from Western Christendom. So, too, did his visits to Ethiopian church services, where, he says, many of the clergymen "did nothing but sing, dance, and jump, that is to say, leaping upwards. While jumping like this they constantly touched their feet with their hands, first one, then the other." The king asked the Portuguese if priests sang and danced like that in their own country: "We answered no, because our singing was very slow and quiet, both the voice and the movement of the body, and they did not dance or leap. Upon this he sent to ask whether as that was not our custom we thought theirs bad. We sent word that the service of God, in whatever manner it was done, seemed to us good."

13

During these months the task of composing Lebna Dengel's letters to King Manoel and his viceroy in India was slowly going forward. This was a solemn and momentous project. The royal clerks needed a great deal of time, Alvares says, "because their custom is not to write to one another, and their messages, communications, and embassies, are all by word of mouth." Constantly referring to the New Testament as a guide to suitable style, the king and his learned men produced their text with excruciating hesitancy. Then Saga za Ab read it aloud, a few phrases at a time, to Pero da Covilhã, who translated it from the Amharic language of Ethiopia to Portuguese; Padre Alvares, who by now had learned quite a good deal of Amharic from Covilhã, polished and revised Covilhã's version, and João Escolar, the secretary of the embassy, wrote it down. At the same time an Arabic translation was being produced. Then the two letters, in their three versions, Amharic, Arabic, and Portuguese, went to the scribes to be written properly in letters of gold on sheets of parchment, everything in duplicate for safety's sake. The whole process took some three months. The letter to King Manoel began in this fashion:

"In the name of God the Father, as always was, in whom we find no beginning. In the name of the Son, one only, who is like him without being seen; light of the stars, from the first before the foundations of the ocean sea were founded: who in former times was conceived in the womb of the Virgin without seed of man or making of marriage: so was the knowledge of his office. In the name of the Paraclete, spirit of holiness, who knows all secrets, where he was first in the heights of heaven, which is sustained without props or supports, and extended the earth, without its being from the beginning, nor was it known nor created from the east to the west, and from the north to the south; neither is the first nor the second, but the Trinity joined together in one Creator of all things, for ever by one sole counsel and one word for ever and ever. Amen.

"This writing and embassy is sent by the Incense of the Virgin [Lebna Dengel], for that is his name by baptism, and when he became king he was named King David, the head of his kingdoms, beloved of God, prop of the faith, a relation of the lineage of Judah, son of

David, son of Solomon, son of the Pillar of Sion [King 'Amda-Seyon], son of the Seed of Jacob [King Zar'a Yakob], son of the Hand of Mary [King Ba'eda-Maryam], son of Nahum [King Na'od] in the flesh; emperor of the high Ethiopia and of great kingdoms, lordships and lands, King of Xoa, of Cafate, of Fatigar, of Angote. . . . This letter goes to the very powerful and most excellent King Dom Manoel, who always conquers, and who lives in the love of God, and firm in the Catholic faith, son of Peter and Paul, King of Portugal and the Algarves, a friend of the Christians, an enemy of the Moors and Gentiles; Lord of Africa and Guinea, and of the mountains and islands of the moon, and of the Red Sea, and of Arabia, Persia, and Ormuz, and of the great Indies, and of all its towns and islands; Judge and Conqueror of the Moors and strong pagans, lord of the Moors and very high lands. Peace be with you King Manoel, strong in the faith, assisted by our Lord Jesus Christ to kill the Moors, and without lance or buckler you drive and cast them out like dogs. Peace be with your wife, the friend of Jesus Christ, the servant of our Lady the Virgin mother of the Savior of the world. Peace be with your sons at this hour. . . . Peace to all your people and populations who are in Christ. Peace to your great cities and to all those that are within them that are not Jews or Moors, only to those who are Christians. Peace to all the parishes which are in Christ and to your faithful grandees. Amen."

Lebna Dengel then retells the peregrinations of the ambassador Matthew at great length, describing his great joy when Matthew's labors culminated in the arrival of a party of Portuguese in Ethiopia, since there were ancient prophecies "that a Frank king should meet with the King of Ethiopia, and that they should give each other peace, and I did not know if this would be in my days and time or in another." Never before had Christians come to him, only "pagans and Moors, dirty sons of Mafamede [Mohammed], and others [who] are slaves who do not know God; and others worship sticks and fire, and others the sun, and others serpents." But now the way was open for a holy alliance between the two Christian kings, "and I and you will not be other than very joyful on account of His goodness, because He has given us everything. And now," Lebna Dengel continues, "do you not cease to make your prayer until God gives into your hands the Holy House of Jerusalem, which is in the hands of rebels against Christ, and they are Moors, and heathens, and heretics." For his own part he pledges, "I will give a thousand times 100,000 drachms of gold, and as many fighting men, and moreover I will give wood, iron and copper to make and equip the fleet, and an infinite quantity of supplies." He has special words of praise for Padre Alvares, whom he hopes King Manoel will nominate as bishop of the lands bordering the Red Sea, because he is "a just man and very truthful in speech, and in all matters which concern the faith." This diocese was at the moment entirely populated by Moslems, but the king prays that Alvares be granted strength to convert them. He asks also that Alvares go to the Pope "with my obedience, which is a matter directly for me." Whether he meant by that obscure phrase to place Ethiopia under papal authority is difficult to say. The king grants permission to the Portuguese to settle on Ethiopia's frontiers, especially at Massawa. Lastly, he says, "Send me craftsmen who can make figures of gold and silver, copper, iron, tin, and lead, and send me lead for the churches: and craftsmen in type-founding to make books in our characters for use in church; and craftsmen in gilding with gold leaf, to make the gold leaf; and this soon, and let them come to stay with me here and in my favor. And when they wish to return of their own free will, I will not detain them, and this I swear by Jesus Christ, Son of the living God. . . . I take courage to make requests of you, and do not hold this to be shameful, for I will pay for it. Because when a son begs from his father, he cannot say him nay, and you are my father, and I your son: and we are joined together as the stone-blocks in a wall, and also we are both joined, one heart in the love of Jesus Christ, who is the Head of the world, He, the Lord Jesus Christ, and so all those who are with Him joined like stone-blocks well fixed together in a wall."

The letters were ready at last on February 11, 1521, each tied up in a small brocaded bag and packed in a leather-lined basket. The time of departure had come, not only for the Portuguese envoys but for the assorted Genoese and Spaniards and others who had lived in Ethiopia since their escape from the Turks four years earlier. (Lebna Dengel had not, however, granted Pero da Covilhã permission to go.) At the ceremony of leave-taking, the king first bestowed on the former Turkish prisoners rich cloths of silk and damask, and thirty ounces of gold to be divided among the thirteen of them. Then Padre Alvares received a silver cross and an inlaid crozier, symbolizing the bishopric Lebna Dengel hoped he would be granted. Dom Rodrigo de Lima was given thirty ounces of gold, and another fifty were awarded to those who had come with him; the king specifically instructed that Jorge d'Abreu and d'Abreu's followers were to have their share of it. The king's other gifts included thirty mules, a hundred loads of flour, a hundred horns of mead, and much else. As a special present for King Manoel, Lebna Dengel offered his own crown, a large one of gold and silver.

They set out for Massawa on Shrove Tuesday, February 12, 1521. Relations between Dom Rodrigo and d'Abreu were so strained that the two men traveled separately, each with his cluster of friends. Two of the Portuguese remained behind, having been persuaded by Lebna Dengel that Ethiopia had need of their skills: these were João Bermudes, the physician, and the painter, Lazaro d'Andrade. Pero da Covilhã, Alvares tells us, rode as a guide with Dom Rodrigo and his group, and with him came "his black wife and some of his sons, who were gray." Saga za Ab accompanied d'Abreu's party.

It was a troublesome journey. "Sin began to excite fresh quarrels," says Alvares, who was with Dom Rodrigo. On the second night João Gonçalves, the factor, fell into a dispute with his assistant, João Fernandes, and struck him furiously with a stick. The next day Fernandes lay in wait for the factor and speared him twice with a lance, almost killing him. Dom Rodrigo had Fernandes seized and bound, but in the night someone freed him, and he ran off to join d'Abreu. Next came difficulties in a town of Moslems tributary to the Ethiopian king; they attacked one of Dom Rodrigo's servants and knocked out two of his teeth, and stoned a man who went to his rescue. An Ethiopian official rounded up the guilty parties, made them pay seven ounces of gold in reparation to the two injured men, and sent them on to Lebna Dengel, who had one Moslem flogged and another beheaded. Meanwhile the Portuguese proceeded on into the province of Tigré, where villagers again stoned them. Here they were met by two great lords of the court, who showed the greatest displeasure over the feuding between Dom Rodrigo and d'Abreu, which they thought "a very scandalous thing." They seemed disinclined to conduct the Portuguese any farther toward the coast unless peace were made among them. At length a glum reconciliation took place for the sake of avoiding trouble with their hosts, but by this time the winds had shifted in the Red Sea, and there was no hope that the fleet would have remained at Massawa to pick them up. (In fact, the fleet had not managed to get to Massawa at all that year.) The trip had been in vain.

While debating their next move, the stranded Portuguese emissaries took lodgings in the town of Debarwa, the capital of the province ruled by the *bahr nagash*. Here the quarrels broke out again. Dom

Rodrigo refused to share his provisions with the faction of d'Abreu. Thereupon d'Abreu and his men burst by night into the houses where the other group was lodged, breaking down doors and firing muskets wildly; a desperate and ludicrous battle ensued, everyone running around shouting in the dark. The uproar was so great that it drew Ethiopian soldiers to the scene, who arrested all of the Portuguese. The local officials sent them to the *bahr nagash*, who chided them for their behavior and "shouted a good deal at the ambassador and at Jorge d'Abreu," according to Alvares. "He told the ambassador to give up to him at once the crown of the Prester, and the letters which he was carrying for the King of Portugal and the Captain Major [the viceroy]. Between the ambassador and Jorge d'Abreu some very ugly words passed." The *bahr nagash* had the Portuguese escorted back to Lebna Dengel's court, taking the precaution of keeping the hostile parties separate en route. They reached the no doubt surprised monarch late in the summer of 1521.

14

Although the Portuguese envoys had bungled their departure from Ethiopia, news of their presence there had reached their mother country. In April 1521 caravels from India arrived in Lisbon, bearing letters from the viceroy describing his friendly meeting with the *bahr nagash* near Massawa, and telling of the dispatch of Dom Rodrigo's mission to the interior of Ethiopia. On May 8, King Manoel sent a jubilant letter to Pope Leo X, declaring, "With the favor of divine clemency we have at last found that most powerful bishop of the Indian and Ethiopian Christians, Prester John, Lord of the Province of Abyssinia." The letter was swiftly published in Latin and in a dual Latin-French edition, so that all of Europe might know. At the same time there appeared in Lisbon a little book entitled, *Letter of the News That Came to the King Our Lord of the Discovery of the Prester John.* This told of the visits of the Portuguese fleet to the Red Sea and the departure of the embassy for the interior; it gave a good deal of information about Ethiopian life and religion; and it made public the letter from Queen Eleni to King Manoel that Matthew had delivered in 1514, asking military alliance between Ethiopia and Portugal.

There was general excitement over the attainment of Prester John's kingdom. In the Vatican, papal officials promptly drew up five letters to be sent to that land by the next ambassadors. One was addressed to "Dearly beloved son in Christ, David, illustrious King of Ethiopia and Abyssinia and the Nile," one to "Dearly beloved daughter in Christ, Helen [Eleni], illustrious Queen of Ethiopia and Abyssinia and the Nile," two to "Venerable brother Mark, Patriarch of Alexandria," and one to "All the archbishops, bishops, abbots, provosts, and other prelates, and the princes, clergy, and all the people of the kingdoms of Ethiopia, Abyssinia, and the Nile." But these documents, so optimistically conceived, never were delivered.

Meanwhile the envoys in Ethiopia now had the opportunity for a leisurely exploration of Prester John's country, for they had no way to leave until the spring of 1522, at the earliest. They wandered about a good deal, generally following the court of Lebna Dengel and remaining perpetually divided into two glaring factions. In 1522 no Portuguese fleet came to Massawa, and so they found themselves with another year to kill.

Padre Alvares, at least, seems to have enjoyed his enforced stay. He visited most of Ethiopia's outstanding tourist attractions: the ruins of Axum, the rock temples of Lalibela, the great churches, and the numerous hermitages where holy men passed their lives under conditions of quite remarkable privation. He also journeyed to the all but inaccessible *amba*, or sheer-faced mountain, on which the kings of Ethiopia imprisoned members of their families who might otherwise be rivals for the throne. This extraordinary custom was long established in Ethiopia. Since succession to the throne traveled in the male line, from royal father to eldest son, the king's daughters and their descendants had no hereditary rights to the crown and were permitted to live freely wherever they chose. But when a new king was crowned, he immediately shut up his brothers and their families atop the royal *amba*, which was, Alvares says, "a rock sheer like a wall, straight from the top to the bottom; if a man goes to the foot of it and looks upwards, it seems that the sky rests upon it. They say that it has three entrances or gates, on three sides, and no more." Here the royal exiles lived forever isolated from the country, under constant guard and forbidden even to send messages to those below. In this way they passed decades in luxurious idleness, the most pampered prisoners in the realm. The system not only insured domestic tranquillity but helped preserve the dynasty, for the royal *amba* was a storehouse of princes, and if the king died without leaving sons it was a simple matter to reach into the *amba* and draw forth one of his brothers, or even an uncle, to succeed him. Many times in Ethiopian history some Rip Van Winkle of a prince was brought down from the *amba* after twenty or thirty years of seclusion to occupy the throne; had the princes been left free to hunt lions or do battle against the Moslems, the dynastic line might quickly have been broken. While Alvares was at the court, a monk who had spent sixteen years on the *amba* escaped from it with a message from one of the princes; supposedly it was an appeal to the Portuguese to liberate the royal captives. The message was intercepted and the monk was flogged by relays of executioners until he died; two hundred of the *amba's* guards were brought down and flogged too, in order to discover which of them had permitted the monk to get free. Later, a sixteen-year-old brother of Lebna Dengel managed to flee from the mountain and went to his mother's house; but the queen mother, knowing the penalties for harboring a royal fugitive, turned him over to the king, who sent him back to the *amba*.

Ethiopia was sorely plagued by locusts in Lebna Dengel's time. Alvares tells us, "Their multitude, which covers the earth and fills the air, is not to be believed; they darken the light of the sun." In one province they devoured the crops along a path eight leagues wide. Since the prayers of Ethiopia's own priests seemed unavailing against them, Alvares volunteered in 1523 to help: he asked the natives to capture a quantity of locusts and bring them before him, and then he read to the insects "a requisition and denunciation of excommunication besides, that within three hours they should begin to set out on their way, and go to the sea, or to the country of the Moors, or to mountains of no profit to the Christians: and should they not do so, [I] called upon and invoked the birds of the air and the animals of the earth, and the stones and tempests to disperse and break and devour their bodies. . . . I thus made this denunciation to those present, in their names, and those of the absent ones, and ordered them to be let go in peace. It pleased Our Lord to hear the sinners. When we were returning to the town, because their road was to the sea from whence they came, there were so many [locusts] coming after us, that it seemed as though they wanted to break our ribs and heads by pelting us with stones, such were the thumps they inflicted on us. . . . Meanwhile a great storm arose from the sea, which met them, confronting them with violent rain and hail, which lasted quite three hours. . . . The next day in the morning there was not a single one alive in the whole country." The happy Ethiopians hailed Alvares' expulsion of the locusts as a miracle, though a few whispered darkly that he had done it by sorcery.

Alvares observed with some interest the practices of the Ethiopians during Lent. Fasting on bread and water was general for the full six weeks, and other penances more severe were performed by the pious: he saw monks trussed into iron girdles in Lent, and some who remained standing the whole season, and some who confined themselves in wooden boxes, while at Axum a multitude of monks and nuns passed Lent neck-deep in a great tank of cold water. One way to avoid these rigors was to get married on the Thursday before Shrove Tuesday, for newlyweds were allowed a month's dispensation from fasting; and, since polygamy was permitted in Ethiopia, Alvares says, "Some of my friends used to marry new wives on the Thursday before Lent, merely to have the privilege of eating meat." But this was not a wide-spread habit.

The priest took careful notes also on court etiquette, the Ethiopian code of justice, the structure of the provincial governments, and other such matters. And, like Mandeville or any of the other medieval fabulists, he set down an account "of the countries and kingdoms which are on the frontiers of the Prester John," the chief difference between his and theirs being that his was based on reliable information. Some of the surrounding kingdoms were Moslem, some were pagan; most paid tribute to Ethiopia, though some, such as Adel and Harar, frequently caused trouble. From Damot, a kingdom of pagans and some Christians west of Lebna Dengel's domain, came most of the gold in Ethiopia, of which there was an immense quantity. (Covilhã told Alvares that in one of the royal treasuries, a cache near his estate, there was enough gold to buy the world: every year huge amounts were put in, and none was ever taken out.) South of Damot, Alvares had heard, lay the kingdom of the Amazons. But he was skeptical of this, for the Amazons he had read about—he mentions the *Book of the Infante Dom Pedro* as one of his sources—mated with men only a few months of the year, while these women "have husbands universally throughout the year, and universally they at all times pass their lives with each other. They have not got a king, but have a queen; she is not married, nor has she any particular husband, but still she does not stop having sons and daughters, and her daughter is the heir to the kingdom. They say that they are very strong women of a very warlike disposition, and

they fight on very swift animals that resemble cows, and are great archers, and when they are little they dry up the left breast in order not to
hinder drawing the arrow."

15

On April 15, 1523, Padre Alvares sang a requiem Mass in memory of
Queen Eleni, whose long life had reached its end the year before.
While the ceremony was taking place, performed in a big new white
tent with silken curtains, messengers from the coast arrived, bearing
two packets of letters for the Portuguese. They had been sent by Dom
Luis de Meneses, who introduced himself as the brother of Dom Duarte
de Meneses, the new Viceroy of Portuguese India in succession to
Diogo Lopes de Sequeira. Dom Luis said that he had arrived in the
Red Sea in January 1523, commanding a fleet of Portuguese ships; and,
coming to Massawa, he had learned that Dom Rodrigo de Lima and
the rest of the envoys still had not been picked up. Therefore he instructed the envoys to come to Massawa at once; he would wait for
them, he promised, as long as he dared without risking the unfavorable
summer winds. If they did not come to him by the date he specified, he
would sail for India without them. The deadline he set was April 15,
1523.

Since the Portuguese were eight days' journey from Massawa just
then, they realized they had missed the boat again. Dom Luis' letters
contained bad news of another sort, too: King Manoel the Fortunate
had died in December 1521, word of his passing having reached Portuguese India the following August. This was a shattering blow to the
emissaries; weeping, they donned mourning clothes and even adopted
the Ethiopian expression of grief by shaving their heads. Lebna Dengel
sent two monks to learn what had happened, and Alvares replied,
"Tell His Highness that the stars and the moon have fallen, and the
sun has grown dark and lost its brightness, and we have no one to shelter or protect us; we have neither father nor mother to care for us, except God, who is the Father of all: the King Dom Manoel our lord
has departed from the life of the world, and we are left orphans and
unprotected." The king displayed his sympathy by proclaiming three
days of national mourning, in which no business could be transacted.
When the three days had elapsed, Lebna Dengel sent for Dom Rodrigo

and asked who would inherit the Portuguese throne. The ambassador replied that the prince Dom João, Manoel's son, was now King João III, to which Lebna Dengel cheerfully responded, "Do not be afraid, for you are in a Christian country, the father was good, the son will be good, and I will write to him."

Some of the Portuguese, thinking Dom Luis and the fleet might yet be waiting for them at Massawa, wanted to set out for the coast at this juncture. Lebna Dengel gave them permission to go, but yet it was necessary for them to remain patiently with the court while the new letter to King João was being composed. That endeavor required a month and a half for its completion. In his letter Lebna Dengel made use of the customary flamboyant rhetoric to vouchsafe his grief over the death of João's father and to offer the new king his fraternal love. To console João for having come to the throne at an early age (he had been, in fact, nineteen years old at Manoel's death) Lebna Dengel observed, "The King Solomon reigned at twelve years, and had great strength and had more knowledge than his father. I also, when my father Nahu [Na'od] died, was very little, and succeeded to his seat, and God gave me greater strength than my father, and I have got all the people of my kingdoms and provinces under my hand, and I am at rest." He urged an alliance upon João: "I have got men, gold, and provisions like the sands of the sea and the stars of heaven. Both of us together we will destroy all the Mourisma [Moslems]." He voiced his regret at not having another Christian king close at hand, and added, "I, lord brother, am not pleased with the Kings of Frankland [Europe], who, being Christian, are not of one heart, and are always fighting with one another. If I had a Christian king for a neighbor, I would never separate from him for an hour." And with a disarming lack of guile he told João, "Lord king and brother, always send me your embassy and write to me, because seeing your letters it seems to me that I see your face, for much more love exists between those who are distant than between those that are near, on account of the desires they feel, as is mine, who do not see your treasures and love you well always in my heart." The letter concluded with a welter of allusions to such biblical figures as "Noe," "Moises," "Rica" [Rachel], and "Sidrac, Misaac and Abdenago."

As the Portuguese departed for the coast, bearing this and the earlier letters, the king gave them rich clothes, mules, heavy gold chains, and other valuable things as the latest in the series of farewell gifts he had bestowed on them over the years. They made the useless journey to Massawa, discovered as they expected that the fleet of Dom Luis de Meneses had sailed on schedule some months before, and returned to the court. Dom Luis had left some pepper for them at Massawa, and a letter telling them that on no account should they stray far from the sea, since he would make another attempt to rescue them in the spring of 1524 and did not want another missed rendezvous.

One tends to think that Dom Rodrigo and his band, who were beginning their fourth year in Ethiopia, would have established themselves in Massawa and not stirred from the island until the fleet showed up. But instead they continued to accompany Lebna Dengel wherever he wandered, and the early months of 1524 saw them far from the coast, at the town of Dara in the central province of Shoa. The king had now suddenly taken up the study of geography and had brought out the map of the world given him by Dom Rodrigo in 1520. Now he asked Alvares to transliterate the name of each country on the map into Amharic script, which the priest did with the help of the monk Saga za Ab. When this was done, the map was presented again to Lebna Dengel, who was astounded to discover that the mighty kingdom of Portugal from whom these emissaries had come was in truth the merest tiny sliver of territory at the edge of Europe. His own land, by contrast, was immense on the map, for the Portuguese cartographer, having no idea of Ethiopia's actual boundaries, had shown the dominions of Prester John as occupying about half of the African continent. The king's faith in Portugal's power was considerably shaken, and he suggested to Dom Rodrigo that it might be best if Portugal joined with France and Spain in occupying the Red Sea, for surely so small a nation could not control it alone. Chagrined, Dom Rodrigo pointed out that Ethiopia's size on the map had unavoidably been exaggerated through ignorance, whereas "Portugal and Spain are in the map of the world as things that are well known." He asked the king to consider how small such undoubtedly important places as Rome, Venice, and Jerusalem appeared on the map, before attempting to judge the strength of Portugal by its area. At this Lebna Dengel was much relieved, and abandoned thought of bringing in France and Spain.

A few days after the episode of the map, the king declared he wished to write a letter to the Pope, whom he called "the King of Rome and Head of the Popes." Because he was unsure of the proper phrases to use in addressing a Pope, Lebna Dengel asked the Portuguese to help in preparing the text. Dom Rodrigo, who seems also to have been unnerved by the prospect of framing a letter worthy of the papal attention, replied that they had not come to Ethiopia to write letters, nor was there anyone among them able to write to the Pope. But the indomitable Padre Alvares volunteered for the assignment. Reporting to the place where the king's scribes and scholars had gathered, Alvares found that as usual they had assembled a mound of learned books to guide their choice of words. Where, they wondered, were Alvares' own books? He told them serenely that he could write letters without the aid of books, and that if they would only inform him of what the king intended to convey to the Pope, he would sit down straightaway and make a beginning. Was such a thing possible? Yes, yes, of course, said Alvares, and as the amazed scribes looked on he took pen and paper, put down "Blessed Holy Father" as salutation, and rattled off the opening paragraphs of a perfectly adequate letter.

With the aid of Saga za Ab and the king's chaplain, Alvares drafted the Portuguese text, which was done into Amharic and shown to Lebna Dengel for approval, then inscribed on parchment in the traditional letters of gold. To Alvares' great joy, the king wished to inform the Pope that he recognized his primacy and herewith made submission to him, hoping that the Holy Father would extend his blessing to him. In a second letter composed in a similar way several days later, Lebna Dengel reiterated his obedience to the Pope and asked for messengers from Rome, as well as for technical assistance. Alvares interpreted these letters to mean that Lebna Dengel planned to have Ethiopia adopt the rites of the Roman Catholic Church, but it is most unlikely that the king had any such thought in mind; Lebna Dengel was merely sending his compliments to one of the great princes of Christendom, and his offer of "submission" was no more to be taken literally than his calling King Manoel "father" and King João III "brother."

Lebna Dengel had decided also to send Saga za Ab as his ambassador to the King of Portugal, which pleased Alvares, "because he was a man who got on well with us, and we with him, and he had no need of an interpreter." The monk accompanied them on their journey to Massawa in the spring of 1524; and in midsummer he accompanied them back to court, for no fleet had come that year. Nor did the ships come for them in 1525. By now Dom Rodrigo was keeping two men permanently stationed by the sea, so that there would be no chance of missing the fleet if ever it came again. On the eve of Easter Sunday, 1526, these two rushed "desperate and senseless" into the Portuguese lodgings in Debarwa and cried out, "There are no Portuguese there [at Massawa] to come for us, nor are there in India, for all are routed and India is lost." They had had this frightful news from the crewmen of three Moslem ships recently arrived at Massawa; disembarking "with much sounding of music and festivity, and very rich merchandise," the Moors told the distraught Portuguese that their country's fleet in the Indian Ocean had been wiped out and all of the Portuguese settlements along the perimeter of that sea were in ruins.

"Father," Dom Rodrigo remarked to Alvares, "let us say Mass tomorrow very early, and commend ourselves to God."

Alvares was too disturbed to conduct the ceremony, and so at dawn the grim and despondent Portuguese filed into Debarwa's chief church to take part in an Ethiopian Easter service. A melancholy Easter dinner followed; then Alvares, excusing himself, went off beside a secluded stream to weep alone. After more than an hour of this, he regained his usual equanimity and told himself: "Now this comes from God, and He is served by me in this land: if it is His will that I should remain here, the Lord always be praised! I know this country better than any native of it does, because I go in pursuit of game, and know its mountains and waters, and the land which is good for cultivation and which will give all that is planted or sown in it. I have got good slaves and fourteen cows, and I have got rams which I will exchange for ewes. I shall go off near to some water, and have a strong bush fence made to keep off the wild beasts, and I shall pitch my tent in which I can shelter with my attendants, and I will make a hermitage within, and each day I will say Mass, and commend myself to God, since the Lord is pleased that I should be here. I will order the bushes to be cut so I can make gardens, and I will show grain of all sorts: and with my crops and game I will support myself and attendants and servants." Greatly comforted, Padre Alvares returned to his companions and found Dom Rodrigo and the others discussing their plight. Dom Rodrigo saw no option but to make the trek back inland to the court's present site and throw themselves on the charity of Prester John. But Alvares explained his scheme of settling as gentlemen farmers in this coastal province, and all but Dom Rodrigo were immediately infected by his enthusiasm, declaring, "We will grow rich, and we will make a town of our own in which we will breed cattle, and we will make big tilled fields."

Through that day and the next they planned their colony—some to farm, some to seek markets for their goods by land, some by sea. Then they went hunting, returning with a haul of hares and bustards, and were enjoying a hearty dinner on Monday night, April 2, when Abetai, one of Alvares' native servants, burst in, gasping, "Sir, sir, the Portuguese on the sea!" Abetai had heard the news from a man just arrived from the coast, who had gone to tell the *bahr nagash*. Alvares hurried to the palace of that potentate, but the guards would not admit him, and he waited there with Abetai until the cocks crowed. Then a man came out. Alvares asked, "Are you the man who saw the Portuguese on the sea?" He answered, "I did not see them with my eyes, but I heard with my ears, on Easter morning, firing of bombards at Dahlak, and I bring this message from the Sultan of Arkiko to the *bahr nagash*."

The firing at Dahlak might have been anything—even the Turks or Arabs celebrating the downfall of Portuguese India. The marooned emissaries spent an uneasy day, "neither believing nor disbelieving either the good or the bad news," and on Tuesday night, says Alvares, "there came to us a letter from Eitor da Silveira, Captain Major of the Indian Sea, who had come for us, and was stopping in Massawa. Here I do not know how to say how pleased we all were, except that we went out of our senses, so great was the joy."

16

Dom Rodrigo was all for setting out for Massawa in the morning; but Alvares pointed out that it was unseemly to travel during the Easter season, and, sending a messenger to Silveira to make certain he would wait for them, they remained at Debarwa until Monday, April 9. Then they hastened to the coast, a journey of fifty or sixty miles. Silveira assured them that the story of a Portuguese defeat in India was merely a malicious lie: there had been no defeat, nor even a battle.

On April 28, 1526, the fleet sailed out of Massawa—three royal galleons and two caravels. They reached the island of Kamaran on May 1, and there the wind failed them for three days; while they waited, Alvares sought out the grave of Duarte Galvão, the first ambassador, who had died on Kamaran nine years before, and reverently exhumed his bones so that they could have a proper interment in a Catholic churchyard. The remains had to be smuggled on board, for the superstitious sailors would not gladly have transported a skeleton. But as soon as the box of bones was hidden on the ship the wind changed, as if for Galvão's sake, and off went the fleet. By November the emissaries were safely across the Indian Ocean in Goa. From there they went to Cananor and then to Cochin, where Alvares delivered Duarte Galvão's remains to his son Antonio, the captain of a ship that soon would be leaving for Portugal as part of a company of three vessels carrying pepper and cloves.

The first of the three sailed on January 4, 1527, bearing Dom Rodrigo de Lima and his fellow ambassador, Saga za Ab; Alvares went with Antonio Galvão's ship, which departed on January 18, and the last ship set forth in the first week of February. The vagaries of maritime travel brought the three ships together, to the amazement of everyone, on April 2, and they sailed as a fleet for a few days, until Antonio Galvão's vessel fell behind the others. The ships were united again in the Azores and went on to Portugal. Lisbon came into view on July 24, 1527.

Padre Alvares had been away from his homeland for twelve years; some of the others, who had had prior service in India before volunteering for the embassy, had been absent even longer; none had been home in at least eight years. But the moment of happy homecoming was not yet at hand, for as they sailed into the mouth of the Tagus River, which forms Lisbon's harbor, "a caravel came out with a message from the king our lord, saying that His Highness ordered that those who came with the embassy of the Prester John were not to land in Lisbon because it was prevented by the plague." They were instead to transfer to riverboats that would take them up the Tagus to Santarem, where they could obtain transportation to Coimbra, the king's place of refuge while the epidemic raged.

These men newly returned from subtropical Ethiopia and tropical India disembarked at Santarem, Alvares tells us, "in the greatest heat I ever felt." Saga za Ab and the servants that had come from Ethiopia were "half dead with heat," and Alvares feared he would succumb to sunstroke himself; he staggered into an inn where the keeper comforted him with cucumbers and cool wine, and he soon felt better. The emissaries had brought back with them a pair of Arab pilots who had been captured off India, and Dom Rodrigo had outfitted them in Portuguese garb—shirts, waistcoats, jackets, trousers—so that they could be presented to the king. Both Arabs collapsed in the heat of Santarem; one died that night despite elaborate attempts to save him, and the other remained in delirium. A royal official, hearing that a member of the party from Ethiopia had died, suspected the plague might be loose among them and conducted an inquiry: the envoys swore "that we were in good health and very sound, and from a very wholesome country, and that we had not entered Lisbon, or any other infected country." As for the Arabs, Alvares explained that, "although they belonged to hot countries with great heats, they were not accustomed to going about clothed and shod, but wore only a cloth round them from their bodies," and so the dead man had suffocated in his European garments. Nevertheless, the travelers were permitted to come no closer to Coimbra than a town five miles south of it, and they stayed there in quarantine for a month before they were allowed to see the king.

At last Diogo Lopes de Sequeria, the former viceroy of India "who had taken us to the country of the Prester John, and looked upon this embassy as a thing of his own," came to embrace them all and conduct them to King João. Alvares relates how "the Marquis of Vilareal led the ambassador of the Prester John [Saga za Ab] by the hand until he kissed the hands of the king and queen our lords, and of the cardinal and the infantes, and we all kissed them in the same way. The king asked the ambassador how the Prester John his lord was, if he was in health, and so the queen his wife, and his sons. The ambassador answered that all were in good health, and very anxious to learn and hear good news of His Highness and of the queen, and his brothers." The first meeting at court went no further than this exchange of politenesses. Two days later Saga za Ab delivered the crown that Lebna Dengel had sent for King João, and turned over the letters addressed to the king and to the late King Manoel.

The king provided Saga za Ab with mules, furnishings, and a generous expense allowance, and kept him at court to await the next letter in the royal correspondence between Portugal and Ethiopia. But Ethiopia was of less concern to João III than it had been to Manoel, and Saga za Ab shortly found himself relegated to limbo, a picturesque but obscure figure at the court whose purpose in coming to Portugal was quite forgotten by most of those around him. Months dragged into years, and there was no sign of any letter from João III to Lebna

Dengel, nor was Saga za Ab able to gain the Portuguese king's attention. Uneasy in these foreign surroundings, unable to adapt to the
alien religious practices of these Catholic Christians, woefully bored
by his idleness, Saga za Ab adopted a most unmonklike and scandalous
licentiousness as his medicine for despair. Alvares, too, was having
problems. He had hoped to be sent quickly on to Rome to give the Pope
the letters from Lebna Dengel that had been entrusted to him; but
João III kept him in Lisbon, asserting that the war then going on between Portugal and France made the roads unsafe. In 1529 the king
dispatched an ambassador to the Pope to negotiate the establishment
of a branch of the Holy Inquisition in Portugal; Alvares begged to be
permitted to go along, but João would not let him. Until the question
of the Inquisition was settled, the king wanted no other Portuguese
in Rome to distract the Pope. From time to time, Alvares writes, "I
reminded His Highness about sending me to complete the journey
which I had promised and sworn to the Prester John to make, namely,
to carry his letters and a cross of gold and his obedience to the Holy
Father in Rome." João found one excuse and another, and eventually
told Alvares that he would shortly be sending another embassy to Rome
headed by a member of his family, Dom Martinho de Portugal: Alvares
could go when Dom Martinho did, but not before.

Dom Martinho's embassy finally departed for Rome in 1532, five
years after Alvares' return from Ethiopia. In January 1533, Alvares at
last came into the presence of the Pope at a grand consistory held in
the cathedral of Bologna. Even though he had been to the ends of the
earth and had looked upon the face of Prester John, this must have
been an awesome moment for the old priest. Here on a lofty throne
sat Pope Clement VII, Giulio de' Medici. Beside him was no less a per-
sonage than the Emperor Charles V, ruler of half of Europe. Cardinals
and archbishops and lesser prelates were on hand in throngs. Dom
Martinho spoke first, presenting a letter from King João III to the
Pope in which the Portuguese monarch told of his country's close relationship with Ethiopia, of its feats in propagating the faith in
India and Africa, and of Portugal's penetration of the Red Sea, "never
before sailed by Christian fleets." Then Dom Martinho gave the Pope
copies of the letters from Lebna Dengel to King Manoel and King
João. Now Alvares came forward and offered the two letters from
Lebna Dengel to the Pope that he had helped compose, nine years
before, in a land so strange and far away that it was coming to seem

only a dream to him. The papal secretary read the letters aloud in Latin. Alvares then took out Lebna Dengel's gift for the Pope, a cross of gold, and made a brief speech of presentation in Portuguese, which the papal secretary also translated:

"Most Holy and Blessed Father, the most serene and powerful lord David, king of the great and high Ethiopia, by the masses called Prester John, no less eminent in his observance of the true religion than in power, wealth, and kingdoms, sent this ambassador of his to Your Holiness with these letters which he delivered to you, together with the command that he render to Your Holiness as true vicar of Christ, successor of Peter, and supreme pontiff of the universal Church, true obedience and submission in the name of His Majesty and of all his kingdoms with all humility, as he has in fact done, and that he offer to Your Holiness this little gift of a gold cross, which should be esteemed not so much for its value, which is slight, as for the veneration due that cross on which Our Lord Jesus Christ deigned to suffer for us, at the same time beseeching you humbly, in the name of that prince of his, to deign to accept all these things with the pious affection of a father from his most devoted son."

The Pope instructed his secretary to reply that the Holy Father, and all the cardinals as well, were pleased to accept the Ethiopian king's declaration of obedience and were grateful for the gift. He praised the Portuguese for having made possible this contact between himself and these distant Christians, and promised to look into the matter of a full union between the Roman and Ethiopian churches. With that the meeting was dismissed. But Pope Clement, who had spent most of his reign wrestling with King Henry VIII of England over the matter of Henry's wish for a divorce, was too deeply preoccupied with the problem of English rebellion against papal authority to do anything about the Ethiopian situation. When he died, in September 1534, Ethiopia had not been brought into the Church of Rome, but England had left it.

17

Things had not gone well for the realm of Prester John since the departure of the Portuguese envoys. Adel and Harar, the Moslem kingdoms east of Ethiopia which Lebna Dengel had defeated so shatteringly

15. Biet Giorgis, one of the stone churches of Lalibela. PHOTO COURTESY
OF ETHIOPIAN AIRLINES.

16. Ethiopian church art. PHOTO COURTESY OF ETHIOPIAN AIRLINES.

17. Shielded from the sun by an ornate umbrella, flanked by assistants carrying elaborate crosses, a priest walks in a procession through the streets of Axum. WIDE WORLD PHOTO.

18. Aerial view of Lalibela, site of eleven thirteenth-century churches carved from solid rock. The mountains, rising to more than 13,000 feet, are characteristic of the rugged Ethiopian topography. WIDE WORLD PHOTO.

in 1517, had recovered their strength under the leadership of an extraordinary general named Ahmed ibn-Ibrahim el-Ghazi, known to Ethiopians as Ahmed Gran, "Ahmed the Left-Handed." This charismatic warrior was revered by his troops as though he were a saint: "He is neither sultan nor emir," his followers declared, "but an *imam* of the faithful, the *imam* of the end of the world!" He had allied himself to the Turks who had conquered Egypt in 1516, and had received from them not only detachments of experienced soldiers but also firearms, which the Ethiopians did not have.

Not many months after the Portuguese had left Massawa, Ahmed Gran began his holy war against Christian Ethiopia, invading the eastern provinces with a great horde of Somali tribesmen led by about two hundred Turks armed with matchlocks. An Ethiopian army that came to meet them was smashed in 1527; the Ethiopians burst into panicky flight as Turkish bullets cut them down. The invincible Gran advanced into the highland plateau of central Ethiopia, occupying the key provinces of Amhara and Shoa, sweeping through Tigré, taking the mountains of Lasta. Those Christians who would not accept Islam were put to the sword. The treasures accumulated by the Ethiopians in their centuries of isolation were destroyed. At Axum, at Lalibela, in the hills of Amhara, churches and monasteries and libraries went up in flames. In Biet-Amhara Gran's forces sacked the great church of the Holy Trinity, Makana-Selassie, the whole vast interior of which was covered with gold and silver plaques inlaid with gold; the invaders plundered it and burned it, and Gran, happily surveying the smoking ruins, declared, "Is there anywhere in the Byzantine Empire, in India, or in any other land, a building such as this was, containing such figures and works of art?" More than a thousand years of Ethiopian culture perished in less than a decade.

Lebna Dengel fought valiantly, but his men could not stand against Gran's, and he was driven from place to place, a miserable fugitive scurrying through mountain retreats. Many of his most trusted aides, seeing the fall of the kingdom as inevitable, defected to the Moslems. His eldest son was slain in combat, and another one taken prisoner. His queen, Sabla Vangel, hid in one of the most inaccessible of the *ambas*. Amba Geshen, however, the peak on which the brothers and uncles of the king were kept, was scaled by the invaders, who massacred all those princes of the line of Solomon. Lebna Dengel continued to fight, while Gran's immense army gradually closed the circle on his small, desperate band of loyalists. All Ethiopia was aflame, and the only thing postponing the king's certain doom was the difficulty Gran found in driving him from the lofty fastnesses of the interior.

Who would help him in this time of chaos? No neighboring prince, surely; but what of his distant royal brother in Christ, Dom João III? Perhaps the ambassador Saga za Ab would return with a grand Portuguese fleet and many soldiers. The Portuguese had guns. Not even Ahmed Gran could withstand their might. But Saga za Ab did not come, and sent no word of what he might be doing in Europe; nor had there been any message from the King of Portugal via some other emissary. There was little time left for waiting. It was 1535 now; Gran had been upon the land for nine years. Lebna Dengel resolved to send another ambassador to the Portuguese to ask for help.

The man he chose was João Bermudes, the barber-turned-physician who had elected to remain in Ethiopia when the rest of Dom Rodrigo de Lima's party went home. Bermudes slipped through the Moslem lines into Egypt and went overland up the Nile Valley to the Mediterranean—a risky route, but the quickest one between Ethiopia and Portugal. In the autobiography that he wrote many years later, he claimed to have undergone many vicissitudes making this journey, but in fairly short order he reached Rome, late in 1536 or early in 1537. There he sought audience with Pope Paul III before going on to Portugal.

Bermudes introduced himself to the Pope not merely as an envoy sent by the King of Ethiopia but as the newly appointed head of the Ethiopian Church. This was a remarkable claim to make, considering that Bermudes was not only not a communicant of the Ethiopian rite but had not even been a priest when he entered Ethiopia. He had an explanation, though. Marcos, the venerable Ethiopian *abuna* who, according to Alvares, was well over a hundred years old, was close to death at the time Lebna Dengel dispatched Bermudes to Europe. Because of the disruptions caused by Gran's invasion, it was impossible to procure a new *abuna* from Egypt as tradition dictated, and so Ethiopia faced a prolonged period without a spiritual leader. Therefore, Bermudes' own account declares, the "faithful and good Christian called Onadinguel [Lebna Dengel], being Emperor of the kingdoms ôf Ethiopia, which they vulgarly call those of the Preste John . . . told that patriarch [Marcos] that he begged him before his death to institute me, in accordance with his use, as his successor, and as Patriarch of that country, as he heretofore had been. The said Patriarch did this, first ordaining me in all the sacred orders. I accepted this on the condition that it was confirmed by the High Roman Pontiff, successor of St. Peter, whom we all have to obey. The said Emperor replied that he was well content, and further asked me to go to Rome to yield obedience to the Holy Father on my own part, for him, and for all his kingdoms. . . ."

Pope Paul thus was asked to believe that in a single burst of benedictions the Abuna Marcos ordained Bermudes a priest, carried him up through the ranks of bishop and archbishop, and appointed him head of the Ethiopian Church. Bermudes wishes us to know that the Pope accepted this astonishing claim at face value, for he tells us that the Holy Father "received me with much clemency and favor, and confirmed me in what I had brought thence, and at my request rectified all, and ordered me to be appointed to the chair of Alexandria,* and to be called Patriarch and Pontifex of that see." There are, however, no documents on file anywhere to prove that the Pope actually acknowledged Bermudes' claim. Bermudes insisted that he was given papal letters confirming his rank, which he said he lost after his return to Ethiopia; if these had actually existed, copies of them should have been preserved in the Vatican archives, but they have never been discovered there. Nor does anything in the state records of Ethiopia give credence to Bermudes' claim. In any case, that claim would have seemed wildly improbable to anyone of his day who was familiar with the customs of the Ethiopian Church. The *abuna* never appointed his successor; he had the privilege of ordaining only priests and deacons, and all Ethiopian clerics of higher rank, from bishop to *abuna*, could be named solely by the parent Coptic Church in Alexandria. *Abunas* were always Egyptians; no matter how desperate Lebna Dengel's situation may have been in 1535, it is difficult to imagine him departing so widely from this tradition as to procure the appointment of a Portuguese Catholic to the post. Even if he had, one cannot see how the Ethiopians themselves could have been made to accept so revolutionary a choice. Then, too, Bermudes constantly refers to himself as "Patriarch of Abyssinia," a case of faulty usage, for in the Coptic hierarchy the *abuna* was not considered a patriarch: Ethiopians recognized only one patriarch, and that was the Patriarch of Alexandria, the *abuna*'s supe-

* A slip of the pen: Bermudes must have meant "Abyssinia" here.

rior. Bermudes may, perhaps, have wangled the rank of priest or deacon in Ethiopia by taking part in one of those mass ordinations described by Alvares; but we must regard his *abuna*-hood as an enterprising and audacious imposture.

Going on from Rome to Lisbon, Bermudes presented himself to King João III, who received him warmly, "as befitted my dignity." One of his first tasks was to confront Lebna Dengel's previous ambassador, Saga za Ab, who, Bermudes says, "had been there twelve years without negotiating anything, through his own mere neglect. For which reason the Emperor Onadinguel had instructed me to deprive him of the office of ambassador, to arrest him, and bring him back with me a prisoner. I brought a letter from the Emperor to this effect, which I gave to him in Lisbon where he was. He took it, kissed it, and recognized it as genuine; through it he acknowledged me as his Patriarch and superior, and kissed my hand, and resigned to me his office without another word. I ordered him to be detained with two iron chains on each arm, according to the custom of his country, which I removed a few days later at the request of his highness, although it was contrary to the Emperor's orders, who had directed me to act thus." Having dealt with Saga za Ab, Bermudes delivered his message from Lebna Dengel to João III: "The said Emperor asked for his perpetual friendship and brotherhood, and therefore requested that their children might be married the one with the other: that one son might go from Portugal to marry his daughter and reign in his kingdom after his death, in order that this alliance between the Portuguese and himself, and also the submission to the Pope, might be strengthened and might endure. Also, he asked him to send troops to defend him from the King of Zeila [Ahmed Gran], who was overrunning his kingdom, for which he would send him great riches, as he very well could. Also, to send him quarrymen to dig through a hill where his ancestor, Eylale belale [Lalibela], formerly diverted the Nile, in order to turn it there again and damage Egypt." Quite possibly all of this except the part about sending troops was the product of Bermudes' own fertile imagination.

Bermudes declares that King João resolved to send 450 soldiers to aid Lebna Dengel. But if the king really felt as much concern for Ethiopia's plight as Bermudes says he did, he took an oddly casual way of offering help; and in fact the Portuguese troops that eventually did reach Ethiopia seem to have gone there more as the afterthought of a viceroy than at the king's direct order. As Bermudes tells it, the relief mission was supposed to go to Ethiopia by way of India, aboard Portugal's India-bound fleet of April 1538. But as that fleet was about to sail, Bermudes fell ill—poisoned, he hints darkly, by minions of Saga za Ab— and his departure (along with the troops for Ethiopia!) had to be postponed a full year. Restored to health, Bermudes finally did leave for India in the spring of 1539, arriving that fall. The viceroy, Dom Garcia de Noronha, "received us with much joy and did me much honor," Bermudes asserts. "Recognizing me as Patriarch, they paid me the honor due to my dignity." The viceroy told him "he would send me to the Preste John with great honor, and would give me a considerable fleet to help him. But, just at this juncture, as ill-luck would have it, he sickened of a dysentery and died. He was succeeded in the governorship by Dom Estevão da Gama. I at once required him to dispatch us, and send me to the Preste John, with the assistance which his highness had ordered. He replied that he could not, as one hundred thousand cruzados, or more, were needed for this purpose, which sum perchance would never be recovered. I replied that all this was nothing for the Preste John who, without missing it, could spend a million of gold and more, for his riches are innumerable." Bermudes goes on to describe how he persuaded the reluctant Estevão da Gama to send an expedition to Ethiopia after all, which landed at Massawa in February, 1541—six years after the beleaguered Lebna Dengel had sent for help.

So far as we can reconstruct what actually happened from various Portuguese official documents, it appears that Bermudes' version of the story varies considerably from the facts. Bermudes says that King João decreed that an army of "450 matchlockmen and pioneers" be sent to rescue Lebna Dengel, but no trace of this decree can be uncovered in Portuguese documents of the period. At best, perhaps, Bermudes was given leave to recruit a force of volunteers in India to go to Ethiopia. Nor was Dom Estevão da Gama reluctant to launch an Ethiopian expedition; he simply had no official knowledge of any such project. When he became viceroy in 1540, he did discover in his predecessor's papers a plan for invading the Red Sea and destroying its Turkish-held ports, and ordered that this be carried out; the Ethiopian campaign developed almost incidentally out of that enterprise.

When Dom Estevão's fleet reached Massawa early in 1541, Bermudes writes, "we heard the news that Onadinguel, Emperor of the Preste John, had died a natural death. All of us were much troubled, I more than any, as the one it touched most nearly; and doubtless the

sorrow I suffered from this was so great that I was near desiring death."
Lebna Dengel, exhausted and defeated, had died with only a few attendants at his side at a hilltop monastery on September 2, 1540. His
reign of thirty-two years, which had commenced in glory, had ended
in disaster; no chained lions now adorned the court of Prester John,
and most of his realm was under Moslem rule. The throne went to his
oldest surviving son, Galawdewos, whom the Portuguese called "Clau-
dius." The new king, who had only sixty or seventy loyal retainers, was
promptly driven from Tigré to Shoa, where he managed to find refuge.
From his headquarters there he sent repeated requests to the Portuguese for succor, letters which one of the Portuguese described as "more
than piteous and miserable, on all of which above his signature was
depicted Our Lord Jesus crucified."

Dom Estevão—the second son of Vasco da Gama—had as his
principal goal of the moment the bombardment of Suez, not the liberation of Ethiopia. Therefore he headed up the Red Sea toward Suez
with his lighter vessels on February 18, 1541, leaving the heavier ones
behind at Massawa in the care of his kinsman, Manoel de Gama, and
giving no orders for any Ethiopian expedition. Bermudes, who also remained at Massawa, agitated constantly for such an expedition all
spring, especially after messengers from Galawdewos began to arrive
asking for military assistance. Manoel da Gama replied that he had no
authority to send troops into Ethiopia, and that nothing could be done
in any event until Dom Estevão returned from Suez. He continued to
take this attitude even after the current *bahr nagash*, one Isaac, came to
plead his country's cause.

Life at Massawa was grim for the Portuguese. The island's heat
and humidity were all but unbearable; an epidemic spread through the
ships and took many lives; the food supplies gave out, forcing them to
buy provisions from the natives at exorbitant prices. "Besides the
heat," wrote one of the sailors, "we suffered so from hunger that a hen
was paid for in gold, and everything else in proportion. Well might the
men consider the time that they spent here as the worst in their lives."
Bermudes continued to extol the beauties of Ethiopia, just across the
way: its cool climate, its green hills and fragrant valleys, its boundless
wealth, which Prester John would surely share with any man who went
to his rescue. Thus he tempted the men to abandon the miseries of
Massawa for the sake of doing heroic deeds in Prester John's realm.

They begged Manoel da Gama for permission to cross to the mainland, but he continued to refuse it, warning them that anyone who attempted to leave Massawa before Dom Estevão came back would be put to death. But week followed dreary week, and Dom Estevão did not reappear. At length about a hundred men, losing patience, decided to desert and offer themselves to the Ethiopian king. They stole a boat and left by night; sentries sounded an alarm and Manoel da Gama sent a boatload of armed men in pursuit, but they were sympathetic to the aims of the deserters and allowed them to reach the Ethiopian shore unmolested. But a guide that the Portuguese hired on the mainland perfidiously led them straight into an ambush set by the troops of Ahmed Gran; all were slain except* one man, who feigned death until the Moslems moved on, then managed to make his way back to Massawa with the terrible news. It was, said Manoel da Gama, a fitting fate for the disobedient.

But on May 22, Dom Estevão returned from his successful raid on the Turkish Red Sea ports and learned of the massacre. He also was approached by the *bahr nagash,* who, weeping, implored him to grant Galawdewos' request for aid. Bermudes, naturally, joined the appeal; and on the spot Dom Estevão decided to organize a relief expedition. He would send four hundred volunteers armed with matchlocks to help Prester John, and as captain of the party he selected his own brother, Christovão da Gama, the fourth of Vasco da Gama's six sons. Dom Christovão was twenty-five years old: bold, vigorous, intelligent, a capable leader, a warrior of proven valor. The four hundred volunteers instantly flocked to Dom Christovão's banner. Dom Estevão equipped them with six hundred matchlocks, one hundred larger guns, and eight pieces of heavy artillery; and they had 130 slaves to carry their burdens and to play the trumpets, kettledrums, and bagpipes on the battlefield. On July 9, 1541, Estevão da Gama bade his brother farewell; Dom Christovão and his band of soldiers began their march toward the Ethiopian interior, and the Portuguese fleet sailed back to India. The cycle of the legend thus was complete: for centuries, Europe had looked to the fabled Prester John for deliverance, and now a European army was on its way to save Prester John.

18

Two accounts of Christovão da Gama's expedition written by men who took part in it have come down to us. One is the work of João Bermudes, published in 1565 under the title, *This is a Short Account of the Embassy which the Patriarch Dom João Bermudes Brought from the Emperor of Ethiopia, Vulgarly Called Prester John, to the Most Christian and Zealous-in-the-Faith-of-Christ King of Portugal, Dom João III*. Written long after the events it purports to describe, and concerned as much with inflating the importance of its author's role and defending his tenuous claim to be head of the Ethiopian Church, it is not the most reliable of documents. Much more trustworthy is *A Discourse of the Deeds of the Very Valorous Captain Dom Christovão da Gama in the Kingdoms of the Preste João*, published in 1564 but written at least twenty years earlier. Its author was Dom Miguel de Castanhoso, a native of the Portuguese town of Santarem, who was one of the officers of Dom Christovão's expedition.

Castanhoso tells us that King Galawdewos was in the far-off southern province of Shoa when the Portuguese entered Ethiopia, so that it was necessary for them to cross the whole devastated country to reach him. For the first few days, because of the heat, they traveled by night. "Dom Christovão marched with all on foot, as there were no riding animals. The artillery, munitions, and supplies were carried on camels and mules, which the Barnaguais [*bahr nagash*] had brought with him; but we often unloaded them and carried the baggage, and even the artillery, on our backs, through very rugged defiles, where laden camels and mules could not pass. In this labor, which was very heavy, Dom Christovão showed the great zeal and fervor that animated him in this holy enterprise: for he was the first to shoulder his burden." At length they emerged into the cooler air of the Debarwa tableland and were welcomed at the *bahr nagash*'s capital by tearful monks, who led them to prayers at a ruined monastery. The rainy season was now under way, and at the *bahr nagash*'s suggestion Dom Christovão decided to camp in Debarwa until the dry season, some three or four months hence, before attempting to join forces with Galawdewos.

The *amba* on which Lebna Dengel's widow, Sabla Vangel, had taken refuge was only one day's journey away. Dom Christovão invited the queen to leave her mountain and accept Portuguese protection. The only access to the *amba* was by way of a large basket pulled up on leather ropes—one wonders how the first climbers scaled it—and two of the Portuguese captains were hauled to the top to assist the queen mother in her descent. She had spent four years on the *amba* and wept for joy that God had sent Christian warriors to deliver her country from the Moslem peril. The noble lady entered Debarwa at the head of a grand procession, with the *bahr nagash* beside her, a lion skin around his shoulders; Dom Christovão greeted her formally and explained how he had come in answer to the appeal of "the Preste your son." To her delight the Portuguese staged a drill for her, "armed with glittering and shining weapons," Castanhoso writes, "with fife and drum, and all in ranks with lances and matchlocks."

During the rainy months the little army constructed carts for the ammunition and carriages for the heavy guns; Dom Christovão took part in the work "as if he had been a carpenter all his life." For diversion the Portuguese subjugated a couple of neighboring towns that had given their allegiance to the Moslems, and, with the queen mother's permission, carried off mules, bullocks, and cows to use as beasts of burden. During this time two spies from Ahmed Gran were discovered in town; Dom Christovão put them to the torture in order to learn the size and location of his enemy's army, and then had them publicly ripped to pieces to discourage any others. In August a letter came from King Galawdewos, offering thanks for Dom Christovão's arrival and saying that his people "had a prophecy, made many years before the kingdom was overrun, that it would be recovered by white men come from far, who were true Christians."

The rains ended in mid-December, and the Portuguese set out to effect a junction with the king. It was a difficult march through high, broken country. "In many places where the oxen could not draw the carts," says Castanhoso, "we had to pull them up ourselves by main strength and on our shoulders." At Christmastime they halted a few days; Bermudes, who had convinced his companions that he really was the "Patriarch of Abyssinia," performed a solemn Mass embellished by the music of bagpipes, kettledrums, flutes, and trumpets, while the queen mother and her ladies looked on in delight and amazement. Resuming the march, they came shortly to a precipitous place that, to their Ethiopian guides, seemed impossible to cross. "Dom Christovão, seeing that the carts could not be dragged over it, ordered us to take every cart to pieces," Castanhoso relates, "and remove the artillery and munitions from them. We then carried all these things on our backs, little by little, with the very greatest labor." Castanhoso compares this operation favorably to Hannibal's crossing of the Alps. A three-day climb brought the Portuguese to the summit of the mountain, where they found a hermitage. In it were some three hundred mummies of white men "sewn up in thongs of dry and worn-out leather. The bodies were almost perfect, with only nose, lips, and some fingers missing." Castanhoso reports that "the people of the country said that these men had come to that country many years before, and had conquered it in the time of the Romans; others said they were saints; the patriarch, Dom João Bermudes, said also that they were saints, who had been martyred here, and that he had heard this said when he had passed there on another occasion." Some of the men collected bones as holy relics, and they went on, through a region of terrible cold and down into a broad plain. Here they camped for eight days, while the chieftains of districts that had been conquered by the Moslems came to pledge allegiance to the legitimate Ethiopian government. The feast of the Epiphany occurred during this time, and it was necessary for Bermudes, as "patriarch," to preside over the ceremony of ritual bathing that had so horrified Alvares. This was northern Ethiopia, however, where the rite was not so nude an affair as it was in the south, where Alvares had seen it. Castanhoso tells us that "the patriarch and all the ecclesiastics went to the river, and the patriarch blessed the water where the queen and the others were to bathe; after the blessing, the queen, all covered with many clothes, so that she could not be seen, went undressed into the water and bathed, and thence went to her tent, and her ladies did likewise. The patriarch and all the friars and priests went a little apart and washed themselves, and then went to say Mass with great music and festivity, in which the whole day was passed; on the following we marched."

Now they were approaching a formidable *amba* held by 1500 Moslem troops. Gran had taken it by treachery years before; there seemed no other way to conquer it, for any ascent had to be made in full view of its defenders. "When Dom Christovão heard that this hill lay on his road he enquired about it," says Castanhoso, "and determined to take it in order not to leave any danger behind him. When the queen heard of Dom Christovão's intention she sent for him, and told him that he should not think of daring such a great deed with so small an army;

that they should march and join the Preste, and then they could do everything—that it was less difficult to fight twelve thousand men in a plain, and destroy them, than to capture that hill." But Gama would not hear of making a detour, and gave orders to do battle. The Portuguese surrounded the *amba*, drawing a barrage of stones and arrows from above; at dawn on February 2 the "patriarch" offered absolution, and Dom Christovão led a furious charge. The heavy artillery of the Portuguese drove the Moslems back as the attackers scrambled toward the top; there was frenzied hand-to-hand combat at the summit, but the Portuguese forced their way in and sent their foes leaping in panic to their deaths over the side of the cliff. When the last Moslem was dead, Dom Christovão liberated the Christian villagers who had been held captive, and knelt in thanksgiving at the mountaintop church, which the Moslems had turned into a mosque and which he now reconsecrated as the Church of Our Lady of Victory. Eight Portuguese had been killed in the fray, and forty wounded.

The Ethiopians rejoiced at this miraculous triumph. Gran, clearly perturbed, decided to make an end of these troublesome intruders before they had a chance to join forces with the king, and led his immense army toward the Portuguese. Dom Christovão was faced with an awkward choice: to clash with Gran's troops unaided, or to retreat into the hills and await the coming of Galawdewos. The first, obviously, held grave dangers; but so did the second, for if he shirked a battle with the Moslems he would lose the reputation for invincibility that his victory at the *amba* had gained him, and the Ethiopians, thinking him a coward, might stop supplying him with provisions. "It was far the greater risk to chance famine, and losing our prestige, than to fight the Moors, for victory is in the hands of God," Castanhoso asserts. Besides, though the Portuguese were greatly outnumbered, they had twice as many muskets as the Moslems.

Gran made camp less than a day's march from Gama and sent him a mocking message, expressing his astonishment that Dom Christovão had the audacity to appear before him with so small a force, especially since rumor said he "seemed to be a mere boy and innocent without experience." But, Gran went on pleasantly, he would pardon Dom Christovão's grand temerity in invading Ethiopia if the Portuguese commander would abandon this folly of fighting on behalf of the Ethiopians, or else return to his country. With the letter Gran enclosed a friar's cowl and a rosary, implying that his enemies were not true warriors but mere monks. Dom Christovão replied that the great Lion of the Sea, King João, having been informed "that the most Christian King, the Preste, his brother in arms, had been defeated and driven from his kingdom by the infidels and enemies of our Holy Catholic Faith, had sent the small succor that was here, which still sufficed against such evil and bad persons." And Gama sent along with his letter a small tweezers for the eyebrows and a looking glass, thus making his foes out to be women.

A few days later—April 4, 1542—the Portuguese began to advance toward the waiting Moslems: 15,000 infantrymen, 1500 cavalry, and the 200 Turkish arquebusiers. Gran's men, seeing the 400 Portuguese come forward, "raised such a noise of shouting, trumpets, and kettledrums, that it seemed as if the world were dissolving; they showed great joy, thinking they had us already in their net. At this," Castanhoso goes on, "we began to do our duty with matchlocks and artillery, which played continually on all sides, so that we cleared the plain as we advanced." The horses of the enemy were frightened by the bombardment, but the hordes of footsoldiers threw themselves energetically at the Portuguese, and the Turkish matchlocks did great damage; Dom Christovão was among those wounded by bullets, though he continued to fight. By midday the weary Portuguese saw the battle going against them. But then Ahmed Gran led a charge that carried him within close range of the Portuguese guns, and one of Gama's matchlockmen fired a shot that pierced Gran's thigh and killed his horse. Seeing their leader fall, the Moslems at once gave the signal for retreat and carried him from the field, while the Portuguese, falling upon the withdrawing foe, administered great slaughter.

Afterward the queen mother and her ladies ministered to the wounds of the Portuguese. Eleven men were dead; but thirty of the special force of Turks had perished, and hundreds of Somalis. Five days later, seeking to sustain his momentum, Gama attacked the Moslems a second time. Gran, still suffering from his wound, directed his army from a litter. An overconfident Moslem captain attempted to lead a cavalry charge, thinking to break the Portuguese ranks, and, says Castanhoso, "had all his men followed his example, they would indeed have done us much hurt." But, seeing the damage the Portuguese artillery was doing, many of the horsemen held back, and the bold captain and his lieutenants were skewered on the pikes of Gama's front line. The failure of the cavalry assault demoralized the Moslems and they fell into wild disarray; the Portuguese chased them until they were out of sight. This battle cost fourteen Portuguese lives.

Two days later a party of men whom Dom Christovão had sent to Massawa to look for some promised reinforcements returned. The hoped-for fleet from India had not arrived, but the *bahr nagash* had come to join Gama's forces, bringing with him forty cavalrymen and five hundred footsoldiers. Dom Christovão was eager for another encounter with Gran, but the Moslem leader, unwilling to chance a third battle with these surprisingly fierce Portuguese, was in retreat across Ethiopia. Gama pursued him without succeeding in overtaking him, and at the end of April the rainy season returned, turning the country into such a mire that warfare was impossible. Gran settled down atop one of the *ambas* and sent an urgent demand to the Pasha of Zebid, one of the Turkish rulers on the Arabian side of the Red Sea, for experienced arquebusiers and above all for heavy artillery. Gama was unable to intercept the Moslem messenger and, late in the time of rains, the Turkish aid reached Gran.

The rains prevented Dom Christovão from uniting with Galawdewos. Somehow he had persuaded himself that the king had a large army; but an Ethiopian Jew who came to Gama to ask that the Portuguese liberate his province told him that Galawdewos had only a handful of men about him. Castanhoso tells us that "when Dom Christovão learnt how small a force the Preste had with him, he became very dispirited and disquieted, and went to the queen to learn if it was true that her son had so small a force; when it was confirmed by her he became still more downcast, without, however, letting her know it." He realized now that he was Ethiopia's only real bulwark against Gran.

During the time of rains the Portuguese achieved one more victory: Dom Christovão and a hundred of his men destroyed the Moslem garrison controlling the Jewish district and seized a great many horses and mules and cattle and slave women. We are told that the Jewish chieftain was so impressed by the ease with which the Portuguese won the battle that he became a Christian on the spot, with twelve of his brethren. Returning in triumph to his main camp, Dom Christovão was greeted by an unpleasant surprise: out of the night came cannonballs crashing down near their tents. Gran had his reinforcements, and he was about to attack.

The battle began the next day, August 28, 1542. A thousand Turks were in the vanguard, and they rushed forward fearlessly, firing their weapons with deadly accuracy. "When Dom Christovão saw the great hurt they did us," writes Castanhoso, "and that the palisades of our camp were not strong enough to be defended, he decided to sally out frequently and attack them, and then retreat. It appeared to him that in this way he would secure victory, for they could never stand against the first charge of any body of Portuguese." The strategy was successful: as one Portuguese captain and then another and then another led his men from shelter for a quick and furious assault, the Turks gave ground. But the Portuguese losses were heavy; each charge cost five or six lives, and many men were wounded, Dom Christovão again taking a bullet in the leg. Yet Gama continued to urge his men on. "It is on such days," says Castanhoso, "that leaders show what they are made of. I know of no words to describe his courage, nor do they exist." The queen mother, too, showed her bravery: she and her ladies set up a hospital in a tent at the side of the field and bound the wounds of the fallen even though bullets and cannonballs were landing all about them. For a time the battle went with the Portuguese. "Truly, had we the horses which were on the way, the victory was ours," Castanhoso declares; "but we deserved for our sins that this should befall us, to happen what did happen. While our men attacked they drove the Moors like sheep, but they were now so weary they could not bear the fatigue." Finally, his ranks severely thinned, Dom Christovão had to call for a retreat, and as he pulled back from the heart of the battle he was struck by a bullet that broke his right arm, causing him great pain. The enemy, cheered at this, launched a ferocious new drive, and some of the more practical Portuguese felt that flight, rather than mere retreat, was now in order. One of the first to act on this conclusion was Bermudes. Castanhoso notes that "when the patriarch saw affairs in this state, he mounted a mule, and retreated to a hill on our flank." Bermudes might ignominiously withdraw, but Dom Christovão was determined to hold his ground even if he died in the effort, and only the insistence of his comrades forced the badly injured commander to leave the field. Under cover of darkness the battered Portuguese clambered up a steep hill, leaving their camp, their munitions, and more than forty injured men to the Turks.

Dom Christovão and fourteen companions became separated from the others and wandered all night on the hillside, descending at dawn into a valley. There they found a little waterfall and refreshed themselves, and, lacking ointments, killed Dom Christovão's mule to use its fat in dressing his wounds. While they rested, they were discovered by a party of Turks and Arabs sent out by Gran to look for the Portuguese leader. The devil, Castanhoso asserts with conviction, led them to him. They brought Gama to Ahmed Gran, who happily showed him a pile of more than a hundred Portuguese heads. Then Dom Christovão was stripped and flogged, and his beard was plucked out, and his eyebrows too were plucked with the tweezers he had sent to Gran, and many other torments and insults were heaped on him, "all of which he bore with much patience," Castanhoso says, "giving many thanks to God for bringing him to this, after allowing him to reconquer one hundred leagues of Christian country." After a while Gran offered to release him if he would defect to the side of Islam, but Dom Christovão, contemplating a glorious martyrdom, of course refused this suggestion with defiant words, and Gran, drawing his scimitar, beheaded him. A spring of healthful water, Castanhoso tells us, burst forth from the place where Dom Christovão's blood was spilled, and at the very moment of his death a large tree in a nearby monastery ripped itself from the earth of its own accord and stood on its branches with its roots in the air.

19

Half the Portuguese were dead, and Vasco da Gama's headless son lay in a Moslem grave with a dead dog by his side, and Prester John's land still was in the grip of Ahmed Gran. That king, believing himself secure, sent his Turkish auxiliaries back to Arabia and returned to his favorite camping place beside Lake Tsana, the source of the Blue Nile, in central Ethiopia.

But Gama's victories had driven the Moslems from several strategic *ambas* which they could not now recapture, for they were again occupied by Ethiopian defenders. One of them, the hill in the Jewish district, became the place of refuge of the Portuguese survivors. About 120 of them, led by the queen mother, gathered there to await the expected arrival of King Galawdewos; some fifty more, going astray on an unfamiliar road, wandered off into the mountains and eventually found themselves in the province of the *bahr nagash*, where they settled while awaiting word from the others.

In October, Galawdewos and his sparse retinue at last appeared. The king, who was about nineteen, displayed great grief at the news of

Dom Christovão's death and greeted the survivors in a princely way, telling them not to feel as though they were strangers in his country, for the kingdom and he himself belonged to their lord, his royal brother, King João. Galawdewos provided mules for the Portuguese, a tent for each two men, silken tunics and breeches, servants, carpets, and other things. All through November and December loyal Ethiopians flocked to the place of rendezvous, offering their services to their king and his valiant Portuguese allies; by Christmas some 8000 footsoldiers and 500 cavalrymen had gathered. Saltpeter and sulfur were available on the hill, and the Portuguese made a good deal of gunpowder for use in their next attack on Gran, while messengers were sent off toward the *bahr nagash's* territory to locate the fifty men who had strayed. In January the messengers returned without them; it seemed that the fifty, having heard nothing from their countrymen, had gone on to Massawa in the hope that a Portuguese fleet would come and take them back to India.

On February 6, 1543, the Ethiopian army began its march. The 120 Portuguese, some of them still nursing open wounds, led the procession, carrying the flag of Our Lady of Mercy. Galawdewos had asked them to appoint a new captain, but they would not, saying that no one could replace the one they had lost. From a party of Moslems whom they ambushed and defeated they learned that Gran was camped only five days' journey away, beside Lake Tsana. "We continued marching," Castanhoso writes, "until we caught sight of it [the lake]; it is so large that we could see it from a distance of six or seven leagues. When we came in sight of the Moors we pitched our camp opposite theirs. They were amazed to learn that the Preste and the Portuguese had come in search of them after the great defeat; this put them in some fear. They began at once to prepare as best they could; they understood well that we had only come to avenge the past. And because we had news of the Portuguese who had been to Massawa, but had not found shipping, that hearing of us and the Preste, they were marching after us, with all speed, the Preste decided in council of all not to join battle until their arrival, as they were near us; and in that country fifty Portuguese are a greater reinforcement than one thousand natives."

Daily skirmishes took place while the Christian army awaited the coming of the fifty. Skirmishes of a different kind were being fought between King Galawdewos and the supposed patriarch, Bermudes. Confronting the king in the royal tent, Bermudes made a long speech reminding Galawdewos that, as Bermudes' own memoirs put it, "The most Christian King your father, now in glory, asked me to go to Rome . . . to give submission to the High Pontiff. . . . Your father recognized him as the successor of St. Peter, chief of the apostles of Christ, and Vicar of his universal Church, in whatever part of the world it may be established; and that he considered himself subordinate to him, with all his kingdoms and lordships." Now, said Bermudes, it would be proper for the new king to make the same profession of obedience to Rome, as a preliminary to the adoption of Catholic rites in Ethiopia. The king, in some irritation, replied, "You are not our father, nor a prelate, but Patriarch of the Franks, and you are an Arian, for you have four Gods,* and you are not in future to call yourself my father." Bermudes writes, "I turned and told him he lied, for I was not an Arian, and had not four Gods; and that as he would not obey the Holy Father, I held him to be excommunicate, and accursed; and that I would no longer be with him, or speak to him; and with that I got up to go. He replied that I was excommunicated, not he." Leaving the tent, Bermudes told some Portuguese outside "that the king would not obey the Roman Church, but was a heretic like Nestor and Dioscero; that therefore I ordered them by virtue of their obedience, and under pain of excommunication by me . . . in no way to obey that king, or any other of his faction, or do anything whatever to help him." If we can believe the story as Bermudes tells it, the Portuguese thereupon declared they would not serve the heretic king if the patriarch forbade it, and even after Galawdewos sent them three thousand ounces of gold to win back their affections they replied that "they could not accept his favors, because of the differences between him and me." Then the queen mother, much distressed, came to Bermudes "and begged me, by the death and passion of Jesus Christ, to take no notice of the ignorance of her son, who was a boy, and it was not well that, considering his extreme youth, he should be utterly condemned." At her urging Bermudes went to the king's tent and found that he had repented. "With great humility he took my hand and kissed it, asking my pardon for what he had said. We all three sat down, and he said he was content to obey the High Pontiff, and that for this the submission that his father had given me was sufficient." Bermudes insisted that Galawdewos make his own submission, declaring in writing the supremacy of

* Ethiopians, being Monophysites, regarded the theories of other Christian factions concerning the Trinity and the dual nature of Christ as something close to polytheism.

the Pope, and "this document one of the chief men of the kingdom must read, seated aloft in a chair or in some high place, in a loud and clear voice, before all the people there with him. He did this, and ordered it to be carried out with solemn pomp and at the sound of trumpets." And so peace was made between king and patriarch. We may be sure that the king's version of the story would be somewhat different: doubtless he looked with some bewilderment on Bermudes' claim to be the *abuna,* and whatever concessions to the authority of Rome he may have made were perhaps granted for the sake of humoring a madman.

20

The fifty Portuguese who had been to Massawa had not yet arrived; but events forced Galawdewos to begin his attack on Gran without them. A certain popular and gallant Ethiopian officer had been shot dead from ambush while going out to parley with two Moslems who came under a flag of truce; the death of this man so upset the other Ethiopians that, Castanhoso tells us, they "began to lose their courage, so much so that many advised retreat, victory seeming impossible. When the Preste heard of this, and found it true, he . . . determined to give battle the next day, as he felt that if he waited longer, all his men would disperse through fear."

There were the usual prayers at dawn for divine mercy; then the army set forth, the Portuguese again in the vanguard, followed closely by 250 Ethiopian cavalrymen and 3500 footsoldiers; Galawdewos brought up the rear with another 250 horsemen and 4000 more infantry. Against them came Ahmed Gran leading a vanguard of 200 Turkish matchlockmen, 600 horsemen, and 7000 footsoldiers, with a rear guard of 600 horsemen and 7000 footsoldiers more. In the first charge the Moslems prevailed, but then a small band of mounted Portuguese led a counterattack, and, Castanhoso reports, the Ethiopians, "ashamed to see them fight thus, threw themselves in so vigorously that they left a track as they went. When the king [Gran] saw that his men were losing ground, he in person led them on, encouraging them, and with him was his son, a young man, helping him; they came so near that he was recognized by the Portuguese, who, seeing him close, fired at him with their matchlocks. As all things are ordered by the Lord God, He permitted that one ball should strike him in the breast, and he fell over his saddlebow and left the press; when his followers knew that he was wounded to the death, they lost heart and took to flight."

Gran's flamboyant defiance of the Portuguese guns had cost him his life and his war as well. His panicky horse galloped from the field with the mortally injured old general slumped across its neck and a young Ethiopian soldier in close pursuit. In the rout that followed, all but forty of the Turkish elite troops were slain, and vast numbers of the Somalis. The Ethiopians, not known for mercy to defeated foes, accepted no surrenders, but slaughtered and mutilated every Moslem they could catch, sparing only women and children to be made slaves. In Gran's camp were many Christian women who now were set free, "which caused the greatest possible pleasure and contentment: for some found sisters, others daughters, others their wives, and it was for them no small delight to see them delivered from such captivity." While the division of the booty found in the Moslem camp was taking place, the youth who had ridden after Gran's horse returned, holding between his teeth a bloody head clenched by the hair. The head was Gran's; and the young man brought it proudly to Galawdewos, who had pledged his sister as a bride for the slayer of the enemy leader. The youth said he had caught up with Gran and struck him down; but Galawdewos, making inquiries, learned that Gran had had his fatal wound from a Portuguese matchlock on the field. Merely cutting off the head of a dying man did not earn one an imperial princess, he said, and refused the reward to the young soldier. Nor did he give his sister to a Portuguese, for no one could say who had fired the mortal bullet. Gran's head was set on a spear and carried through all of Ethiopia, so that the people might see that the man who had terrorized them for seventeen years was indeed dead. Castanhoso declares that the tree which had uprooted itself when Dom Christovão died miraculously replanted itself upon Gran's death.

Now began a season of rejoicing and reconciliation. The fifty Portuguese from Massawa arrived, too late for the battle but in time for the feasting. Chieftains who had given their allegiance to Gran hastened to renew their loyalty to the Ethiopian throne; among them was the father of the *bahr nagash*, who lamely explained that he had defected to Gran's side "because it appeared to him that the realm would never be restored." Galawdewos pardoned these renegades, for, as Castanhoso observes, "if he had put all of them to death, he would have

had no men left." Only a few whose crimes against Ethiopia were particularly unforgivable were executed. To Galawdewos, now, also came
common folk by the thousands, who hailed their heroic young king and
enrolled in his army. Many of them were deserters who had fought in
Gran's forces but who, with equal opportunism, switched sides again
when it seemed appropriate. Within a couple of weeks Galawdewos
commanded 26,000 soldiers. With the aid of God and a few hundred
Portuguese, the Moslem threat to Ethiopia had been ended.

The Portuguese spent Easter of 1543 at Lake Tsana, marveling
over such creatures as the hippopotamus: "In this lake are bred certain
creatures like seahorses, which they must be," Castanhoso says; "they
are as large as big horses, and of the fashion and color of elephants;
their heads are exceedingly broad, with very wide mouths." Then the
king began a grand progress through his reconquered realm, with the
Portuguese accompanying him. In August, on the first anniversary of
Christovão da Gama's death, Galawdewos held a great memorial service for him, in which more than six hundred Ethiopian priests took
part. By this time some 100,000 people were following the king from
place to place. Since peace had been restored, the Portuguese began to
think of leaving; Castanhoso says, "As there was nothing to be done
in the country, which was quite freed, and I suffered from my wound
[a bullet in the arm], which would not heal, and there was none to
cure me, I sought the Preste's permission to go to Massawa to wait for
our vessels which were then due." Galawdewos was reluctant to see
any of his Portuguese go, for, although the war was over, the country
was in a devastated state and much work of rebuilding had to be done.
Therefore he asked Castanhoso to stay, using the pretext that he was
not yet wealthy enough to give him a proper farewell present and did
not want him to go empty-handed out of Ethiopia; but Castanhoso
pointed out that he might die of his wound if he did not have treatment
soon, and he could not get the proper treatment in Galawdewos' land.
At this the king yielded, and bestowed on Castanhoso twenty ounces
of gold, two mules, and a handsome green velvet cloak in gratitude for
his services. At this fifty other Portuguese pressed the king for leave to
go, and, seeing he could not hold them, he emptied his churches of
silver chalices and crosses and took bracelets and ornaments from his
womenfolk so that they could be paid. At the end of the year they departed for Massawa, where they found no fleet, but only one very small
ship that had been sent out to learn what had become of Christovão da

Gama and his men. The little vessel had room for only a few extra passengers, and so it was decided that all of the veterans of the Ethiopian campaign should remain to await the fleet, except Castanhoso, who would go with the small ship on account of his wound and because he carried letters from Galawdewos to King João.

"On the morning of the following day, Sunday, February 16, 1544, I embarked," Castanhoso concludes, "leaving my companions very desirous to do the same. They and those in the small craft took leave of each other with many good wishes; they remained saying a prayer to the crucifix on their banner, and afterward turned with sobs, and, mounting their horses and mules, rode inland towards where the Preste was. . . . We sailed on to India, where it pleased the Lord God to bring us in safety. We arrived on April 19th of the said year: thanks be to Him, who was pleased to remember me, and may He bring them back in safety."

21

Among those who stayed in the land of Prester John was the self-styled Patriarch of Abyssinia, João Bermudes. Galawdewos derived little cheer from his presence. On the eve of the climactic battle against Ahmed Gran, the king had been willing at least to pretend that he recognized Bermudes' authority, for the sake of avoiding a troublesome squabble; but once the war was won he wanted no more of this folly of a Portuguese *abuna*. He found Bermudes ignorant and presumptuous, and bluntly refused Bermudes' demands that the Roman rite should be introduced in Ethiopia and that all the clergy should be reordained by him. Bermudes then stirred up his fellow Portuguese against the king, and matters grew so vexed that there was actually a minor battle between the Portuguese and Galawdewos' troops over the question of Bermudes' patriarchal decrees. The king managed to calm things, and shrewdly avoided further trouble by awarding estates to the Portuguese in such a fashion that they were scattered all through the most remote districts of the land. Meanwhile he sent off to Alexandria for a genuine *abuna*.

Galawdewos also had complained to King João about Bermudes' antics in one of the letters carried by Castanhoso. The Portuguese king sent a brisk reply by way of India, under date of March 13, 1546: "As to what João Bermudes has done there, whom the king your father [Lebna Dengel] sent to me as his ambassador, I disapprove greatly, for they are things very contrary to the service of Our Lord, and by reason of them it is clear that he cannot be given any help or assistance, nor do I know more of him than that he is a mere priest. Of the powers which he says the Holy Father granted him I know nothing." King João went on to suggest, though, that Bermudes should not be punished harshly for his usurpation, out of respect for "that dignity of patriarch which he has chosen to usurp, though no one gave it to him." And João promised to send "to you and for your kingdom, with the permission of God, a person for patriarch, who shall be such and of such zeal and good walk of life, that in these matters he may be able to know how to serve Our Lord well, from whom you may receive great contentment. . . ."

Now that the Portuguese king himself had repudiated Bermudes, Galawdewos no longer hesitated to deal with him. From Alexandria came a proper Coptic *abuna* named Joseph, whom Galawdewos immediately installed as head of the Ethiopian Church, saying that Bermudes could go on functioning as patriarch of the Catholics in Ethiopia, if they would have him; he was banished from the court and sent to live in a frontier province, from which he was shortly driven out by a pagan uprising. Thereafter Bermudes seems to have lived an obscure and discredited life, wandering through the Ethiopian hinterlands, until in 1555 he learned that the Pope had sent an officially accredited "patriarch" to bring Catholicism to Ethiopia. That destroyed the last vestige of Bermudes' claim to primacy, and he slipped out of the country via Massawa, reaching Portugal in 1558. He spent the remaining years of his life in retirement, emerging only in 1565, when, to counter the publication of Castanhoso's narrative, he issued his own account of the Ethiopian campaign. Bermudes died in 1570, and, according to a contemporary historian, he died a very holy death.

22

In Europe the question now was not one of finding Prester John, or of striking up friendly relations with him, but of converting him and his people to the true and only Church, that of Rome. For, thanks to the researches of the distinguished humanist scholar Damião de Goís, it was now clear beyond all doubt that Prester John, this bulwark of the Christian faith, was both schismatic and heretic and much in need of enlightenment.

Goís was a twelve-year-old page in the court of King Manoel when Matthew the Armenian arrived in Lisbon in 1514; listening to the doctors of the Church interrogate the Ethiopian ambassador concerning the doctrines of Christianity as it was practiced in that country, the boy contracted a passionate interest in matters Ethiopian. Nine years later, when King João III sent him on diplomatic business to Antwerp, Goís collected a great deal of information about Ethiopia in that busy Belgian port from Portuguese involved in the spice trade. There he came into possession of a manuscript text of the interrogation of Matthew and other details of Matthew's journey to Portugal, and translated this material into Latin. Later, Goís showed these documents to a friend, Cornelius Grapheus, whose brother, a printer, published them in 1532 without Goís' knowledge or permission. The book, entitled *Embassy of the Great Emperor of the Indians, Prester John, to Manoel, King of Lusitania* [Portugal], was the first extensive printed account of Matthew's visit to Lisbon, and included a wealth of data about the kingdom and court of Ethiopia, its religion, its "patriarch," and such things. Interesting though the book was, its contents would have been almost wholly obsolete on the day of publication had Padre Francisco Alvares, who had returned from Ethiopia five years before, made known what he had learned there. But none of Alvares' knowledge was accessible, for the publication of his memoir was still eight years in the future, and Goís' book served meanwhile as the most up-to-date account of Ethiopia.

Goís himself was aware of the deficiencies of his book, publication of which embarrassed him; but from 1523 to 1533 he had been absent from Portugal, serving his king in Belgium, Denmark, and Poland, and he had had no opportunity to question Alvares or any of the other emissaries who had come back from Ethiopia. Recalled to Lisbon in 1533, though, Goís sought out Saga za Ab, the hapless Ethiopian ambassador who was stranded in Portugal, homesick and neglected. From him Goís learned that the account of Ethiopian religion that Matthew the Armenian had given was naïve and inaccurate. Matthew, after all, had been a layman and a foreigner; Saga za Ab was by profession a theologian. He offered to explain things properly to Goís and found that brilliant scholar to be an eager listener. When they parted, Goís asked

Saga za Ab to prepare a written exposition of Ethiopian religious thought and practice for him.

The monk compiled the work in the spring of 1534 and sent it on to Goís, who by that time had gone on to Padua for advanced study at the university. Saga za Ab described all those Ethiopian rites that Catholics would find so strange: the circumcision, the ritual bathing, the chanting and dancing in church, the Saturday Sabbath, and much more. However, whether accidentally or out of fear of upsetting Goís, he neglected to discuss the most basic theological point separating Ethiopia and Rome, the Monophysite doctrine; his text was vague on the potentially troublesome subjects of the nature of Christ and the definition of the Trinity. Still, the picture of Ethiopian religion that emerged was a decidedly exotic one. But Goís, though Catholic himself, did not find it in the least disturbing that the Ethiopians should practice a species of Christianity so alien from that of Europe. He was no narrow dogmatist; he had been the pupil of Erasmus, and the German arch-heretics Luther and Melanchthon were among his friends. Saga za Ab's manuscript seemed fascinating and not at all shocking, and Goís happily translated it into Latin and published it in 1540 under the title of *Faith, Religion, and Manners of the Ethiopians*.

It was not a good era for free intellectual discourse of the kind Goís relished, though. In England Henry VIII was trampling on the authority of the Pope and in the German-speaking countries the Lutheran heresy was spreading like a plague; defenders of the old order, seeing the Catholic world collapsing, worked frantically to stave off further defections. Any book that indicated that one might be a virtuous Christian even if one did not accept the dictates of Rome was obviously anathema. Goís' work had been published at Louvain in Flanders, where he had settled after taking his degree from Padua; a copy of the book reached the Cardinal Infante Dom Henrique, Grand Inquisitor of Portugal, who found it full of forbidden thoughts and banned it. Goís, from Louvain, protested: what harm could there be, he asked, in telling people about Ethiopian religious customs? The Grand Inquisitor replied that, although he still regarded Goís "as a good man and a good Christian," the book was too dangerous. It implicitly advocated a kind of world-wide confederation of Christians, made up of independent churches that followed each its own style of worship, and denounced the attempts of any branch of the Church to interfere with the practices of another branch: "It is very unworthily done," Goís had quoted Saga za Ab as saying, "to reprehend strangers that be Christians so sharply and bitterly, as I have been oftentimes reprehended myself."

Although Goís' *Faith, Religion, and Manners* was reprinted at Paris in 1541, appeared again at Louvain three years later, and found its way into English and other languages, it remained suppressed in Portugal until 1791, by which time presumably it no longer was necessary to conceal the fact that Prester John was a heretic. Goís himself was summoned to Lisbon in 1545 and strongly rebuked by the Inquisition; thereafter he remained suspect as a propagandist for heresy, and as late as 1571, when the Inquisition ordered him confined to a monastery, he was still being forced to pay for his purely intellectual curiosity about Ethiopian religion. The Catholic Church, meanwhile, was busy trying to convert Prester John.

In particular the newly founded Society of Jesus, the most zealous of all Catholic religious orders, wished to accept the Ethiopian challenge. Ignatius of Loyola, who had organized the Jesuits in 1540, would gladly have gone to Ethiopia himself, but his administrative duties forbade that; when King João of Portugal asked the Pope in 1546 to nominate a patriarch for the Ethiopians, Loyola sought and won permission for a Jesuit to have the title. Bureaucratic delays in Rome held up the appointment until 1555, when João Nuñez Barreto, a Portuguese Jesuit, was consecrated as Patriarch of Ethiopia. André de Oviedo and Melchior Carneiro, Spanish and Portuguese Jesuits respectively, were named as his assistants, with the rank of bishop. These three, along with an ambassador from the King of Portugal, set out for Ethiopia by way of India, as was usual, traveling with Portugal's India-bound fleet of 1555.

To prepare the way for them, some Jesuits already stationed in India were sent to Ethiopia for the purpose of discovering whether King Galawdewos was really inclined to welcome a Latin patriarch. The leader of this group, which arrived at Arkiko, opposite Massawa, in the spring of 1555, was Mestre Gonçalo Rodrigues. They presented themselves to Galawdewos, and Padre Rodrigues informed him that the patriarch promised by King João would soon arrive. Galawdewos, who for some years had had a perfectly satisfactory and legitimate *abuna*, seemed a bit puzzled at how to respond to this, but finally he replied diplomatically that he was, of course, deeply grateful to his royal brother of Portugal. Then he went off for a month's sojourn in another province.

Rodrigues, who remained behind in the house of one of the Portuguese survivors of Christovão da Gama's army—except for Castanhoso and a couple of others, they had all been compelled to settle in Ethiopia— passed the time composing a treatise entitled *The Errors of Ethiopia and the Truth of Our Holy Faith.* This he blithely presented to Galawdewos upon the king's return. Galawdewos was not pleased. Ethiopia has no errors, he told the Jesuit, to which Rodrigues replied, "Your Highness has none, but your subjects have." In some wrath, the king asked when God had ever indicated His disapproval of the practices and teachings of the Ethiopian Church. Rodrigues invited him to make submission to the Pope, and the king said that he would not. Nor had he any use for the "learned and religious men" that were coming to him from Europe; he had a sufficiency of learned and religious men in his own realm. Well, then, the dismayed Rodrigues asked, would he allow the Portuguese patriarch to Ethiopia at all? Becoming more amiable, Galawdewos answered that the patriarch could certainly come, if he wished, and would be received in a friendly manner.

The Jesuit scouts hastened back to India with a discouraging report. Prester John is such a heretic, Rodrigues said, that he thinks *we* are heretics and *they* are good Christians! The viceroy, pondering Rodrigues' conversations with Galawdewos, decided that it might not be wise to send the patriarch to Ethiopia just yet: better to dispatch one of the bishops, who might induce in the king a more receptive attitude. Patriarch Barreto therefore stayed in India, and in fact died there some years later without ever having seen his appointed province; across to Ethiopia early in 1557 went Bishop Oviedo, a thin, ascetic, and saintly Castilian, along with three fellow Jesuits and two other priests.

They arrived just in time to witness the beginning of a new era of troubles for Ethiopia. The Turks, who had been extending their control southward along both shores of the Red Sea all through the sixteenth century, now seized Massawa, which had been subject to Ethiopia for some time. A small Turkish garrison was in possession of the island when Oviedo landed; they did not molest the priests, and let them cross unhindered to the mainland, but not long afterward a much larger force of Turks occupied Massawa, closing the main route of access for Portuguese going to Ethiopia.

In March 1557, Oviedo and his companions reached Debarwa, where they were greeted by the survivors of the Christovão da Gama expedition and spent some time hearing confession and performing marriages. Then they went on to see Galawdewos, who received them reclining on a couch and dressed in a tunic over a Moorish shirt and trousers of Persian cotton. He was, Oviedo wrote, "a broad black man, with large eyes and an imposing presence," who appeared "noble and discreet and friendly to the Portuguese," and he listened with evident interest to the bishop's exegesis of Catholic theology. But the king was not about to embrace Rome. His father, Lebna Dengel, seems to have been attracted to Catholicism, even if his "submission" to Rome was more a deed of politeness than anything else. But Galawdewos was convinced of the superiority of the Ethiopian kind of Christianity and was capable of arguing his position clearly and succinctly. The learned Jesuits were able to outflank the *abuna* and his clergymen in theological discussion, but they met their match in Galawdewos. Debating religious matters with Oviedo seemed to amuse him, and they spent hours together in lively argument. The bishop would cite a list of Ethiopian heresies; the king would reply with passionate defenses of each practice that was attacked. Circumcision? Merely a native custom, like the decorative scarification of the face common in so many parts of Africa. The Saturday Sabbath? Likewise not a borrowing from the Jews, but only a national habit. Distinguishing between clean and unclean meats? That seemed a harmless thing to Galawdewos. He parried every thrust; once, after an exceptionally difficult session with the king, Oviedo burst from the royal tent in visible distress and protested to his colleagues, "That man is a great heretic!"

No matter how sorely Oviedo harangued him, Galawdewos remained unfailingly courteous and generous in his treatment of the missionaries. There was only one moment of real tension, when two Ethiopian monks succumbed to Oviedo's persuasions and declared their adherence to Catholicism. Their abbot ordered them to return to their monastery, but the Jesuits refused to hand the converts over, and Galawdewos was forced to intervene. He demanded that Oviedo let the monks go. Oviedo said he would not. "No?" Galawdewos roared, and turned on the bishop with such rage that Oviedo expected to be struck down. Meekly he awaited the fatal blow, but the king halted, laughed, and clapped his hands. "You think that you will die a martyr at my hands?" he asked. "I will not give you that glory. Go, and take your monks. Give them eggs on Friday, and you can be bishop of two monks."

While Galawdewos played host to the Jesuits the Turks were encroaching on his coastal domain. From their base at Massawa they crossed to the mainland, defeated the *bahr nagash*, and seized Debarwa; they might have gone much farther had not an epidemic sprung up among the invaders and wiped out practically all of them. There was also trouble on Ethiopia's southeast flank, where the Moslems of Harar had gone on the warpath again under the leadership of Ahmed Gran's successor, Nur-ibn-Mudi al-Wazir. When Nur invaded an Ethiopian border province in March 1559, Galawdewos went forth to repel him. They met in battle late that month, on Good Friday, which Ethiopians considered an unlucky day for making war; and unlucky it was, for Galawdewos went to a hero's death surrounded by enemies, as did a number of Portuguese who fought beside him. The Moslem force then withdrew, because domestic troubles had broken out in Harar. Galawdewos was succeeded by his brother Minas, who had been captured by Gran in Lebna Dengel's time and who had spent many years as a prisoner among the Moslems. This captivity, perhaps, was the cause of his irascible and fanatic nature. The first to feel his violence were the Jesuits.

Minas despised Catholicism and regarded all its communicants in his realm as dangerous aliens. He confiscated the lands that his brother had bestowed on the companions of Dom Christovão and forbade the Ethiopian wives of Portuguese settlers to continue to follow their husbands' religion, a practice that Galawdewos had permitted. Any Ethiopian who entered a Latin church, Minas decreed, would be banished. He threatened to burn the Jesuits alive and told Oviedo he would cut off his head if the bishop did not stop preaching. Oviedo replied that he would preach the true faith as long as he had breath; the king, in frenzy, seized the Jesuit and would have throttled him if the queen had not interceded. Oviedo was sent instead to an *amba* in the wilderness.

But the king's rages fell also upon the Ethiopians, and in 1561 a cabal of nobles attempted to overthrow him, with some encouragement from the Portuguese settlers. Minas defeated the rebels in battle, though their leader, the *bahr nagash*, escaped and went off to seek an alliance with the Turks. The dangers inherent in this did not escape Minas' attention, and he embarked on a policy of reconciliation, recalling to court those Portuguese who had remained loyal and even allowing Oviedo to return from his mountaintop exile. None of this helped him when the *bahr nagash* led a Turkish army into Ethiopia in 1562;

the royal forces were trounced and Minas died shortly afterwards. The northern provinces passed into Turkish control.

Minas' son, Sarsa Dengel, became king. He neither persecuted nor encouraged the Jesuit missionaries; rather, he paid no attention to them, regarding them as holy men who were doctrinally unsound and not worth heeding. Oviedo and his colleagues now dwelled in straw huts in the town of Fremona, near Axum. Although he had succeeded to the patriarchate in 1562 upon the death in India of Barreto, the prelate was forced to grow his own vegetables and make his own bread, and for writing paper he had to tear blank leaves from his breviary. But this life of holy poverty only sustained and enhanced his saintliness, and a good many Ethiopians became Catholic out of sheer admiration of his virtue. He lived quietly in Fremona until his death in 1577.

23

Sarsa Dengel was a valiant warrior and his reign was a successful one. He put down the rebellion of the *bahr nagash*, drove back the Turks, kept Harar in check, and did battle against the Gallas, an unruly pagan tribe of the south. During the thirty-five triumphant years he occupied the throne, there was no contact at all between Ethiopia and Portugal or Portuguese India, for the Turks controlled the Massawa gateway and forbade Christians to pass. One priest who tried to enter Ethiopia was captured at sea by the Turks and enslaved; another, discovered at Massawa, was cut to pieces. In 1588 two more Jesuits, both Spaniards, made the attempt: Pero Paez, a Castilian, and Antonio de Monserrate, a Catalan. They planned to land at Zeila on the Somali coast, but a storm drove their ship to Arabia, where they were seized and led off to captivity deep in the desert. They spent seven years as prisoners, undergoing many strange adventures, before being ransomed and returning to India, where Monserrate shortly died. A Jesuit of Arab extraction, Father Abraham de Georgiis, was the next to seek Ethiopia, in 1595, hoping that he could pass through Massawa posing as a Moslem, but he was betrayed and the Turks put him to death.

Meanwhile the last of the five priests who had accompanied Oviedo to Ethiopia had died at Fremona in 1597, leaving the Catholics in that country without a spiritual leader. There was still a substantial colony of so-called "Portuguese" there: a few of them were veterans of the

Christovão da Gama campaign, now in their seventies and eighties, but most were the half-breed sons and grandsons of those men, who clung to their Portuguese identity even though they were Ethiopian by birth, color, and customs.

Sarsa Dengel also had died in 1597, having greatly strengthened and enlarged the kingdom he had inherited from Minas. A dynastic crisis developed upon his death, for all of his living sons were children, and an assortment of grandsons and great-grandsons of Lebna Dengel attempted to gain the throne. After a period of some confusion a young prince named Za Dengel, nephew of Sarsa Dengel and that king's own preferred choice as successor, came to power. And a few years later—in 1603—a Catholic missionary finally succeeded once again in penetrating the land of Prester John.

He was Pero Paez, the same Spanish Jesuit who had been detained seven years in Arabia on his previous attempt. The fluency in Arabic that he had acquired during that sojourn had served him well: returning to India after being ransomed, he had used it in striking up a friendship with a Turkish merchant from the Sudan. Posing as an Armenian, Paez asked the Turk's help in getting back to his purported homeland, and the Turk offered to see him as far as Jerusalem. Thus Paez obtained passage aboard a Turkish vessel bound from India to the Red Sea. When the ship stopped in Massawa, he casually asked if he could go ashore to pick up some property waiting for him there; disembarking, he slipped quietly into Ethiopia and sent a message ahead to the Portuguese settlers, who met him and guided him to Fremona.

Neither a patriarch nor a bishop, Paez had no need to present himself at court, nor did he make any claim to official status in the land. Thus he aroused none of the hostility that had met the attempts of Bermudes and Oviedo at converting the Ethiopians. Instead, living peacefully at Fremona, he employed his considerable charm and intelligence to win the love and support of the populace. Paez quickly mastered Amharic, the Ethiopian vernacular, and Ge'ez, the scriptural language; then, opening a little school—he was his own architect, mason, and carpenter—he set about teaching those languages to the children of the Portuguese colony and to those Ethiopian children whose parents chose to entrust them to him. As word spread that the instruction Paez gave in Ge'ez was superior to that provided by the native clergy, many members of the nobility enrolled their offspring with him. By no accident, the chief textbook of this school was a Catholic catechism in the form of dialogues which Paez had translated into Ge'ez; hence as the little scholars repeated their grammar lessons they painlessly absorbed the essential doctrines of the Church of Rome. This tactic seems to have stirred no suspicions; indeed, by the middle of 1604, Paez' reputation as a pedagogue glowed so brightly that King Za Dengel, curious and fascinated, asked to have this wonder brought before him. Paez came with two of his star pupils, who staged a theological discussion that dazzled and baffled the clergymen of the court; then the Jesuit delivered an hour-long sermon in flawless and eloquent Ge'ez, and celebrated Mass for the king. Za Dengel, deeply moved, asked Paez for private instruction in Catholicism, fell under the spell of the Spanish priest's dynamic personality, and shortly announced his conversion. This was no token giving of allegiance, either: the king promptly issued decrees abolishing most of the native rites that were at variance with the teachings of Rome.

Such a radical step, though, exceeded the limits of Za Dengel's somewhat precarious grip on his throne. Followers of an opposing faction of the royal family used his new-found Catholic zeal as an excuse for rebellion; civil war broke out and the rebels induced the *abuna* to excommunicate the king, thereby freeing the people from their oath of allegiance to him. Za Dengel's army left him and he was slain in December 1604. Another period of dynastic confusion ensued, as two princes of the line of Sarsa Dengel claimed the crown; order was not restored until 1607, when a nephew of Sarsa Dengel named Susenyos gained sole power.

Susenyos was a man of great force and stature, who, unlike most Ethiopian princes, had avoided the stultifying isolation of life in one of the mountaintop eyries where those of royal blood usually were confined. As a child he had been captured by the pagan Galla tribe and was raised among them as a chief's foster son; this exposure to barbarian ways gave him a less parochial outlook than he might have developed growing up in the cloistered, ritual-bound orthodoxy of the princely *amba*. After his rescue, he managed to establish himself as one of Sarsa Dengel's generals; thwarted in an attempt to succeed that king, he spent the decade after Sarsa Dengel's death planning his own ultimately successful seizure of the throne. While still a prince, Susenyos had been attracted to Paez and spent a good deal of time with the Jesuit and several of his colleagues who had now joined him. When he became king, he installed Paez as a court favorite and gave him a daily audience, even permitting the priest the extraordinary privilege of dining at the royal table. Religion was the principal topic of their conversations; Susenyos quickly and eagerly embraced Catholicism.

It was not primarily the theology of the Church of Rome that brought about his conversion, although, like almost all Ethiopian monarchs, he greatly loved abstruse discussions of the nature of the Trinity. What drew him most strongly was his high regard for the vigor, dignity, asceticism, and scholarship of Pero Paez. The Ethiopian clergy had fallen into a lamentable slovenliness of soul, body, and intellect in his time; Susenyos saw on the one hand his own ignorant and corrupt priests, and on the other the Jesuits busily teaching, studying, striving to bring enlightenment. They had set up a printing press on which they produced their Amharic translations of the Gospels and their commentaries, in Ge'ez, on the Scriptures as a whole. They also laid out roads, built bridges, constructed churches, taught the Ethiopians how to erect two-storied buildings of stone and cement, and designed a handsome lakeside palace for the king—in which Paez provided a clever secret chamber that saved Susenyos' life during an assassination attempt. If these men were so capable in so many different ways, the king reasoned, then probably their brand of Christianity was as superior to the Ethiopian kind as they were to the native clergy.

But, having seen Za Dengel undone by his conversion, Susenyos moved slowly in making Ethiopia a Catholic land. He remained outwardly loyal to the traditional religion during the first five years of his reign, though he did not conceal his admiration for Paez and permitted him to preach openly throughout the country. Once he had consolidated his power, Susenyos grew less cautious. In 1612 he tested the temper of the country by allowing his brother, Se'ela Kristos, the governor of the province of Gojjam, to announce his own adherence to Catholicism. When no violent reactions followed, Susenyos took another step: he summoned the leaders of the Ethiopian priesthood to take part in a theological debate with the Jesuits. This contest, which lasted for days, was hopelessly one-sided, for the Ethiopians were unable to cope with the formidable techniques of argument that even then were a Jesuit specialty. Balthazar Telles, a Portuguese Jesuit who wrote a history of the Ethiopian mission later in the seventeenth century, declares that "these heretics had never studied logic, nor were they versed in syllogisms, enthymemas, and modes of argument, nor had they any knowledge of the subtleties of scholastic theology." When the Jesuits had finished their annihilation of the Ethiopian clergymen, Susenyos decreed that inasmuch as the doctors of the native Church had been vanquished his subjects were thenceforth required to believe that there are two natures in Christ, one human and one divine, each distinct from the other but both divinely united in the person of the Saviour.

The *abuna*, who had not taken part in the debate, promptly excommunicated the king. He had the support of Emana Kristos, one of the king's half brothers, who coveted the throne; so the quarrel was not entirely a spiritual one. Susenyos threatened the *abuna* with beheading if he did not withdraw the excommunication, and the *abuna* hastened to comply. The king then reissued his decree, adding that death would be the penalty for those who disagreed with his views on the dual nature of Christ. Sixty monks immediately flung themselves from a cliff in horror. Emana Kristos and some of the other nobles took the more direct approach of trying to murder Susenyos, but it was this attempt that was foiled by Paez' architectural cleverness. As the conspirators rushed toward the king, he stepped into his secret chamber and slammed the door in their faces; a cunning spring lock fashioned by Paez prevented them from following him, and they fled.

Susenyos crushed the rebellion that ensued; the *abuna* and several other ringleaders were slain and Emana Kristos was imprisoned. The king then made it unlawful for Ethiopian Christians to continue observing the ancient Jewish Sabbath on Saturday. This produced another rebellion, led by Jonael, the governor of the province of Begamedr, who compared Susenyos to the Roman Emperor Diocletian, a savage persecutor of Christians, and called the Jesuits "the kin of Pilate." Susenyos quelled this uprising also, and Jonael took refuge among the Gallas, who cut off his head and sent it to the king. These events took place in 1620.

The king still had not publicly professed Catholicism, nor had he renounced the Coptic Church; he had merely promulgated a few innovations in doctrine and observance. "I have not changed my religion," he told his people, "I have only improved it. I do not hold my faith because it is that of the Portuguese, nor because it is the faith of Rome, but because it is the true faith. And do not deceive yourselves—for this faith I am prepared to die if necessary, but all those who contradict it will die first." Open acceptance of Catholicism was the logical next step. In 1622 he let it be known that he had gone to Paez for confession, and that he had renounced all of his wives except the first one; in a lengthy proclamation he affirmed the truth of the Catholic doctrines and exposed the vices of the recent *abunas,* who, he said, were guilty of buying their sees, of keeping concubines, of raising their hands in warfare against their lawful prince, and much more.

The violent manifesto by which Susenyos turned Ethiopia over to the Church of Rome sent shock waves rolling across the seas. Pietro della Valle, an Italian traveler who was visiting Portuguese India in 1623, heard the surprising news and noted in his journal that "*Prete Janni,* King of *Aethiopia* and the *Abissins,* was by means of the Jesuits reconciled to the Roman Church, and became a good Catholic, intending that his whole country should do the same; which, if true, is indeed a thing of great consequence." Had the wise and beloved Pero Paez lived longer, perhaps that thing of great consequence would have come to pass; but it was Susenyos' ill luck that Paez died only a few months after the king's public conversion, depriving him of his most prudent adviser and most inspiring preacher. "The virtuous Reverend Padre Pero Paez," Susenyos wrote, "was father of our soul, bright sun of faith lighting the darkness of Ethiopia. Since our sun has been eclipsed and set, our joy is turned to sadness, and our happiness to mourning."

24

Now came another Jesuit, the stern and righteous Padre Afonso Mendes of Portugal, in response to a request from Susenyos that the Pope nominate a patriarch for Ethiopia. Mendes, a forty-three-year-old doctor of theology and professor of Latin, was consecrated as patriarch in Lisbon in May 1624 and reached Ethiopia in June of the following year, entering by way of the tributary Moslem kingdom of Danakil on the coast south of Massawa. His first act was to demand an unambiguous wholesale act of submission from the Ethiopians. At a grand ceremony on February 17, 1626, Susenyos knelt before the new patriarch and swore fealty to him as representative of the Catholic Church, declaring, "The Pope of Rome, lawfully elected, is the true successor of St. Peter the Apostle . . . and we do promise, offer, and swear true obedience, and subject, with humility at his feet, our person and empire to him." The imperial princes, the nobles and officials of the court, and all the important priests and monks then were required to take the same vow. After this Mendes pronounced excommunication on those who broke the oath and threatened with death any who would not observe the Roman rites.

Paez had won Ethiopia with love, understanding, and tact. Mendes endeavored to keep it through logic and stringency. Questions had been raised about the conduct of the last few *abunas;* Mendes therefore ruled that the ordinations they had performed were invalid and suspended all priests until they could be reordained at his hands. All churches had to be reconsecrated and altars of the Roman form erected in them. The traditional arks of the covenant were taken out of the churches and images of the saints, which Ethiopians considered idolatrous, were put up. Circumcision was forbidden. Everyone, adults and children alike, had to be rebaptized according to Catholic practice. Holidays not in the calendar of the Roman Church were stricken from the roll. The bodies of saints not recognized by Rome were disinterred and destroyed. Polygamy and divorce were prohibited. Prosecutions for witchcraft were initiated, for, while the Ethiopians did not believe in witches, Patriarch Mendes did. Use of the Ge'ez liturgy was proscribed and services thenceforth were to be conducted in Latin. Dissenters to any of these decrees had their tongues cut out or were burned or hanged.

Susenyos himself was more than a little dismayed by the single-minded fury of Mendes' dismantling of the Ethiopian Church, but at first he took issue with only a single reform: the substitution of Latin for Ge'ez. It was unreasonable, he argued, to ask his people to pray in a language they could not understand, and Mendes, yielding just on this, gave permission to continue celebrating the holy rites in Ge'ez. Otherwise, the extirpation of Coptic ways proceeded apace, and, when the people resisted, soldiers of the government carried out the penalties for heresy decreed by the patriarch. Catholicism was imposed on Ethiopia by terror and force.

The Ethiopians rebelled. The uprisings of 1615–20 had been inspired by ambitious princes eager to take Susenyos' place on the throne; those of the late 1620s were genuine popular insurrections, the response of an outraged kingdom to the violent supplanting of its ancient religion. Susenyos marched endlessly from province to province, suppressing one revolt after another, but there was no end to the disturbances. Rebellion grew into civil war as the anti-Catholic forces coalesced. The climax came in 1631 when Susenyos led the royal army against a force of 25,000 rebels and in a day of terrible slaughter routed them completely, taking 8000 lives. But the victory was a bitter one. The next morning, when Susenyos went out with his son and heir Fasiladas to inspect the field of carnage, the prince turned to him and said, "The men you see strewn upon the earth were neither pagans nor Moslems, but your own subjects, your compatriots, some of them our kinsmen! This is no victory that we have gained. In killing them you drive the sword into your own entrails. How many men have you slaughtered? How many more will you kill? They cannot understand this faith of Rome. Leave them, father, to the ways of their ancestors!"

It was a somber moment for Susenyos. He remained convinced of the truth of the Catholic faith, yet Fasiladas' words were unanswerable. He went to Mendes, hoping the patriarch would authorize some lessening of the campaign against heresy, would tolerate the return of a few of the more harmless traditions. But Mendes upbraided him severely for such talk of compromise, and Susenyos saw that his position had become impossible. His attempt at religious reform had led only to a national tragedy. The king wished no more bloodshed, yet he could not repudiate the faith that had cost Ethiopia so many lives. Abdication was the only solution. On June 24, 1632, heralds carried this proclamation through the land:

"Hear us! Hear us! Hear us! We first gave you the Roman faith thinking it to be a good one. But countless men have gone to their deaths because of it: Yolyos, Gabriel, Takla Giorgis, Sarsa Kristos,* and a multitude of peasants. We therefore restore to you the faith of your forefathers. Let the clergy return to the churches, let them set up their own altars, let them say their own liturgy, and let all of you rejoice. As for myself, I am now old and worn out with war and infirmities, and no longer capable of governing; I name my son Fasiladas to reign in my place."

In a single day thus fell the whole structure of Ethiopian Catholicism. Susenyos had hoped, by abdicating, to preserve the Church of Rome as the faith of at least some Ethiopians, but that was not to be. The king died, still loyal to Rome, three months after his abdication, and Fasiladas set about at once undoing his father's work. The princes and nobles were instructed to give up Catholicism, and those who would not were banished or executed. The paraphernalia of Roman worship came out of the churches. The Jesuits were interned at Fremona. Too late, Mendes offered to take a softer stand on the coex-

---

* Leaders of the anti-Catholic rebellion.

istence of Coptic and Catholic Christianity in Ethiopia, but Fasiladas, regarding the Roman Church as a source of infection in the body politic, was determined to oust it entirely. In 1634 he ordered all Catholic priests out of the country. Mendes protested, indignantly maintaining that he had served God faithfully and properly, and pointing out that he had taken a vow never to leave Ethiopia. "Your Lordship is not leaving Ethiopia," Fasiladas replied. "It is Ethiopia who has left Your Lordship." Mendes and his colleagues were expelled the following year; some were caught and killed by the Turks at Massawa, but Mendes succeeded in reaching India, where he ended his days. A handful of Jesuits chose to stay in Ethiopia, living as fugitives and ministering to underground Catholic congregations. One by one these were caught and hanged.

So ended Europe's long involvement with Prester John. There would be no alliance between Christian Europe and Christian Ethiopia against the menace of Islam; there would be no conversion of the Prester and his people to the faith of Rome; there would be no contact at all between that exotic realm and the Europeans who had for so many centuries pried into its secrets. Suspicion of outsiders became again a national trait, as it had been hundreds of years earlier. The agonies of Ethiopia's Catholic period were not to be repeated. The land would be sealed against missionaries and against "Franks"—Catholics—in general. When the Pope, hearing of the collapse of the Jesuit mission, mistakenly concluded that the Ethiopians objected to Portuguese Jesuits rather than to Catholicism itself, he sent a company of French Capuchins to right matters, but the Ethiopians put them to death. In 1648 three more Capuchins landed at Massawa; they, too, were executed by order of Fasiladas. A party of Franciscans smuggled themselves into the country later in the century, but they were detected and stoned. The only European to visit Ethiopia in the late seventeenth century was a French apothecary, Charles Poncet, who was allowed to enter in 1699 to treat the king's skin ailment. He left the following year. In 1735 some Greek silversmiths who had been living in Cairo embarked for India but ran out of money and got no farther than Massawa; when the king heard of them, he hired them to assist in the decoration of his new palace, and they remained permanently in Ethiopia. Then, in 1769, there arrived the astonishing James Bruce, a towering Scot who had come looking for the source of the Blue Nile. His gift for languages, his phenomenal courage, and his fierce hatred of Catholicism, stronger even than the Ethiopians', saw him safely through a two-year visit in which he became the confidant of the king and took part in an intricate civil war. Beyond these few intruders, Ethiopia admitted no one, and until modern times managed to preserve its lunar solitude.

In any case, the Portuguese experience had convinced Europe for all time of the folly of the Prester John myth. Prester John had been found, and he was no king of miracles, but only a black-skinned chieftain of a wild and primitive land, who dined on raw beef and imprisoned his brothers on mountaintops. Reality had destroyed the golden vision. Thenceforth, men would have to pursue other phantoms.

SEVEN

Was Prester John an Ethiopian?

Fᴏʀ those who still preferred to have the myth, mythmakers obligingly continued to ply their trade even after the publication of Padre Alvares' report in 1540 had revealed Prester John to be a mere mortal monarch. The popular appetite for tales of the Prester remained unabated. And so in 1590 there appeared in England a book entitled, *The Rare and Most Wonderful Thinges which Edward Webbe, an Englishman Borne, Hath Seen and Passed in His Troublesome Travailles in the Citties of Jerusalem, Damasko, Bathelem, and Gallely; and in the lands of Jewrie, Egipt, Grecia, Russia, and in the land of Prester John.*

Edward Webbe, the author of this work, was an adventurer who had gone to Russia in the 1560s, at the age of twelve, with a party of English merchants. When the Tatars burned Moscow in 1571 he was carried off to the Crimea as a slave; ransomed, he returned to England, then sailed to the Near East only to be captured by the Turks and enslaved once more. He pulled oars in Turkish galleys, served in the Turkish army in Persia and Syria, and took part in the Turks' attempt to conquer Ethiopia's Red Sea coast. Eventually he won his freedom and, after running into some more trouble with the Inquisition in Italy, came back to his native country in May 1589.

Webbe may well have seen at least the shores of Ethiopia, but his account of that country is a concoction of familiar tales going back four full centuries, to the original Prester John letter. "This Prester John," he declared, "is a king of great power and keepeth very beautiful court . . . he hath every day to serve him at his table, sixty kinges wearing leaden crowns on their heads, and those serve in the meat unto Prester John's table: and continually the first dish of meat set upon his table is a dead man's scull, cleane picked, and laid in black earth; putting him in mind that he is but earth, and that he must die, and shall become earth again." Webbe goes on to report that "in this Court of Prester John there is a wilde man—whose allowance is every day a quarter of raw mutton; and when any man dyeth for some notorious offence, this gentleman's diet is changed to a quarter of man's flesh. . . . There is also in the Court of Prester John a beast called *arians*, having four heads." And, he adds, "I have seen, in a place like a park, adjoining Prester John's Court, three score and seventeene unicorns and elephants . . . and they were so tame that I have played with them as one would play with young lambes."

This tale of wonders must have found an appreciative audience, for three publishers released editions of it in 1590 alone. But serious students of geography had only contempt for it. Richard Hakluyt snubbed Webbe's narrative when assembling his immense three-volume collection of voyages and travels in 1598, and Samuel Purchas, Hakluyt's successor, not only excluded Webbe from his even larger collection of 1625 but dismissed him as "a mere fabler."

In fact, the deflation of the Prester John mythos had been under way since the first half of the sixteenth century. We have already noted three significant examples of this. Valentim Fernandes, in his 1502 edition of Marco Polo, pointedly declared that the ruler of Ethiopia "is the king whom we consider to be Prester John, and he is not Prester John. For Prester John is out there in Cathay." Alvares, addressing Pope Clement VII in 1533, spoke of "the most serene and powerful lord David, king of the great and high Ethiopia, *by the masses called Prester John.*" And the title of the memoir that Patriarch Bermudes published in 1565 included the phrase, "*the Emperor of Ethiopia, Vulgarly Called Prester John.*" Among educated men of the sixteenth century, then, it was understood that "Prester John" was merely a colorful way of referring to the Ethiopian king, a kind of shorthand introduced by fourteenth- and fifteenth-century travelers who imagined that they saw in him the monarch of the old myth. Scholars of the seventeenth century usually took the same attitude. Purchas, in 1625, commented that the Negus of Ethiopia was "called Priest John, by error of Covilanus [Pero da Covilhã], followed by other Portugals in the first discoverie, applying by mis-conceit through some like occurrents the Relations in M. Polo and others touching Presbyter John, in the North-east parts of Asia." The English astronomer Edward Brerewood examined the same point in a book of 1614, *Enquiries Touching the Diversity of Languages and Religions Through the Chief Parts of the World*. He considered and rejected the possibility that the Ethiopian Prester John, so called, was descended from the Asian Prester John whom Marco Polo had found in Tenduc on the Mongolian steppes. The idea, Brerewood wrote, "that it was the King of the *Habassines* that inlarged his dominion so far in the northe east of Asia, till hee was driven into Afrique by the Tartars, hath neither any foundation at all in historie, nor probability in reason. Namely that a King in Afrique should subdue the most distant parts of all Asia from him, and there hold residence, all the regions betwixt belonging to other Princes. Moreover it is certainly known of *Presbyter John* of Asia, that hee was a Nestorian, whereas hee of *Habassia* was, and still is, a Jacobite." Hiob Ludolf of Germany, the foremost seventeenth-century authority on Ethiopia, wrote in his *History of Ethiopia* (1681) that it was Covilhã who wrongly saddled the Ethiopian king with the burden of being Prester John—although, as we have seen, that error had established itself long before Covilhã's time. Ludolf remarks that Covilhã, traveling "in some of the Ports of the Red Sea, heard much talk of a most Potent Christian King of the *Abessines*, that us'd to carry a Cross in his Hands; as also of his Subjects, who were great Favourers if not Followers of the Christian Religion. Believing it therefore to be of little moment whether this famous Monarch liv'd in *Asia* or in *Africa*, he certainly persuaded himself, as being Ignorant both in History and Geography that this was the Prince so much sought after. . . . These glad Tidings the *Portugals* sooner believ'd, than consider'd, and so spread the News all over *Europe* for real Truth; Credulity gaining easily upon those that are ignorant of Foreign Affairs and Kingdoms."

But at the same time that some scholars were saying that the identification of the Ethiopian king as Prester John was an error of the ignorant Portuguese, others were endeavoring to prove that "Prester John" was merely a distorted version of the Ethiopian king's actual title, and therefore that the identification of that king as Prester John was etymologically and historically sound. Prester John, according to this school of thought, had *always* been the King of Ethiopia, and the displacement of the Prester to Asia in the early days of the story had been a mistake.

To prove this required some ingenuity. The Ethiopians who had visited Europe in the fifteenth century had denied any knowledge of the use of "Prester John" as a royal title in their land. Even when they did begin accepting the European usage of that title, it was obvious that they did so only for the sake of easier communication with those who persisted in calling their king by that name. Still, scholars can be resourceful in the face of almost any kind of challenge.

The earliest of these excursions into imaginative etymology appears in a small book entitled *Embassy of David, King of Ethiopia, to the Most Holy Pope Our Lord Clement* VII, published in Bologna in 1533. This volume is primarily an account of Padre Alvares' report to the Pope on his mission in Ethiopia but includes some supplementary material, such as the information that the king of the Ethiopians "is not called by them Prester John (as the masses falsely believe) but *Gyam*, which in their language means 'powerful,' for he is in truth most powerful."

Seven years later, when Damião de Goís brought out his *Faith, Religion, and Manners of the Ethiopians*, he offered a derivation of the "Prester" part of the title. It had nothing to do with "priest" or "presbyter," he said, but was merely a corruption of the Latin word *pretiosus*, meaning "high" or "exalted." Goís declares that his informant, Saga za Ab, told him that "our Emperor is always called Pretiosus Ioannes, and not Presbyter Ioannes, as is everywhere mooted." Not that the Ethiopians actually used the word "pretiosus." That was merely the Latin equivalent of the native words meaning "high," which were, according to Saga za Ab, *belul* in the vernacular Amharic tongue and *encoe* in the liturgical language, Ge'ez. Thus, said Goís, the Ethiopians call their king "Ioannes Belul" or "Ioannes Encoe."

Explaining "Prester" in this roundabout fashion still begged the question of the derivation of "John," unless one accepted the 1533 *gyam* etymology. Soon the 1533 explanation was confirmed by Portuguese returning from Ethiopia, who reported that the natives did indeed call their king by a title variously transcribed as *jan*, *gian*, or *zan*, which meant "powerful" and was pronounced "zhan." That seemed to settle the issue. *Jan Belul*, which could be translated as "Precious John," was the Ethiopian appellation of rank that had found its way into European tongues as "Prester John."

2

It was not so simple, though. Early in the seventeenth century Pero Paez, no mean linguist, offered his own version of why Europeans used the name of Prester John for the Ethiopian king, discarding entirely the *pretiosus* theory:

"It may possibly be due to the fact that as the Emperor is usually a deacon, some Greeks call him Presbyter, and then adding to this the title of *zan*, which, as I have said, is given to the Emperor, they came to say *Preste zan*, and foreigners, who are often wont to corrupt names, accommodating them to their own language, thus called him Prester John. This name Zan is of ancient usage in Ethiopia, for, in order to describe some of the offices still held by the descendants of those officials whom Solomon gave to his son Menelik, it is still employed; for they speak of the officials of *zan*, as we should say officials of the Emperor. Thus, the master-of-the-horse of the Emperor is called *zan beleu*, and the chief armor is called *zan xalami*."

The next significant attempt at analyzing the use of the title appeared in the *History of High Ethiopia or Abassia*, written by the Portuguese Jesuit Manoel de Almeida between 1628 and 1646. Almeida, born in 1580, had become a Jesuit novice at the age of fourteen and in 1602 was sent to India. In 1622, after Paez had succeeded in bringing about King Susenyos' public adherence to Catholicism, Almeida was transferred to Ethiopia and made a difficult journey there that took nearly a year and a half. He witnessed the anti-Catholic uprisings of the 1620s and early 1630s, and, after the abdication of Susenyos, left for India in April 1633 as the patriarch's secret emissary, carrying news of the attack on Ethiopian Catholicism by the new King Fasiladas. He spent the rest of his life in India, dying at Goa in 1646.

His long and valuable history of Ethiopia begins with a chapter entitled, "The Name Prester John," and opens with the sentence, "It is so common in Portugal and Europe for the Emperor of the Abyssinians to be called by this name that anyone who undertakes to write the history of Ethiopia and of the Abyssinian empire must necessarily give some explanation of it." Almeida then recapitulates the history of Prester John, noting that the name "was at first given to a Christian, but Nestorian, emperor who ruled in the interior of Asia. His ordinary name or title was Jonanam, derived from the prophet Jonah (this name has been erroneously changed by Europeans into John). This name was common to the rulers of that monarchy as that of Pharaoh was to the Kings of Egypt. They called him Presbyter because of the cross that he always carried aloft before him, as among us Archbishops and Primates do."

Next, Almeida asserts, the name of Prester John was transferred to the Ethiopian king by the error of Pero da Covilhã. This, of course, is incorrect, since Europeans had been calling that king Prester John for nearly two hundred years before Covilhã's arrival in Ethiopia in 1493. But, Almeida says, Covilhã "was persuaded that he had found him and that this was the Prester John whom his king had sent him to find, and he wrote to him from Cairo to this effect. The news, welcomed in Portugal, spread throughout Europe, and caused the Emperor of Abyssinia from that day to this to be commonly called by all Prester John."

But, Almeida continues, "The truth of the matter has never, up to today, been doubted, nor will it be so by anyone in Ethiopia, for either they are ignorant that their Emperor is known by this name, or if we mention it they become alarmed and seek information, but are unable to find anything corresponding to the term or title in their language." True, he says, Damião de Góis did learn from Saga za Ab that the Ethiopian king was known as Jan Belul, which could be translated as "Precious John." But Almeida asserts that Saga za Ab and another Ethiopian identified as "Pedro" who had come to Europe with him had deliberately misled Góis: "They pretended what they liked and said that the name Prester John had been taken from Belul and Jan and that this meant Precious Jan and that our people had corrupted Jan into John. All this is fiction without foundation in fact."

Almeida declares, "There is no doubt that the Abyssinians call their Emperor Jan, and sometimes they call him Belul also, but the one is never joined with the other; among them it would be a solecism and a very barbarous expression if someone were to say 'Belul Jan' or 'Jan Belul.' To each of these two names, in fact, the word 'qhoj'* is usually added, which means the same as the word 'my' among us when it is used to signify love or tenderness, as one says to a child, as an endearment, 'my sweetheart, my prince, my king.' This is nearly what the Abyssinians mean when they address their King as 'Janqhoj,' 'Ianqhoj,' or 'Belulqhoj,' though this second name is less used among them than the first. To come to the root from which they were derived, it is this. They say that in the ancient language of Ethiopia 'Jan' means 'elephant,' and because this animal is so powerful and terrible compared with the rest, they applied its name to the King as a title of honor and grandeur. So those who call out at the gate of the Emperor's enclosure for him to grant their suits or send someone to hear their complaints at some injustice that has been done to them, they name him by this name if they are Amharic, shouting at the tops of their voices 'Janqhoj, Janqhoj' until the Emperor sends a servant to see what it is they want.

"The name Belul is less common. Properly speaking it means a certain jewel like an earring, which on the death of the reigning ruler and election of a new Emperor, was entrusted to an official, whose duty it was to go and communicate the news to the elected Emperor and place the ornament in his ear, the certain and infallible sign of his election; hence some called the new Emperor after the name of the ornament 'Belulqhoj,' which is equivalent to 'my jewel' or 'my chosen' as it is the sign of his election.

"But as I have already stated, the two words Jan and Belul are not in any case used together, neither are they as a rule used without the addition of the word 'qhoj'; it is thus clear that there is no foundation whatever for the statement that the name Prester John is derived from them."

Later scholars took no serious issue with Almeida's argument, except to point out that the proper meaning of the Amharic word *zan* or *jan* is "judge," not "elephant." Nevertheless, the use of the suffix *qhoj* or *hoy* with *zan* seems to reinforce, rather than deny, the presence of *zan* at the bottom of the notion that the King of Ethiopia was Prester John, at least in the view of James Bruce. Bruce, the eighteenth-century Scottish traveler, whose grasp of Ethiopian was exceptional, provided the final etymological twist in the account of his journey that he pub-

* Pronounced *hoy*.

lished in 1790. Discussing the Ethiopian custom of allowing litigants to call out in loud appeals to the king to hear their cases, he wrote, "These complaints, whether real or feigned, have always for their burden, *Rete O Jan hoi*, which, repeated quick, very much resembles Prete Janni, the name that was given to this prince, of which we never yet knew the derivation; its signification is, 'Do me justice, O my king!' "

In 1923 the Rumanian medievalist Constantine Marinescu re-examined the whole Prester John story and concluded that the royal title *zan* had indeed given rise to the name. He suggested that Italian merchants in the Near East, hearing this title, had understood it to be "Gianni," the short form of "Giovanni"; they had also heard of the alleged priestly powers of the Ethiopian king, and from these two items they concocted "Preste Gianni" as his name—hence the English "Prester John." According to Marinescu, this process must have taken place sometime prior to 1145, when the name of Prester John first appears in the written literature of Europe.

This line of reasoning has some seemingly fatal flaws, though. The use of *zan* or *zan hoy* as a royal address appears to go back no earlier than the sixteenth century; before that the word used, we are told by students of Ethiopian literature, was *danzo*, meaning "noble" or "brave." This would explain why the Ethiopians who came to Italy in 1441 were unable to recognize "Prester John" as any sort of appellation for their king; surely if *zan* had already been in use (pronounced, as noted, "zhan") they would have mentioned it. Then, too, even if *zan* had been used in Ethiopia as early as the twelfth century, it seems strange that a minor title of respect would have come to the notice of foreigners, but not any accurate information about the location or religious beliefs of the place where that title was used. Why, after all, would Bishop Hugh of Jabala have identified Prester John as a Nestorian from India, if he knew he was the Monophysite Zan of Ethiopia?

So one is forced to assume that the name of Prester John was coined in some mysterious fashion in the twelfth century, perhaps by one of the processes described earlier in this book, and that it had no connection originally with any Ethiopian words. The Portuguese then fell into the habit of calling the Ethiopian king by that name, either because he was a Christian who ruled over an exotic kingdom, or because some variant of the *zan hoy* appellation sounded to them like "Jan" or "Janni." Prester John *was* an Ethiopian, then—but only because Europeans said he was.

3

And what did it all mean, this centuries-long quest for the land of Prester John, this search that occupied so many explorers and missionaries and scholars? Was it, as one historian has said, "one of the blind alleys of history"? Was it only a foolish and self-deluding pursuit.of an unattainable mirage?

I think not. Certainly the quest has its foolish aspects, as when Prester Johns were being discovered in every corner of Asia and Africa. Certainly those who placed their faith in the coming of an invincible Christian monarch out of the East were naïve. Certainly the search for Prester John was a foredoomed enterprise, like all such romantic endeavors. Yet the story has its noble side. It was not, as was the superficially similar quest for El Dorado, a mere hunt for gold. There were no material benefits to be had from finding Prester John, except, perhaps, that of locating an ally for Christian Europe against the hordes of Islam. In the main it was a pure and abstract seeking after knowledge. Men gave years of their lives to know the home of Prester John. Men died in the quest. They were given a bundle of misty myths, and out of it they drew a familiarity with the strange continents that lay beyond Europe's eastern edge.

The story of Prester John begins in dreams and fantasies. It begins with tales of mysterious palaces, of bizarre rites, of miracles and wonders, of unicorns and unipeds, of a king whose realm borders on Eden itself. Through centuries of effort that story was purged of its mysticism and mythology. The seekers found *a* Prester John, if not *the* Prester John, and in the process of the search mankind moved out of medieval credulity and toward the modern age of rational thought. Within the structure of the developing quest for Prester John it is possible to trace the outlines of the evolution of the scientific era. We begin with rumor and hyperbole; we end with Jesuits poring over the subtleties of Ethiopian philology. What is lost to the imagination is the intellect's gain.

For all its absurdities, then, the search for Prester John was a struggle out of darkness toward the light. Our ancestors' obsession with him was at once ridiculous and sublime, for, in their constant adjustments and refinements of the myth, their shuttling of Prester John about from place to place, their redefinitions of his qualities, their gallant attempts to make this chieftain or that fit his robes, they were in fact engaged in the hardest of all human tasks, which is to see through the webwork of illusion and delusion we spin about ourselves, and to discover the nature of the objective reality that lies beyond the myths. In this they ultimately succeeded, and so the quest ended, for it was now apparent that the true Prester John of legend could never be found. By giving up the hopeless search Europe accepted reality. And yet, though Prester John eluded his pursuers and doled out only disappointment and disillusionment to those who undertook the chase, we must not think of him as insubstantial or unreal. He was and remains a metaphor for all human striving, a symbol of the hunger to know the unknown, and in that sense there can be no end to our quests for him, for the Prester John of dreams, for the regal figure in glittering armor and a gilded crown, for the king of the shadowy realms at the ends of the earth, the monarch of the lands of romance and magic and mystery, the ever-enduring prince of the impossible.

BIBLIOGRAPHY

ALVARES, FRANCISCO. *The Prester John of the Indies.* Translated by Lord Stanley of Alderley, revised and edited by C. F. Beckingham and G. W. B. Huntingford. Two volumes. Cambridge: The Hakluyt Society, 1961.

AZURARA, GOMES EANNES DE. *The Discovery and Conquest of Guinea.* Translated by C. R. Beazley and Edgar Prestage. London: The Hakluyt Society, 1896.

BARBOSA, DUARTE. *The Book of Duarte Barbosa.* Translated by M. L. Dames. Two volumes. London: The Hakluyt Society, 1918.

BEAZLEY, C. RAYMOND. *The Dawn of Modern Geography.* Three volumes. London: John Murray, 1906.

——, editor. *The Texts and Versions of John de Plano Carpini and William de Rubruquis.* London: The Hakluyt Society, 1903.

BECKINGHAM, C. F. *The Achievements of Prester John.* London: School of Oriental and African Studies, University of London, 1966.

—— and Huntingford, G. W. B., editors. *Some Records of Ethiopia, 1593–1646. Being Extracts from The History of High Ethiopia or Abassia, by Manoel de Almeida.* London: The Hakluyt Society, 1954.

BREREWOOD, EDWARD. *Enquiries Touching the Diversity of Languages.* London: John Bill, 1614.

BROWN, LLOYD A. *The Story of Maps.* Boston: Little, Brown & Co., 1950.

BROWN, RAYMOND E., editor. *The Gospel According to John.* Two volumes. Garden City: Doubleday & Co., 1966, 1970.

BRUCE, JAMES. *Travels to Discover the Source of the Nile.* Five volumes. Edinburgh: Robinson, 1790.

BURTON, RICHARD F., translator. *The Thousand Nights and a Night.* Sixteen volumes. London: The Burton Club, no date.

BUXTON, DAVID. *The Abyssinians.* London: Thames & Hudson, 1970.

CHAPMAN, WALKER. *The Golden Dream: Seekers of El Dorado.* New York: Bobbs-Merrill, 1967.

——. *Kublai Khan: Lord of Xanadu.* New York, Bobbs-Merrill, 1966.

CRAWFORD, O. G. S., editor. *Ethiopian Itineraries, ca. 1400–1524*. Cambridge: The Hakluyt Society, 1958.

DELLA VALLE, PIETRO. *The Travels of Pietro della Valle in India*. Translated by G. Havers. Two volumes. London: The Hakluyt Society, 1892.

DORESSE, JEAN. *Ethiopia*. New York: Frederick Ungar, 1959.

ENSLIN, MORTON SCOTT. *Christian Beginnings*. New York: Harper & Brothers, 1938.

EUSEBIUS. *The History of the Church*. Translated by G. A. Williamson. Harmondsworth: Penguin Books, 1965.

HAKLUYT, RICHARD, editor. *The Principal Navigations Voyages Traffiques and Discoveries of the English Nation*. Modern edition, twelve volumes. Glasgow: James MacLehose & Sons, 1903–5.

HAMILTON, FRANKLIN. *The Crusades*. New York: The Dial Press, 1965.

HERRMANN, PAUL. *Conquest by Man: The Saga of Early Exploration and Discovery*. London: Hamish Hamilton, 1954.

JOINVILLE, JOHN DE. *Memoirs of the Crusades*. Translated by Sir Frank T. Marzials. New York: E. P. Dutton & Co., 1958.

JONES, A. H. M., and MONROE, ELIZABETH. A *History of Ethiopia*. Oxford: Oxford University Press, 1955.

JORDANUS OF SEVERAC. *The Wonders of the East*. Translated by Henry Yule. London: The Hakluyt Society, 1863.

KOSMAS INDICOPLEUSTES. *The Christian Topography*. Translated by J. W. McCrindle. London: The Hakluyt Society, 1897.

LACH, DONALD F. *Asia in the Making of Europe*. Vol. One: *The Century of Discovery*. Chicago: University of Chicago Press, 1965.

LANDSTRON, BJÖRN. *Columbus*. New York: The Macmillan Company, 1967.

LAYARD, AUSTEN HENRY. *Nineveh and Its Remains*. Two volumes. London: John Murray, 1849.

LEO AFRICANUS. *The History and Description of Africa*. Translated by John Pory. Three volumes. London: The Hakluyt Society, 1896.

LETTS, MALCOLM. *Sir John Mandeville: The Man and the Book*. London: The Batchworth Press, 1949.

LUDOLF, HIOB. A *New History of Ethiopia*. Translated by J.P., Gent. London: Samuel Smith, 1684.

MAJOR, R. H., editor. *India in the Fifteenth Century*. London: The Hakluyt Society, 1857.

MANDEVILLE, SIR JOHN. *Mandeville's Travels*. Edited by Malcolm Letts. Two volumes. London: The Hakluyt Society, 1953.

MARKHAM, SIR CLEMENTS, editor. *Book of the Knowledge of all the Kingdoms, Lands, and Lordships That Are in the World . . . Written by a Spanish Franciscan*. London: The Hakluyt Society, 1912.

NEWTON, A. P., editor. *Travel and Travellers of the Middle Ages.* London: Routledge & Kegan Paul, 1926.

NOWELL, CHARLES. "The Historical Prester John." *Speculum,* 28: 435–45, 1953.

OLSCHKI, LEONARDO. *Marco Polo's Asia.* Berkeley and Los Angeles: University of California Press, 1960.

OPPERT, GUSTAV. *Der Presbyter Johannes in Sage und Geschichte.* Berlin, 1864.

PANKHURST, RICHARD, editor. *Travellers in Ethiopia.* London: Oxford University Press, 1965.

PARKER, JOHN. *Books to Build an Empire.* Amsterdam: N. Israel, 1965.

PENROSE, BOIES. *Travel and Discovery in the Renaissance.* Cambridge, Mass.: Harvard University Press, 1955.

PHILLIPS, E. D. *The Mongols.* London: Thames & Hudson, 1969.

PLINY. *Natural History.* Translated by John Bostock and H. T. Riley. Six volumes. London: Henry G. Bohn, 1856.

POLO, MARCO. *The Travels of Marco Polo.* Translated by Ronald Latham. Harmondsworth: Penguin Books, 1958.

———. *The Book of Ser Marco Polo.* Translated and edited by Sir Henry Yule. Third edition, revised by Henri Cordier. Three volumes. London: John Murray, 1929.

PRAWDIN, MICHAEL. *The Mongol Empire.* London: George Allen & Unwin, 1940.

PRESTAGE, EDGAR. *The Portuguese Pioneers.* London: Adam & Charles Black, 1933.

PURCHAS, SAMUEL. *Purchas His Pilgrimes.* Modern edition, twenty volumes. Glasgow: James MacLehose and Sons, 1905.

RAVENSTEIN, E. G., editor. *The First Voyage of Vasco da Gama.* London: The Hakluyt Society, 1898.

ROGERS, FRANCIS M. *The Quest for Eastern Christians.* Minneapolis: University of Minnesota Press, 1962.

———. *The Travels of the Infante Dom Pedro of Portugal.* Cambridge, Mass.: Harvard University Press, 1961.

RUNCIMAN, STEVEN. *A History of the Crusades.* Three volumes. Cambridge: Cambridge University Press, 1951–54.

SANCEAU, ELAINE. *The Land of Prester John: A Chronicle of Portuguese Exploration.* New York: Knopf, 1944.

SHEPARD, ODELL. *The Lore of the Unicorn.* New York: Barnes & Noble, 1967.

SILVERBERG, ROBERT. *Bruce of the Blue Nile.* New York: Holt, Rinehart & Winston, 1969.

———. *The Great Wall of China.* Philadelphia: Chilton Books, 1965.

SLESSAREV, VSEVOLOD. *Prester John: The Letter and the Legend.* Minneapolis: University of Minnesota Press, 1959.

SYKES, SIR PERCY. *The Quest for Cathay.* London: Adam & Charles Black,
1936.

TAFUR, PERO. *Travels and Adventures.* Translated by Malcolm Letts. New
York: Harper & Brothers, 1926.

THORNDIKE, LYNN. *History of Magic and Experimental Science.* Eight
volumes. New York: Columbia University Press, 1923.

WHITEWAY, R. S., editor and translator. *The Portuguese Expedition to Abyssinia in 1541–1543, as Narrated by Castanhoso, with some Contemporary Letters, the Short Account of Bermudez, and Certain Extracts
from Correa.* London: The Hakluyt Society, 1902.

WITTFOGEL, KARL A., and CHIA-SHENG, FENG. *History of Chinese Society:
Liao.* American Philosophical Society, *Transactions,* Vol. 36, 1946.

WRIGHT, JOHN KIRTLAND. *Geographical Lore of the Time of the Crusades.*
New York: American Geographical Society, 1925.

YULE, SIR HENRY. *Cathay and the Way Thither.* Second edition, revised by
Henri Cordier. Four volumes. London: The Hakluyt Society, 1913–15.

ZARNCKE, FRIEDRICH. "Über eine neue . . . Redaction des Briefes des
Priester Johannes." *Berichte über die Verhandlungen der königlich
sächsischen Gesellschaft der Wissenschaften zu Leipzig, Philologische-
historische Classe,* Vol. 29, 1877.

———. "Der Priester Johannes." *Abhandlungen der philologisch-historischen
Classe der königlich sächsischen Gesellschaft der Wissenschaften,* Vol.
7, 1879.

———. "Der Priester Johannes." *Abhandlungen der philologische-historischen
Classe der königlich sächsischen Gesellschaft der Wissenschaften,* Vol.
8, 1883.

Index